## DATE DUE

| | | | |
|---|---|---|---|
| 4-30-00 | | | |
| | | | |
| APR 1 6 | 6/ | | |
| | | | |
| | | | |
| | | | |
| | | | |
| | | | |
| | | | |
| | | | |
| | | | |
| | | | |
| | | | |
| | | | |

Demco No. 62-0549

# THE BLUESTOCKING CIRCLE

*Nine Living Muses of Great Britain. (Detail).* Portraits in the Characters of the Muses in the
Temple of Apollo by Richard Samuel. *c*.1779. National Portrait Gallery, London.
*left-hand group:* seated is Angelica Kauffman with Elizabeth Carter and Anna L. Barbauld
behind her.
*Centre:* Elizabeth Anne Sheridan (née Linley).
*right-hand group:* seated are Catherine Macaulay, Elizabeth Montagu, and Elizabeth Griffith
with Hannah More and Charlotte Lennox behind them.

# THE
# BLUESTOCKING
# CIRCLE

## Women, Friendship, and
## the Life of the Mind in
## Eighteenth-Century England

SYLVIA HARCSTARK MYERS

CLARENDON PRESS · OXFORD
1990

*Oxford University Press, Walton Street, Oxford* OX2 6DP
*Oxford New York Toronto
Delhi Bombay Calcutta Madras Karachi
Petaling Jaya Singapore Hong Kong Tokyo
Nairobi Dar es Salaam Cape Town
Melbourne Auckland*

*and associated companies in
Berlin Ibadan*

*Oxford is a trade mark of Oxford University Press*

*Published in the United States
by Oxford University Press, New York*

*British Library Cataloguing in Publication Data*
*Myers, Sylvia Harcstark*
*The Bluestocking Circle : women, friendship, and the life
of the mind in eighteenth-century England.
1. English literature. Bluestocking Circle
I. Title    820.9006
ISBN 0-19-811767-1*

*Library of Congress Cataloging in Publication Data*
*Myers, Sylvia Harcstark.*
*The bluestocking circle : women, friendship, and the life of the
mind in eighteenth-century England / Sylvia Harcstark Myers.
p.    cm.
Includes bibliographical references
(Oxford University Press)
1. English literature—Women authors—History and criticism.
2. English literature—18th century—History and criticism.
3. Women and literature—England—History—18th century. 4. Women
authors, English—18th century—Biography. 5. Friendship—England—
History—18th century. 6. England—Intellectual life—18th
century. 7. Salons—England—History—18th century. 8. Women—
England—Intellectual life.    I. Title
PR448.W65M94 1990      820.9'9287'09033—dc20      90-30542
ISBN 0-19-811767-1*

*Typeset by Downdell Limited, Oxford
Printed and bound in Great Britain by
Bookcraft Ltd., Midsomer Norton, Bath*

*This book is dedicated
to the women,
past, present, and future,
who struggle for a life of the mind.*

# PREFACE

My interest in the bluestockings began some years ago, when I read Doris Mary Stenton's discussion in *The English Woman in History* (1957) of an eighteenth-century woman, Elizabeth Carter, who, Stenton explained, was conscious of the oppression of women. Stenton's observation was new to me; at that time there seemed to be a gap between the early eighteenth-century feminist, Mary Astell, and the late eighteenth-century feminist, Mary Wollstonecraft. So I pursued the comment and found Montagu Pennington's statement in his *Memoirs* of his aunt that Elizabeth Carter had an 'extreme partiality for writers of her own sex' and that 'She was much inclined to believe, that women had not their proper station in society, and that their mental powers were not rated sufficiently high' (i. 447–8).

I was intrigued by Elizabeth Carter's views, which were so different from the attitudes and ideas of the standard eighteenth-century novelists and essayists, and began to research her life and works, a pursuit which soon brought me into contact with her friends—Elizabeth Montagu, Catherine Talbot, Hester Chapone, the Duchess of Portland, Mary Delany, Elizabeth Vesey, and the younger members, Hester Thrale, Fanny Burney, and Hannah More. I became aware of the term 'bluestocking', and tried to work out its changing uses and their implications.

As I worked with the printed works of the women of this group, with their volumes of published correspondence, and with a mass of unpublished materials, I gradually came to realize that the bluestockings were credited with a limited accomplishment—the popularization of the salon in London—but that their underlying motives, their aspirations to a life of the mind, and in some cases to the vocation of writer, were generally overlooked.

Furthermore, I discovered that discussions of the bluestockings were often steeped to a surprising degree in an unacknowledged bias against women intellectuals and that, conversely, those who spoke favourably of them had an agenda in support of the idea of aspiring women. And I found that the impact of these underlying views has persisted into the twentieth century.

During the period around World War I pro-woman and anti-woman attitudes affected scholarship on the members of the bluestocking circle. Ethel Rolt Wheeler, who wrote *Famous Blue-Stockings* (1910), celebrated the extraordinary women of the eighteenth century who, she believed, established the salon in England, and left as their memorials their innumerable memoirs and volumes of correspondence. Chauncey Brewster Tinker, in *The Salon and English Letters: Chapters on the Interrelations of Literature and Society in the Age of Johnson* (1915), was less enthusiastic. He traced the origins of the term 'bluestocking' back to the Italians. But Tinker was not sympathetic to the idea of women with literary ambitions. He believed their contribution *should* be to create salons as centres in which men were to develop their literary talents. He believed that the contributions of the French women were superior to those of the English in this regard, and faulted the bluestockings for not measuring up to the more supportive attitudes of the French *salonières* towards the men who frequented their salons. Tinker's general view is most clearly shown in a statement he makes about the publications in defence of women at the end of the seventeenth century:

In any case, this flood of feeble defenses seems to show that woman had forgotten her high office as inspirer and patron of letters, which she had hitherto always taken for granted, and had decided to occupy herself with vague questions of equality and natural capacity. (99)

The men should be the focus of interest, and Tinker says the nearest approach to a true salon in England was the dining-room at Streatham, with Samuel Johnson reading aloud from the *Lives of the Poets* in the best French tradition (164).

The first full treatment of the bluestockings was a pioneering one. In 1947 Mary L. Robbie, in her Ph.D. thesis, 'Discovering the Bluestockings: A Neglected Constellation of Clever Women' (Univ. of Edinburgh), made a thorough survey of the lives and works of many members of the bluestocking circle. Yet she did not see them as aspiring intellectuals but as reformers who preferred conversation to cards; she found that their correspondence formed for the most part their most interesting contribution to literature.

The traditional view which stresses the importance of the bluestockings as *salonières* persisted in *The Family, Sex and Marriage in England, 1500–1800* (1977) by Lawrence Stone. He argued that 'the rise of the blue-stockings . . . as leaders of salons which included the most distinguished intellects and wits of London is proof of how at any rate some women were now forcing themselves upon male society and holding their own there' (341). Stone described a 'middle-class intellectual blue-stocking [as someone] who challenged and threatened men on their own ground of the classics' (358). His emphasis on male hostility prevented him from recognizing any influence that men might have had as mentors in encouraging the women to study and write; he also did not consider that the bluestockings may have been important in encouraging other women to educate themselves. He claimed that the bluestockings had no real influence, yet he showed that women's attitudes towards their education changed from a 'humiliating sense of their educational inferiority in 1700 to a proud claim of educational superiority in 1810' (359).

Since the full development of feminist scholarship, which has been one of the results of the most recent women's movement, some literary feminists have taken an interest in the blue-stockings as women striving for independence. Evelyn Gordon Bodek's 'Salonières and Bluestockings: Educated Obsolescence and Germinating Feminism' (1976) recognized that the blue-stockings in England were a group held together by friendship, and that the English 'blues' were not as dependent on male opinion as the French *salonières*. The French salons had male stars; the English 'blues' had a sense of solidarity as women, unlike the French. Bodek argued that the blues challenged the idea of women's inferiority; they were not feminists but individualists who claimed intelligence for women.

Marilyn L. Williamson, in 'Who's Afraid of Mrs. Barbauld? The Blue Stockings and Feminism' (1980), argued against Stone's views in *Family, Sex and Marriage*. She claimed that Stone's discussion of the attitudes and activities of Mrs Barbauld and the bluestockings is limited, even biased. Yes, she said, the bluestockings did threaten men—not by intruding into their circles, but by showing that women were capable of leading autonomous lives. Williamson found that the lasting influence of the bluestockings was to provide examples of virtuous, domestic women with intellectual interests.

Yet some feminists continue to emphasize the salon aspect of the bluestocking contribution. In her article on 'George Ballard's Biographies of Learned Ladies' (1980) Ruth Perry called them 'earnest amateurs, determined to substitute good conversation for the nightly card games which were otherwise their lot' (91). And the *Norton Anthology of Literature by Women: The Tradition in English*, edited by Sandra M. Gilbert and Susan Gubar (1985), has no examples of the writings of the bluestockings except for Fanny Burney. The anthology skips from Lady Mary Wortley Montagu, born in 1689, to Charlotte Smith, born in 1749, and goes on to Fanny Burney, born in 1752. The writings of Elizabeth Carter, Elizabeth Montagu, and Catherine Talbot of the first generation of bluestockings, and those of Hester Thrale Piozzi and Hannah More of the second generation of bluestockings, are omitted, although the editors mention that 'a small circle of aristocratic ladies, imitating the salons of French hostesses, became renowned for learning and grace' (56).

And yet the bluestockings were participants in the long history of aspiring women. As I worked on the bluestockings I began to realize that, although separated from them by differences of time, place, beliefs, and customs, I had a strong feeling of recognition. After all, women of my generation, who were educated in the period before and after World War II, also had the experience of being 'put down' for their intellectual interests and of being deprived of opportunities to carry them on.

To speak personally, as a girl growing up during the depression and World War II, I loved school and study. But somehow, though I often received praise, I was also viewed with some disdain, and spoken of as 'just a book girl'. Apparently, something of the old attitudes towards women with intellectual interests still lingered on. Graduate school after World War II was not much different. In general, women were accepted, but with a degree of reserve or indifference. Most of the young women would probably marry. We were not expected to work after marriage, and certainly not after having children. There-fore, people let us know that our advanced education would probably be a waste of time and effort.

Those of us who tried to pursue careers in academia before the most recent feminist movement began in the early 1960s experienced at first hand the kind of uneasiness generated by prejudices against women with intellectual interests, without really understanding the cause of our unease. Therefore, it has been very satisfying to me to have lived through a time when the old assumptions have been re-examined. I have tried to present the lives and works of the bluestockings against the old traditions which prevented women from becoming educated and from taking full, active parts in intellectual life. And I wish to dedicate my book to the women of my generation who struggled, often without much success, to share in the life of the mind.

S.H.M.

*Berkeley, California*

# EDITOR'S NOTE

Sylvia Myers died from a heart attack three months after the Preface was written. Her manuscript was complete, except for the Acknowledgements, and only a few final corrections had to be done. This task was assumed by her husband, and he found a brief outline which he used to construct the following Acknowledgements. He apologizes for any omissions.

# ACKNOWLEDGEMENTS

The author would like to thank Robert Halsband, Edith Larson, and Ralph Rader for scholarly assistance. Portions of her manuscript were read by Joanne Lafler, Janice Rossen, Claire Still, and Jayne Walker, and she would like to thank them for their criticism and encouraging her to complete this work. Her interest in women writers was stimulated by two organizations: the Institute for Research on Women and Gender, Stanford University, and the Institute for Historical Study, San Francisco. She was an affiliated scholar with both of these.

Her research required the co-operation of a number of libraries. These included the Bedfordshire County Record Office Archives, the British Library, the Henry E. Huntington Library, the Lewis Walpole Library, and the university libraries in Berkeley, Edinburgh, Manchester, Nottingham, and Oxford. While in Edinburgh she was affiliated with Edinburgh University's Institute for Advanced Studies. She must give special thanks to the Huntington for making available the Montagu Correspondence and for their readers' assistance staff led by Virginia Renner.

Most of the library work in England was made possible by her receiving the 1982 Ellen Moers Memorial Fellowship of the Tulsa Center for the Study of Women's Literature. She would like to thank Germaine Greer for awarding her this fellowship.

Important eighteenth-century materials were made available to her by Gwen Hampshire, Prof. John S. Macauley, and Barbara Rutherford. Their co-operation was greatly appreciated. Some people assisted her with translations from French, and these included Nicole Courtet, and Patricia Barlow and Josette.

Her husband received great support from the staff at the Huntington for the assembling of the final manuscript. The people who directly helped him with this project were Virginia Renner, Mary Robertson, and Leone Schonfeld. He would also like to thank the Rt. Hon. the Lady Lucas, the Bodleian Library, the British Library, the Houghton Library, the

Huntington Library, the John Rylands Library, and the University of Nottingham Library for granting permission to quote from manuscripts in their collections.

# CONTENTS

# LIST OF ILLUSTRATIONS

# Prologue

## Learning, Virtue, and Friendship: The Making of the Bluestocking Circle

RECENT feminist scholarship has shown the various ways in which patriarchal tenets worked to dissuade women from attempting learning, and has brought into the light women who persisted in such attempts to share the male life of the mind. *Female Scholars: A Tradition of Learned Women before 1800*, edited by J. R. Brink, contains essays on scholars like Anna Maria van Schurman, Bathsua Makin, Sor Juana Inés de la Cruz, and Elizabeth Elstob. Brink reminds us that the woman scholar was 'for the most part an oddity, labeled "unnatural" by women as well as men' (5). In *Beyond Their Sex: Learned Women of the European Past*, edited by Patricia H. Labalme, the focus is on women in various times and places in Europe. In her Introduction Labalme indicates the ways in which family status, the ambitions of male mentors, and the religious commitments of the women combined to help them be productive. But, as she points out, they lacked the support of mutual society, their works were few, and their confidence fragile (6-7).

Margaret L. King, in her contribution to *Beyond Their Sex*, 'Book-Lined Cells: Women and Humanism in the Early Italian Renaissance', shows that there were a number of learned women in the period 1350-1530. These women came from courtly or learned families, and were free to study when they were young, but as they became adults they had to choose: marriage and a life in the world or singlehood and withdrawal from the world (68-9). Only a few continued their studies after youth. And although they had some achievement and some recognition, they were partly defeated

by their own self-doubt, punctuated by moments of pride; and by their low evaluation of their sex, which undermined their confidence further and which was confirmed by the behavior of other women for whom the intellectual strivings of a few threatened their condition of comfortable servitude. (74)

We will see that similar conditions led both to the ambitions of the women who came to be called the bluestockings and to their difficulties, while changes in attitudes and customs made possible their lasting influence.

The informal group of men and women interested in literature and other intellectual matters which we call the 'bluestocking circle' flourished in England in the last half of the eighteenth century. Why and how did it happen at this point in the history of women that a group of women was able to gain some general acceptance for the idea of women as intellectuals? Like the women of the 'book-lined cells' described by King, the women of the bluestocking circle were determined to combine their learning with virtue—a term which covers such traits as chastity for single women, fidelity for married ones, and Christian piety. As with earlier generations of learned women, the bluestockings' reputation for virtue shielded them from some deliberate attacks by those prejudiced against learned women. There were, furthermore, Enlightenment views developing in late seventeenth- and eighteenth-century England which were beginning to consider the condition of women and to advocate more equitable treatment for them. The bluestockings had, in addition, the benefits of the mutual society which, as Labalme indicates, the women of early modern Europe lacked.

The success of the bluestockings—and of course it was only a partial success—came not only out of their dedication to both learning and virtue, but also out of their capacity for the male and female friendships which provided the supporting structure for their efforts. By close attention in this book to their personal development, their friendships, and their writings, I hope to show how the bluestockings functioned, what they accomplished, and what their limitations were. In Part I I will discuss the youth and early friendships of the first bluestockings (1740–58). In Part II I will discuss their decisions regarding marriage and their developing views on the condition of women. In Part III I will consider the writings which gave them their reputations as women of letters (1758–75). In Part IV I will present the nature of bluestocking fame (1775–1800). In the Epilogue I will show the varied uses of the term 'bluestocking' as a legacy from 1800 to the present.

When King Lear raged about the cruelty of his daughters, he wanted to have Regan anatomized, and thus 'see what breeds about her heart. Is there any cause in nature that makes these hard hearts?' (III. vi.). Reviewing the long history of writings against women, one might well ask the reasons why men have carried on persistent cruel treatment of them. The psychological basis for this mistreatment, with its complex motives of fear and hatred of women, seems as difficult to fathom as Regan's mistreatment of her father. Yet in *The Creation of Patriarchy*, Gerda Lerner argues that there is in fact no mystery, that the subordination of women had its origins in early history as a means of assuring the survival of small kingdoms, and that the mythology of writing against women developed to strengthen patriarchal systems. Lerner sees the educational deprivation of women as one of the ways of assuring their subordination. 'Women have not only been educationally deprived throughout historical time in every known society, they have been excluded from theory-formation' (5). The story of the bluestockings thus begins in an atmosphere of educational exclusion.

The arguments against learning for women took a variety of forms by which parents of eighteenth-century girl children could be influenced. If they read their Bibles carefully, as many still did, they might be affected by the story of Adam and Eve. As Lerner shows, 'The most powerful metaphors of gender in the Bible have been those of Woman, created of Man's rib, and of Eve, the temptress, causing humankind's fall from grace' (182). The New Testament would also give arguments for the subordination of women. Parents could take seriously the teachings of Paul, that woman was created for the sake of man, and had to acknowledge his authority (1 Cor. 11: 3–15), or that 'A woman must be a learner, listening quietly and with due submission. I do not permit a woman to be a teacher, nor must woman domineer over man; she should be quiet' (1 Tim. 1: 11–13). Worldly parents might read or attend plays; they would be exposed to satiric attacks on learned women which dramatists provided from Molière's *Femmes savantes* on. Both male and female playwrights created such ludicrous characters. The extravagantly literary Phoebe Clinket is in *Three Hours*

*After Marriage* by John Gay, Alexander Pope, and John Arbuthnot; the extravagantly experimental philosopher Valeria is in *The Basset-Table* by Susanna Centlivre. Novels could also be a source of such prejudice. A learned lady might be, as was Narcissa's aunt, a character in Smollett's novel *The Adventures of Roderick Random*, unkempt, unclean, out of touch with reality.

More significantly, a connection was often made between learned women and sexual laxity. In 'Book-Lined Cells' Margaret L. King quotes from an anonymous attack on Isotta Nogarola, a prominent woman scholar of the Italian Renaissance, in which an enemy asserts that 'an eloquent woman is never chaste; and the behavior of many learned women also confirms its truth . . .' and goes on to accuse Nogarola not only of promiscuity but also of incest (76–7). A similar assertion that learned women are lewd appears in Aubrey's *Brief Lives*, where the author describes the learned atmosphere of Wilton House and adds slanderous remarks about the supposedly lascivious conduct of Mary Sidney Herbert, Countess of Pembroke (138). The admonitions given by Alessandro Tassoni, an Italian poet of the seventeenth century, are another example of this sort of argument. His harsh view of learned women was quoted in a long note to the article on Baptiste Guarini, the author of *Pastor Fido*, in Bayle's *General Dictionary*, as late as 1737:

there is no doubt, but that study is an occasion of exciting lust, and of giving rise to many obscene actions; because, together with the reading of amorous adventures and stratagems in loose books, and especially in the solitude and leisure which study requires; obscene images present themselves, with unchaste thought and desires, under the appearance of pleasure and delight, to which the inquisitive mind abandons itself. Hence as I suppose, it is, that we find, in Euripides and Juvenal, that the learned women of antiquity were accused of immodesty, who, by perusing loose books, and conversing, upon the specious pretence of learning, more freely with men than was proper for the weakness of their sex, grew bold; so that their lust became inflamed by Idleness, and the utmost sagacity of their wit was employed to apologize for their libidinous conduct.[1]

Considering the long history of such pressures against education for women, it is not surprising that eighteenth-century women were afraid to appear too learned or too interested in learning. When Lady Mary Wortley Montagu was corresponding with her daughter, Lady Bute, from Italy, she agreed that Lady Bute should encourage her daughters to read if they enjoyed reading, but advised her to teach them not to expect applause. 'Let their Brothers shine . . .' (*Letters*, ii. 449–50). In her later years Hester Piozzi advised her adopted son not to 'breed your Girls to Literature: *My* Happiness was almost all made by it, but it is not the *natural* Soil, where Females are likely to find or form a permanent Felicity' (Houghton MS Eng. 1280, iii. 126).

A more obscure woman with intellectual interests, Jemima Campbell, later Marchioness Grey, an early and close friend of Catherine Talbot, one of the bluestockings, as a young married woman expressed her sense of unease at the idea that she might be suspected of being a learned lady. In the winter of 1744–5 Lady Grey was eating a solitary dinner in her London house when the Bishop of Oxford, Thomas Secker, called on her. Secker was Catherine Talbot's 'foster father', and had been a mentor of both young women. He offered to lend Lady Grey a new translation of Horace. The book, in four thick octavos bound in blue paper, came while she was making tea next morning for 'Fine Gem'men'. (She used these words herself in describing the incident to Catherine Talbot.) Naturally, the books were first presented to her husband, Philip Yorke, eldest son of Lord Chancellor Hardwicke, but he disowned them and referred them to his wife, who had to confess that the Bishop had said he would send them. She was rather alarmed at this accident:

An English Translation is always one should think Unexceptionable, —but then it had Latin of One Side, & *which* I read you know may be doubtful: besides an Old Latin Poet in any Dress I fear by no means belongs to a Fine London Lady.

Then Mr Wray, another gentleman at the breakfast, talked about 'Electrical Experiments' and setting a day for Lady Grey to observe them. She swallowed her tea and escaped, hoping she did not leave behind her 'the Character of *Précieuse*, *Femme Sçavante*, Linguist, Poetess, Mathematician, & any other name that any Art can be distinguished by' (Bedfordshire County Record Office, Lucas Papers, L 30/9a/4, pp. 30–32). We need to note that Lady Grey used terms which had been employed to ridicule learned women in the past, but she did not use the term 'bluestocking' because its meaning in the sense of a woman with intellectual interests had not yet been invented.

The history of the origin and changes in the use of the term 'bluestocking' illuminates both the dissatisfactions of women with the state of their opportunities to have an intellectual life at all, and the underlying attitudes of those who resisted change. When the term 'bluestocking' first appeared in Elizabeth Montagu's correspondence in 1756, it was used simply as a joke about Benjamin Stillingfleet, scholar and botanist, a well-educated but eccentric gentleman (he was the grandson of a bishop) who lacked preferment. He seems to have worn blue worsted stockings to gatherings where white hose might have been expected. 'An elegant leg in a white silk stocking was an important part of fashionable appearance' (Buck, 31). White silk hose was the mark of the gentry, or of a successful London tradesman; blue knitted wool hose was the dress of the working man (Buck, 138; 149). Blue dye, made from the leaves of the European herb woad, was the dye which was least expensive to produce, and was used for the uniform of such charity schools as the Bluecoat School (Ewing, 35).

There was a certain amount of teasing about Stillingfleet's blue stockings among Mrs Montagu's friends of the late 1750s. Samuel Torriano wrote to her (13 Nov. [1756]):

pray Madam be so good as to tell Stillingfleet I neither can nor will answer his questions till he returns to Clarges Street. Monsey swears he will make out some story of you & him [i.e. Stillingfleet], before you are much older. You shall not Keep Blew stockings at Sandleford for nothing. (MO 5153)[2]

The tone of this letter suggests the jocularity of a spa friendship, and, as I will show, these spa friendships were important to the creation of the bluestocking circle. Torriano seems to imply that Dr Messenger Monsey, an eccentric physician who wished to ingratiate himself with Mrs Montagu, was jealous of Stillingfleet, who was then visiting at Sandleford, the country home of the Montagus. In March 1757 Mrs Montagu wrote to Dr Monsey that Stillingfleet 'is so much a man of pleasure, he has left off his old friends and his blue stockings, and is at operas and other gay assemblies every night' (Doran, 270).[3]

But if Stillingfleet had even temporarily abandoned his blue stockings, the term itself remained alive, and was used in the letters of Elizabeth Montagu and her friends during the 1760s in two different ways. Most frequently it was applied to men with intellectual interests whose friendships were valued by the women as helping to develop their own studies through conversation and correspondence. Writing to George, Lord Lyttelton, on 22 November 1763 from Newcastle upon Tyne, where she had gone with her husband to oversee his extensive holdings in estates and coal-mines, Mrs Montagu contrasts her visitors in Newcastle and London:

I have not stirr'd out of my room for some days, & the fireside, which if in London would be incircled with beaux esprits & blue stocking philosophers, is now filld by stewards & people who are in the business of the Mines. Virgil, Milton, & Fingal are forgotten, of the sublime & beautifull I have at present no taste . . . (MO 1428)

Elizabeth Vesey (called by her friends The Sylph), one of Mrs Montagu's favourite companions when both were in London during the season, enjoyed the term and used it in her letters written from her home in Ireland. Mrs Montagu's reply to a letter in which Mrs Vesey described bluestocking activities in Ireland (17 [Feb. 1764]), plays with meanings of the term:

I receive such charming letters from the blue stocking Lodge, that I begin to be jealous for the Original Society. You seem to imitate the Jesuits of Paraguay, who became infinitely more rich & great than the Country from whence they went out a small colony. The imitation of Dr. Young is admirable, I may say the imitation is inimitable for it has all possible marks of resemblance and yet is not mere mimickry & that is hard to hit. I find Mr. O'Hara reveres as he ought the blue stockings of the Peripatetick philosophers; Mr. Caulfield the blue hose which encircles the nimble & taper leg of une jolie paisanne. I am not sure therefore that he is worthy of our society, however as he may be only an elegant spectator of forms, or consider blue stockings as the least deviation from the simplicity of the golden age, I am glad he is received into the Lodge, & I think we may admit him of the Colledge in time. (MO 6375)

Evidently Mrs Montagu was sceptical of the nature of Mr Caulfield's interest in the blue stockings of a 'pretty peasant', but was at least willing to consider him capable of platonic attitudes.

The Bluestocking philosophers were a source of entertainment and learning. On 2 February 1768 Mrs Montagu in London wrote to Mrs Vesey:

Mr. Montagu passd ye Xmass at Sandleford, I with the blue stocking philosophers. I had parties of them to dine with me continually, & had my Sylph been of ye party, nothing had been wanting. I have got a new blue stocking with whom I am much pleased, a Mr. Percy who publish'd ye Reliques of ye ancient Poetry, he is a very ingenious man, has many anecdotes of ancient days, historical as well as Poetical. (MO 6393)

During these years the friends had also begun to use the term to indicate a point of view—'blue stocking doctrine' or 'blue stocking philosophy'. Writing presumably in 1764, Mrs Montagu forwarded to Elizabeth Carter a letter from Mrs Vesey in Ireland: 'I introduce la chere Sylph to you, she has nobly discharged the postage to me by half a sheet of excellent epistle, she longs to be again with the blue stocking Philosophy; she was not made for ordinary society' (MO 3061, prob. after 26 June 1764). Writing to Elizabeth Carter (17 [Aug. 1765]), Mrs Montagu speaks of Mrs Vesey's problems and their cure:

She complains of stomach, & says she is languid, but I hope the late hot weather may have occasiond her languor more than any thing else. Philosophical blue stocking doctrine apply'd to her ear is the best cure for all her complaints. Sensible & ingenious minds cannot subsist without variety of rational entertainment; & then the languor of mind is charged on that most innocent Hulk ye body. If a person is robust enough to bear a course of hard study they may live in any place, with dull society sometimes, or in retirement without any society at all; but in a delicate state of health it wont do . . . Poor Vesey complains of want of rational conversation. (MO 3151)

Elizabeth Montagu saw bluestocking philosophy as a resource against the tough world of politics. After a long account to Mrs Vesey of Parliamentary debates, Mrs Montagu wrote, 'I design for the future to addict myself intirely to the Blue stocking philosophy which treads not the paths of ambition' (MO 6387). To this remark Mrs Vesey replied that she thought her friend's character 'too animated to retire to blue Stocking or any other exclusive Philosophy . . .' (MO 6276).[4]

At the end of one London season Mrs Montagu bewailed the dispersion of her friends:

& oh barbarous cruel desertion Some blue stocking philosophers went to fish for polypes in ditches, others to cull simples in the fields; the Poets to gather new blown similes in the meadows & gardens; Prose writers to meditate & reason in solitude. (MO 6376, 5 June 1764, to Elizabeth Vesey)

In the 1760s, therefore, Elizabeth Montagu and Elizabeth Vesey were using the term 'bluestocking' to refer to men with intellectual interests with whom they had friendships, and to the idea that women needed rational entertainment. But by 1774 Mrs Montagu could refer to the bluestocking circle without seeming to restrict the term to men. In a mood of disenchantment with literary interests, she wrote to Mrs Vesey on 6 August 1774 that she was temporarily giving up her interest in the Muses for a concern with Hygea, 'sweet Goddess of unthinking Mien', at least until Mrs Vesey would return to London. At the moment Mrs Montagu is choosing simple health, 'let ye delicate aspire to the more elegant joys of the blue stocking circle' (MO 6439). At this point Mrs Montagu seems to be thinking of both men and women as members of the 'Muses Coterie'. In 'Bas Bleu, or Conversation', published in 1786, Hannah More referred to men and women of the circle. As late as 1791 Hester Chapone was still using the term in this sense—symbolizing the intellectual companionship of men and women:

Are you in Town my dear Miss Burney? & do you remember an old Soul that used to love your Company? if you will give it me next Thursday Eveng you will meet Pepyss—Boscawen & so you may put on your blue Stockings. if you have got any *boots* to walk about in the mornings, *I* shall like you as well in *them*. (BL Egerton 3698, fo. 119, 27 Dec. [1791])

Mentioning a male friend (Pepys, or she may mean a married couple), and a female friend (Boscawen), Mrs Chapone was suggesting that the term itself was not something she took seriously.

But commentators on the bluestockings had begun to focus on the feminine gender by the late 1770s. Hester Thrale's references to the 'blues' in *Thraliana* are all to women. In 1779 she noted that Fanny Burney's play 'The Witlings' was not staged because of 'fear of displeasing the female Wits—a formidable Body, & called by those who ridicule them, the *Blue Stocking Club*' (*Thraliana*, i. 381 n. 3). In April 1781, describing the events just before her husband's death, Hester Thrale recounted a visit to 'Webber's Drawings of the S: Sea Rareties —we met the Smelts, the Ords, & numberless *Blues* there, & displayed our Pedantry at our Pleasure . . .' (*Thraliana*, i. 488 and n. 3—she is referring to John Webber's work as an artist on Cook's third voyage). On 17 May 1781, after her husband's death, Mrs Thrale wrote resentfully that Elizabeth Montagu was encouraging her to continue with her duties at the brewery: 'the *Wits* & the *Blues* (as it is the fashion to call them) will be happy enough no doubt to have me safe at the Brewery—*out of their way*' (i. 494).

Why did the term 'bluestocking' change its gender? Why did it not at least continue to refer to men *and* women, as it seems to have done in the late 1760s and early 1770s? Hester Thrale observed that the 'female wits' were called bluestockings by those who ridiculed them. This ridicule is instructive. The transformation of the term's meaning reflects an awareness of the fact that women had broken the taboo against learning, and the taboo against their taking a public part in intellectual life.

Of course, there were other women who had been writing and publishing, and were continuing to do so. But they often led retired and rather isolated lives, or, if they engaged in theatre or journalism, were suspect as members of a rough masculine world. In *The Celebrated Mary Astell: An Early English Feminist*, Ruth Perry has described Astell's cadenced and sober life in Chelsea (121). But her exemplary life did not prevent attacks on her for her *A Serious Proposal* in the *Tatler*, Nos. 32 and 63 (228–30). In *The Rise of the Woman Novelist: From Aphra Behn to Jane Austen*, Jane Spencer has shown that writers as different as Aphra Behn and Delariviere Manley were linked together as 'erotic and immoral women writers . . .' (53) because they did not suit burgeoning ideas of what women writers should be and do.

As it happened, the work of the first bluestockings came at a time when moral teaching and respectability were becoming central to the acceptance of women's writing, as Spencer argues (75–6); the bluestockings exemplified these values. The first bluestockings were not consistently productive, but they managed a significant number of publications between 1758 and 1775: Elizabeth Carter's translation of Epictetus (1758), her *Poems* (1762), Elizabeth Montagu's *Essay on the Writings and Genius of Shakespear* (1769), Catherine Talbot's posthumous *Reflections on the Seven Days of the Week* (1770) and her *Essays on Various Subjects* (1772), and Hester Chapone's *Letters on the Improvement of the Mind* (1773) and her *Miscellanies* (1775). Their 'fame' as scholars and writers, discussed in newspapers and periodicals, combined with interest in and gossip about their social gatherings, brought into public notice the idea that respectable women could study, write, and publish. Henceforth, used sometimes in a complimentary way, still often in a derogatory one, the term 'bluestocking' would refer to women with intellectual interests.

For the bluestockings themselves, learning, virtue, and friendship *were* inextricably linked. In their own eyes to be a bluestocking meant to be an impeccable member of an intellectual community which included both men and women. Elizabeth Montagu wrote to Elizabeth Vesey (21 Sept. 1781):

We have lived much with the Wisest, the best, & most celebrated Men of our Times, & with some of the best, most accomplish'd & most learned Women of any times. These things I consider, not merely as pleasures transient, but as permanent blessings, by such Guides & Companions we were set above the low temptations of Vice & folly, & while they were the instructors of our Minds they were the Guardians of our Virtue. (MO 6566)

The women of the first circle formed the model and point of departure for others, so that by the 1770s and 1780s knowledge of the bluestocking circle had spread widely, and many women were imitating their social and literary activities. Hester Thrale, Fanny Burney, Hannah More, as members of the second generation, came on to the scene when the idea of bluestocking interests had already been established, and some progress had been made. Although the pressures against the idea of the intellectual woman never vanished entirely, its expression changed, and the ways in which negative attitudes were displayed were in general not as scurrilous as they had been. These second-generation bluestockings could regard themselves as women who were carrying on a complex of literary and social activities which were a known and accepted part of their society, though they were still conscious that reproof might be expected.

Furthermore, the word 'bluestocking' developed a life of its own as women in other countries began to engage in similar pursuits. By the early nineteenth century the term 'bluestocking' had made its way into at least five European languages—French, German, Dutch, Danish, and Swedish.[5]

As I shall show, controversies aroused by the idea of the bluestocking continued from the late eighteenth century into the nineteenth century. Bluestockings were attacked as being affected, but they were also defended because they demonstrated that women had an equal right to education with men and, moreover, were equally capable of intellectual effort. As education for women became more widely accepted later in the nineteenth century and into the twentieth, stresses and difficulties continued to affect the intellectual woman, who often continued to be called a bluestocking. But, despite the resistance implied by some uses of the term, the efforts of the bluestockings to gain for themselves and others the 'female right to literature' succeeded at least in creating an image of the educated woman as a respectable member of society.

# PART I

# The First Bluestockings: Mentors, Families, and Friends (1740–1758)

# Introduction

ATTENTION has often been paid to the social activities of the female bluestockings without recognizing the extent to which the bluestockings were innovative in their personal development. The social activities and ease of the bluestocking circle were the by-products of a way of life which these women created, in which friendships supported the intellectual interests and the independent views of a group of women drawn from several levels of society and different parts of the country. The personal development of these women was the end result of a process of decision-making which had started in girlhood, when they had begun to try to shape their lives in a particular direction. This direction was affected by mentors, family ties, marriage or its absence, and by friendships.

A recent study of the development of women, *In a Different Voice* by Carol Gilligan, helps to throw light on this process. Gilligan has shown that the developmental stages of females proceed differently from those of males. Gilligan argues that a young woman, as she develops, sees herself not as an entity achieving separation from the mother and purposefully ascending a series of stages (as a young man does), but as an individual with a continuing need for relationships that, extending from herself as a centre, form a 'female web of experience'. Even for women of the present time, autonomy follows rather than precedes connectedness; with the greater emphasis on autonomy, a modern woman has to learn how to mediate her drive towards autonomy with her need for connectedness.

For these eighteenth-century women autonomy also followed connectedness. Although, as I shall show in Chapter 5, these young women did not really have a sense of a feminist tradition, they had some role models whom they could follow, they knew some writers on the condition of women by whom they were influenced, and they had the support of mentors, family members, and friends who encouraged them in the direction of autonomy.

Growing up female in the middle of the eighteenth century

in England of course meant being moulded, sometimes with subtlety, more often with unquestioning demands, to the requirements of its society. But there evidently was leeway for developing interests and initiative in particular cases. As in the case of previous generations of learned women, the status of the family, the interest of an educated father, the presence of brothers who were being educated, might make it possible for a girl growing up in England during the 1720s and 1730s to receive a careful, sometimes even a solid, education.

Gina Luria, writing in *Signs* in 1978, pointed out the important part which generous male mentors have played in helping women to pursue a life of the mind. She argued that since the dissolution of the convents in the fifteenth century, and the absence of formal education for women in the following centuries, most English women who turned to intellectual life did so with the help of learned men. Such male mentors show the

existence of an important support for women living in sex-stratified cultures, the honorable alliance possible between men and women which has served, at least in part, to counteract just those societal constraints against the female mind which every woman writer has had to face and find a way around. (376)

In the generation which produced the first bluestockings, mentors (most often fathers or brothers) were influential in helping these girls to read and study. In such cases the interest was mutual: the girls were bright, curious, generally assertive by nature; their male mentors felt some commitment to helping them become educated by sharing their books and knowledge, and enjoyed doing so.

The bluestockings took their family ties seriously. Irene Q. Brown has shown the importance of the ideal of rational affection in the upper-class eighteenth-century English family in 'Domesticity, Feminism, and Friendship: Female Aristocratic Culture and Marriage in England, 1660–1760'. She points out that the ideal of rational domesticity helped to liberate the individual within a supportive family framework (415). In the cases of the women I will discuss, parental relationships were important; there were varying degrees of closeness and of stress. Girls were often close to both their brothers and sisters, but again there were instances of friction and sometimes conflict. Yet some family members evolved into lifelong 'friends'. The talent for friendship was exportable; other friendships developed outside the family circle. When they were young, these women were able to make female friends who sometimes acted as mentors and helped in developing autonomy by offering opportunities for self-awareness and self-expression.

In *Women's Friendship in Literature*, Janet Todd analysed the presentation of female friendships in a number of eighteenth-century novels. She separated these friendships into five categories: sentimental, erotic, political, manipulative, and social (4). Because real-life friendships show a mixture of elements, I prefer to use the term 'supportive' for the bluestocking friendships. Sometimes bluestocking friendships did involve sentimental effusions. Sometimes friends made efforts in regard to practical matters, such as patronage, which verged on the political. In a few instances there were manipulative tendencies. These elements were actually combined with what Todd called 'social' or nurturing friendships. The category which is not represented is the erotic.

In general, the bluestockings resisted the erotic element, although they were aware of its importance to other members of their society. They particularly disliked conventional male 'gallantry' in which women were treated in a flattering way as sex objects. As respectable women of the eighteenth century, committed to virtue and chastity, the bluestockings resisted the intrusion of eroticism into both their male and female friendships.

Mrs Montagu shows in her letters awareness of sexual deviancy. In a letter to the Duchess of Portland which Elizabeth Robinson wrote in her youth she was puzzling about a homosexual scandal, probably at Tunbridge Wells:

I heard of a scandalous story that except as it is scandalous is not fit to report to a Lady, of the younger Mr Byng, whose name I think is Ned, they say he is to be prosecuted for some particular fondness of a Barber, but I don't know what they mean, I am afraid to mention his name the Gentlemen laugh so much & the Ladies don't seem quite ignorant of it. (MO 260, 4 Sept. 1736)

As a young married woman she was exercised about an

overly affectionate relationship between two women which seems to have been the subject of gossip, again at Tunbridge Wells. She said that a certain Mrs Cotes was well rid of her charge, and it was being reported that Mrs Lyttelton had taken that person to live with her:

> which I must confess I am sorry for, as it will add to the jests the Men made on that friendship, & I own I think those sort of reports hurt us all, And fall in their degree on the whole Sex: and really if this nonsence gains ground one must shut oneself up alone; for one can not have Men Intimates, & at this rate the Women are more scandalous, so we must become Savages & have no friendships or connextions . . .

The friendship referred to was between 'Mrs L– – & Miss R', who made a 'parade of their affection', which Mrs Montagu thought would give some people opportunities to make up lies (MO 5719, 18 [?Sept. ?1750], to Sarah Robinson). The significant point here is that Mrs Montagu felt that sexuality interfered with friendships both between men and women, and between women.

The current views of feminists who stress a relationship between female friendships and lesbianism are leading to some serious distortions about friendships among women in general, and the bluestockings in particular. Although I agree with Adrienne Rich's argument in 'Compulsory Heterosexuality and Lesbian Existence' that female friendships are one way in which women have been able to rebel from or evade the demands of patriarchal societies, I do not think these friendships necessarily meant that these women were excluding themselves from friendships with men or were erotically attracted to other women. Certainly, I do not think her term 'lesbian continuum' (648) as an umbrella term covering all women who had strong female friendships is appropriate for the study of eighteenth-century women.

Bonnie Zimmerman discusses the problem of definition in 'What Has never Been: An Overview of Lesbian Feminist Literary Criticism'. She offers three definitions. The most conservative is that of Catharine R. Stimpson in 'Zero Degree Deviancy: The Lesbian Novel in English', which limits lesbianism to 'carnal' relationships. (In the article Stimpson says that a lesbian 'is a woman who finds other women erotically attractive and gratifying' (364).) At the other extreme is the definition of Adrienne Rich proposing the 'lesbian continuum', which Zimmerman thinks is very broad. Zimmerman finds that the definition of Lillian Faderman in *Surpassing the Love of Men: Romantic Friendship and Love between Women from the Renaissance to the Present* takes a middle ground. Zimmerman warns that all-inclusive definitions of lesbianism like that of Adrienne Rich 'risk blurring the distinctions between lesbian relationships and non-lesbian female friendships, or between lesbian identity and female-centered identity' (205). Zimmerman also finds problems with Faderman's framework as it relates to actual cases. I agree, and will discuss Faderman's view of the Carter–Talbot friendship in Chapter 3.

Following Rich, Moira Ferguson in *First Feminists* has characterized a whole range of female friendships as on a 'lesbian continuum' (23). Attempting to fit the bluestockings on this range leads to misconceptions about their relationships. I think the friendships between these women should be called 'supportive', and the term 'lesbian' should be restricted to overt sexual female relationships—a kind of relationship of which eighteenth-century women like Mrs Montagu were certainly aware.

As we have seen from Mrs Montagu's letters quoted above, young eighteenth-century women were not totally ·sheltered from awareness of social realities. Actually, perhaps without realizing the consequences, their society fostered customs which were helpful in allowing for the development of female autonomy. The activities of the year were organized according to the seasons and the weather. Women who had some financial ability to travel could be actively involved in social life during long stays in London in winter and early spring, and then have the advantage of retreat to other homes in the country during late spring, summer, early autumn. Month-long visits to spas, relatives, or friends varied the scene. These customs eventually helped to create a cadence to both male and female bluestocking friendships. In their visits to each other during the season in London, or at spas like Tunbridge or Bath, and by their long-enduring correspondence from distant country places, they

wove a fabric of connectedness which supported their autonomous interests. The evolving pattern of bluestocking interests is
foreshadowed in the early friendship of Lady Margaret Cavendish Harley (later Bentinck, the second Duchess of Portland)
with Elizabeth Robinson (later Montagu).

# 1 · The Importance of Bulstrode

IN the summer and autumn of 1740 Elizabeth Robinson, just past her twentieth birthday, made her first long visit to Bulstrode, the country home of Margaret and William Bentinck, the second Duke and Duchess of Portland. This visit marked an intensification of the friendship between Elizabeth and her friend, the former Lady Margaret Cavendish Harley, that had begun some time before 1732, when Elizabeth was twelve and Lady Margaret was seventeen. Now Bulstrode, as a setting for congenial family and friends with social and intellectual interests, made a lasting impact on its young visitor.

Elizabeth's friendship with Lady Margaret had begun in another stately home, Wimpole Hall, the seat of Lady Margaret's parents, Edward Harley, the Earl of Oxford, and his wife Henrietta (familiarly called Harriet), Countess of Oxford. Born in 1715, Lady Margaret was an only daughter, and their only surviving child. Lady Henrietta was herself the only child and heiress of John Holles, Duke of Newcastle of the second creation. She brought to her marriage the great estates of Welbeck Abbey in Nottinghamshire, Wimpole Hall in Cambridgeshire, as well as extensive properties in London. Lord Harley, as he was then known, was the son of the powerful Tory politician, Robert, Earl of Oxford, Chancellor of the Exchequer and Lord Treasurer during the reign of Queen Anne; after the death of Queen Anne and the accession of George I, Oxford was impeached and imprisoned by the Whigs.

Lord Harley participated only marginally in political life before the death of his father. When he became Earl of Oxford in 1724, he avoided active politics altogether. He had inherited a substantial collection of books and manuscripts gathered by his father and grandfather, and it was to collecting that Lord Oxford devoted much of his energies and a large part of his wife's fortune. In addition to books, pamphlets, manuscripts, documents, he also collected pictures, engravings, coins, and objects of antiquity. People wrote to him about prospective purchases for his library; he also travelled through England to observe sights, visit great houses, and examine antiquities. He lent books and manuscripts to scholars and friends. In his account of Lord Oxford in *Earls of Creation*, James Lees-Milne gave the general size of the library as 50,000 printed books, 8,000 volumes of manuscripts, 41,000 prints, and 350,000 pamphlets (181).[1]

When Lady Margaret was a child, her family lived at Wimpole during part of the year. A country house of red brick, Wimpole had begun as a seventeenth-century mansion built by Sir Thomas Chicheley. In 1710 it was bought by John Holles, Duke of Newcastle, and on his death was inherited by Lady Henrietta. After his marriage in 1713 Lord Harley had begun to enlarge the house and to improve the landscape. His architect, James Gibbs, added a west wing, a chapel in the east wing, and a library designed to house the Harleian collection. The chapel was decorated in baroque style by James Thornhill. The great room for the library, a room 50 feet long by 23 feet wide, was finished in 1730 (National Trust, *Wimpole Hall*, 18). That summer Alexander Pope wrote to Lord Oxford expressing his enthusiasm for the new room.

I will fancy I am standing on the Stone-Steps at the Great door to receive you, & that I have just been Setting the Bells a-ringing in your parish church. I am impatient to follow you to the New-roof'd Library, & see what fine new lodgings the Ancients are to have. (*Correspondence*, iii. 114)

Young Elizabeth Robinson, visiting the house with her parents several years later, was probably impressed by the great library room and the brilliant chapel.

Lady Margaret was the child of careful and loving parents. The letters of Jonathan Swift, Alexander Pope, and Matthew Prior to Lord Oxford show an attentiveness to Lady Margaret (called Peggy by Prior) which must reflect the interest and concern the parents themselves showed their only child. Swift congratulated Lord Oxford on Lady Margaret's recovery from smallpox (*Correspondence*, iii. 393). Pope showed an attentiveness to her presence and graces. Once when he was ill during a visit to the Oxfords, Pope enjoyed Lady Margaret's 'obliging, sweet, & Thisbean Conversation thro a Wainscote Wall'

(*Correspondence*, iii. 187). Matthew Prior was a frequent guest at Wimpole when Lady Margaret was a child. She remembered him, and said he had made himself beloved by everyone in the house (Porter, 29–33; Lees-Milne, 195–6). He wrote for her the well-known poem, 'My noble, lovely, little Peggy', in which he urged her to be a 'devout Christian and a good daughter' (Lees-Milne, 196).

We know little about Lady Margaret's education. She had a governess, Miss Philippa Walton, and learned French and Italian. Her mother had her own library of books, some of which had been given her by her husband and by the men of letters who were friends and recipients of patronage. Among the books she marked as having read in the 1720s and 1730s were *Poems* of Katherine Philips, Sir John Denham's *Poems*, Dryden's *Works*, Beaumont and Fletcher's works, Sidney's *Arcadia*. She also read books of travels, and in later years noted having read Theobald's edition of Shakespeare, Shelton's translation of *Don Quixote*, Pope's *Works*, Clarendon's *Rebellion*, Aubrey's *Antiquities of Surrey*, and Dr C. Deering's *Catalogue of Nottingham Plants* (Goulding, 14–17). She probably shared her interests in literature, history, and botany with Lady Margaret, whose interests followed similar lines.

It is not known to what extent Lady Margaret browsed in her parents' libraries, but we do know that she accompanied them on trips that might be said to have had educational purposes. In 1730, when Lady Margaret was fifteen, Lord Oxford received a Doctor of Civil Law degree at Oxford University. His wife and daughter were present for the ceremony. Conyers Middleton, Elizabeth Robinson's step-grandfather, a scholar and librarian at Cambridge, was a member of the party, and received a second Doctor of Divinity degree at the same time.

When Lady Margaret was seventeen, her father took his wife, daughter, her governess, and his nephew, Lord Dupplin, on a trip through parts of the counties of Suffolk, Norfolk, and Cambridgeshire. They made a systematic tour of the area, visiting country seats, the remains of abbeys, as well as churches and towns.

The family party covered 208 miles in ten days. Lord Oxford's notes reveal a downright, rather plain-spoken, often critical landowner and collector. He judged gentlemen's estates in terms of their architecture, furnishings, art, and improvements; towns he viewed in terms of churches, civic buildings, extent of trade, cleanliness, and treatment of the poor. He copied churchyard inscriptions. Once he noticed some large birds called bustards which he believed to be rare, and which were being hunted because of their rarity, and expressed the wish that they should not be molested. His notes mention the ladies only once—when he and Lord Dupplin rode out to visit Lord Townshend, and left the ladies to come in their own time two hours later.

This trip may be taken as the young woman's equivalent of the Grand Tour. Sons of noblemen might be sent on an extensive tour of Europe—but these parents had no son, for their only other child, Henry Cavendish, born on 18 October 1725, lived only four days. Lady Margaret was an heiress to immense wealth, and it does seem that by sharing with her their observations and travel, her parents were training her to deal with the world in a direct and practical way.

But the model for her independent interests seems to have come from her father rather than her mother. Lord Oxford had his collections, his travels, his friendships with and patronage of scholars and men of letters. Lady Oxford was also a collector —but a collector of a special kind. After her death Horace Walpole remarked that during her widowhood, except for doing many just and right things, Lady Oxford spent her time 'in collecting and monumenting the portraits and reliques of all the great families from which she descended, and which centred in her' (xxxv. 271). In the variety of her collecting interests, in her patronage of scientists, and in her friendships, Lady Margaret was her father's daughter.

As she matured, marriage was what her parents wanted for Lady Margaret and what she herself welcomed. Lady Margaret's bridegroom was William Bentinck, second Duke of Portland, a descendant of Hans William Bentinck of Holland. I will discuss the details of the Portlands' marriage in Chapter 4, for the financial arrangements show what a union of wealth and title involved, and make a clear contrast between Lady Margaret's situation and that of Elizabeth Robinson.

Lady Oxford was clearly a dominating mother, and her

daughter was aware of her domination and resisted it. She may have discussed the restraints of her condition with her friends. Writing to Catherine Collingwood before Lady Margaret's marriage, another friend, Anne Vernon, expressed her happiness that Lady Margaret's marriage would release her '*out of her prison*' (Delany, 1st ser., i. 482). As a married woman writing to her friend Elizabeth Robinson, the Duchess expressed her distaste for her mother's formality and protectiveness. It was a burden to have to be prompt to meals during a family visit at Welbeck, and especially to be prevented from going out. 'I am not to Stir out of sight Least I should Break my nose or Tumble into the fire & if I was to go out I might be Stole for a Great Fortune . . .' (MO 197).

Given her family circumstances, it is hardly surprising that Lady Margaret took up her married life with the handsome Duke with buoyancy. The Portlands participated in some Court functions, but the Duchess did not enjoy formal visiting. The Duke did not take an active part in politics. He was elected a Fellow of the Royal Society in 1739, and was installed a Knight of the Garter on 20 March 1741. The usual custom of the Portlands was to live with their family at their country house, Bulstrode, near Gerrard's Cross in Buckinghamshire, during the summer, autumn, and part of the winter. Later winter and early spring were usually spent at their town house in Privy Garden, Whitehall. They were especially fortunate that Bulstrode was not a long journey from London, so visitors could come up, or on occasion they could go down to London if business required. Taken speedily, the journey from Bulstrode could be made in three and a half hours. Mary Pendarves reported, 'We set out from Bulstrode at eleven, and were in town by half an hour after two, over hills of snow and heaps of ice; but our horses flew as if each had been Pegasus—four coaches and six, with twelve horsemen attending' (1st ser., ii. 23).

As her father had formed a world out of interests supported by friendships, so the Duchess expanded her domestic life by cultivating her interests and friends. The Duchess was also fortunate in that her husband was a good-humoured man, who enjoyed participating in the social activities of the house. Notes written to his old tutor, Mr Achard, who remained a member of the household, show that the Duke enjoyed his children, and paid attention to their education (Univ. of Nottingham Library, MS PC PwC 71–96). In addition to supervising his properties, hunting, and nursing the painful attacks of gout which began to trouble him in his early thirties, the Duke read and conversed with the various friends whom his wife attracted to Bulstrode. Among her women friends were Mary Pendarves, later Delany, her sister Anne, later Dewes, Anne Donnellan, and the young Elizabeth Robinson, whom his wife called Fidget because of her quickness of movement. Fidget amused the Duke. Writing to Mr Achard from Bulstrode, 30 December 1740, Portland recounted an ingenuous remark the young lady had made. They had been talking about Dr Sandys, a prominent physician, who had recently married. Lord George (the Duke's brother) thought the doctor's marriage would interfere with his practice: 'wt says Fidgett is Dr. Sandys wife to be brought oftner in a year than an other woman and so he be taken up entirely wth her; this occasioned a great laugh as you may easily imagine' (Univ. of Nottingham Library, MS PC PwC 81). Life in the country could be dull, and the Duke evidently enjoyed the young woman who brought the sparkle of youth and the charm of *naïveté* into the family circle. Elizabeth Robinson was just finishing her first long visit to Bulstrode at the time of the Duke's letter. Her background, family situation, and financial resources were very different from those of the second Duchess.

Born on 2 October 1720, in York, Elizabeth was the fourth child and first daughter of Matthew Robinson and Elizabeth Drake Robinson. Matthew Robinson, holder of landed property in Yorkshire, and a commoner at Trinity College, Cambridge, had married Elizabeth Drake, heiress to property in Cambridgeshire and Kent, when he was eighteen. Robinson was a lively, sociable gentleman and a skilled painter. He is seen 'in a suit of greyish-gold, laced with silver' at the centre of a portrait by Gawen Hamilton called 'A Group of Vertuosi' (1735), reproduced by Anne Buck in *Dress in Eighteenth-Century England* (30). The original is in the National Portrait Gallery, London. Elizabeth Drake Robinson was a strong, rather stoical woman. Doran claimed she had been educated at Bathsua Makin's academy at Tottenham High Cross, which was known for its solid education for girls (6); if so, she probably encouraged her daughters to study and may have helped in their education. Mrs Robinson's letters, written in a firm angular script which is almost print, are sensible, thoughtful, but not emotional. As we shall see, she gave her daughter stiff, rational advice at a time when others were more sympathetic. She was very concerned about the careers of her sons. Later she bore her terminal illness, breast cancer, and its treatment by surgery, with stoical endurance.

When Elizabeth was about seven, her mother inherited property in Kent and the family moved to a house called Mount Morris at Horton near Hythe. The nine surviving children—seven boys and two girls—were raised there.

But there were long visits to Cambridge. Elizabeth's maternal grandmother, Sarah Morris Drake (c.1673–1731), had been widowed, and as her second husband she had married (c.1710) Dr Conyers Middleton, fellow of Trinity College, Cambridge, controversialist and later principal librarian. In his 'Anecdotes Relating to Dr. Conyers Middleton', Horace Walpole claimed that Middleton was at first Lord Oxford's librarian, but the exact nature of Dr Middleton's duties, and the period when he took them up, have not been established (xv. 291-2 nn. 3,4). The appointment seems to have been informal, in any case, and seems to have involved only occasional residence at Wimpole. Dr Middleton wrote his first controversial pamphlet, *A Letter to Dr. Waterland*, which raised suspicions of his religious scepticism, in 1730. When his authorship of the pamphlet was discovered, Lord Oxford took umbrage and the friendship seems to have cooled.

Dr Middleton relinquished his fellowship on his marriage; according to William Cole, Mrs Middleton's fortune made it possible for the couple to live in an 'excellent house adjoining Caius College and looking into the Theatre Yard, and near St. Mary's Church, in the most cheerful part of the town' (Walpole, xv. 305). There were family visits from the Robinsons; writing to Elizabeth after her marriage Dr Middleton reminded her that her three youngest brothers were 'all born under my roof' (Montagu (1810-13), ii. 201). Evidently, Mrs Robinson came to her mother's house to have her last children.

Elizabeth's long visits in the house of this learned gentleman between her sixth and thirteenth year must have been influential. Her nephew, Matthew Montagu, claimed that as a child Elizabeth had been encouraged by Dr Middleton to listen to 'learned' conversation and later required to summarize the talk (Montagu (1810–13), i. 3–4). This practice may have been something Mrs Montagu told her nephew about years later; there seem to be no references to such a custom in her letters. In one of his congratulatory letters to Elizabeth Montagu on her marriage, Dr Middleton did say that he had observed her 'amiable qualities from her tenderest years' (MO 1551). Later he reminded her that Cambridge University had educated Mr Montagu, and that Cambridge had had a share in her education (Montagu (1810–13), ii. 202). I don't think it was a case of formal instruction. Elizabeth was pretty and vivacious. If some of her brothers were away at school, she would have been one of the older children, and certainly she was the oldest girl. Dr Middleton probably found amusement in encouraging her. His attention and praise would stimulate her towards learning. A few years later she wrote about him in a derogatory manner, but her letters to Dr Middleton after her marriage are very respectful.

The friendship of Lady Margaret Harley and Elizabeth Robinson must have begun during those family visits to Cambridge. Elizabeth's parents probably called at Wimpole Hall, eight miles from Cambridge. Elizabeth may have stayed the night there. The first letter we have in a long correspondence between the two friends was received at Wimpole on 24 February 1731/2, when Elizabeth was not yet twelve, and Lady Margaret was seventeen. Written in a careful, immature hand, the letter tells of pain Elizabeth has had in her face, and that the pain may seem greater because she lacks her Ladyship's 'company and compassion' which she had had at Wimpole (MO 235). In typically mercurial fashion, the young girl first expounds on Lady Margaret's condescension in asking Elizabeth to write to her, but ends flippantly, 'I am in great hopes that when your ladyship sees any impertinent people at London it will put you in mind' of her humble self. The bright, rather excitable girl appealed to her affectionate, fun-loving older friend, and a friendship began which continued, though not without strains, through the lives of both women.

Elizabeth was the eldest daughter, but had three brothers

older than herself—Matthew, seven years older, Thomas, six years older, and Morris, five years older. Robert was about a year younger than she. Sarah, her only sister, was three years younger. Between the time she was six and thirteen, three more brothers were born. Elizabeth had fond memories of growing up with her brothers as her 'playfellows', and with her sister as a close confidante. Elizabeth's interest in developing her abilities and in 'showing off' seems to have come from her childhood in this large, active family dominated by brothers. The children were so vociferous that Mother was required to moderate, and was dubbed 'The Speaker' for her services. But Elizabeth Montagu also recalled with pain the room in which her father used to chide the children. Mrs Montagu wrote to her sister, 'I have in my nature such an aversion to scolding that I [cannot] think of ye room where Papa used to scold all dinnert[ime] without a frisson', although 'that room in which we lived in such tender harmony will always be dear to me.' Sometimes gaiety made their home a palace; at other times tyrannical caprice and peevishness made it a prison (MO 6006, 12 [July 1777]). These complaints were directed at her father. In later life Elizabeth Montagu had open quarrels with him.

Elizabeth also got an early sense of the limitations she would have to accept as a woman in contrast to her brothers. She was eager to share their activities, but when they hunted birds' nests together, she would not, or could not, climb as high as they. (Perhaps her clothing interfered.) She remembered the limitation as an adult, writing to Lord Lyttelton that 'if I had been a boy, when I had gone a birds nesting, I should have indeavour'd to have climb'd to the Eagles Ayerie' (MO 1428, 22 Nov. 1763). She was aware of the limitations involved in being female when she was sent to stay with another country family because of an outbreak of smallpox at home. Her eldest brother had visited her and was going on to Bath. She writes, 'I wish I could metamorphosis myself into a Brother from a Sister to go with him . . .' (MO 281, 10 Sept. [1739]).

As she was growing up, she must have often been reminded of the restrictions inherent in being female. When she was in her early teens, the eldest brother, Matthew, went to Cambridge. Morris and Thomas went to London to study law. Soon afterwards, Robert, who was younger than she, went to sea. Elizabeth remained in the country. Her father got testy in winter from the sheer boredom of a country existence, but he usually delayed their visits to London until early spring, and kept them short. Finances were probably the reason. The Robinsòns did not have a house in London and had to take lodgings. A short visit reduced the expenses. Her parents sometimes teased Elizabeth about her eagerness to be off to London. Of course, her brothers could go to London alone, but she had to wait for her parents' company.

For Elizabeth the tedium of living in the country was lightened by local dances, visits to Tunbridge Wells, and her letters from her friend. Lady Margaret offered warmth and compassion, and in exchange the bright young girl sent epistolary amusements based on the dullness of her life in the country and on any little adventures which her father permitted her. The correspondence between the great heiress and the young daughter of the gentry—respectable, with inherited land, but not wealthy and with seven sons and two daughters to think of—was surprisingly fresh and outspoken. Elizabeth had the spirit of a young caricaturist and entertained her friend with titbits of gossip and country scandals, the excitement of visits to Tunbridge Wells, the Canterbury Races, an occasional coach accident or near-accident. At Tunbridge Wells she looked for verses to send her friend, but could find none, even though 'at the latter end of the season when the garrets grow cheap that the Poets come down, there is commonly plenty' (MO 240).

Although differing in age, family situation, and prospects, the friends developed a correspondence which seems to have amused and entertained them. On at least one occasion Elizabeth wrote an effusive letter describing her excessive feelings of love towards the Duchess, but in general the tone was light and humorous. Somewhat surprisingly, Dr Middleton, Elizabeth's supposedly esteemed relative, served as a convenient scapegoat. They exchanged gossip about Dr Middleton's latest marriage, the physical peculiarities of his wife, an expected child, Dr Middleton's pride in his performance, and the eventual loss of the child. The letters also suggest a particular irritation with Dr Middleton's controversial religious views, and in fact a general tendency to find the learned people of Cambridge who came to Wimpole a source of humour.

As the young women were sharing with each other their growing knowledge of the world, adultery also became a source of humour. In 1735 Elizabeth shared some bits of scandalous gossip with the Duchess of Portland about an adulterous couple. It seemed that Sir George Saville was going to sue for divorce because he had found his wife in bed with Mr Levans. The fourteen-year-old correspondent remarked that the husband first suspected his wife's infidelity when he saw a black spot on her arm which Mr Levans had given her 'by a loving squeeze . . .'. Elizabeth thought he should have handled her more gently (MO 249). Her informant had also told her that five more gentlemen were going to get divorces, but to the Duchess's request for specifics, Elizabeth later had to reply that she was unable to give any names. The person who told her said he had forgotten them (MO 256). Several years later she wrote that she had sat up until 2 a.m. (after everyone had gone to bed) to write a letter which included gossip about the scandal involving Theophilus Cibber and his wife (MO 273, 17 Dec. [1738], Mount Morris).

After Lady Margaret's marriage in July of 1734, her governess sent Elizabeth some wedding-cake (MO 246). During the next few years Elizabeth began to have a share in her friend's London life and in her growing family, usually in early spring when the Robinsons took lodgings in London for a visit. Probably it was in the spring of 1738 that Elizabeth was invited to stay on at Whitehall with the Portlands. The Duchess was expecting a child, and Elizabeth told her father that she had been asked to help receive with her during the formal ceremonies which would follow the birth. His daughter would be meeting 'all the people of quality of both Sexes' and would also go about with the Duchess in town. Therefore she needed a new 'Suit of Cloaths', whose value she left to her father to decide (MO 4756).[2]

Mr Robinson sent his daughter twenty pounds. Revealing the pecuniary prudence which was to become a lifelong characteristic, Elizabeth bought a fabric with a damaged portion. As she explained to her mother,

I have obey'd your commands as to my cloaths & have bought a very handsom blue & silver Ducape within the twenty pound, a little accident which had happen'd to the silk in the Lomb made it a great deal cheaper & I believe it will not be at all the worse when it is made up, the colour in some places is a little damaged but that will cut for the tail & the rest is perfectly good . . . (MO 4707)[3]

In the spring of 1739 Elizabeth again visited London and stayed with the Portlands after her family returned to Kent. That the relationship was close is indicated by the tone of the Duke's letters to Elizabeth. Elizabeth had returned home before the birth of Lady Margaret in July 1739. The Duchess was very ill after that birth, and the Duke wrote notes to keep Elizabeth informed of the state of his wife's health, and that of 'her little known & unknown friends' (MO 443, 15 Sept. 1739).

From the literary point of view the Duchess was already finding her friend's letters bright and cleverly expressed. She especially enjoyed Elizabeth's letters from Bath. The Robinsons had gone there in the autumn of 1739 for the health of both Elizabeth and her mother. Although Elizabeth claimed to find this visit boring, she wrote the Duchess some amusing letters about the customs of the place:

Lord Aylesford comes to the Rooms every night like Beau Clincher in a Blanket, he wears a nasty red rugg great Coat, with a belt to comfort his bowels or prevent a rupture I don't know which; his daughter Lady Ann is as good natured, as merry, as fat, & as awkward, as any Lady of her age in England. . . . The Dowager Dutchess of Norfolk bathes, & being very tall she had like to have drown'd a few women in the Cross Bath, for she ordered it to be fill'd till it reach'd her chin, & so all those who were below her Stature as well as rank were forced to come out or drown, & finding it according to the Proverb in vain to strive against the Stream they left the Bath rather than swallow so large a draught of water. I believe a Husband may be necessary for those Ladies who are apt to turn topsy turvy, but for us who can stand upon our own legs I think it by no means necessary . . . (MO 289)

Elizabeth's reference to husbands reflects her increasing aware-ness of the problem of marriage, and her determination not to be pressured into a marriage which did not suit her.

In the spring of 1740 Elizabeth was again in London with her parents and sister; when they went home to Kent, Elizabeth stayed on with the Portlands. Elizabeth and her sister Sarah (or Sally) had been so close that they were called the two 'peas'. Sally's return to Kent with her parents was the beginning of the first really long separation of the sisters. Elizabeth wrote to the Freinds—William Freind (son of the Revd Dr Robert Freind, Headmaster of Westminster School), and his wife, her cousin Grace Robinson, 'think of the cruel divisions of the Peas on sunday morning and sigh sympathetically . . .' (MO 1001, 22 [May 1740], Leicester St.). Elizabeth was ambivalent about being apart from her sister. She missed her company, but was eager to take up the opportunities associated with her friend-ship with the Duchess. So she promised Sarah 'you will be acquainted with her Grace next winter, & Mrs Pendarves & the rest of my friends . . .' (MO 5553, 22 [Sept. 1740], Bulstrode). But, although Sarah met her sister's friends, she never became a member of the group. When the girls were young, the cause may have been resistance on the part of the Robinson parents to having the younger girl join her sister in this higher life. Later, after Sarah had developed her own writing interests and had had the painful experience of her marital separation, she maintained her friendship with her sister, but showed definite resistance to living her life in her sister's orbit.

During the stay in London which preceded the visit to Bulstrode, Elizabeth sat for her picture at Mr Zincke's, visited Mary Pendarves at Sir John Stanley's at North End, and went to Lord Oxford's ball (MO 4708, to Elizabeth Drake Robinson, [27 May 1740, London]). She wrote to her mother that she was taking a course of cold bathing for her health. She had become aware that differences in the social standing of her friends affected relationships. When she called on a Kentish friend (Mrs Knight) in London, the Duchess set her down at the door. The coach with its liveried footmen and its ducal insignia must have been rather intimidating; Elizabeth thought Mrs Knight's reception of her was 'constrain'd'. Elizabeth visited a second time, because she was afraid her friend 'shou'd say that now I ke[pt] company with great folks I did not remember little ones . . .'. She added that she had dined at Lord and Lady Oxford's in Dover Street, and worn her new 'head'—a head-dress that was a gift from the Duchess. Elizabeth thought it 'extreamly hansome, very broad & the lace has more thin work in it than has been made till this year . . .' (MO 4710, [17 June 1740, London]).

The pleasures of London were interrupted by the illness with smallpox of the Portlands' friend, Lady Wallingford, and the sudden death of her husband, Lord Wallingford. Although the Portlands' return to the country was delayed by these events, they finally left for Bulstrode at the end of June.

Bulstrode Manor was an estate with a history dating back to the thirteenth century, when it was owned by the Knights Templars (*Victoria History of the Counties of England*, iii. 280). Horace Walpole called the house a 'melancholy monument of Dutch magnificence', but added that it had a 'brave' gallery of old pictures and a chapel with 'two fine windows of modern painted glass' (xxxii. 233). Perhaps Walpole found the house sad because it had been built by the notorious 'hanging' judge, Baron Jeffreys, in 1686. Walpole had of course not forgotten that the first Earl of Portland, who bought the property in 1706 from Jeffreys's son-in-law, was originally Dutch. Other visitors mentioned the natural beauties of the park in which the house stood, the menagerie, the aviary with many beautiful birds, and the gardens. On a visit in later years, Mrs Philip Lybbe Powys remarked that 'her Grace is exceedingly fond of gardening, is a very learned botanist, and has every English plant in a separate garden by themselves' (120–1). William Gilpin described the custom of feeding families of hares on the lawn at Bulstrode (187–91). The Duchess became very attached to the place; after her husband's death she exchanged residences with her eldest son—Welbeck Abbey for Bulstrode—so that she could remain at Bulstrode.

Elizabeth Robinson's responses to Bulstrode were enthusiastic. After a swift but dusty journey from London in the Duke's coach, Elizabeth found 'the most charming place I ever saw, a magnificant House fine Gardens & a beautifull Park'. She was impressed by a solid marble table in the hall sixteen feet long and she added, 'a slice of the Apartment I live in would make you and I a comfortable House in the State of our Virginity when we are poor Old Maidens . . .' (MO 5529, 25 [June 1740]). Her letters to her sister from girlhood to old age were the ones in which she revealed her feelings most openly. Here she was expressing her pleasure in the spaciousness of the room in which she was staying, her response to the beauty of the furniture, and also her anxiety about the future. The long visit to Bulstrode initiated Elizabeth into the charms of the Duchess's rural life. The Duchess herself listed some of her pastimes as working (i.e. handiwork), spinning, knotting, drawing, reading, writing, walking, and 'picking Herbs to put into an Herbal' (MO 176, 30 June 1738, Bulstrode). The Duchess also made objects in jet and amber by 'turning'. In a letter to Catherine Collingwood, Mary Pendarves described a slightly different routine at Bulstrode in 1736, when she herself was making one of her earliest visits there. Besides reading, working, and drawing in the morning, there were 'billiards, looking over prints, coffee, tea, cribbage', and playing with 'pretty Lady Betty' (Delany, 1st ser., i. 574).

Elizabeth enjoyed the country-house life at Bulstrode. She took the cold bath, dressed, and walked in the garden before breakfast. At one point Lord and Lady Oxford came to visit, which increased the formality of the house. Just at this time Lord Oxford was having financial difficulties because of his uncontrolled expenditures on his collection, and was forced to sell Wimpole Hall. There is no mention of this event in Elizabeth's letters, but her reference to a 'fuddled' peer indicates that she was aware of the heavy drinking with which Lord Oxford was reacting to his embarrassments (MO 5553). Elizabeth explained to her sister that happily she was not wanted for the 'Cabinet Council,' conducted by Lady Oxford, so she had her mornings to herself. In the afternoon she had to participate in formal conversation, but she did handiwork and could think her own thoughts (MO 5543). At her request her father sent her a pattern for an embroidered apron she wished to work for the Duchess (MO 5544, 4754). She walked out with Mary Pendarves and talked with her about the pleasures of sisterly friendship (MO 5569). Mrs Pendarves also had a close friendship with a sister—Anne, recently married to John Dewes.

Her visits to Bulstrode were an important part of Elizabeth's education, both in terms of worldly experience and of study. The Duchess tried to have interesting people to stay, in order to entertain her and each other. But there were times when she had tedious formal visits from the great, and from less important people. Elizabeth kept a sharp eye out for the vagaries of the visitors. To her sister she wrote (10 [Sept. 1740]) that some of these people 'outcharacter Caractura' (MO 5551). One example was a neighbour, Lady Shadwell, whose curtsies exactly reflected the importance of the person to whom she was curtsying. When she came to Elizabeth, 'a private Gentlewoman', Lady Shadwell's curtsy was very short (MO 5534, 23 July [?1740], Bulstrode).

Elizabeth's visit seems to have quickened her sensitivity to the inequities of life. Writing to her sister, she adapted the opening lines of Shakespeare's Sonnet 66:

> Tir'd with all these, for restful death I cry,
> As to behold desert a beggar born,
> And needy nothing trimmed in jollity

explaining that she has seen 'Desert a beggar born and Gaudy nothing trimm'd in jolity' (MO 5573, [12 Dec. 1740, Bulstrode]).

But there were compensations: the pleasures of country living in an elegant house—playing with the children, becoming acquainted with accomplished people, and engaging in individual and group study. The visit of the poet Dr Edward Young brightened the days. Elizabeth enjoyed his company. Dr Young was an old acquaintance of the Portlands, who were attempting, but eventually failed, to get him the kind of church preferment he wished for. Dr Young's wife had died the previous January, and he had been seriously ill in August, but his visit in the autumn struck the young visitor as very pleasant. Sarah had objected to the satires on women which Dr Young had included in his *Universal Passion*. But Elizabeth defended him, explaining that he 'honors the best of them [women] extreamly & seems delighted with those who act & think reasonably' (MO 5556). To Anne Donnellan Elizabeth wrote (17 Oct. 1740), 'This our Dread Satirist is the best natured Man living. I am in platonick Love with him . . .' (BL, Portland Loan 29/325, p. 13).[4] His ability to introduce new subjects of conversation was very helpful to country life. Once she explained to her sister that she had intended to write a letter to her, but 'Dr. Young came in & entertain'd my Mental faculties with a feast of Reason and a flow of Soul till Six . . .' (MO 5557). In quoting Pope's 'Imitation of Horace' (I. ii. 127), in which Pope

expressed his joy at country pleasures and companions, Elizabeth was adapting both Horace's and Pope's praise of country
life to express her own appreciation of Bulstrode as an ideal
community.

As the autumn days went on Elizabeth read a variety of
works. She wanted to read Italian, but the Duke's library was
not well furnished with Italian books, and she was not able to
choose according to her inclination. So she was reading the
'Decameron de Boccace a celebrated and much esteem'd
Author'. The Duchess was 'renewing' her Italian, and Elizabeth was sure she would get some good books in the future.
Elizabeth was also joining the Duchess in the rather old-
fashioned custom of reading sermons; 'you may expect me to
be an Excellent Preacher in a little while for we are to read
Dr. Samuel Clarkes Sermons' (MO 5561, [1 Nov. 1740, Bul-
strode] to Sarah Robinson). Much time was spent in writing
letters, long ones to her sister, shorter ones to her brothers,
occasional letters to her mother, and serious, rather sententious
ones to Anne Donnellan.

The association with the Portlands continued, as Elizabeth
returned to London with them. She was to participate in their
social life and was looking forward to 'Operas & delight'
(MO 5575, 26 [Dec. 1740, Bulstrode]). On 1 January 1740/[1]
Elizabeth wrote to Anne Donnellan that she was to be with the
Duchess 'till March & then I vanish to the Shades of Kent our
family will not be in Town which grieves me much, in which
I feel my own part of vexation & my Sisters too' (MO 813).
Elizabeth found the Duchess a thoughtful friend. On 9 January,
she was dressing to go to Court with the Duchess when the
Duchess read in the paper about the death of Lady Knatchbull,
a family friend of the Robinsons in Kent. She sent to Golden
Square to confirm it, before telling Elizabeth 'in the tenderest
manner' (MO 5593 to Sarah Robinson).

Elizabeth stayed in town with the Portlands until February,
when her father came to London (MO 4757). The Duchess
sent him thanks for letting Elizabeth stay. Elizabeth explained
that the Duchess's health was bad, and she would have been
anxious to have left her. The Duchess was expecting a child.
After the birth of Lady Frances in April 1741, the Duke wrote
to Elizabeth to let her know that his wife and 'the Babe' were

doing well. The Duke complimented 'Fidgett' very much on the excellence of her own letter to him, and assured her that she was a very marriageable young lady; he jocosely compared her to Dame Partlett of either the 'little Bantam kind, or of ye ruffled friesland kind', whom any Chanticleer would strive to possess (MO 445, 25–8 Apr. 1741, Whitehall).

That spring, after Elizabeth had returned to the 'shades of Kent', she was banished from home because her sister had come down with smallpox. She felt lonely. 'I am left wholly to myself & my books & both I own too little to possess me entirely what's Cicero to me or me to Cicero as Hamlet would say . . .' (MO 816, [20 Apr. 1741], to Anne Donnellan). With the encouragement of her friends, however, she became more interested in reading the classics as a resource against the difficulties of life.

Her relationship to the Portlands and an overlapping visit to Bath had given Elizabeth the opportunity to develop a friendship with Anne Donnellan (c.1700–62). Anne was the daughter of an Irish judge who had been Chief Baron of the Exchequer. He had died in 1705, and after several years her mother had married Philip Percival, brother of the first Lord Egmont. Ann Donnellan and Mary Pendarves were old friends and had made a long visit to Ireland together. Anne Donnellan was also an old friend of Bishop Berkeley; in a letter written to her friend Gilbert West when Bishop Berkeley died, Mrs Montagu claimed that Berkeley had proposed to Anne Donnellan, but she had refused him (MO 6697, 28 Jan. 1753). Anne Donnellan, who was now an unmarried woman in her early forties, made her home in London with her mother and stepfather. She had some financial independence, as her sister Catherine had married Robert Clayton, later Bishop Clayton, who had inherited a fortune, and turned Catherine's dowry over to Anne (McGowan, 3).

Anne was musical and had a good singing voice. She was interested in the classics and in religion. She was an occasional correspondent of Jonathan Swift and in one letter (10 May 1735) had claimed to be 'a great asserter of [women's] rights and privileges' (Swift, iv. 332). The letters Anne and Elizabeth exchanged dealt much with reading. Anne brought out Elizabeth's serious side and encouraged Elizabeth in her efforts at

education. Some years later she was recommending to Elizabeth a new translation of Pliny's letters, 'which does for us poor
ignorant women who cant read it in the original, as some
learned ladies can' (MO 786, 28 Oct. [1748], Kings Weston).

Ignorance of the classical languages was a sore point. Elizabeth never learned Greek, but did learn enough Latin to enable
her to quote Horace in the original in her *Essay on Shakespear*.
She early became fluent in French, and read French writers in
the original. Later, she sometimes depended on French or
Italian translations of Greek drama. In her letters to the
Duchess and to Anne Donnellan she now began to discuss
works she and they were reading. She had read a translation of
Cornelius Nepos, became interested in the character of Atticus,
and intended to read the French translation of Cicero's *Epistles
to Atticus*. Anne Donnellan had recommended that she read
Horace; Elizabeth explained that she had read his work before,
but depending on going to her brother's copy to read again,
finds he has not got it with him. She is very impatient to read
Dacier's French translation of Homer and plans to ask her
brothers to bring it with them during the next vacation
(MO 816, [20 Apr. 1741]). With the Duchess she discussed Dr
Middleton's book on Cicero, and said she liked his chapter on
Cicero's religion best because the author discussed the ancient
schools of philosophy and Cicero's relationship to the different
sects (MO 311).

On 16 June 1741 Lord Oxford died in London, and Elizabeth's letters attempted to comfort her friend. The Duchess
shared her sadness with Elizabeth, and her sense of being
unable to carry on her usual duties. At the end of August the
Duchess wrote that she was to entertain the Duchess of Kent
and Lady Mary [Grey], her relatives by marriage, and was
afraid she would not feel up to talking and to answering all
their questions (MO 185, 31 Aug. 1741, Bulstrode). She was
unwell, but did not think she was pregnant, and hoped that
that would not happen again. She was hoping for another visit
from Elizabeth, and regretted to hear that Elizabeth's parents
seemed unwilling to part with her (MO 186, 2 Sept. 1741,
Bulstrode). On 7 September she was looking forward with
discouragement to having to entertain her mother, who was
coming for a visit. She was still mourning the death of her

father. The Duchess wrote that she did everything she could to lessen her grief, but when she was alone she felt it very strongly (MO 187).

Finally, Elizabeth wrote that she had received permission for a second visit to Bulstrode (MO 310, 7 Oct. 1741, Mount Morris). Her parents had been very nervous lately. 'Our Speaker is much to be pittied. at present she is quite low spirited.' Elizabeth was not well; a cold had swelled her face, and her mouth was 'broke out' (MO 311). But by 19 October she was back in 'this Region of peace' and getting into better health (MO 5606, [1741]). During her second visit Elizabeth met at Bulstrode, in addition to Mrs Pendarves, Mrs Dewes, and Dr Young, Dr Alured Clarke, Dean of Exeter, Dr Thomas Shaw, Regius Professor of Greek at Oxford, traveller, botanist, and conchologist, and Mr and Mrs Gilbert West. West (1706–56) was a poet and translator of Pindar.

Reading aloud was one of the group's usual entertainments. At different times Elizabeth reported that they were reading Swift's and Pope's letters (MO 5617), Middleton's new edition of his *Letter from Rome* (MO 5617), Colley Cibber's *Life* (MO 5618). They investigated nature with a microscope provided by Mr Achard (MO 5627; 5628). Elizabeth reported being entertained by the disputes of the clerical visitors on sermon subjects, especially metaphysics and morality (MO 5619), and reading an *Account of the Life and Writings of Homer* (MO 5625). She wrote enthusiastically to Anne Donnellan:

Dr. Shaw is just come he is full of Laughter & communicates it. Dr. Clarke is with us also, he is a very agreable Companion: Dr. Young makes up the Triumviri of Divines, he is all three together he has a head of wisdom, a heart of honesty, & mind of chearfullness. Think how the hours fly in our Society! . . . (MO 812)[5]

On New Year's Day Elizabeth wrote to Anne Donnellan that 'Our happy Society is just breaking up . . .'; Elizabeth went with the Portlands to London on her way to Kent. Elizabeth hoped to return for between two and three months, beginning in March of 1742 (MO 830, [1 Jan. 1741/2]). Elizabeth did return to London that spring with her sister and parents. The friends exchanged affectionate notes; the Duchess sent tickets

for a play box (Univ. of Nottingham Library, MS PC PwE 33).
But Elizabeth stayed in Jermyn Street, not at Whitehall. The
negotiations which led to her marriage must have been under
way at this time.

Her visits to Bulstrode and her friendships with the Duchess
and with Anne Donnellan encouraged in Elizabeth a sense of
the value of learning. She was aware of the taboo against
learning for women and resented it. When William Freind
recommended books to her (she was then about seventeen), she
explained that she was happy to have his advice, 'but there is a
Mahometan Error crept even into the Christian Church that
Women have no Souls, & it is thought very absurd for us to
pretend to read or think like Reasonable Creatures' (MO 1000,
[?1737]). Her solution, she claimed, would be to take care not
to let anyone know that she had ever read anything but 'my
Grandmothers receipts for Puddings & Cerecloths for Sprains'
until she knew that person very well. Here we see the unease
about being known to be educated which the taboo against
learning for women instilled.

She also knew the common terms used to disparage learned
women. She implied that certain young ladies of Canterbury
who were celebrated for their learning were slovenly in their
dress:

to exceed in Learning & Hoop seldom happens to the same person we
have two or three Sapho's at Canterbury but in Dress & fashions they
never exceeded a farthingale & instead of having their Hair moutonne
it is in Boileau's Phrase Herissé de Grec . . .[6]

Elizabeth explained that she surprised

one of 'em once with a Visit when she was in a Learned Deshabile &
she said by way of Apology that the Cultivation of her mind had
hinder'd the Adjustment of her person but she Believed I was such a
Friend to Litterature I shou'd easily excuse the faults of Apparel for
the Rectitude of well informed Ideas.

Elizabeth must have felt some rivalry with this young woman.
She claimed that a two hours' conversation with the schoolmaster of her youngest brother the day before had provided her
with adequate responses to what she felt was the contemptuous
conversation of the young woman, 'but really Considering a

Certain Vermin may Live upon the wisest uncomb'd head I was afraid she would rather Communicate one of her well fed Animals—than her well Informed Ideas . . .' (22 May 1741 to Anne Donnellan, BL Portland Loan 29/325, p. 38). These aspersions about slovenliness echo traditional slights put on learned ladies, of the sort Smollett was to dramatize in *Roderick Random* in 1748.

Nevertheless, Elizabeth enjoyed languages and literature. Her brothers had encouraged her to share their learning. Matthew and his sister corresponded in French while he was at Cambridge, and he assured her that there were not three people of her sex in England who could write their own language as well as she did French (MO 4819, 16 Jan. [*c.*1734], Cambridge). Later, writing from Bath *c.*1738, he lets Elizabeth know that he has been reading the *Arcadia* and thinks his sister as worthy as Sidney's dear sister (MO 4826). Her oldest brother's compliments and interest must have strengthened her drive towards learning.

Elizabeth herself, writing to her sister (evidently from Bath in 1739), described her eagerness to read a collection of Prior's poems which had been lately published, and wrote a critique explaining her disappointment with the edition. In that letter she went on to muse about the vagaries of literary survival. She observed that time had dropped authors of great reputation, but

as ye eighteen first years of your life were not spent in receiving Greek & Latin in ye shape of Blows, buffets, & whippings perhaps you may not much regret them, tho' there are two whose loss I am sure you will be concern'd for, Madam Sappho a woman of great fame, tho' but half reputation, & the Mother of ye famous Gracci, Cornelia, whose letters were in great repute among the Romans . . .' (MO 5525, 12 Nov. 1739).[7]

Even at this early age, she was identifying with women writers and sharing that interest with her sister.

The Robinson sisters were accustomed to pursue their intellectual interests independently. The examples of the Duchess and of Anne Donnellan probably reinforced this practice. Elizabeth encouraged her sister to study as a sensible relief from the trivialities of life in the provinces. On 1 November

1740, she wrote to her sister from Bulstrode, 'I admire your Classical life, what a variety does study make, what a difference is there between the Rhetorick of Livy & that of our friend Mr B-- how different is Mrs Pyot from Cornelia & Mutius Scevola from the delicate Mr C--k' (MO 5561).

Elizabeth Robinson clearly had a variety of male and female mentors who contributed to her development. In later years she thanked her father for permitting her to be educated, but said nothing about the nature of the education. The extent to which she was influenced by her mother and by Dr Middleton cannot be determined, but as Elizabeth seems to have been a bright, clever girl, both probably encouraged her. Elizabeth's brothers certainly encouraged her learning, and shared their books with her. Anne Donnellan later was a source of encouragement.

Her mentors and friends pointed her in the direction of learning, but the catalyst for Elizabeth Robinson's aspirations was Bulstrode. Its inhabitants, way of life, visitors, customs, created an ideal on which Elizabeth Robinson began to fashion her life. Interest in literature, friendships with unusual women, acquaintance and even friendships with men with intellectual interests, could be developed within the context of a domestic existence. Some years later Mrs Montagu herself wrote of the importance of her friend's example:

I shall always remember the countenance and protection you gave my youthful state, & in those advantages I less reckon the honor your rank might do me, than the benefit it must be to a young & inexperienced mind to receive ye precepts & ye example of a virtuous & laudable conduct. Much perhaps of ones future life depends on ones first friendships & I reflect upon it as a happiness that mine was with the Duchess of Portland. (Univ. of Nottingham Library, MS PC PwE 32, 29 Dec. 1751, Sandleford)

In 1779, when she was almost sixty, and again wished to compliment her friend, she looked back on her days at Bulstrode as the happiest time of her life, a happiness that was not just the result of youth, but 'your Grace's conversation and example led me to a way of thinking which makes the happiness of all times and all seasons. You taught me neither to admire nor covet what was not really good' (Montagu (1904), i. 347; 1 Dec. 1779, Hill Street).

In later years Elizabeth Robinson became an indefatigable London hostess, famous for large, glittering parties. But the appeal of Bulstrode was not that of the crowded assemblies of her later life; it was the appeal of a small society of congenial people, entertaining each other with the 'feast of reason and the flow of soul'. It was this ideal which was the incentive for Elizabeth Montagu's interest in what she and Elizabeth Vesey came to call their 'bluestocking' friends in the late 1750s, and which formed the basis for their later efforts.

# 2 · Elizabeth Carter's London Career

WHILE Elizabeth Robinson was growing up in Kent and visiting Cambridge, Tunbridge Wells, London, and Bulstrode, another Elizabeth, who was later to become a close and influential friend, was also growing up in Kent—at the seaport village of Deal—from which she made visits to Canterbury and to London. In the spring of 1738, about the time Elizabeth Robinson was developing a social existence under the wing of the Duchess of Portland, Elizabeth Carter, a clergyman's daughter, came to London to write for the *Gentleman's Magazine*. Years later the friendship formed by these two women was to influence the creation and social acceptance of the 'bluestocking' circle.

Elizabeth Carter, born on 16 December 1717, was the eldest of the five children of Margaret and Nicolas Carter. The other children were Nicolas, James, John, and Margaret. Mrs Carter, an heiress who lost her money in the South Sea Bubble, died when Elizabeth was ten. Elizabeth as the eldest daughter must have helped with the care of the younger children. After her father married again several years later, Elizabeth also helped with the care of Mary (Polly) and Henry, the children of his second family. In fact, she later tutored Henry in the classics to prepare him for Cambridge.

Deal, a village on the Channel near Dover, had no real harbour, but was an important port for the many vessels that anchored in the 'Roads', finding safe harbour in the shelter of the Goodwin Sands, except when the wind blew from the south or south-west, when vessels might be blown ashore. There were usually 300 to 500 ships anchored there (Cozens). The village consisted of three unpaved and unlighted streets parallel to the sea. It was an open, breezy place. Deal had a naval yard, built boats, carried on rescue operations during times of shipwreck, and was also a centre for the smuggling of goods from the continent which was prevalent during the eighteenth century. Elizabeth grew up burdened with family responsibilities, but she also enjoyed a great deal of physical freedom in this small village by the sea. She was a strong walker and took long walks on the sea-shore and inland in the countryside. As a country woman, she sometimes walked the distance between Canterbury and Deal (about sixteen miles).

A young woman of learning and poetic gifts—considered something of a prodigy in her abilities and interests—Elizabeth Carter came to the *Gentleman's Magazine* about the same time that Samuel Johnson did. Of course, it was unusual for a respectable young woman to be permitted the opportunity to work in London as a woman of letters, but Elizabeth Carter was probably given that opportunity because of the special views and hopes of her father. Revd Dr Nicolas Carter, Perpetual Curate of the Church of St George the Martyr at Deal, and one of the Six Preachers at Canterbury, a strong-minded and rather contentious cleric, had given his sons and daughters the same classical education. Elizabeth learned Greek, Latin, and Hebrew with her father. She resided with a French protestant family in Canterbury for a year to learn French. She also learned German at her father's urging. She taught herself Italian and Spanish. In later years she worked on Portuguese and Arabic.

In raising his eldest daughter, the Revd Carter seems to have encouraged her to think of herself as an independent person capable of taking risks. Father and daughter carried on a correspondence, some of it in Latin, on occasions when he was away from home. The Revd Carter was an encouraging mentor. As early as 8 October 1729, when Elizabeth was twelve, he wrote to her from Bath, where he had accompanied his local patron, Sir George Oxenden, and Lady Oxenden, that he could not help showing her letter to Sir George, who had complimented Elizabeth on her exact spelling and use of appropriate expressions (Hampshire collection).[1] Later, when Elizabeth was in London, she did errands and made purchases for her father and the family. His willingness to let her make her own decisions is shown both in small and in important .matters:

when you are determined to come down [from London] give me timely notice, and you may have my chaise, either to come wholly to London, where staying one day to refresh the cattle it may return with you—and so home. Or if you like it rather it should meet you at Tunstall, or at Rochester—whatever you chuse, let me know in time

. . . Before you come down, when it suits you, you must buy sugar of all sorts, according to your judgement, except that of the very coarsest kind. . . . Powder blew and stone blew. Starch according to your will, and whole rice. Flower of Mustard, Sallad Oyl, Nutmegs, Cloves. Anchovies, Icing-glass. Peper. Morells. Best Almonds. Raisins; Coffee. And anything else, of whatever kind you think is wanting. Your brother will receive money from me, and you may have from him what you want. (Collins, 8)

Her father's willingness to let her follow her own judgement, a practice he persevered in later when they were faced with more serious issues such as marriage proposals, had an important effect on her personality.

Edward Cave, publisher of the *Gentleman's Magazine*, was a friend of the Revd Carter; Carter also had a brother in trade in London, and a sister who was married to Mr Vere, his partner. Elizabeth probably lived at her uncle's in Bishopsgate, but also spent time at Cave's house in St John's Gate. The sixteenth-century Gatehouse of the Priory of the Order of St John in Clerkenwell (now a museum) had a large vaulted room which housed Edward Cave's printing works and offices. Elizabeth may have dined there on a regular basis. In her later letters to Cave she sent compliments to his wife and daughter. Although Nicolas Carter's exact motives in sending his daughter to live in London are not clear (and may not have been entirely clear to him), he was a clergyman with a small income and a large family, and seems to have been attempting to publicize himself and his daughter as a means of gaining preferment. He had Cave print a collection of his sermons, and encouraged his daughter to print a small collection of her verses to distribute to friends. He undoubtedly felt in a vague way that a young woman who wrote poetry and read Greek and so many other languages would be helped eventually to improve her situation in life. Sir George Oxenden seems to have promised that he might find her preferment at the Court of George II. It was he who had urged her father to have her learn German. In a letter of 27 March 1738, Revd Carter told his daughter that he had explained to the Dean of Canterbury that she was in London to improve herself (Stebbing/Rutherford extract).

Cave evidently treated his young associate in a fatherly and

teasing manner. She had been busily refurbishing her ward-
robe, and reported to an unknown correspondent, 'Cave told
Savage he saw me to a disadvantage because I had not my little
Straw Hat on' (27 Apr. 1738, Deal County Library, Stebbing
extract). Later Elizabeth wrote with pleasure of the adventure of
being introduced to Thomas Wright (1711–86), an astronomer
and mathematician, and to Dr John Theophilus Desaguliers
(1683–1744), an experimental philosopher.[2] She reported with
amusement that Dr Desaguliers's house was very strange and
'appears very much like the Abode of a Wizard' (23 June 1738,
St John's Gate, Deal County Library, Stebbing extract). In
July she had a walk through 'delightful meadows' from Richmond to Twickenham and a sight of Pope's Gardens, 'by the
Interest of one of our Company with his celebrated man John.
of all the Things I have yet seen of this sort none ever suited my
own Fancy so well' (Hampshire, 221). This visit was soon com-
memorated in Latin and English verses in the pages of the
*Gentleman's Magazine*.

Elizabeth Carter had in fact been contributing poetry to the
*Gentleman's Magazine* from the time she was seventeen. Begun in
1731, the *Gentleman's Magazine* had established a loyal reader-
ship all over the country. Cave encouraged young poets and
printed the verses in which they often responded to and praised
each other's contributions. The young lady in Deal joined the
group of contributors. Her riddle on fire ((Nov. 1734), 623)
was praised by John Duick, writing under the pen-name of
Sylvius ((June 1735), 321).[3] Duick encouraged 'Miss Cart–r'
to join her 'sister muses' in the pages of the magazine. In her
reply, 'To Sylvius', the young poet explained that she wished
to write about the lofty subjects of life and death, but felt too
inexperienced to do so ((July 1735), 379).

In September 1735 there appeared her first translation from
the Greek, Anacreon's Ode XXX, 'The Muses once intent on
play' (553). After an interval of more than a year she published
in April 1737 a poem 'On the Death of Mrs. Rowe' (247).
Elizabeth Singer Rowe (1674–1737) was the closest thing to a
female role-model for a person of Elizabeth's interests and
attitudes. A well-known poet, Mrs Rowe published her first
volume of poetry in 1696, under the name of Philomela, and
continued to write and publish verse and prose throughout her

lifetime. She was well read in English literature, and in religious and philosophical works. She read Italian literature in the original, but did not know the classical languages. In 1710 she married Thomas Rowe and was widowed five years later. She was a close friend of Frances Thynne Seymour (1699–1754), Countess of Hertford, and later Duchess of Somerset. Mrs Rowe lived mainly at Frome, where she devoted her life to religion and good works, and wrote prose and verse of a devotional nature (Stecher). Mrs Rowe's devotional poetry had an intensity that verged on passionate feeling, and Nicolas Carter, while he acknowledged Mrs Rowe's worth as a poet, felt it necessary to warn his daughter against her enthusiasm.

In November 1737 Elizabeth Carter published her translation of Horace's Ode 10, Book II, 'Would you, Licinius, chuse the surest way' (692)—a poem which praises moderation—and in February 1738 her forceful and imaginative poem, 'A Riddle', beginning, 'Nor form nor substance in my being share' (99). In this poetical riddle on dreams the poet shows the paradoxical ways dreams confound conventional modes of perception. In March 1738 she printed an imitation of Horace's Ode 22, Book III on integrity, 'The virtuous man, whose acts and thoughts are pure' (159).

The riddle on dreams had drawn the praise of a new contributor to the *Gentleman's Magazine*—Samuel Johnson—who wrote to Cave, 'I have compos'd a Greek Epigram to Eliza, and think She ought to be celebrated in as many different Languages as Lewis le Grand' (Johnson, *Letters*, i. 11). Johnson's epigram appeared in Greek and in Latin in the *Gentleman's Magazine* for April 1738 (210). She replied in Greek and Latin in the following issue (May 1738 (272)). Hers are the first verses known to have been addressed to Johnson (*Works*, vi. (1964), 44–5).

The April issue also had an imitation by 'Eliza' from the Spanish of Quevedo, ''Tis true, my form no *Tyrian* purples grace' (211). In May she offered a satire, 'Fortune', with an epigraph from Juvenal (272). In the June issue her poem, 'While clear the night, and ev'ry thought serene', with an epigraph from Virgil, 'Felix qui potuit rerum cognoscere causas', muses on the nature of the physical universe. Influenced by her acquaintance with Wright and Desaguliers, the poet wonders about the orbs of the Galaxy,

> Where ev'ry star, that cheers the gloom of night
> With the faint tremblings of a distant light,
> Perhaps illumes some system of its own
> With the strong influence of a radiant sun.

In a passage which she cut from the version later printed in her first collection, she speculates that sentient beings may live on other planets:

> And yet, perhaps, while we our station prize
> Blest with the warmth of more indulgent skies,
> Some cold *Saturnian*, when the lifted tube
> Shows to his wond'ring eye our pensile globe,
> Pities our thirsty soil, and sultry air,
> And thanks the friendly pow'r that fixed him there.

Reviewing the magnificent order of the Universe, the poet deduces that it must be the work of God. She finishes with a final compliment to her scientific friends:

> All view the happy talents with delight,
> That form a *Desaguliers* and a *Wright*.
>
> (315–16)

In seeing the universal order as a work of God, Elizabeth Carter was following the popular viewpoint of the time (Meyer).

The visit to Pope's garden inspired a nice outburst of occasional poetry. In July 1738 appeared (p. 372) a Latin epigram ascribed to Samuel Johnson, 'Ad Elisam Popi Horto Lauros carpentem'.[4]

This epigram was followed in the August issue by three English translations. The third of these has been ascribed to Samuel Johnson (*Poems*, 82–3):

> As learn'd *Eliza*, sister of the Muse,
>    Surveys with new contemplative delight
> *Pope*'s hallow'd glades, and never tiring views,
>    Her conscious hand his laurel leaves invite.
>
> Cease, lovely thief! my tender limbs to wound,
>    (Cry'd *Daphne* whisp'ring from the yielding tree;)
> Were *Pope* once void of wonted candour found,
>    Just *Phoebus* would devote his plant to thee.

Directly below these lines is Elizabeth Carter's reply in Latin and English, of which the English is:

> In vain *Eliza's* daring hand
>   Usurped the laurel bough;
> Remov'd from *Pope's*, the wreath must fade
>   On ev'ry meaner brow.
>
> Thus gay Exotics, when transferr'd
>   To climates not their own,
> Lose all their lively bloom, and droop
>   Beneath a paler sun.

By August 1738 Cave had published a slim quarto of Elizabeth Carter's poems. Although neither author's nor publisher's name appeared on the title-page, a cut of St John's Gate, clearly labelled as such, indicated the work's relationship to Cave. *Poems upon Particular Occasions*, with a motto from Euripides, contained only a few of her poems—'In Diem Natalem', an earnest and reverent poem written on the occasion of her eighteenth birthday, two translations from Horace, the 'Dream' Riddle, the poem on 'Fortune', and a poem 'On the Death of Her Sacred Majesty Queen Caroline', which was presented to George II by Sir Robert Walpole through the agency of Sir George Oxenden, then one of the Lords of the Treasury (Carter, *Memoirs*, ii. 22 n.). The concluding poem to Stephen Duck is interesting because it shows the young woman anticipating her return to Deal:

> On the bleak Margin of the Sea-beat Shore,
> When *Richmond*'s Scenes shall charm my Eyes no more,
> Thy Verse the gay Ideas shall renew,
> And all the beauteous Prospect glad my View.
>
> (22)

But that time was not yet at hand. In the autumn and winter of 1738 the young poet was kept busy with translations and with the friendships she was making by her literary work. In the long run the friendship with Samuel Johnson was to have a positive, supportive influence on her life. Conversely, the friendship with the Revd Thomas Birch was to prove troublesome, and may have led to her retreat from London in the following year.

Elizabeth Carter was evidently encouraged by her associates at St John's Gate to undertake translations. First she did a translation from the French of a work by Jean Pierre de Crousaz, professor of mathematics and philosophy at the University of Lausanne, who had criticized Pope's *Essay on Man* in a work called the *Examen de l'essay de M. Pope sur l'homme.* The translator supplied some explanatory notes for the text of this work, and also some critical remarks.

Both Birch and Johnson read Carter's translation of Crousaz. Johnson read the work in progress and praised it, evidently in what Elizabeth thought was a disinterested manner; on 26 September 1738, the Revd Carter wrote to his daughter that he was 'glad your Translation goes on so briskly, and yt Johnson has given it his Suffrage, free from Biass' (Hampshire collection). On 27 November 1738 Birch complimented her in Latin on the 'perfection, the elegance, and the correctness of the style in a most difficult task' (BL Add. 4302, fo. 72; trans. Ruhe, 495).

Both Johnson and Birch had suggestions for Carter's further work. Johnson wrote to Cave that Carter should translate Boethius's *Consolation of Philosophy*, and put her name to the work. (Many years later he made the same suggestion to the young Mrs Thrale.) Birch recommended a translation from the Italian of Francesco Algarotti's *Il Newtonianismo per le dame*, published in Naples in 1737. Birch knew Algarotti personally; Algarotti, whose social and intellectual life spanned both professional and aristocratic circles, was a friend of Lord Hervey and Lady Mary Wortley Montagu, and a fellow member with Birch in the Royal Society and the Society of Antiquarians. Elizabeth Carter settled on the Italian work. Her translation, for which she supplied a number of explanatory notes and the original English verses of which Algarotti had given Italian versions, appeared in May of 1739 as *Sir Isaac Newton's Philosophy Explain'd for the Use of the Ladies,* in *Six Dialogues on Light and Colours.* Algarotti's friendship with Lady Mary Wortley Montagu had blossomed into love on her side. When Lady Mary left for the continent with the hope of joining Algarotti, she had in her luggage copies of both the Italian and the English editions of Algarotti's book (Halsband, 180).

This translation of Algarotti, although it appeared without

Elizabeth Carter's name on the title-page, was widely known to be by her. In the *Gentleman's Magazine* of June 1739, Dr J. Swan published a long poem 'To Miss Carter' in praise of her work. He acknowledged Algarotti's contribution in providing a clear and easy explanation of Newton's ideas, and especially praised the effect of Carter's translation:

> Now may the *British* fair, with *Newton*, soar
> To worlds remote, and range all nature o'er; . . .

The poet regarded Miss Carter as the one who has made it possible for British women to understand science:

> Ah why should modesty conceal thy name?
> The attempt were vain to hide such worth from fame;
> The polish'd page *Eliza's* hand betrays,
> And marks her well-known softness, warmth, and ease.

(322)

The Revd Birch contributed a long article on Carter's translation of Algarotti to the *History of the Works of the Learned* (Art. XXXI, June 1739). The reviewer pointed out that the translation was by a young lady, daughter of Dr Nicolas Carter of Deal in Kent, author of an excellent volume of sermons published in London, 1738, and reviewed in *Works of the Learned* in July, 1738. Birch seemed to want to recommend himself to both father and daughter:

This Lady is a very extraordinary Phaenomenon in the Republick of Letters, and justly to be rank'd with the Cornelia's, Sulpicia's, and Hypatia's of the Ancients, and the Schurmans and Daciers of the Moderns. For to an uncommon Vivacity and Delicacy of Genius and an Accuracy of Judgment worthy of the maturest Years, she has added the Knowledge of the ancient and Modern Languages at an Age, when an equal Skill in any one of them would be a considerable Distinction in a Person of the other Sex. (392)

The reviewer also mentioned Carter's talent for poetry as instanced by a poem of hers prefixed to the *Miscellaneous Works* of Elizabeth Singer Rowe. The poem was a revision of Miss Carter's poem on Mrs Rowe; the revised version appeared in the *Gentleman's Magazine* in March 1739 (152). Birch also reprinted Carter's answer to Johnson's epigram, 'Ad Elizam in

Popi horto Lauros carpentum', from the *Gentleman's Magazine*.
Birch then went on to give an extensive exposition of the
*Dialogues*.'
  Birch's publicizing went even further. He included Elizabeth
Carter's poem on Mrs Rowe and his complimentary state-
ments  about Miss Carter's abilities in the article on Elizabeth
Singer Rowe which he provided for Bayle's *General Dictionary*
(viii. 798).
  The excessively flattering tone of these reviews, and Birch's
mingling of the personal with the intellectual in his praise of
Elizabeth Carter, reflect an intensity of interest and a lack of
tact which Miss Carter probably found embarrassing.
  What was the relationship between the Revd Thomas Birch
and Elizabeth Carter? Thomas Birch kept extensive records in
Latin in his diaries (now in the British Library) of his meetings
with Elizabeth Carter during the months of the London season
of 1738-9. Birch recorded many letters to Elizabeth (to which
she rarely replied), and various meals at which Johnson was
sometimes present. In the 1950s Edward Ruhe discussed the
entries in Birch's diaries, and took it for granted that many of
these activities were carried on *tête-à-tête*. He outlined a shadowy
'affair' in which Birch and Elizabeth Carter spent much time
alone together, and even took a trip to Oxford 'without
company of any kind' (Ruhe, 497). Here is an instance of a
scholar following in a long tradition and suggesting that
Elizabeth Carter, as a learned woman, may not have been as
virtuous as she seemed. This view of a 'romantic episode' has
been carried on in a recent biography of Thomas Birch by
A. E. Gunther (29-30).
  Certainly, if Birch were helping Miss Carter with the
Algarotti translation, as some of her notes indicate, frequent
meetings might not be unexpected. But in fact, as we shall see
in Chapter 4, both Elizabeth and her father were puzzled by
Birch's overtures. Dr Carter was concerned about her reputation; his earnest letters to his daughter indicate that Birch's
strangely uncommitted yet persistent attentions created a great
deal of anxiety.
  Birch may have pressed for *tête-à-tête* dinners, and his journal
entries may seem to suggest such frequent meetings, but on the
whole such dinners were not very likely. A practice closer to the

custom of the time would be that Birch was dining at Cave's in St John's Gate in company with various literary colleagues— sometimes Carter, and sometimes Carter and Johnson; in the self-centred privacy of his journals Birch may have noted only those persons on whom his attention was focused. His attention was focused on Elizabeth Carter.

Birch's diary entry describing the visit to Oxford is an instance of his practice. In Birch's entry it sounds as if the couple travelled alone, and Ruhe took it that way. But there were at least three others in the group with Elizabeth, and in point of fact she did not enjoy the trip. She had consulted her father, who had given her permission to go to Oxford if she wished (3 May 1739, Hampshire Collection). Many years later she confided to Elizabeth Montagu that she had gone to Oxford once, but had not enjoyed the visit:

For want of some companion with that critical taste and glowing imagination, which give distinction and spirit to objects, I found myself very little improved or amused by the sight of Oxford and Blenheim, when I was there many years ago. I went with a set of very well meaning folks, but some of whom were dull, some were peevish, and some were in love; and most of them even in their natural state would have considered a consular statue of Cicero, and a waxen image of Queen Anne, in pretty much the same light, as merely something to look at. In short, as I had neither the aid of society, nor the freedom of my own solitary thoughts, I scarcely recollect anything of the expedition, but that it made me heartily weary. (Deal, 8 July 1762, Carter, *Letters* (1817), i. 162)

That dry 'some were in love' probably refers to Birch.

The Revd Thomas Birch (1705–66) was a scholar and clergyman—a self-made man who had achieved clerical orders without a university education; he was, in fact, an enthusiast in the field of letters. He had been born in Clerkenwell, and when Elizabeth Carter came to London was living on St John's Lane. He was then in his middle thirties and had been a widower for about ten years. Birch had an extensive circle of acquaintances and carried on a heavy schedule of literary work. He was responsible for over six hundred articles in the English edition of Bayle's *General Dictionary*, then in process of publication (Osborn). Years later Boswell noted that Birch was active and diligent, but Johnson was supposed to have said that Birch had lots of anecdotes but his writing was dull (Boswell (1934), i. 159 n. 4). Horace Walpole wrote of Birch after his death that he was 'a worthy good-natured soul, full of industry and activity, and running about like a young setting dog in quest of anything, new or old, and with no parts, taste or judgment' (*Correspondence*, ii. 186).

I suspect that the indefatigable Birch, self-important and purposeful, especially irritated the young woman by his excessive attention. Elizabeth Carter hated flattery. She even felt that Johnson's appreciation in his epigram, 'Ad Elisam', had been too strong. But, as she wrote to her friend, Mrs Underdown, she did not really fear that Johnson's flattery would make her vain: 'Flattery operates on me as Laudanum does upon other People; If given in a moderate dose tis ten to one but the poison might take, but administered in too large a proportion intirely loses its dangerous Effect . . .' (Hampshire, 222). Birch's assiduous attention and flattery came to a peak with the June 1739 review of Algarotti. He used his public writing to praise a woman in whom he seemed to have a personal interest. But, as we shall see, there seems to be no evidence that he actually proposed. He wrote to her for the last time in June and she replied from Deal. Elizabeth Carter had returned to her 'sea-beat shore'.

During the time she had been working in London, Elizabeth Carter seems to have developed an awareness of herself as a woman poet relating to other women poets. The expanded version of her poem 'On the Death of Mrs. Rowe' speaks of the way intrigue works 'to blacken the records of female wit'. She found Mrs Rowe to be a shining example of the moral poet; Elizabeth Carter expressed a sense of dedication to follow in Mrs Rowe's footsteps:

> Fix'd on my soul shall thy example grow,
> And be my genius and my guide below:
> To this I'll point my first, my noblest views,
> Thy spotless verse shall regulate my Muse.
> And oh! forgive (tho' faint the transcript be
> That copies an original like thee)
> My highest pride, my best attempt for fame,
> That joins my own to *Philomela*'s name.[5]

But by June 1739 Elizabeth Carter was back in Deal, and the adventure of being in a regular 'professional' life in London was over.

For a while Elizabeth Carter did conduct something of a literary life from her country home. In some interesting letters to Edward Cave in the British Library (MS Stowe 748) she is asking Cave to order a book for her, returning a pamphlet which belongs to Mr Birch, asking Cave to send a copy of Algarotti to Mrs Brereton (24 June 1739). She returns Mrs Masters's verses with corrections, and apologizes for being too late for the July magazine, because she has been taken up by visitors from Canterbury. She goes on to state that she does not think her corrections make any great addition, but they are at his service (31 July 1739). Her 'compliments' in these letters are of interest: to Mr and Mrs Cave, Miss Cave, Mr Birch, Mr Johnson, Mr Savage, 'if he sees him before he leaves London', and Mrs Masters, when Cave writes to her. She comments on new publications: Dr Cheyne's new work on *Regimen*, Mrs Masters's book, the 'Hymn to Science' in the October magazine. She complains about a crude epigram Cave printed in the October issue: 'wretched Epigram', she calls it. She finds it difficult to work on the new translation she is engaged on. The name she gives is 'Maurocordate', possibly Alexandros Maurokordatos, *Pneumaticum instrumentum circulandi sanguinis* (1664). On 29 November 1739 she writes that she has given up the idea of translating this work, as she has found that it is not highly regarded. In December she writes to inquire rather urgently about the author of a recent pamphlet, *Woman not Inferior to Man*, published under the pseudonym, 'Sophia', and to let her know as soon as he conveniently can. 'I have some particular Reasons for my Curiosity in this point & I cannot my self form the least probable Conjecture to satisfy it' (1 Dec. 1739). Elizabeth Carter's curiosity is hardly surprising, for the author of the pamphlet quoted extensively from the praises Birch had sung of her in his review of her Algarotti translation in the *History of the Works of the Learned*. The pamphlet consists of material from François Poulain de la Barre's *De l'égalité des deux sexes* (1673) with additions (Ferguson, 266). But 'Sophia', if she existed, has never been identified, and if there was a connection with Birch, that too has not been established.

The reasons for Elizabeth Carter's retreat from a professional life in London were undoubtedly complex. Sir George Oxenden had been hinting to her father a year earlier that Elizabeth cheapened her work by appearing too often in the pages of the *Gentleman's Magazine*; her works would be better appreciated if they were more scarce (Hampshire Collection, Malton, 12 July 1738). Literary life at St John's Gate had its darker side, and was evidently a disillusioning experience. She had encountered Richard Savage (?1697–1743), the poet and playwright who claimed to be the illegitimate and neglected son of Lady Macclesfield and Earl Rivers, when Savage was coming to the end of his erratic life in London. Savage was on the verge of leaving for an imagined happier life in Wales (Clifford, 207–8), but he was to die a few years later in Bristol gaol. Samuel Johnson, who had become a close friend of Savage, wrote the *Life of Savage* (1744) after Savage's death.

Samuel Johnson himself, who was in his late twenties in those years, was also struggling with poverty, but Elizabeth Carter had been impressed from the beginning of their friendship with his worth and integrity. On the other hand, the friendship with Birch was disturbing. He was a successful literary man, but even setting aside the marital ambitions he may have had, he was insensitive to Elizabeth Carter's modesty and diffidence, and to her privacy. She complained about some person she knew who was unscrupulous in copying her letters and circulating her letters and manuscripts; it may very well have been Birch. He left his papers to the British Museum; these contain copies of Elizabeth Carter's letters from those years.

Health may have been another factor. The first mention I have found to the headaches which intermittently made her ill in the course of her long life comes in a letter from her father to her in London in which he says he has heard that she has been having headaches, and advises her not to study so hard (Stebbing/Rutherford, 2 Jan. 1738/9). The question of the intensity of Elizabeth Carter's application to study and its effect on her health is a difficult one. Montagu Pennington is the source for the story that learning came hard to her, but that she persevered with great application which laid the foundation for her headaches (Carter, *Memoirs*, i. 9). Pennington's comments imply that the headaches started very early, but the language of her father's letter does not suggest a long-standing problem, but one that had recently appeared. Elizabeth Carter's lifelong struggle with migraines may have begun when she was in London working on the translations. People often assumed that her headaches were caused by study, but as Oliver Sacks has indicated in his work on *Migraine* (1985) the physiological and psychological causes of debilitating headaches have even now not been ascertained. Eventually, Elizabeth Carter decided that it was better to live with this complaint, rather than allow physicians to attempt to 'cure' her.

The retreat to Deal may also have had something to do with whether or not Elizabeth Carter planned to marry. Later, her father expressed the view that if she did not plan to marry, she should probably live in a retired manner, as such a life would be less expensive. Furthermore, her own admiration for Mrs Rowe may have suggested that she could function better as a virtuous woman poet in Deal rather than in London. In fact, the next poem she printed in the *Gentleman's Magazine* was a poem on melancholy (Nov. 1739, 599). It is a 'graveyard' poem in which the poet speaks of the transient illusions of the 'painted cheat' of the senses, which the truths of religion counter with prospects of eternal bliss after death. She sent this poem with the proviso that her authorship was to be kept a secret, as neither her father nor her London friends knew about it (Robert B. Adam, iii. 54).

Her father's practical attitudes, his patron's protective concern for her respectability, the excessive adulation of Birch, her feelings of disenchantment with a regular London life, her admiration for Mrs Rowe, probably all helped to bring Elizabeth Carter back to Deal. In essence, her retreat to the 'sea-beat shore' meant that she had found no way to employ her talents in London which satisfied her. It was better to remain in Deal. Given her experiences, her return to Kent offered compensations. She could participate in family life and local friendships. She could turn to her books. She could muse on the sea-shore about her brother and another friend who had died in distant parts of the world. She could walk in the countryside, or make long visits to Canterbury, where she had several good women friends, and where she could participate in the social life of dances, plays, and race week if she wished. For Elizabeth

Carter, then, the 1740s were in general a period of retirement —with an increasing reliance for comfort on the letters and company of women friends. Two female friendships were especially important—that with Catherine Talbot and, towards the end of this period, with Hester Mulso. In the long run Elizabeth Carter was to achieve a degree of satisfying independence which was supported by her friendships. The friendship with Catherine Talbot, which began in 1741, was to be especially important in reinforcing her sense of her own interests and in getting her started on a new project.

Her father's gift of a classical education had created for Elizabeth Carter an unusual but interesting way of life. If there was not really a place for her in London as a learned woman, then she was determined to fashion her life in her own way in a kind of retirement.

# 3 · Chosen Friends: Jemima Campbell, later Marchioness Grey, Catherine Talbot, Elizabeth Carter, and Hester Mulso

THE concept of 'chosen friends' was important as a preparatory stage for the first bluestockings. This view of friendship as a medium leading to supportive relationships between individuals of different backgrounds irrespective of gender and social class has been traced by Irene Q. Brown to the philosophical movements of the second half of the seventeenth century, in which particular men and women were appealing to the use of reason to 'reconcile religion and science, authority and liberty, women and men . . .' (416). The first bluestockings had as examples for such friendships the relationships described in the poems of Katherine Philips and the writings of Jeremy Taylor. He had assured his friend Philips, to whom his *Discourse of the Nature, Offices and Measures of Friendship, with Rules of Conducting it* (1657) was addressed, that women as well as men were capable of maintaining true friendships. The friendship of Catherine Talbot with Jemima, Lady Grey, and those of Elizabeth Carter with Catherine Talbot and with Hester Mulso, show a reaching out across distances of space and, to a certain extent, of class to create connections of friendship based on similar interests and similar problems.

Like Elizabeth Carter, Catherine Talbot was a clergyman's daughter, but the circumstances of her life differed greatly from those of Miss Carter. Catherine Talbot was of a higher class than Elizabeth Carter, having aristocratic and high clerical connections. But the significant fact of Catherine Talbot's life was that she was fatherless. Her father, the Revd Edward Talbot, Archdeacon of Berkshire, and Preacher at the Rolls, died of smallpox in December 1720; she was born on 21 May 1721. Mary Talbot, the grieving widow, found aid with a friend, Catherine Benson, who later helped her care for her infant daughter, also named Catherine. They continued to live together. The widow seems to have been left in narrow circumstances, and there are no indications that her late husband's family was interested in helping her. When Catherine Benson married Thomas Secker, another clergyman, in 1725, Secker declared that the widow and her child would always have a home with them. This act of charity and friendship was to determine the rest of Catherine Talbot's life.

The Revd Thomas Secker was an interesting and powerful personality. Born into a dissenting family, he had first studied divinity at various dissenting academies. But he began to doubt his commitment to his religion, and turned to the study of medicine in London and Paris. In Paris he met Martin Benson, brother of Catherine. Another friend with whom he corresponded was Joseph Butler, whom he had met while a student at a dissenting academy. He returned to England in 1720 and was introduced by Butler to the Revd Edward Talbot, whose father was then Bishop of Salisbury, later Bishop of Durham. Having decided to take orders in the Church of England, Secker went to Leiden for a medical degree, then entered Exeter College, Oxford, for a Bachelor of Arts. It is said that the son recommended his friends Benson, Butler, and Secker to his father, Bishop Talbot, on his deathbed, and in fact all three men achieved high places in the church. Secker received preferment from Bishop Talbot in 1724, when he was made Rector of Houghton-le-Spring, Durham. His rise was steady. He became Bishop of Bristol, then Rector of St James's, Piccadilly; while holding this office he was also Bishop of Oxford. He resigned the Rectorship to become Dean of St Paul's, but continued as Bishop of Oxford. Finally he was appointed Archbishop of Canterbury (Porteus).

Secker was an unusually active and able man, both as a parish priest and as a scholar. He knew Greek and Latin well, and had an extensive knowledge of Hebrew. Works of Hebrew scholarship were submitted to him for criticism (Porteus, pp. lxxx–lxxxv). He carried on the ceremonial duties of his various positions with diligence, and also found time to study sacred writings and documents of Church history. He was a vigorous person, who worked at retaining his contacts and friendships with people he met at different times and places. He took an interest in the practical details of life. He was energetic and methodical in the use of his time.

Catherine Benson Secker seems to have suffered many ill-nesses during the course of the marriage. The couple was child-less, and it turned out that Catherine Talbot became a sort of daughter to them, although, of course, the term 'foster father' was not used by the family members. Catherine always referred to Secker in her journals as the 'dear friend' whom providence had brought to assist her and her mother in their distress. Catherine seems to have enjoyed a relationship with Mrs Secker which had warmth and lightness of touch. Catherine also seems to have admired and been awed by her 'foster father'.

As part of the family of Thomas Secker, 'pretty Kitty Talbot' changed her residence as her foster father moved from one clerical preferment to another. His wife's ill health also meant visits to Bath. Catherine was a bright, volatile girl who wrote poetry and sent her female friends witty, incisive observations in her letters. Some of her poetry circulated in Bath, and she acquired a minor reputation as a clever girl. A poem printed in the *Gentleman's Magazine* (1741), 'On Miss Talbot's conversing with a Lawyer at Bath', made a connection between Catherine Talbot and her uncle, then Lord Chancellor of England, and claimed that the beauty of 'this accomplish'd fair' equalled the wisdom of the Chancellor on the bench (Carter, *Letters* (1808), i, p. xii).

Secker encouraged Catherine's intellectual interests in the classics, in English and French literature, in history. In 1733, just before he became Rector of St James's in London, he wrote to her (she was about thirteen) that he was pleased with the appointment partly because he thought it would be of advantage to her:

One of my greatest pleasures, in the new preferment I am to have, is, that it may be of advantage to your improvement; and it shall always be my business to give you all the improvements I can, and to adjust and regulate those which other persons give you.

You are the only child of a very good woman, our dear friend, and in stead of a child to my wife and me. The affection we all have for one another is united in *you*: for ourselves, all we can expect is, some continuance of our present happiness; but *You are our growing hopes*. The only way our enjoyment of life can much increase, is by seeing your mind, and temper and behaviour coming near to what we wish it.

In this letter Secker cautioned her to have 'absolute confidence in us'. He expressed the feeling that a time was coming when it would be difficult for her to judge correctly. He counselled her to resolve to follow good sense, and to rely on the fact that her 'old experienced friends are more to be trusted than the most officious new ones, who can desire to recommend themselves'. He cautioned her that human happiness is usually slight and interrupted; therefore, 'let your rule be to act right, expect little, and take cheerfully the good, and patiently the evil, that comes to your share.' The desire for happiness would be fully satisfied in a future world (Butler, 577–81).

As a mentor, Secker provided Catherine with some intellectual training, and of course he taught her reliance on her religious faith. As part of his evident love and protectiveness, he also seems to have feared her developing womanhood. Another poem from a Bath visit has survived which was written to chide Secker for 'Advising Miss Talbot Not to Mind what the Men Said to her':

> Why will you strive to make the fair
>   So blind to ev'ry charm,
> Alone unknowing of their pow'r
>   Which ev'ry bosom warm?

> No, Secker, no, in reason's spight
>   Thy arts must not prevail;
> Here overcome, and only here,
>   Thy eloquence must fail.
>           (Carter, *Letters* (1808),
>           i, pp. xiii–xiv)

His warnings were evidently forceful, for his admonitions seem to have imprinted on her mind tendencies to self-scrutiny and self-abasement which later had a painfully dampening effect on a lively spirit. While Nicolas Carter was bringing up his eldest daughter in such a way that she had a sense of freedom and ease about herself and her decisions, Catherine, who was more imaginative and romantic, was growing up with a sense of uneasiness about her own worth.

St James's was a fashionable church which had been built in the late seventeenth century by Sir Christopher Wren. Residence at the Rectory of St James's brought Catherine into contact with the congregation, which included both members of the aristocracy and people of literature and fashion. Fortuitously, it brought her into especial contact with two girls of about her own age who lived for part of the year in the Duke of Kent's family home on St James's Square, a short walk from the Rectory. The girls were Lady Mary Grey, youngest daughter of Henry Grey, Duke of Kent, by his first wife, and Jemima Campbell, his granddaughter by his eldest daughter, who had died when Jemima was five. Jemima's father was John Campbell, Lord Glenorchy, heir to the Earl of Breadalbane. Lord Glenorchy was envoy extraordinary to the Court of Denmark. Jemima was born in Denmark on 20 October 1722. A few years later her mother became ill and Jemima and her brother returned with their mother to Wrest, the Bedfordshire estate of the Duke of Kent. Lady Glenorchy died early in 1727; the son died later the same year. Jemima's grandmother, the Duchess of Kent, died the following year, leaving her youngest daughter, Lady Mary, who was then nine.

The two motherless girls were close in age and were more like sisters than aunt and niece. While they were living at St James's Square they struck up a warm friendship with Catherine Talbot. The Revd Secker had evidently been asked by the Duke to look in on the girls in London while he was at his country estate in Bedfordshire with a new young family (Godber, 7–14).

Catherine's happiest memories centred on her companionship with the two girls, which was enhanced by mutual intellectual interests. Their friendship began when they discovered they were reading the same book—Rollin's *Roman History* (Bedfordshire County Record Office, Lucas Papers L 30/9a/75). They soon found that mutual interests made it possible for their relationship to develop from a mere formal acquaintanceship to an intimate girlish friendship. The girls were interested in educating themselves; they shared their reading when they were together, and wrote about it when they were apart. Later on, Jemima recognized that their friendship had really meant an assertion of individuality, when she said she was glad such a friendship *could* be formed outside the confines of a 'narrow family circle', and that 'Minds are free to choose their own associates' (Bedfordshire County Record Office, Lucas Papers L 30/9a/5, p. 153).

We have some of Catherine Talbot's early letters to Jemima Campbell and Lady Mary because Thomas Birch made copies of them which he left with his other manuscripts to the British Museum. The letters—written between 1735 and 1739—are those of a girl with both literary and social interests. On 17 July 1735, when Catherine was fifteen, Jemima thirteen, and Lady Mary about sixteen, Catherine wrote Lady Mary a long letter based on her reading of the *Iliad*. (They were probably reading Pope's translations: *Iliad*, 1715–20; *Odyssey*, 1725–6.) Catherine was glad Miss Campbell liked the *Odyssey*, but asked her not to name that or any book alongside the *Iliad* (BL Add. 4291, fos. 254$^v$–255). There were inquiries about Virgil and Rapin, but Catherine said that 'Baken' was going along very slowly at home.

The emotional side of their friendship flourished as well. Feelings were exchanged in those early days, about real and fictional events. The girls recalled weeping in Catherine's dining-room over Charles Johnson's tragedy, *Caelia; or, The Perjur'd Lover*—'we three and the Kittens' (Bedfordshire County Record Office, Lucas Papers L 30/9a/50). Significantly, the girls were weeping over a play that foreshadowed *Clarissa*, in which a young woman has been stolen by Mr Wronglove from the house of a family friend. The lady is pregnant but he will not marry her. He arranges to send her to Mrs Lupine, who he claims is a midwife, but who is actually a brothel-keeper. In the end Caelia dies, a sacrifice to love.

Real anxieties also aroused emotions. In a long letter written probably in 1736, Catherine expressed her worries about a serious illness of Mrs Secker (BL Add. 4291, fos. 256–257, Bath, 16 Aug. 1736). But visits to Bath also brought the usual references to balls, visits, and puppet shows. The girls' pleasures alternated between the excitement of social events and a sentimental appreciation of solitude, quiet friendship, and good books.

In 1740 came a significant change. The Duke of Kent decided to make Jemima his heiress—all his male issue having failed— and he also wanted her to be married to Philip Yorke, eldest son of the Lord Chancellor, Lord Hardwicke. (Secker, who was one of the chaplains to King George II, knew the Lord Chancellor, and may have helped to arrange the match.)

Jemima was a realistic young woman who believed in taking life as it came, and she seems to have assented readily. The bride was seventeen; the groom was twenty, and had to be recalled from Cambridge for the ceremony, which took place on 22 May 1740. Shortly after the marriage her grandfather died, and Jemima became Marchioness Grey, owner of Wrest Park. (Her grandfather had received a special dispensation to have his name continued in the female line.) About three years later Lady Mary married Dr David Gregory of Oxford University (Godber, 17–18; 25).

The warmth of Catherine Talbot's attachment to her girlhood friends, especially Lady Grey, did not alter, although there seems to have been a temporary estrangement from Lady Mary. But Jemima's marriage did raise for Catherine the question of whether their friendship could continue as it had been. At the same time, she was also tormenting herself about a secret romantic attachment of her own. For a while it seemed to Catherine that she would have to live much of her life apart from her old friends, but in fact her contacts with Jemima continued to be close throughout her lifetime. They corresponded during the months when they were apart, and saw each other frequently in London. Lady Grey's older daughter, Lady Amabel, copied transcripts or extracts from her mother's correspondence into nine bound volumes, probably at some time after her mother's death in 1797. These volumes, which are now on deposit in the Bedfordshire County Record Office, contain portions of many letters from Jemima to Catherine, but only a few letters from Catherine to Jemima. Her daughter thought that Catherine's letters must have been in a box of papers which was destroyed accidentally while the papers were being sorted. But the extracts which remain show evidence of a close friendship in which literary interests and feelings continued to be shared.

Catherine visited Jemima and her husband at Wrest a number of times. In the early days, she joined in the literary projects in which Jemima's husband and his brother Charles Yorke were engaged. Over the years, Catherine became an intimate of the Yorke–Hardwicke circle, and an affectionate honorary aunt to Jemima's children, Lady Amabel and Lady Mary, to whom she wrote appealing, humorous letters.

However, if minds were free to choose their own associates, as Jemima had perceived, in the early years of Jemima's marriage a new friendship, of a sort that had nothing to do with the social set with which Catherine was usually engaged, might also be welcome. Thomas Wright, who knew both Elizabeth Carter and Catherine Talbot, probably because he had taught them mathematics and astronomy, thought they would be congenial. Thomas Wright was a self-taught scientist who after early struggles had published several works and acquired as patrons a number of aristocrats including the Duke of Kent. Wright stayed at Wrest in the summer of 1736 to teach mathematics 'to the ladies of the family' ('Biographical History of Mr. Thomas Wright', 11),[1] presumably Jemima Campbell and Lady Mary; Catherine Talbot may possibly have been visiting at that time. We know from her letters that Elizabeth Carter had visited Wright in London and carried on a correspondence about mathematics with him. He had a reputation for enjoying fantasy. Elizabeth Carter's letter to Wright on 28 January 1741 (Carter, *Letters* (1808)) indicates that she had seen Catherine Talbot on the previous Sunday—probably at St James's. She was eager to meet her, but her claim, 'Miss Talbot is absolutely my passion; I think of her all day, dream of her all night, and one way or other introduce her into every subject I talk of', seems to be a romantic exaggeration written to entertain Thomas Wright. The young women finally met in February 1741, probably at the London residence of Elizabeth's Canterbury friend, Hon. Mrs Rooke. (Pennington thought they had met at Mrs Rooke's house in Canterbury, but as both were in London that winter, the London meeting seems much more probable.) Catherine was impressed by this sensible, well-educated, talented, and rather independent young woman. Elizabeth was also enthusiastic about her new friend, of whose literary abilities she had heard.

But, after their introduction in 1741, Elizabeth and Catherine did not meet again for at least six years. Elizabeth was spending her time at Deal and Canterbury; Catherine was dividing her time at the Rectory of St James's in winter and spring, at the Bishop's residence at Cuddesden near Oxford in summer and autumn. There was a difference in their movements in that Elizabeth moved freely between Deal and

Canterbury, whereas Catherine travelled, except for a couple
of visits to Wrest, always with her mother, the Bishop, and Mrs
Secker.

The opening of this epistolary friendship shows Elizabeth's
diffidence. She feels that her difficulties in writing come from
having sunk into ignorance. She also develops a fantasy. She
tells Catherine that she is planning a 'romantic voyage to the
Goodwin sands' with Mr Wright in which she may be drowned.
Therefore she thinks Catherine will prefer 'the impertinence of
a letter, rather than run the hazard of being suprized by a
posthumous visit' (Carter, *Letters* (1808), 16 Aug. 1741). In her
reply Catherine also acknowledges difficulty in writing. She
adds that 'the pleasure your acquaintance gave me last winter,
was more than my utmost vanity could expect, but this is so far
from satisfying me, that I am only more desirous of having it
repeated this year . . .' (15 Sept. 1741). The following winter
Catherine was still urging her new friend to come to London,
but Elizabeth went to Canterbury instead. Then Catherine was
ill and did not write for six months. The young women made
efforts to maintain this friendship in letters, although there
were long gaps when one or the other was ill or unhappy, and
did not write.

The letters they exchanged over a period of almost thirty
years came into the possession of Elizabeth Carter's nephew,
Montagu Pennington. He published them in 1808. The
originals have disappeared. Pennington later brought out the
letters of his aunt to Elizabeth Montagu in 1817. When we
compare Elizabeth Carter's letters as they appear in this edition
(her letters to Mrs Montagu are also missing) with the original
replies by Mrs Montagu now in the Huntington Library, we
can see discontinuities. Alterations and omissions were made
by the editor. The same was probably the case for the Carter–
Talbot collection. Still, the letters as we have them convey the
interests, attitudes, emotional problems, dilemmas of both
women. They reveal their personal characteristics and the way
their friendship functioned as a positive and supportive relationship.

From the beginning the friends wrote about their emotions
and the conditions of their lives. Having given up her work at
St John's Gate, Elizabeth evidently felt a sense of relaxation,

for she explained that she had idly passed the 'whole summer in the care of my health, and the utter neglect of my intellects' (Carter, *Letters* (1808), 5 Nov. 1741). One brother, a lieutenant in the Royal Navy, had died overseas. Elizabeth spoke of her sorrow, and described her melancholy walks in the moonlight by the sea. A couple of years later she was still explaining that she was doing all the things she had not done as a young girl: working ruffles, knitting, dancing. It seemed odd to some people that 'a person who thought of little but books at fifteen, should at five and twenty run mad after balls and assemblies' (1 Jan. 1743). She seems to have been trying to experience pleasures she had ignored when young.

Both women were interested in writing and in literature, so it was natural that they discussed literary matters. Mme de Sévigné offered a model for their correspondence. They read her letters in French and carried on some of their discussion in French. Elizabeth Carter thought Mme de Sévigné's deep attachment to her daughter was for the most part the source of the beauties of her spirit, and regretted that Mme de Grignan's letters had not been preserved. 'La vivacité de la mère auroit fait un contraste fort agréable avec la froideur de la fille' (9 Oct. 1744). Catherine Talbot agreed that there was nothing more agreeable or interesting than the maternal tenderness which the letters revealed. But Mme de Sévigné's attachment was too intense for this world (15 Nov. 1744). Replying, 5 Dec. 1744, Elizabeth Carter said that she thought Mme de Sévigné's fondness was probably carried too far. She had a lively temper, which had not been restrained by a regular education.

A staple of their letters was accounts of the daily readings of Catherine Talbot's family. On 28 December 1747, in a letter from Cuddesden, Catherine described how they read *Clarissa, en famille*, at set hours, and spent the rest of the day speaking of it. 'One can scarce persuade oneself that they are not real characters, and living people.' (The first two volumes had been published on 1 December 1747.) The friends also discussed Fielding, whom Elizabeth liked especially. Catherine Talbot explained that their family readings had to be in English, but both Talbot and Carter themselves read and referred to French philosophy, memoirs, histories, and plays in their letters.

As the women got to know each other better, they also

shared their interest in the writing which both were doing; the letters themselves became a repository for humorous, descriptive, or analytical writing. They were interested in moral teaching through literature, and shared their strong interest in the *Rambler*, their interest in the composition of *Sir Charles Grandison*, and Catherine's accounts of her friendship with Samuel Richardson.

By way of contrast to herself, Catherine Talbot was very much interested in the kind of life which Elizabeth Carter was living in Deal and Canterbury. Elizabeth Carter described her studies, her walks in the Kentish countryside, her responses to the sea which was so pervasive a presence at Deal, and the ways of her country neighbours. Catherine Talbot countered with light, humorous descriptions of people, and enthusiastic sketches of gardens and the Oxford countryside. Catherine described her life in the country—visiting a circle of about eighteen families around Oxford, musing in the garden, drawing, painting, teaching children the catechism, doing handwork, reading, and writing. During the London season she saw Jemima, Lady Grey, and participated in some of the London social life, attending operas, concerts, plays. When she felt cheerful she could write,

I love society extremely, from the fine folks in town, down to the dirty children in a village-school, or day-labourers with their hooks and scythes. I love solitude to excess—I love walking because it is cheerful, and sitting still at home because it is safe and quiet. (4 Sept. 1745)

By this time Catherine and Elizabeth were also writing more openly of their feelings. One of the emotions which they shared was a sense of regret that marriage meant the loss of close women friends. Catherine had struggled with a sense of abandonment when Jemima had married; Elizabeth also felt depressed at the prospect of a good friend's marriage. But, as Catherine assured Elizabeth, it was necessary to accommodate oneself to this change, and she herself had found that her affection for her married friend had continued as it was, although they were not able to see each other as often as they had in the past (27 June 1744).

Both women struggled with a sense of being intimidated by those whom they loved, and who loved them. On one occasion

Elizabeth complained that she had been prevented from taking her walks because of the opinions of other people that it was too cold to walk. Catherine felt that she herself had long been 'broke' to the wishes of others (12 Aug. 1746). There were physical and psychological symptoms which may have been related to this sense of oppression. Elizabeth was still having debilitating headaches. Catherine, on the other hand, suffered from nervous fears. She described to her friend her anxiety in handling a horse which was very spirited.

By returning to Deal Elizabeth Carter had attempted to come to terms with the difficulties in her own circumstances. Catherine Talbot's situation in the Bishop's household also posed difficulties, but there did not seem to be a solution to them. She admitted to sometimes feeling depressed. Partly, it was that she felt her time was not her own; she was bound to carry on the social and practical duties which came to her as a member of the Bishop's 'family'. Catherine had a strong sense that she lacked control over her life:

What should I do if I was engaged in any serious business? I have but three creatures in the world over whom I have a right to exercise any government, a foolish dog, a restive horse, and a perverse gardener, who has lately been put under my direction. In this my small dominion I meet with as many difficulties as ever indolent monarch did. The dog uncontrouled is for ever running after sheep, or jumping upon me with dirty paws; the horse will by no possible persuasion go over the same ground twice; and the gardener is demolishing my beds of flowers, which I meant to have had enlarged. (26 Oct. 1747)

The letters gave both women opportunities to express their discontents; Elizabeth even remarked that having written about her difficulties she felt better. The letters gave them a sense of community. In general, the advice each gave the other was to be sensible, do things as much one's own way as possible, and persevere. To Catherine's complaints about her life, Elizabeth responded with joking, but partly serious advice as to the ways and means to bring her 'rebellious subjects into better regulation'. She suggested that Catherine give her dog to the care of some child ('I have a brother at your service') who would soon tease it into submission; that Catherine send her unruly horse into Kent to take morning walks with her and her friend, as they would eventually tire the horse. But the gardener, 'being a perverse human creature', she did not know how to change (29 Oct. 1747).

In the spring of 1748 Elizabeth Carter came to London for several months. She probably stayed at her uncle's house, but spent much time with Catherine. During this time Mrs Secker died. Elizabeth offered consolation and long walks. When Catherine returned to Cuddesden for the summer, she remembered her happy times with Mrs Secker in that place. The loss was very painful to her; what was also painful was that she felt the necessity of trying to comfort her mother and the Bishop, while they maintained such strict composure that she had difficulty bringing the subject up. Usually Elizabeth's letters were shown to the others. The extent of Catherine's anxiety is shown by the fact that in this instance she asked for a letter of advice from Elizabeth to be addressed to one of the maids, so that she wouldn't have to show it to the Bishop (8 June 1748).

Elizabeth stayed in London during that summer, living either at her uncle's residence in town (he had moved to Devonshire Street) or sometimes at his country home in Enfield. When Catherine returned to London in November 1748, the friends again had the opportunity for personal visits. It was during this time that Elizabeth Carter had the marriage proposal which gave her much anxiety, and that Catherine Talbot asked her friend to begin the translation of the *Works* of Epictetus for her personal use. After her long stay, Elizabeth Carter left London in April, spent a week at Canterbury, and then started home. Her letter from Deal, 5 May 1749, describes her walk home:

On Wednesday I took my place in the Deal coach, but finding it stuffed with six queer-looking people, in a hot dusty day, it was agreed the man should take me up at the end of some miles, where he was to discharge one of his passengers; but it seems he took it so much in dudgeon that I should resist his persuasions of making the seventh, that he drove quite away, and left me to trudge on; so I procured an honest country lad to accompany me, and performed the sixteen miles with great alacrity, only now and then reposing on a green bank, and under a shady tree, where I treated myself and my swain with plumb cake.

This brief scene shows Carter's vigorous independence and her use of romantic language for humour.

Catherine Talbot's travels at this time were with the Bishop and her mother. In the spring of 1750 the Bishop offered Catherine an opportunity to visit the sea. He spoke of Portsmouth in particular but left the decision to her. She chose a visit to Deal so that she could spend some time with Elizabeth. The family party went to Canterbury, where Elizabeth met them, then on to Dover, and then to Deal. They preferred to stay at an inn during the visit. Elizabeth had been asked by Catherine to keep the fact of the Bishop's visit quiet, so that he would not be waylaid by the clergy in Canterbury. Catherine enjoyed her week's visit and was grateful to Elizabeth for letting them meet her friends and relations (14 May 1750).

In 1750 Secker resigned the Rectorship of St James's for the Deanship of St Paul's, while remaining Bishop of Oxford. For Catherine this meant that she and her mother had to leave the old house in Piccadilly in which they had lived for so long, for a home in the City. During 1752 and 1753 Catherine had several losses which depressed her: the deaths of Bishop Butler, Bishop Benson, and Bishop Berkeley. Catherine had been particularly attached to Martin Benson, Bishop of Gloucester, the brother of her beloved Catherine Secker. In Catherine's journals she gives him the name 'Marcus' and describes him as a person with an 'inimitably easy amiable Manner so mixed of merry Cheerfullness, Sweet Goodness & thorough Seriousness . . .' (BL Add. 46690, fo. 17). Catherine noted the times when he gave her mother and her his company—they spent happy hours reading separately while sitting together, and talking casually when something came up which they wished to share (fo. 48$^v$).

During the 1750s Elizabeth Carter was again mainly in Deal —preparing her brother Henry for the University, working on her translations of Epictetus, and sewing shirts. There were some visits to London, during which Elizabeth had lodgings near St Paul's, and spent much time with her friends at the deanery. She was a good friend of Mrs Talbot, and they made a congenial family party. Mrs Talbot sent her 'tender love to her daughter Betty' (19 June [1753]). Invitations to Elizabeth Carter's relatives were also forthcoming; her father, brother, and sister dined at the deanery at different times. Secker was called on to help various members of Elizabeth Carter's family, so that in the long run her friendship with Catherine Talbot was useful to them.

The personalities and attitudes of the two women were well suited to be supportive of one another. Catherine was bright and witty, but subject to depressions and feelings of lack of self-worth; Elizabeth was realistic, patient, and diffident. Of course, Catherine continued to express her complaints to her old friend Lady Grey, who spent much time trying to argue her out of her depressions. She advised Catherine to begin to live in the present, forget the past, take life as it came. The sadness of life should be noted, but 'gayer landscapes' should be included. Lady Grey was tough-minded. She remarked that when travelling over Hounslow Heath she did not think it always necessary to look at the man hanging in chains on the gibbet (19 Oct. 1745, Bedfordshire County Record Office, Lucas Papers L 30/9a/4, pp. 71–2). Elizabeth was more sensitive and compassionate. Catherine was continually attacking herself for frivolity and waste of time. Elizabeth assured Catherine that she was judging herself too harshly, and that she should accept her weaknesses as such and not try to perfect herself. So this friendship went on, with Catherine struggling against depressions, and Elizabeth struggling with headaches. But, although Catherine could not alter her own situation, she made an effort to try to alter Elizabeth's, for she felt it a pity that Elizabeth should be 'buried' at Deal.

In their biography of Samuel Richardson, Eaves and Kimpel implied that Elizabeth Carter's headaches might have had something to do with an unexpressed sexual orientation (355). Lillian Faderman in *Surpassing the Love of Men* (1981) is more direct in claiming that Catherine and Elizabeth were essentially lovers; she speculates on why they did not live together. In both cases Carter is regarded as a would-be lesbian. I do not agree with this view. In evaluating the nature of the relationship between Elizabeth and Catherine, we need to make distinctions between kinds of female friendships. Faderman defines 'romantic female friendship' as a close, passionate, long-lasting relationship between two women, which she sees as a non-sexual form or precursor of lesbianism. Her paradigm is the relationship of two women of the next generation, Lady Eleanor Butler and Sarah Ponsonby, who eloped from Ireland in 1778 and lived together in Wales for more than fifty years. The relationship of the 'Ladies of Llangollen' is certainly a good example of romantic female friendship; in her journals Lady Eleanor referred to her companion as 'Beloved' and focused on her as an exclusive love-object (Hamwood Papers); Sarah Ponsonby wrote of Lady Eleanor as 'My B.' (Mavor).

But such emotion is not really typical of the friendships of the bluestocking women. There is no evidence that Elizabeth Carter ever felt the sort of exclusive attachment for another woman that the 'Ladies of Llangollen' felt for each other. Of course, the Talbot–Carter friendship had its sentimental aspects. By the summer of 1751 the friendship was close enough so that Elizabeth could ask Catherine for a 'bit of hair'. Catherine would have liked to have sent it in a crystal case, but found such jewellery to be too expensive, so embroidered a case instead (8 June 1751). In her letter acknowledging the gift, Elizabeth Carter assured her she did not intend to make a charm or relic of it.

But I must be allowed to look on it with delight as the gift of a person to whom I owe the highest obligation, that of having endeavoured to render me wise and better; and I think you will be satisfied that the sentiments arising from such a reflection cannot do mischief. (25 June 1751)

It took time for the bluestockings to break through the conventional formalities of friendship to trust and intimacy; these friendships, which developed gradually, were neither passionate nor exclusive. Elizabeth Carter and Catherine Talbot enjoyed each other's company at those times when both were in London, but they never expressed the wish to live together. They shared their friendships—Elizabeth Carter always tried to bring her women friends together—and in some cases the sharing included male friends.

Another indication that the bonding of these women was not an erotic attachment but an effort to create stable, supportive relationships among women is the friendship of Elizabeth Carter and Hester Mulso, whom Carter met at Canterbury in 1749. Hester Mulso was a bright young woman with literary interests and an open, expressive personality. She was born on 27 October 1727 in the village of Twywell, in the county of Northampton. Her father Thomas (b. 1695) was the only son of an old landed family. Mr Mulso married in 1719 a Miss

Thomas, daughter of a Colonel Thomas; both father and daughter were considered handsome people (Mulso, pp. vii–viii). Hester was born in the Elizabethan house near the church which was among the remains of the family's properties. In the unsigned biography which appeared in Hester Chapone's *Posthumous Works* the writer claimed that Hester's mother resented attention being paid to her daughter, and may even have tried to limit her education. Mrs Mulso was an ailing woman, in any case, and her continued illnesses probably did reduce the amount of education Hester received (i. 5–7).

It is not clear how much time Hester spent at Twywell. John Cole, another biographer (1839), thought that Hester lived at Twywell during her early years, but also visited Canterbury, Peterborough, and London. However, according to Rashleigh Holt-White, editor of John Mulso's *Letters to Gilbert White of Selborne*, the senior Mr Mulso became Clerk of the Assizes and lived in London at King Square Court, Soho, from about 1731 (Mulso, pp. vii–viii). It seems likely that Hester resided in London from her early years for much of the time, with visits to Anne Mulso Donne, her aunt who was the wife of a prebendary at Canterbury, and to her uncle John Thomas (her mother's brother), who was first Bishop of Peterborough, then Salisbury, then Winchester. His wife was Mr Mulso's sister Susanna (Mulso, p. viii). Hester's mother lived at least until 1747; in a letter from Hampton on 21 August 1747 her son John mentioned visiting her. There is a gap in his letters until 17 July 1749 and he does not mention his mother again (Mulso, 18–19). According to that chronology, her mother died when Hester was in her early twenties.

The biographer in Chapone's *Posthumous Works* claimed that at her mother's death she began to manage her father's house and to educate herself. She learned French and Italian and some Latin. She liked poetry and philosophy, but did not really enjoy reading history until later in life (i. 8–9). As she explained to Elizabeth Carter, in the days before she chose her own books she read many romances, such as *Le Grand Cyrus* and *Clélie* (i. 34–5).

Hester Mulso is an example of a woman whose development owed much to the interest and companionship of her brothers. She was the only girl in a family with three surviving brothers.

Her brother Thomas was a barrister, her brother John a clergy-man, and Edward a clerk in the Excise office. Both Thomas and Edward figured in Hester's friendship with Samuel Richardson. Her brother John was a college friend of Gilbert White of Selborne, the naturalist, with whom he exchanged visits and carried on a lifelong correspondence. In John's letters his sister Hester appears as a bright, clever girl. Hester also had a friendship with Gilbert White, and there are some hints that John would have liked Gilbert to show a more personal interest in Hester. John referred to his sister as 'Heck', 'Hecky', and, for some reason one can only guess at, as 'Yes Papa' (Mulso, 51). Was her brother teasing his sister about her close relationship with their father? Or was he teasing her because her obedience had a degree of cheekiness? In any case, Hester signed herself 'Yes Papa' in a note she wrote on the bottom of one of John's letters to Gilbert White (Mulso, 51).

John thought his sister a vital, energetic person. He regarded her as a 'bold girl' when she travelled with her father to North-amptonshire and also to Canterbury in an open 'chair' (Mulso, 24; 34). He also reported her colds and vapours, and the times she came to nurse him when he was ill. After he married, she came to help his wife and children (Mulso, 129). At one time when he had a living in the North, Hester travelled alone from London 'in chance Company in the Leeds Machine', a trip her brother regarded as a 'bold undertaking' (Mulso, 198).

Literary activity figured in the correspondence of John Mulso and Gilbert White, and Hester was brought in as a participant. John thought Hester had a good ear for verse, and at his suggestion Gilbert White sent her his poetry to criticize. John spoke proudly of Hester's 'Ode to Epictetus', which appeared in the opening pages of Elizabeth Carter's translation. John told his friend of her acquaintance with Samuel Richardson. 'My Sister & ye Family are got into the Acquaintance of Richardson ye Author of Pamela & Clarissa, in which they take great Delight, for the Man is a Sort of an Original for Goodness & Sensibility' (Mulso, 43). As we shall see, brother John was amused that Hester seemed to have got the better of Richardson in their exchange of letters on the duties of children and parents. John Mulso also reported the friendship with Elizabeth Carter.

From their initial meeting at Canterbury (Hester was visit-ing her aunt, Mrs Donne) Hester Mulso and Elizabeth Carter developed an epistolary friendship which was strengthened by Hester's visits to Deal in 1752 and 1756, and a visit Elizabeth made to Canterbury to see Hester in 1754. In her *Letters on the Improvement of the Mind*, published years later, Hester advised her niece to find a friend eight or ten years older than she who would provide her with the benefit of the friend's greater experience. This was essentially the relationship which began between Hester at twenty-two and Elizabeth at thirty-two.

Poetry was a shared interest, and formed a topic in their correspondence. The friends sent each other poems they had written; Hester asked for free and open criticism. She had a light, incisive prose style and a modest view of her work. She saw writing poetry as a female, albeit an undernourished, creative act. About her writing she said, 'should the scribbling fit ever seize me again, my maternal fondness will, in all likelihood, tempt me to send the brat to you, who seem to have so much tenderness for such poor little half-starved infants' (Chapone, *Posthumous Works*, i. 33).

The friends also discussed contemporary poetry and prose. Hester found Young's *Night Thoughts* difficult to understand, but liked his *Universal Passion*. The friends discussed Fielding. They had both been reading *Amelia*, and showed diverse reactions to the novel. Elizabeth accepted Fielding's characterizations, especially of Booth. She believed that human nature was mixed, and that Booth should be accepted as a frail character. Hester on the other hand thought Booth contemptible or wicked and would happily have seen him hanged (Chapone, *Posthumous Works*, i. 48–52).

When both were reading the *Rambler*, Hester objected to what she believed to be Johnson's 'depraved' view of human nature. She also objected to the contemptuous manner in which the *Rambler* spoke of women, and moreover to the fact that the essays showed more bad female characters than good ones. 'I dare say you will agree with me in this, for you carry your partiality to your own sex farther than I do' (11 Oct. 1752, Chapone, *Posthumous Works*, i. 64). They also discussed Richardson, his views and his letters. Elizabeth Carter and Hester Mulso did not always agree about Richardson. Elizabeth dared to deride Richardson's prolixity, but Hester defended him.

The classics also came into discussion. At one point Hester

was reading Guthrie's translation of Cicero's *Epistles to Atticus*, and thought Elizabeth's favourite, Tully, was excessively vain. Hester felt that she was in general less reverent towards 'great names' than many people were, but would share her open irreverent comments only with Elizabeth, although she expected even Elizabeth to reprove her (Chapone, *Posthumous Works*, i. 47–8).

After her visit to Deal in 1752, Hester wrote an amusing 'thank-you' note. In it she explained how much she valued Elizabeth's friendship. She suspected that Elizabeth's sister thought her an awkward houseworker—even though she was never guilty of more than four odes (Chapone, *Posthumous Works*, i. 54–5). Below she noted, 'N. B. I had like to have been overturned upon Sandown, but thought of the stoic philosophy, and did not squeak' (i. 56–7).

Among Hester and Elizabeth's recurring subjects were religion and the moral nature of man. Hester agreed with her friend that the world was 'more enlightened, as well by the discoveries of human reason, as by the progress of divine revelation' (Chapone, *Posthumous Works*, i. 67). Later Elizabeth sent her something towards proof of the truths of Christianity. In their continuing discussions, Hester wrote to her friend as to a mentor: 'The puzzling question is, whence does sin derive its original?' (Chapone, *Posthumous Works*, i. 80).

Unfortunately, we do not have Elizabeth Carter's letters to Hester Mulso. But from Hester's letters we get a sense that she saw her friend as a serious intellectual who tended to try to emphasize mind too much over feelings. When Elizabeth complained that the 'tender affections' seemed to involve more pain than pleasure, Hester advised her friend, 'Do not then, my dear Miss Carter, quarrel with your heart because you cannot make a stoic of it' (Chapone, *Posthumous Works*, i. 75). She suspected that Elizabeth was not kind to her body, and warned her not to sacrifice her physical well-being to her studies (Chapone, *Posthumous Works*, i. 84–5).

Despite differences in age, situation, talents, attitudes, the friendship between Hester and Elizabeth gave both of them the benefit of something they valued—rational conversation in person and on paper. Writing to Elizabeth to thank her for visiting her in Canterbury, probably in 1754, Hester said:

Your conversation seems to have new-set the spring of my mind, which had been greatly hurt and weakened. Till you arrived I was just in the state which Miss T[albot] so charmingly describes; 'je mourois d'ennui!' but you have restored to me a relish for my existence . . . (Chapone, *Posthumous Works*, i. 83)

These remarks, which Hester Mulso threw off in such a nonchalant manner, are significant for all of these friendships. These women were determined to function, if possible, in a self-directed way. Their friendships helped them to keep the springs of their minds going, and to avoid that common problem of upper- and middle-class women, ennui. Their lives were not the same, nor were they equally linked. But their friendships were important in helping them to create a 'female web of experience' which supported their efforts at autonomy.

# PART II

# The First Bluestockings: Choices and Changing Views

# Introduction

THE prospective bluestockings took their friendships seriously and made them a means of personal development. As they grew into young women, of course, they also faced the issue of marriage. As Anne Donnellan, herself unmarried, assured Elizabeth Robinson when she was on the verge of marrying, marriage 'is the settlement in the world we should aim at, and the only way we females have of making ourselves of use to Society and raising ourselves in this world . . .' (Montagu (1906), i. 113). This astute assessment indicates Donnellan's awareness of the narrow opportunities available to the women she knew. They could make themselves useful by becoming wives and mothers; they could raise themselves by marrying men who had more money or higher status than they.

But marriage as a relationship could also be idealized. In his work on friendship, Jeremy Taylor gave marriage the highest place in friendship; he claimed that 'Marriage is the Queen of friendships, in which there is a communication of all that can be communicated by friendship . . .' (72). This statement epitomizes the ideal of rational domesticity which Irene Q. Brown has shown to have influenced aristocratic English men and women from the Restoration period on to the middle of the eighteenth century and which affected the motives and actions of the bluestockings.

Although the ideal of marriage as a union of friends was developing, in fact the choice of a spouse involved practical realities over which young women might not have a great deal of influence. Since girls were not being prepared for anything but matrimony, their education was usually considered complete when they were fifteen (Trumbach, 112). At that point upper-class girls went out into society: they visited watering-places, attended balls, went to plays. Although entertainment and personal pleasure motivated their social life, they were also being displayed to their social group at large: men who were interested in marriage might observe these young women, ascertain what their financial resources were, and begin to develop some acquaintanceship. Sometimes a personal relationship was not considered at all necessary, and a man could propose marriage to a woman about whom he had only heard. Elizabeth Robinson, Elizabeth Carter, and Catherine Talbot all had proposals of this sort.

But styles of courtship were changing in the middle of the eighteenth century. Young women could be affected by earlier and later styles; their families might also reflect these different attitudes. Women could be influenced by old ideas that marriage *should* be the means of improving the family's fortunes, that parents *should* choose the spouse, with the young woman having veto power only. Newer ideas involved some degree of personal interest and attraction. If people were beginning to think that a lasting marriage *should* be based on the admiration and esteem of the partners, who had begun, and would continue, as friends, then the daughter or son should be permitted to choose, subject to the parents' veto, which was apt to concern itself with financial position and status. Ideas of romantic love were circulating in poems, plays, and novels. Lawrence Stone thinks that despite the emphasis on romantic and sexual love in such works, 'falling in love' was not then a common practice (272–3). Couples 'in love' do figure in Elizabeth Robinson's correspondence, but she tended to disparage them. She herself felt that romantic love was only a pretence offered by a man to marry a woman whom he had actually chosen on other grounds.

The changing styles created uncertainties for the young women who were to become the 'bluestockings'. Should they let their families choose their husbands? And if so, on what basis were they to accept this choice? Was it simply enough to agree that one's family knew best? To what extent should feelings be consulted? How was a young woman to deal with the realities of her economic situation, as it related to the kind of person she might prefer as a spouse? The pressures put on Clarissa Harlowe in Samuel Richardson's novel are only an extreme instance of the more subtle pressures and conflicts which young women felt. Arguments against personal choice could be internalized. Lady Grey and Catherine Talbot discussed Clarissa's problems in their letters; they seemed to agree that Clarissa's right to refuse Solmes should have had its source in duty rather than in personal inclination. Lady Grey thought that the power to refuse was consistent with reason and duty, but insisting on a private choice was not (12 Dec. 1747, Bedfordshire County Record Office, Lucas Papers L 30/9a/5, p. 49). As we shall see, Catherine Talbot also felt a deep commitment to family duty when it conflicted with personal choice.

And, in fact, for each of these young women choice in marriage seems to have come down to a very personal decision. Each woman dealt with her family's wishes, her own feeling for family, her own inner desires, and the economic limitations of her circumstances in a different way.

# 4 · Marriage and the Bluestockings

THE question of marriage for Lady Margaret Harley was on the minds of friends and family very early. When Lady Margaret was fourteen, Elijah Fenton dedicated an edition of the works of Edmund Waller to her with a poem in which he celebrated her beauties and wondered who would be the 'fav'rite youth' who would be her bridegroom. The chosen man would have grace of form, grace of mind, great merit, great lineage, and be 'wise, brave and studious to support the State' (Waller, 1729, sig. A4ʳ).

In fact, her father's views on the sort of man he wanted for Lady Margaret were much the same as the poet's. In a letter of 8 August 1734, after the marriage, Lord Oxford explained to Jonathan Swift the careful search which the parents had made for a husband for their daughter. He was now convinced that they had chosen an exceptional young man, free of such common vices as 'gaming, sharping, pilfering, lying, Etc' (Swift, iv. 244). Lord Oxford thought the bridegroom seemed to be the soul of honour, an exceptional person in mind and body, who got along well with his family. In his reply Swift expressed his pleasure that Lord Oxford seemed to have 'disposed' of his daughter so well. Swift had known the bridegroom's father, whom he thought good-natured but 'expensive'; he thought Lord Oxford's account of the sobriety and good sense of the son suggested a pleasant prospect. 'I was always a diligent observer of My Lady Margaret, and consequently could not but be an admirer of her Virtues which she discovered so early, and so abundantly' (iv. 248).

Lady Margaret's bridegroom was William Bentinck, second Duke of Portland, a descendant of Hans William Bentinck of Holland, who had been a devoted aide of Prince William of Orange; the aide came to England when his patron became King William III. The King rewarded his friend with important preferments and the title of Earl of Portland. His son, Henry, married Lady Elizabeth Noel, eldest daughter of Wriothesley Baptist Noel, Earl of Gainsborough. Henry was created first Duke of Portland by King George I in 1716. But

the first Duke lost a great deal of money in the South Sea
Bubble, and took a post as governor of Jamaica in order to
recoup his losses. He died in 1726 at the age of forty-five.
William, born on 1 March 1708/9, was thus seventeen when he
succeeded to the Dukedom (Turberville, ii. 1–17).

During the years between 1728 and 1730 the young man
spent some time studying at Leiden in the company of his
tutor, John Achard. In letters to Mr Achard William's mother
expressed her happiness at his tutor's good reports of him. She
evidently found William a pleasant contrast to his brother
George, who had recently been rather 'wild' but was getting
better. The dowager Duchess urged her son to stay at Leiden
until he had mastered his studies, and then to visit other parts
of Europe (Univ. of Nottingham Library, MS PC PwC 28).
Reports from Mr Achard indicated that he and his pupil got on
well together, which pleased but did not surprise his mother, as
his son's temper was 'so good' (MS PC PwC 30).

The marriage of Lady Margaret Harley and William, Duke
of Portland on 11 July 1734 was certainly an arranged one, an
example of the ways in which noble landed families could
increase their estates by marriage or bring in much-needed
cash; it was also an example of the sort of marriage a wealthy
woman could make. Scholars have corroborated the perceptions
of novel-readers that, as Christopher Clay put it, 'generally
speaking a girl's marriage prospects depended on the size of
her portion' (507). Lady Margaret was a great heiress, and her
husband, according to Thomas Hearne, was 'reported to be
the handsomest man in England'. Hearne believed that Princess
Amelia, daughter of the present king, George II, was supposed
to have been 'wonderfully in love with him, and would fain
have had him if she could' (Hearne, *Remarks*, xi. 361).

In *The Rise of the Egalitarian Family*, Randolph Trumbach
claimed that the average sum a woman who married a peer
brought was £25,000 in money rather than land (81). In the
previous generation Lady Henrietta had had a dowry of
£20,000 and lands worth £5,000 a year by her father's will
(Nulle, 12). The original marriage-settlement of the Duke and
Duchess of Portland has recently come to light among a collection of documents sent to the Portland Collection at the
University of Nottingham Library from the solicitors' offices in

London, where they evidently had been stored since they were written. The marriage settlement stated that 'Twenty Thousand Pounds of good and lawful money of Great Britain' was to be paid to the Duke as the marriage portion of Lady Margaret. The settlement then went on to list the properties owned by the Duke, including Bulstrode, property in London, and property in Kent. The total value mentioned was about £36,000, though the value of all the properties was not mentioned. The cash brought by the bride seems to have been equal to about half the value of the groom's landed properties. According to the customs of the times, Lady Margaret was assured 'pin money' (Trumbach, 82). But in this case Lady Margaret's personal income of £500 a year in quarterly payments was to come from the rents and profits of properties held in trust by the Earl of Oxford, money with which 'the said Duke her intended Husband is not to intermeddle or to have any controlling power over.' The Duke himself was allocated a yearly income from the Oxford rents beyond this sum. The agreement also specified property from which the yearly rent charge of £1,600 was to be paid as Lady Margaret's jointure, the provision for her maintenance after her husband's death. The settlement also provided for sums of £20,000 for any children, and a sum for the yearly maintenance of William's brother George (Univ. of Nottingham Library, MS PC P1 D).

The Oxford properties which were held in trust to provide income for the Duke and Duchess of Portland remained in Lady Oxford's control after her husband's death, for by the terms of Lady Oxford's will, the Duchess of Portland received a life interest in her mother's estates after her mother's death in 1755. The Duke died in 1761. But the third Duke did not succeed to his grandmother's properties until his mother's death in 1785, because his mother retained her life interest in these estates. Her son wanted her to turn over her estates to him in return for an annual rent. In June of 1766 the Duchess wrote to her son that she had been made independent by her mother's will, and was determined to keep herself so (Turberville, ii. 60–6; 154–6).

The financial disagreements between mother and son were the story of the next generation; at the time the marriage must have suited both sides. There were mutual benefits. From the

Portlands' viewpoint Lady Margaret brought the Portland family money and the eventual possession of extensive properties; from the Oxfords' viewpoint, Portland made their daughter a Duchess.

The phrase the Duchess used in writing about the arrangements for her marriage seems strangely accurate in this light. She called it 'making a purchase' and she seems to have been content with hers. In her letters to her girlhood friend Catherine Collingwood a few months after her marriage, the Duchess referred to her new husband as 'Sweet William', and wished her friend knew 'more of that flower, for I am sure you would be quite charmed with it' (Delany, 1st ser., i. 511).

In recent years scholars such as Lawrence Stone, Randolph Trumbach, and Irene Q. Brown have pointed out that new kinds of attitudes towards family life were developing in late seventeenth- and early eighteenth-century England, although there are disagreements as to when the change developed. The ideal was a family life in which parents created a harmonious atmosphere, and cared for and educated their children in a thoughtful, considerate manner. It has been usually assumed that for such a family life to exist, the marriage must have begun in mutual attraction and romantic love. But the Portlands' marriage, an arranged aristocratic one, nevertheless seems to have been an example of the companionate marriage. Both parties seem to have brought to it affection and the desire to create a pleasant family life.

The changes in attitudes towards family life also involved a change in the attitude towards pregnancy. Although the Duchess of Portland found pregnancy a difficult experience, she tried to take a rational attitude to its problems. She is really an early example of the aristocratic women whom Judith Schneid Lewis discusses in *In the Family Way: Childbearing in the British Aristocracy, 1760–1860*. Lewis shows that these women participated in the production of an heir and other children as part of their loyalty to their class, and that they shifted their attitude towards pregnancy from emphasis on the suffering of childbirth, which earlier had been regarded as a passage to adulthood, to concern with the mothering values involved in raising children (58).

The Duke and Duchess of Portland were attentive parents

who took a continuing interest in their children. The Duchess herself combined her close interest in her children and in family life with her own interests as a collector and student of nature. To Elizabeth Robinson she seemed to have an ideal situation.

As a young woman with a small portion, Elizabeth Robinson was aware of the difficulties of her position, but she was determined to do things her own way. A neighbour, referred to as Mr B in her letters (probably James Brockman), claimed to be in love with her, but she refused to take him seriously. She suspected he was not sincere. In any case, he was provincial, and she did not intend to marry a provincial man. She knew her mind in that respect. As the Duchess of Portland continued to produce so many girls, 'Duchesses' as Elizabeth said, she herself would have to start making Fidgets in a few years. But Elizabeth claimed she did not know where to get a handsome pattern. 'I am sure if they were made Kentish fashion neither you nor I should like them, when I set about fidget-making I intend it should be a la mode de Beau, & was I to begin here, it must be a la mode de clown' (MO 278). To Anne Donnellan she complained that some country squires read nothing but 'parish Law & books of husbandry, or perhaps for their particular entertainment Quarles Emblems, the Pilgrims Progress, Aesops fables & to furnish them with a little ready wit jo Miller's jests' (MO 816, [20 Apr. 1741], Hayton).

In this letter the young woman expressed a social distinction. As friendship was founded on a likeness of dispositions, to love calves one should be a calf, and to love country squires one ought to be a country damsel. Having assumed something of a higher character, she found that she did not enjoy the company of calves and damsels. Furthermore, she suspected that calves and country squires would really prefer the dairy maid.

Aware that 'fortune', the amount of money a young woman could bring to her husband, was very important in determining whom she could marry, Elizabeth looked with a satiric eye on the manners of those who were courting and marrying. As early as 1736, she reported that 'love rages upon Barham Downs in the most cruel manner', but she believed that much of the emotion was directed towards property (MO 261). Her treatment of the courting men she observed inclined to the sardonic. Lord Winchelsea, for instance, she thought too old to court at forty; 'there is a time to Ogle & a time to look thro' spectacles, but to do both together is squinting thro' a glass, a moving not a melting sight' (MO 269). She was also critical of those who married for love without regard to money. She was sceptical of the prospective happiness to be had by Miss Clark and Mr Daeth, who, in return for Miss Clark's fortune of £5,000 and a little estate of the groom, were to live on an allowance from his father of £500. She was sceptical of their prospects for happiness in living in a cottage on love. Further, the eldest Miss Daeth was to marry a younger son of Lord Downs, 'a very wild young Gentleman of small fortune & large expences, if her Brother lives in a Cottage she must be content with a Cave' (MO 270).

She had early asserted that matrimony always involved the woman's 'bargain and sale' (MO 259). To Elizabeth, her friend the Duchess of Portland's marriage was an ideal one, a union of love and friendship, but an exception to the general state of the other married couples whom Elizabeth observed. It seemed to her that the obsequious lover turned after marriage into the imperious husband (MO 275). But spinsterhood and the possibility of a poor old age haunted her. We have seen her awareness that a portion of the large room she was staying in at Bulstrode might make an adequate residence for her and her sister when they were poor old spinsters. She felt that Dame Fortune had left her pocket very empty (MO 5566). She hinted to her father that when she got older it might be helpful for her to possess some land. 'Is it not a Sad thing to be brought up in the Patriot din of Liberty and property and to be allow'd neither?' (MO 312). In London, writing to the Duchess, who was going to a play, Elizabeth compared herself to Cordelia— all she had was a small portion and her fidelity (Univ. of Nottingham Library, MS PC PwE 36).

Elizabeth Robinson's marital prospects were thus hindered by her small dowry and her high standards. She observed of another match that

a Man of Merit & a younger Brother is a purchase only for a great fortune, as for those who have more merit than wealth, they must turn the penny by disposing of their useless virtues for Riches, the exchange may sometimes be difficult, virtues not being Sterling, nor merit the Current coin of the Nation. (MO 290)

Her awareness of her lack of negotiability gave her pain. She felt a strong love for the Duchess and asked herself what would happen to her if she fell in love with a man:

while Hymen holds by Mammons Charter my affections would assuredly be slighted, having nothing but myself i' the Scale & some few vanities that make me light, what is a Woman without gold or fee Simple, a toy while she is young, & a triffle when she is [old]. Jewels of the first water are good for nothing till they are set, but as for us who are no Brilliants we are no bodys money till we have a foil & are encompass'd with the precious metal, as for the intrinsick value of a Woman few know it, & no body cares . . . (MO 291)

Elizabeth's visits to Bulstrode had made her aware of the possibility of a 'great' marriage. William Freind, writing to Sarah, had unfortunately suggested that Elizabeth might be suited for a Duchess and Sarah suited for a parson's wife. This letter had been read by Mr and Mrs Robinson, who got angry. (William Freind thought parents should not read their children's letters, and was surprised that the Robinsons had done so.) But Elizabeth disclaimed any wishes towards a marriage of that sort, declaring she had recently decided she would make a silly wife and an extremely foolish mother (MO 1005). A month later, William had a suitor to propose, whom he thought a good prospect. He was a Captain, not noble, but with good qualities, with three or four thousand a year. His estate was in Ireland, but he planned to live in England. Expressing surprise at her conquest, Elizabeth rejected the offer, and claimed that 'a long and intimate acquaintance is the best presage of future agreement' (MO 1009).

Elizabeth's remarks against marriage had evidently frightened her mother, who was afraid that her daughter's demanding attitudes would make it impossible for her to marry. Elizabeth reassured her with a quotation from the Bible (Prov. 31: 10):

I am not at all of your opinion in two things. The first that I shall never marry, & the Second that the wisest & best Men marry for money, I think Sense & virtue in a Man will induce him to chuse prudence & virtue in a Woman, & surely Sense only teaches a Person the true value of things . . . but till I can meet with a Deserving Man who rightly thinks the price of a Virtuous Woman above Rubbies I shall take no other obligation or name upon me but that of being . . . your most Dutifull Daughter. (MO 4716)

Of course marriage was essential. In spite of sardonic comments on the courting styles and ill-founded marriages of others, Elizabeth knew she must marry. The prospect of a meagre spinsterhood was a threat for the future. While visiting at Bulstrode she had written to her sister about the problems of another woman, and remarked that to marry greatly took time, patience, and opportunity (MO 5559). The possibility of such a marriage must have occurred to her. Later she explained to her sister from Bulstrode that the Duchess wanted her to talk to the Duke, who was lame with gout and confined to his chair. Elizabeth remarked that the experience might be good for her if she were to marry a rich man with gout (MO 5607).

In early 1742, as we have seen in Chapter 1, she was looking forward to spending the spring in London with the Duchess and her family. By August 1742 she was married. We know few details about the match. The letters which have remained are essentially silent on the business of Elizabeth's marriage; some pertinent letters may have been taken out and destroyed. Matthew Montagu printed a letter to the Duchess dated 1741 (MO 312) in which Elizabeth said she was to be in Yorkshire next summer because her father had to go to put his affairs in order (Montagu (1810–13), i. 242). Climenson thought that therefore she must have gone. But I have found no indications that Elizabeth went to Yorkshire until her wedding trip in August 1742. It is more likely that the courtship was carried on in London. In a letter provisionally dated 2 March 1741/2 her brother Thomas was teasing her and her sister about their marital prospects. Mr Brockman's father had died, and he would now be seriously looking for a wife. One sister might go there, and the other be chosen 'to provide for ye other elderly Gentleman now in [?town] of whom you have lately had Advice' (MO 4924). During that spring, when Mr Montagu was presumably courting Elizabeth, he was receiving a series of eight letters dating from March 1742 to June 1742 from Lady Mary Wortley Montagu's scapegrace son, Edward Wortley Montagu, who had applied for financial help to Mr Montagu, his father's cousin, while in difficulties with his parents

(MO 2833–40). The letters were all addressed to Mr Montagu in Dover Street, Piccadilly, London.

Edward Montagu, a grandson of the Earl of Sandwich, Lord High Admiral of the Fleet to Charles II, was a bachelor at fifty-one. We do not know whether he met and admired the bright, witty young woman of twenty-two, or whether he had heard of her through friends or relatives. At any rate, he was the good man for whom Elizabeth was waiting—well off, prudent, and willing to accept her with a small dowry.

Something of the financial arrangements seem to be indicated in a letter Elizabeth wrote to her sister years later, just after her father's death, when she was already a widow. She owed her father's estate £4,000, which had been borrowed to purchase lands adjoining their own. But 'Mr Montagu never had any mortgage for ye 1500 that was to come at my Fathers decease'; she went on to refer to these £1,500 as having been stipulated in her marriage. These comments suggest that Elizabeth Robinson's dowry was £1,500 (MO 6043, 8 Oct. [1778]). Sarah's dowry seems to have been the same (MO 5728).

In the summer of 1742, as Elizabeth was preparing for her marriage, the prospective bride's feelings were not joyful. Writing to the Duchess (Univ. of Nottingham Library, MS PC PwE 52) she spoke of the unequal way the matches of this world are made, unlike the matching of shells with their proper kind. She felt melancholy. Then she was preparing her clothes for the marriage, and changing from old maid's pink to bridal pink and silver (MS PC PwE 54). She expressed fears at the coming catastrophe. In another letter she spoke of her 'timorous heart' and the fears that attend 'this alteration' (MS PC PwE 55). She hoped her friendship with the Duchess would go on with better opportunities after her marriage. In her letter of congratulation, the Duchess assured her that her apprehensions were understandable before an event that was to be so decisive for one's life, and that she herself had been frightened before her wedding (MO 192).

Elizabeth Robinson married Edward Montagu on 5 August 1742. Years later she evidently thought she had been too hasty, for she told Lord Lyttelton that she thought *his* daughter should wait until she was twenty-eight; by then she would have seen more of the world and would be ready to settle down (MO 1428,

22 Nov. 1763). But her wish to marry a well-off, disinterested man, and her parents' concern that she marry seem to have coalesced, and in spite of her anxieties Elizabeth became Mrs Montagu.

As a bride Elizabeth Montagu spoke of her husband as 'my friend', a man whose good temper and easiness as a travelling companion contrasted with the unpleasant manners of her father. As it turned out, her early married life was to be a test of her stability and capacity for independent action. Edward Montagu was a Member of Parliament and a man of business with extensive properties in Yorkshire. After the wedding the pair travelled to his house in Allerthorpe, Yorkshire. They were accompanied by Elizabeth's sister Sarah as the bride's companion—it was common practice to take a woman friend for female companionship on a wedding trip. Mr Montagu's Yorkshire house was convenient but old and not handsome. Its owner was often from home, for he had to make frequent business trips in the neighbourhood. There were few people Elizabeth cared to visit. So the bride was much alone with her sister. But she had a keen sense of her own position. Very early in her stay, she had a significant quarrel with one of the servants in the house. Harry had questioned the authority of his new young mistress, and refused to stay after bringing in the tea-table. 'I sent him word that those who would do any thing for me must do every thing, & as he wd not obey all my orders he should have none, & that he must keep intirely out of my sight till your Return' (MO 2139). Her husband backed his wife's authority (MO 1708), and, as Mrs Montagu wrote to her husband, in the sententious but often rather incisive way in which she entertained him in their correspondence:

[Harry has returned to his duties] and he seems desirous to oblige now he finds the other way does not succeed, he design'd the strongest Will should rule, & mine being back'd with the mighty circumstance of power came off Conqueror, & I believe may govern for the future without mutiny or Rebellion . . . (MO 2142)

By October she was pregnant; it was not considered safe for her to travel in the early stages of her pregnancy, but Mr Montagu had to be in London for the opening of Parliament. He went to London alone, and she was left with Sarah as her sole companion, to wait until it was considered safe for her to travel. Then, of course, she and her sister were to make the long journey by coach.

The friendship of the Duchess of Portland and young Mrs Montagu continued, even intensified, in an epistolary way, during the months Elizabeth was isolated in Yorkshire. Mrs Montagu confided to her friend her puzzling anxieties about her condition, and the physical discomfort she was experiencing. At first there was some question whether Elizabeth was actually pregnant, and the Duchess asked several times, 'How often has the Cardinal miss'd paying you a Visit' (MO 198). (Mrs Montagu avoided telling her.) The Duchess wrote a long letter to Sandys about her friend's condition. He was to write to Mrs Montagu. In fact the pregnancy was managed by the post:

I fancy he will not allow you to move till You are Quick which Certainly will be safer as for your Reachings & sickness I Believe they never make any Body miscarry & I Believe you may remember my Complaining of a Violent Pain in my Back which I always have when I am with Child so Don't Allarm your self for I Dare say there is no Danger. (MO 199)

While the Duchess was consoling her friend isolated in Yorkshire, she was also sharing with her the discomfort she herself felt at the prospect of making a family visit to her formidable mother at Welbeck Abbey. As we have seen, Lady Oxford was not a sacred personage in the correspondence of the two women. In her mother's house, as in much of her own life, the Duchess felt that inclination must bow to ceremony (MO 194). Elizabeth was instructed to write a letter 'in form' to her which she could show to Lady Oxford, and to address her more intimate correspondence to Mrs Elstob and Mrs Hog. (Ironically enough, Elizabeth Elstob was the Anglo-Saxon scholar whom the Duchess had rescued from the hard work and penurious existence of running a small school by taking her into her family as governess for the children in 1739: see Chapter 5.) At Welbeck the Duchess was ground down by her mother's insistence on punctuality at meals, by her protectiveness, and by the presence of dull company:

My Understanding was never good but it is now Hammerd Down to the Comprehension of Cocks & Bulls & Idle Riddles & The Sum Total of Wit is a Horse Laugh a Jog of the Elbow & Hah,—are not some peoples Company Delightfull? (MO 200)

Mrs Montagu, isolated in a dreary house, unable to make visits of any distance, dreamed of her days at Bulstrode: 'Oh Bullstrode Bullstrode when I forget thee, may my head & hand forget their cunning . . .' (MO 330). But she settled down to her country exile, wrote letters, and read sermons. She wrote to her husband, to the Duchess, to Anne Donnellan, to her mother. She was trying to keep up with news of politics and the theatre, and asked her husband if he had seen the 'famous actor' Garrick (MO 2152, 10 Dec. [1742]). She asked for books: Shaftesbury's *Characteristics* and Young's *Night Thoughts* (MO 2155). She also was interested in helping her younger brothers, William, John, and Charles, whom her parents had placed in a boarding-school in Yorkshire. She had convinced her parents the boys should be allowed to be at school closer to home, and reported to her husband on her arrangements for their return (MO 2155, 17 Dec. [1742]). By early January 1743, she was packing up. She had worked out a careful plan for her journey, and expected to be in London on the 17th. She had a dilemma to deal with. If travelling disagreed with her she would return to Yorkshire, even though she was afraid of the prospect of being there so far from help in a few months. But she had planned very well. She had courage; her first problem when she began her journey was to cross a flooded road in a boat. After travelling seven days, she and her sister arrived safely in London.

In March Mrs Montagu, in the later stages of pregnancy, experienced the stress of sharing with the Duchess of Portland her grief at the death of one of her children—two-year-old Lady Frances (MO 5632, to Sarah Robinson). During this time Mrs Montagu's parents and sister came to London to visit; the prospective father seems to have returned to his northern properties, although he expected to return to London in time for the birth. Mr Montagu returned to London in May. The baby, a son named John but called Punch, was born 11 May 1743. The mother did not plan to breast-feed her baby, but followed the still prevalent custom of engaging a wet-nurse—a woman from Kent. After the child's baptism the parents left him in London with his nurse and Sarah, and went themselves to Mr Montagu's Berkshire property, Sandleford.

The evolving life-style of the young mother was rather in the pattern of the Duchess. For some part of the year she retired to her husband's country property, Sandleford. She used her country time to read. In one letter to the Duchess Mrs Montagu explained that she had been reading Locke's *Two Treatises of Government* and believed Locke to be a religious, moral, and open-minded man. She recommended the work to the Duchess (MO 357).

Mrs Montagu had also begun to embellish her estate. The Duchess had offered orange trees, which 'will give me great pleasure as they will resemble a little what I have seen at Bullstrode.' Mrs Montagu had turned gardener, but, contrary to current taste, she wished for flowers, and also ordered shrubs to be planted in the wood. She asked about her 'Graces Dairy, etc. have you got your Bees, I design to have some of these Musical Chymists, I think their hum very agreable' (MO 359).

Childbirth had evidently left an aftermath of illness and physical weakness. Mrs Montagu described her complaint to her mother as 'histerick shaking' and explained also that since she had lain in she had had a weakness in her knees. But Mrs Montagu felt that her lovely child compensated for her suffering. 'If you was to see my Young Hercules you would not wonder I should be exhausted with bearing him, he laughs as loud as Dr Shaw already, & is indeed more stout than most Children at a year old' (MO 4727, [*c*.Sept. 1743]).

In those early days Mrs Montagu found her husband a pleasing companion. Alone in the country with her child for periods of time while her husband was in London or in the North, she looked forward to a variety of activities on his return:

we walk, ride, chatt, & read together, & are as suitable in temper & opinions as you will often see two people, we both agree in loving Retirement in the Country, however we are glad to have any friends in the house with us . . . (MO 360, 1 Dec. [1743], to Duchess of Portland)

She appreciated the contrast between her husband, a sober, studious, courteous person, and her father, a rather testy, light-minded, pleasure-loving gentleman. A few years later, when both men were in London, she worried that her father would lead her husband astray into a coffee-house existence.

Enjoying her child and the companionship of her husband, Mrs Montagu, after the child had been successfully weaned (MO 5678), determined to accompany her husband with the child on his next trip to Yorkshire. *Her* mother did not think she should do it. Mrs Montagu wrote to the Duchess that her parents refused to believe she was going to Yorkshire (MO 374).

In August the Montagus were again at Allerthorpe. They had seen Oxford, Stowe, Thoresby, and York. In a week they were to go to Newcastle but would leave their child with the Steward's wife, 'who is very prudent and carefull & will take care no accident shall happen to him' (MO 376, 14 Aug. [1744], to Duchess of Portland). But evidently while Mrs Montagu was still with her child he died of 'convulsion fits, occasioned by teething' (Montagu (1906), i. 191, from ead. (1810–13), ii. 310). Punch had had trouble with teething earlier, and it is possible that he was given medications to alleviate pain which harmed him.

His death was a devastating experience. The letter of condolence written by the Duchess reminded Mrs Montagu of her 'good understanding and submission to the Divine Will': 'What wou'd I give to be with you, my Dear Friend, that you might pour out your whole heart, and utter all your Grief, but it is never in my power to be of any Service to those I love' (MO 216). Then, after the death of her child, as in the days of her pregnancy, Mrs Montagu was left in Yorkshire while her husband returned to London. She returned later, and wrote to the Duchess that she felt desolate and melancholy. Her depression was renewed by the news that her mother had cancer of the breast. Mrs Robinson was operated on in December 1744; at first she thought that surgery had cured her, but it was not to be.

Before her grandchild was born, Elizabeth Drake Robinson had expressed anxiety over Mrs Montagu's health and warned her daughter of the fragility of children:

for my part I love you too tenderly to rejoice abundantly at your being with child you had very ill health all ye time & there must be some hazzard at last, but that is not ye worst children are very precarious Blessings & both Mr Montagu & you are both so passionately fond yt any accident that may happen to it peirces very deep, & at ye best gives you great anxiety in fears . . . (MO 4670, 19 Jan. [1742/3])

Her mother's prediction was correct, and Mrs Montagu mourned a long time for her child. She tried to reason with her daughter. Mrs Robinson said of another woman's grief, 'I am surprized when there is so many & various accidents that must make a fond parent miserable people shou'd make themselves unhappy for want of Children but it is a weakness in human nature always to want Some Thing' (MO 4699, 17 May [c.1745]). (This renunciation was written by a woman who had nine surviving children, but was now suffering from a terminal illness.) A few weeks later, in her letter of 9 June, Mrs Robinson indicated that she had given up reasoning with Mrs Montagu, because her daughter, although a person with more reason than herself, 'will not make use of it on this occasion' (MO 4702).

It was in later years that Mrs Montagu confided the extremity of her grief to Frances Boscawen, the wife of Admiral Edward Boscawen. Mrs Montagu wrote that she had trusted to continual watching of her son but forgotten God's power, and the consequence of her confidence in her own care was that she lost her 'beloved object, & with him my hopes, my joys & my health' (MO 575, 25 Oct. 1757, Sandleford). She seems to have blamed herself for over-confidence.

The summer of 1745 the Montagus were at Sandleford, and Mrs Montagu was spending a great deal of time on horseback. In August 1745 she wrote to the Duchess that she was going to Tunbridge for her health, as Mr Montagu had a lot of business in Yorkshire. 'I hope you don't think there is any imprudence in a Young Woman going without her Husband to such a place' (MO 392). This first venture was to lead to the eventual creation of the bluestocking circle.

In the late 1740s there developed an estrangement between the Duchess and Mrs Montagu which gradually deepened into silence. They stopped seeing each other and stopped writing; there are no letters in the Huntingdon Collection between the friends from 14 September 1753 (MO 432) to 1760 (MO 433). Years later, Mrs Montagu indicated that she thought the Duchess had been tactless in displaying her youngest child, Lord Edward, while Mrs Montagu was mourning the loss of her son. The bitterness was life long. On 11 December [1782] she wrote to Elizabeth Carter about Lord Edward's marriage to an actress,

I used to think her Grace wanted compassion when, just after ye death of my Son, she always set Lord [Edward] before me when I visited her, but my tears are d[ry] & for ye dead one has not to blush. I am sure I wd not have changed Sons with her for many years past. (MO 3542, to Elizabeth Carter)

But the lapse in friendship may also have had something to do with disagreements over Sarah Robinson's choice of a husband. Sarah had fallen in love with George Lewis Scott (1708–80), a mathematician, and the son of an associate of George I. King George I's daughter Princess Sophia was his godmother. In November 1750 Scott was made sub-preceptor to Prince George (afterwards George III) and his younger brothers, perhaps through the recommendation of the Duchess of Portland along with other prominent people (MO 5216; Montagu (1906), i. 280). Scott has been described as a large man, a very hearty eater, and a very sociable and amusing person. But, for some reason, Mrs Montagu distrusted him; Sarah thought she was trying to interfere in the affair by keeping back letters, presumably from Scott (MO 5207). In the summer of 1748 the schedules of Mrs Montagu and the Duchess prevented visiting. The Duchess wrote,

I met Mr. Montagu in the street who was so obliging to come & breakfast with us the next day which I took very kindly of him. He gave me an account of your Health which I shou'd be Happy to hear was better & that You have received great benefit from your new Doctor & Regimen.

The Duchess added:

I am sincerely sorry that any thing shou'd hurt your Health which I think this affair does & therefore since it is to be I wish there was a Conclusion of it & that you wou'd make your self easy about it I heartily pity you both as I dare say it is a great affliction to her to be the cause of any to you & what she can no ways help as people cannot alter their affections as others wou'd have em I don't doubt whatever was in her power she wou'd but this indeed is not. (MO 229, 21 July 1748, Bulstrode)

Resentment'at her friend's advice may have contributed to Mrs Montagu's distancing herself from the Duchess. And the fact that Sarah's marriage broke up after a year probably added to her chagrin. But the Duchess was also clearly angry with Mrs Montagu. When Gilbert West visited Bulstrode in 1753, he reported that the Duchess had not even asked about Mrs Montagu until he mentioned her, and then her inquiries were very cool (MO 6657, 27 Oct. 1753).

About the time the rupture in the friendship with the Duchess was beginning, Mrs Montagu was giving away her child's clothing. In the summer of 1748 Lydia Botham, a cousin who was the wife of an impecunious clergyman, wrote to Mrs Montagu asking her for help on the occasion of the expected birth of her fifth child, a child she said she could have done without. Mrs Montagu evidently sent her an old shirt and shift and some children's things. Lydia was happy to use the old garments to make clothes for the infant, but she did not wish to use the good children's shirts, caps, and 'clouts', because they would be dirtied, and she thought they should be saved by their owner for some future cousins which she hoped would arrive in 'due time'. She spoke of putting the children's clothing aside until she could return it (MO 602). But sending these garments may have been a sign that Mrs Montagu was beginning to accept her childless situation. She and her husband had been doting parents. The death of their child was a loss they absorbed. But Mrs Montagu also felt that child-bearing meant a great deal of pain and suffering. And in fact she had not been well since the death of her son.

The state of her health, the state of the marriage, may have resulted in an explicit agreement or an unspoken arrangement to continue childless. In 1758 Frances Boscawen, whose first child was born in 1744, and who had carried on a committed, but often solitary, life as the wife of an active naval officer, was expecting her fifth and last child (Aspinall-Oglander (1940)). By then Mrs Montagu seems to have placed sexuality and pregnancy at a distance. The birth was evidently delayed, and Mrs Montagu wrote to her sister with irritation, 'I wish it was well over, for my part I look upon it as a strong indecorum for a

Woman of my age to be lying in, surely we should be too wise for such girlish tricks' (MO 5768, 3 May 1758). The wisdom may have consisted in what Jane Austen later called 'the simple regimen of separate rooms' (*Letters*, 480).

Most eighteenth-century gentlemen seemed to believe that every young woman was in want of a husband. Elizabeth Carter was not overlooked as a matrimonial prospect. As early as 27 March 1738, while Elizabeth was working for the *Gentleman's Magazine* in St John's Gate, her father wrote her that the Dean of Canterbury had heard a rumour that she was going to marry a Mr Oliver, which the Dean regretted. But her father was happy to have been able to give the Dean a denial (Stebbing/ Rutherford). By 21 September 1738, however, Elizabeth had evidently had some sort of offer in a letter from a suitor identified only as 'Mr. G.' Her father thought the man was not respectful enough, and that if she entered into a correspondence with him, that might keep off other suitors. Her father wrote, 'It would be one of the greatest Pleasures of my Life to see you married to a Virtuous Man, able to keep you in a decent manner, & of a Temper suitable to your own . . .'. Dr Carter advised his daughter to be

civil to All, but not too Intimate with any; And very reserved with some. Preserve the Character of an Inoffensive, & prudent Woman, & your other very extraordinary qualifications will in Time, I doubt not, produce something desireable. (Hampshire collection)

It was about this time that Elizabeth Carter encountered Thomas Birch; Elizabeth's account of his conduct and letters became a puzzle which her father tried to solve. Birch's goal was probably marriage (he had been a widower for almost ten years), but at that time he had no settled prospects. Was he trying to develop a close friendship with his colleague without committing himself to courtship, or did he really mean to propose in the end? Her father felt that the way he behaved to her might affect Elizabeth's reputation. In a letter of 29 September 1738, Dr Carter advised Elizabeth that there were very few women who had prudence enough to manage the sort of conversation Birch was asking for without prejudice to themselves. Her father said that he had confidence in her judgement and felt she would behave discreetly and not permit any freedoms from 'Mr. B.' of any sort that might expose her to the least censure. But he warned her to avoid too frequent conversation (Hampshire collection).

In a letter of 16 October Dr Carter tried to figure out whether Birch's letters to Elizabeth were in fact courtship. He thought it would be impossible for her to converse with Birch in the manner Birch wished her to without hurting her character, unless she intended to marry him in the end. But he thought that Birch would behave differently if marriage were not his aim (Hampshire collection). At one time Birch had been intending to go to Ireland to live, but gave that up. On 16 April 1739, her father responded to news that Elizabeth was ill with concern and hoped that she would leave London as soon as possible.

If any Thing concerning ye Gentleman with whom we dined at Mr Caves, makes a Part of your Uneasiness, you have my entire Consent to act as you yourself choose. I could not bare the Tho'ts of parting with you into Ireland: But as that Scheme is laid aside by him, I have no further Objection, If he be your Choice.

He suggested that she could invite Birch to Deal if she wished. On 3 May 1739 he wrote that she could go to Oxford if she wanted to; she might also stay in London after Algarotti was finished, but he didn't think it would be useful (Hampshire collection).

Birch not only pursued Elizabeth assiduously, if ambiguously; he publicized his friendship with this unusual learned young lady in his own circle. William Warburton responded that Birch had forgotten to mention a particular that was 'of more importance to her than all her Greek & Latin That is whether she is handsome' (BL Add. 4320, fo. 131, 27 Aug. 1738). Birch sent a copy of Elizabeth Carter's *Poems* to another friend, Joseph Welby, who responded that

I could, methinks be not a little pleas'd to find a nearer relation between two persons of such similar tastes & inclinations as She & You seem to have. Besides I have my own private views; for as you do not intend to change yr condition but with yr circumstances, soon may you be provided for. (BL Add. 4321, fo. 119, 9 July 1739)

That was the rub. Birch had been paying assiduous attention to the young scholar, but his situation had not changed. For that reason he had probably not made any decisive overtures by the time Elizabeth returned to Deal in the summer of 1739. Her references to Birch in her letters to Cave are all friendly and non-committal. But she did not return to London until the winter of 1741, and never went back to working at St John's Gate.

Thomas Birch was a friend of Philip Yorke, who was the eldest son of Lord Chancellor Hardwicke, and the husband of Jemima, Marchioness Grey. Birch had collaborated in the writing of *The Athenian Letters*, to which Catherine Talbot had also contributed. He was an occasional visitor to Wrest, and Jemima had once noted in a letter to Catherine that 'Nothing but [Birch's] spirits could hinder one from hanging oneself at the thoughts of November being return'd in May' (22 May 1744, Bedfordshire County Record Office, Lucas Papers L 30/9a/3, p. 107). After Elizabeth Carter had become a close friend of Catherine Talbot, Thomas Birch became a subject of discussion and some teasing in their letters. In the autumn of 1751 Catherine went to Wrest in the company of Birch, 'almost tête-à-tête, only Jane [her maid] for a Chaperon; and really for people who do not feel the danger of being talked into a consumption, he is an entertaining and instructive companion, as well as a good sort of man' (Carter, *Letters* (1808), i. 286). In her journal for that visit, Catherine noted that

Mr 2.8. [i.e. Birch] is a Man of Universal Learning & very Communicative, Knows too every body in the living World, & is full of Anecdotes. Too Vehement for Me & too perpetual & loud a Talker, but one may learn much from him & he is very good humor'd. Among these the Conversation turned generally on Matters of History & was to me very instructive & entertaining. (BL Add. 46690, fo. 29)

Elizabeth Carter was usually forgiving of human shortcomings. Therefore, her response to Catherine Talbot's account of travelling down to Wrest with Birch was surprisingly harsh; she supposed that they must have been harassed

for forty miles by a 'throat of brass and admantine lungs.' You had no other chance to escape this persecution but a danger of the coach being overturned, the only situation in which I ever remember the hero in question to have been silent, and then for four hours he never spoke a word, and he quietly composed himself to sleep. Seriously however I agree with you in all you say to his advantage, and wish him well settled in the world, if he chuses it, with some good kind of deaf and dumb gentlewoman. (Carter, *Letters* (1808), i. 287–8)

There are both bitterness and humour here on the subject of Birch and marriage. It sounds as if twelve years after her encounter with Birch she was detached enough to joke about it, but was also expressing a lingering anger at his self-centred behaviour.

There were other more definite proposals. On 24 April 1740 her father in Deal wrote to Elizabeth in Canterbury about a possible marriage. About this proposal, Dr Carter seems to have been ambivalent. He did not want 'to part nor yet to keep her' (Stebbing/Rutherford). Elizabeth declined.

In the spring of 1747 Elizabeth in Canterbury had another proposal about which she jokingly told Catherine. This suitor was a gentleman 'whose wig is always in an uproar, his cloaths hung upon every lock and bolt by the extreme trepidation of his pace, and who runs over every body he meets in his way.' He had sent a servant with a written proposal late at night, much to Elizabeth's surprise, who had never had any notice previous to this of his intentions:

however, I had a *no* extremely at his service, but would not detain his emissary, who, I concluded, was to gallop on without loss of time to Deal, to ask my father's consent, and from thence to London for the approbation of my uncle. The next morning, before any soul was up, he returned with the same violence of ringing, and carried back my answer to his master, whom I expect every day to come and fly away with me in a chaise and one, unless he should meet with somebody in his way, and be married upon the road. (Carter, *Letters* (1808), i. 132)

Although this proposal evoked Elizabeth's comic spirit, there eventually came one about which she was undecided. In the spring of 1748, acceding to the urgent wishes of Catherine, Elizabeth came to London and spent the next five months there. During this period Mrs Secker died. Elizabeth remained in London that summer, staying at her uncle's either in London or at his country property at Enfield. Catherine was at Cuddesden with her mother and the widower, Bishop Secker.

Then from November 1748 to April 1749 the friends were both in London, and Elizabeth had her most interesting offer of marriage.

The gentleman is referred to as Mr Dalton or Dr Dalton, and it seems probable that her suitor was John Dalton, who had been tutor to Lord Beauchamp, the Duchess of Somerset's son, who had died of smallpox while on the Grand Tour. During the late 1740s Dalton was an assistant preacher for Bishop Secker, who continued to hold the Rectorship at St James's. Dalton was evidently a pleasant, agreeable man. He had an interest in the theatre and had produced a version of Milton's *Comus* for the stage. Pennington claimed that Elizabeth rejected this suitor's proposal because she had heard that he had been involved in a questionable episode involving the writing of some light verses (Carter, *Memoirs*, i. 29–30). The verses exist—they were an exchange between Dalton and Mrs Henrietta Knight, later Lady Luxborough. Although rather tender, they do not seem to have upset Lady Hertford, later the Duchess of Somerset, who copied them into her commonplace book (Helen Sard Hughes, 169–81). But the reason given by Pennington may be a subterfuge for a much more serious scandal, which Horace Walpole was convinced was fact. Walpole believed that Dalton had had a love affair with Lady Luxborough, and that it was this affair that occasioned Lady Luxborough's separation from her husband, which continued for her lifetime (xi. 65; xxxii. 243–4). In his copy of Lady Luxborough's *Letters to Shenstone* (1775) Walpole repeated this story, and stated that an illegitimate daughter had been born to Mrs Knight in 1736 (*Rothschild Library*, i. 342). Elizabeth must have heard rumours of this scandal; in a letter to his daughter the Revd Carter wrote that he had heard about a certain gentleman's reputation in France in regard to a matter of gallantry. The reference was probably to Dalton, for her father adds that if he is innocent he has been subject to much injury as the topic of scandal (3 Jan. 1748/9, Hampshire collection).

The Revd Carter's further letters in the Hampshire collection chart the progress of the courtship:

This is an Affair in wch you ought to be left to your own Determination. The character you give is agreable. The Prospects seem advantageous. The Judgment of ye World, of wch you do not express any favourable Opinion, is not to be slighted, when there appears no wrong Biass to warp it. (5 Feb. 1748/9)

Her father went on to point out that a settlement arranged with prudence is better than a single life, 'which is errant, & Seldom meets with much Esteem'.

On 6 February he wrote that he had heard that Mr Dalton wanted to see him, and he thought he should go to London. He had heard an advantageous account of the suitor, as far as circumstances, person, character went. But the Revd Carter continued to give his daughter the freedom to make up her own mind. He thought she should consider the matter carefully, but he advised her not to put herself into a great deal of perplexity and distress. He would not condemn her if she could not bring herself to like her suitor (9 Feb. 1749). By 6 March he was writing, 'You say Mr D. is now gone, & yt there is an End of ye Affair.' But this time when she declined 'such an advantageous offer' he could not help venting his disappointment. He felt that he was getting older, was having trouble getting his children established, and that Elizabeth's marriage would have helped the family. It was then that he expressed the view that if she did not intend to marry, as she seemed to intimate in one of her letters, she should live 'retired, and not appear in ye World with an Expence, which is reasonable, upon ye Expectation of getting an Husband; But not otherwise.'

Thirteen years later Catherine reported to Elizabeth (9 Oct. 1762) that she had seen 'poor Dr. Dalton'. He had become very thin, could not walk, but was well and talked 'as cheerfully and as much as ever'. He had found a wife. Catherine described her as an ebullient and joyful person who worked very hard, without complaint, at caring for her husband. It sounds as if by then Catherine felt Elizabeth was right to have refused Mr Dalton; as it turned out, caring for him would have taken up her time.

During most of her life, Elizabeth Carter strove to preserve her independence in her dealings with both men and women. The intervals when she gave her time to other people were always compensated for by periods of time when she could live her life alone as she wished. During the early years of their friendship, Catherine Talbot had been encouraging her friend to marry. She wanted to feel that Elizabeth had an establishment of her own. To this urging Elizabeth replied that she already had a family (her younger brothers and sister) of whom she was taking care and whom she was instructing. But at one time she did remark jokingly that she was wearing her eyes out making shirts for her brother, and when she had been blessed with the family of boys Catherine was hoping for, she hoped they would all learn to make their own shirts (Carter, *Letters* (1808), 25 Jan. 1747).

During the 1750s Elizabeth had begun to insist on the value to her of remaining unmarried. In 1751 her father had a serious quarrel with his congregation over the use of the Athanasian Creed in the services he gave. He objected to this creed, while his congregation upheld it. Elizabeth became involved in the controversy, but she felt disappointed in her father's quarrelling. Elizabeth pointed out to Catherine that her situation might have been much worse, if she had been married to a man of whose actions she did not approve (Carter, *Letters* (1808), 21 May 1751). But Catherine replied that a good man would never require his wife to do unreasonable things (8 June 1751).

Elizabeth Carter's refusal to marry and her reliance on the friendship of women seem to have arisen out of her perception that marriage involved a power relationship in which men dominated women, whereas the friendships with women involved a more trustworthy relationship between equals. Certainly, her experiences with Birch and Dalton were not reassuring. She began to see liberty as her most important value. Very early in their friendship she had told Catherine she was so much against imprisonment of any kind that she could hardly keep a bird in a cage (20 July 1744). She dared not risk the loss of independence, so she settled on the idea that marriage was not suitable for her, although she thought that any of her friends who sought happiness that way were welcome to try the married state. She seems in some ways to have been what Janice Raymond has called in her recent book, *A Passion for Friends*, a 'marriage resister'—a person who consciously chooses not to marry (117), although Elizabeth Carter did not advocate her position as one to be generally followed by others.[1] She chose to be single to maintain her life as a scholar and to preserve her independence. She accepted the consequences, and she was content with the personal and familial friendships which added interest to her life.

*Talbot*

During the crisis of Dalton's proposal, Elizabeth Carter had certainly confided in Catherine Talbot, but it is not clear to what extent Catherine confided in Elizabeth her own emotional attachments to the men in her life. In the early 1740s Catherine had suffered from a romantic infatuation for a man whom she called, in a French journal she kept, the 'Comte de S.' (or it may be the 'Comte de L.'). This gentleman was evidently an Oxford neighbour who had been the focus of her interest for some time, and who she felt had paid some special attention to her in earlier days. In 1743 she felt that her maid even started to 'make Castles in Spain' for her about the relationship. But by 1745 he was married and she had to meet him and his wife socially in the neighbourhood of Oxford. Her infatuation and his marriage gave her intense feelings of anxiety and rejection (BL Add. 46688, fos. 8–9; 10–13).

Aside from this painful infatuation, Catherine does not seem to have taken much practical interest in her own marital prospects. In 1752 Catherine had a proposal which she reviewed in her journal on 31 December 1752. She and the man had never met, but she heard that his character was excellent and his age and rank were suitable. Her friends, Lady Grey, Lady Anson, and Lady Hardwicke, were consulted. They convinced her that the proposal was promising; if she and her suitor liked each other after they met, the marriage would be an appropriate one. But it turned out that the father refused to settle on his son the amount of money her friends thought appropriate. So the scheme fell through. Catherine had heard that he tried to find her in town, but did not succeed, which she was sorry for. But summing it all up, Catherine thought she did not regret the failure of the proposal. She felt happier in having found that Providence did not wish her to make the change; she felt Providence would guide her through life as it best saw fit. 'In that I Cheerfully trust Enjoy my present Freedom & Prosperity, & look forward to the Melancholy & Solitary Scenes of Life without fear or dejection.' She added that 'E:C: that Amiable Friend whose Heart is all Candour & Integrity was our near Neighbour for Four Months & we saw her daily' (BL Add.

46690, fo. 77). She thought she preferred to depend on the close relationships she already had.

However, that year also marked the beginning of a friendship which developed into an emotional attachment that created a conflict in her mind between her feelings for parental authority and her friend. The young man was George Berkeley, son of George Berkeley, Bishop of Cloyne, the philosopher, who was an old friend of Thomas Secker.

In 1752 Bishop Berkeley brought his wife Anne, son George, and daughter Julia to England from Ireland and established a residence at Oxford. His son was just entering the University, and the Bishop wished to supervise his studies. Cuddesden, the Bishop of Oxford's residence, which he usually occupied in summer and autumn, was close to Oxford, and it was inevitable that a family friendship would develop between the Berkeleys and Catherine and her mother. In January 1753 Bishop Berkeley died very suddenly, while having tea with his family, and Secker was much concerned to help the bereaved. That summer the Berkeleys spent much of their time at Cuddesden; Catherine became attached to both brother and sister. She spoke of George as her beloved brother (BL Add. 46690, fo. 93ᵛ); she also confided in her journal the times when George read to her while she painted, or when they went for walks. Julia seems, however, to have been considered more a daughter than a sister, and, in another journal addressed to Julia, Catherine gave her serious advice about using her time in a constructive way (BL Add. 46688, fos. 15–37ᵛ).

George's journal of 1754, which he kept while he was at Oxford, shows his reliance on and affection for the family at Cuddesden. He often joined them for church services, meals, and walks. Years later Catherine reminded him of the pretty rural churchyard at Cuddesden, where they used to meditate on the tombstones (BL Add. 39311, fo. 171ᵛ). In the autumn of 1754 George noted in his journal that Julia's reason was disturbed. She seems to have had a nervous breakdown. Secker helped to make arrangements to get the best medical care for her in London, but Mrs Berkeley eventually decided to take Julia back to Ireland with her (BL Add. 46689, fos. 1–9). George Berkeley must have turned to Secker and the Talbots as family friends, and the friendship between George and Catherine became close. As we shall see in Chapter 8, she discussed her writing with him.

In 1758 there was a significant change in the lives of Thomas Secker and his family. He became Archbishop of Canterbury. Although he was confirmed on 21 April 1758, Secker and the Talbots did not move into Lambeth Palace until the autumn of that year. (Catherine's first letter to Elizabeth from Lambeth is dated 22 October 1758.) Catherine felt some anxiety about moving. The change meant the loss of long stays in summer and autumn at Cuddesden; Lambeth, across the Thames from Westminster, was rather inaccessible to the friends and activities of the city. Eventually Catherine became fond of the old building, with its state rooms, galleries, and old portraits, and of the gardens, which they found could be enriched with flowers. Mrs Talbot seems to have had a portion of the palace as her own house, which her daughter called the Brick House, or Jessamin Hall, where Mrs Talbot gave small musical parties.

At the end of 1758 came the crisis of Catherine Talbot's life: George Berkeley proposed marriage. He had been ordained deacon in 1756; he would take his MA on 26 January 1759 and also be presented to the vicarage of Bray in that year. We know from a letter in French in Catherine's handwriting that is among the Berkeley papers in the British Library that Catherine was deeply affected. She knew she loved him very much and that his friendship was very important to her. But she knew there would be objections on both sides. Addressing him as 'mon Frère,' she claimed that he was far above her in worth:

Pauvre Coer trop aimable et trop aimé, le mien va te répondre. Que parles tu de *Presomption*? Tu me fais trop d'honneur. Selon le Monde il y auroit assez d'Objections des deux Cotés,—Suffit hélas! qu'ils sont insupèrables—Mais dans mon petit moi même Je juge tout autrement que le Monde; Je te vois bien loin au dessus de tout ce que Je puis valois, & Je te remercie bien sincerement *d'un* procédé qui te convenoit bien—Cest tout dire. [Poor Heart so lovable and so beloved, mine is going to reply to you. What do you speak of *Presumption*? You do me too much honour. According to the world there will be enough Objections on two sides. Alas, it is enough that they are insurmountable—But in my small self I judge entirely differently from the World: I see you far above all which I can value, & I thank you sincerely for an action which becomes you well—That is all that needs to be said.] (BL. Add. 39312, fo. 333)

Catherine added that she had perceived what he felt for her, and had tried to open his eyes about it, and about the impossibility which she also saw. She explained that she would have acted if she had not hoped that their friendship would do him more good than harm. She told herself that he was getting older and a little time would bring healing. In the mean time she felt they could take advantage of the influence which he was giving her to offer him consolation, joy, faithful advice.

But her conscience warned her they were on dangerous ground. She was afraid of spoiling better prospects for him. She asked him whether she could atone for having done wrong by depriving herself of his dear friendship, but she asked him to allow her to contribute to his happiness by conversations and advice. She asked him to allow her to be his affectionate sister; if he found that impossible, she was willing to have him keep away, thereby sacrificing what was most agreeable in her life. His happiness came first.

Catherine concluded by assuring George that she was willing to bear loneliness—the loss of his company—if necessary. If she were certain that in that estrangement he would be happier than in her company, as a Christian she would be tranquil. Her last words are an apology:

Ainsi ne songes Cher Ami qu'a ton propre repos, & pardonner lui seulement ce quil y a en dans sa Conduite de blamable, & tout ce qu'elle t'a causé d'inquietûde! S'il se peut. [Thus, Dear Friend, think only that you have your proper repose, and pardon her only for that in her Conduct which has been blamable, and all the uneasiness She has caused you! If it is possible.] (BL Add. 39312, fos. 333–334)

Although Montagu Pennington claimed, in his 'Account of the Life of Catherine Talbot' which he added to the seventh edition of her *Works* in 1809, that Catherine had never had a proposal in mature life, whatever might have been the case when she was younger (pp. xxiii–xxiv; as we shall see, he may have been reacting to publicity about the relationship with George Berkeley), she did have this strong attachment to George, which might have ended in matrimony, if . . . But too much was against it. There was Catherine's lack of money; although she had cousins in the aristocracy, and she had grown up as a member of the Bishop of Oxford's family, she seems essentially to have been a fatherless woman without any dowry. At the time of her previous proposal, her friends had felt that the man's father was not offering enough money. But nothing was said about Catherine's fortune. Although it turned out later that Secker had provided for Catherine and Mrs Talbot in his will, there seems to have been no clear statement earlier about a dowry. Furthermore, there was a marked difference in age. Catherine was thirty-seven, George twenty-five (he was born in 1733). We can suspect that there was some feeling that George should marry a woman more likely to give him children than Catherine, although if her fortune had been good, that might have been overlooked. Alexander C. Fraser thought the Bishop had left his family poor (Berkeley, iv. 355). Another biographer, A. A. Luce, claimed that the son was considered a young man of expensive tastes (183). Why the decision against the proposal was made cannot be positively deduced. Finances must have played a strong part in the decision. In any case, Catherine's reverence for parental authority, in particular for Thomas Secker's authority over her because of his generous care for her, would have made it impossible for her to go against his views.[2]

Her letter shows conflict. She knew that a strong emotional tie had developed; did she hope against hope that the older generation might agree, or did she hope that George himself would turn away from her and save her from the necessity of a decision? As it turned out, trained to obedience, she did the obedient thing, and gave up marriage with George as impossible.

It hardly seems coincidental that Catherine had a severe illness at the end of 1758. Secker thought the illness was a dangerous consumption. Early in 1759 the Talbots and Secker went to Kensington for her health. In March Catherine Talbot went to Bristol for six months with Elizabeth Carter and Mrs Talbot.[3] Even four years later, Catherine was still harking back to her close call with death, a time when she felt she had been a very difficult patient. But at the end of 1760 she was actually back in London, writing to George's mother. George had been visiting her and she could not remember when she had spent ten days more comfortably. He laughed her out of petty disquiets and turned her mind to more important subjects. She was reading John Norris's *Practical Treatise on Humility* (BL Add. 39312, fos. 342–343). In March 1761 George married someone else—Eliza Frinsham, a young woman who was the eldest daughter and co-heiress of the Revd Henry Frinsham (Chalmers, 1812).

During these years Catherine wrote poems about her painful renunciation; George Berkeley had copies of these poems which his wife found after his death. She published two of them. The others, also unusually expressive poems for a woman writing at Catherine Talbot's time, have remained unpublished. I will discuss them in Chapter 8.

Hester Mulso did not take parental authority as seriously as Catherine Talbot. Hester believed in love and romance and tried to live according to those beliefs. In the late 1740s she had become acquainted with Samuel Richardson and had become one of the group of sympathetic women who visited him at his country home at North End, and exchanged letters with him. Her brother Thomas, and his friend, Miss Prescott, were also included. Susanna Highmore made a sketch of Richardson reading the manuscript of *Sir Charles Grandison* to his friends in 1751. The friends were Mr Mulso, Mr Edward Mulso, Miss Mulso, afterwards Mrs Chapone, Miss Prescott, afterwards Mrs Mulso, Revd John Duncombe, Miss Highmore, afterwards Mrs Duncombe (Richardson, *Correspondence*, v. ii). Hester met her prospective husband at Richardson's. John Chapone was an attorney, son of the Revd John Chapone and Sarah Kirkham Chapone, who was the old friend of Anne Dewes and Mary Delany. John Chapone had been recommended to Richardson by Mrs Dewes, who called him in her letter of introduction a 'remarkably sober, good young man' (Cole, 17).

Hester was probably engaged by 1754, for she sent Elizabeth Carter a love poem, and asked for her forgiveness, if not applause. She said that she knew that her friend's opinion of the 'lordly sex' was not a 'very high one'; Hester hoped to convince her some day that 'a man may be capable of all the delicacy, purity, and tenderness which distinguish our sex, joined with all the best qualities that dignify his own' (13 Aug. [?1754], Chapone, *Posthumous Works*, i. 90).

For financial reasons Hester's marriage had to be delayed for a long time, as was her brother Thomas's to Miss Prescott.

On 29 August 1757, Hester was writing to Elizabeth Carter from Canterbury that she looked forward to having a visit from Mr Chapone, 'a *fancied essential* to my happiness' (Chapone, *Posthumous Works*, i. 101). In the summer of 1759 Hester was still waiting to marry, and wrote to Elizabeth Carter, who was at Bristol with Catherine Talbot, that she was 'deep in stoicism'. She was reading the *Meditations* of Antoninus, which she admired. She preferred him to Epictetus because Antoninus was mild and sociable and not against human affections (Chapone, *Posthumous Works*, i. 112).

Hester married John Chapone in London in December 1760, the same day her eldest brother Thomas married Miss Prescott. Hester wished to maintain her friendships with women after her marriage. She wrote to Elizabeth Carter,

> I hope you join with me in the most perfect dissent from an opinion of your favourite Johnson, 'that a married woman can have no friendship but with her husband.' I flatter myself my heart will be improved in every virtuous affection by an union with a worthy man, and that my dear Miss Carter, and all my friends, will find it more worthy of their attachment, and better qualified for the best uses of friendship, than it ever was before. (Chapone, *Posthumous Works*, i. 118)

At first the newly-weds lived in lodgings on Carey Street, which was close to Mr Chapone's chambers. Then they took a house in Arundel Street, far from Clarges Street in Mayfair, where Elizabeth Carter was staying. Elizabeth Carter had lamented the long engagements both Hester and her brother had experienced. The senior Mr Mulso had eventually made the financial settlements which made the marriages possible. In the early days of her marriage, Hester wrote of loneliness. Her husband's business allowed her little of his company except at meals. Of course, when they met it was with 'joy and complacency', as she explained to Elizabeth, and 'If you *can* love a *man*, I expect you will love him, if you ever know him thoroughly' (Chapone, *Posthumous Works*, i. 120).

Hester's letters as a wife contain some regret that she had not seen Elizabeth as frequently in London as she had wished, and she hoped the following winter would set that right. But there was to be no second winter of married life. John Chapone died in September 1761 after a short illness. John Mulso wrote a graphic account of the event in his letters to Gilbert White.

Hester had not been well and had gone with her sister-in-law Mulso to Islington for the benefit of the air and waters. Mr Chapone became ill of a 'sharp Feaver' and died in their lodgings in about ten days (Mulso, 164). Her brother says she bore her 'cruel Loss' with 'patient Resignation' and did not charge God in her distress, but the sorrow was very deep. She moved to a brother's house, caught cold, and was very ill. She seems to have lost her memory and understanding for a while, but the doctors thought she would slowly recover.[4]

During the period of despair and illness after his death, Hester was helped by her friends, the Miss Burrowses, with whom she stayed. Elizabeth Carter wrote to try to strengthen her fortitude. By 6 December 1761 Hester could describe to Elizabeth her suffering, her recognition that her physical illness had rested her emotionally, and her patient return to living. Later, Elizabeth introduced Hester and the Miss Burrowses to Mrs Montagu. Hester spent the summer of 1762 at Sandleford with Mrs Montagu. At first she felt that her own insignificance would keep her at a distance from Mrs Montagu. But Mrs Montagu seemed to be able to offer friendship to women in more narrow circumstances than herself. Returning to town, Hester wrote to Mrs Montagu of her lonely lodgings looking uncomfortable after the 'delightful Society' she had enjoyed (MO 705, (c.1762)). Her future was to be made up of lodgings and visits.

Widowhood, spinsterhood, partial estrangement—the lack or loss of companionate marriages runs like a binding thread through the lives of the women who became the first blue-stockings. While they were growing up, they had been encour-aged towards a degree of self-awareness and self-direction, and they faced the difficulties of their mature lives with some deter-mination. Each woman's life worked out in a different way. The Duchess of Portland was widowed in 1761. She was finan-cially independent and was able to exchange Welbeck for Bulstrode with her son so she could remain at Bulstrode. She continued her life as she had lived it, and later relied on the close friendship of Mary Delany, who was widowed in 1768. Mrs Montagu's marriage remained intact but strained. And yet Mr Montagu steadily maintained his respect for and support of his wife, and was proud of her work on Shakespeare.

After his death in 1775 she had the benefits of wealth and independence.,

Although Elizabeth Carter avoided marriage at least partially in order to be free to continue her studies, she was not very productive. It is possible that marriage to another scholar might have helped her to pursue work in a more systematic way. Catherine Talbot's situation as a spinster in Secker's family confined her in a way that marriage to George Berkeley would probably not have done. Hester Chapone's loss of her husband was one of life's unexpected blows. But she, like the Duchess of Portland and Frances Boscawen, who was also widowed in 1761 (Aspinall-Oglander (1942)), and later Elizabeth Montagu, who was widowed in 1775, did not remarry. Aside from the benefit of independence which widowhood might bring, not remarrying was traditionally considered a tribute to the departed husband. As the *Ladies Library* advised, borrowing from Jeremy Taylor, 'Widowhood is pitiable in its Solitariness and Loss, but amicable and comely when it is adorn'd with Gravity and Purity, not sully'd with the Remembrances of past Enjoyments, nor with the present Desires of a second Bed' (i. 156).[5]

Thus, the marital experiences of the first bluestockings varied. They were single, widowed, or much alone in a marriage. But the significant factor which brought them together seems to have been that they had some control over how they used their time, and where they lived and visited. A woman who married and could not live in London or could not afford to visit in the season seems to have been unable to maintain a 'bluestocking circle' friendship. Susanna Highmore (1725–1812), the daughter of the painter Joseph Highmore, was certainly qualified to belong both by her literary interests and by her friendship with Elizabeth Carter. But after her marriage to John Duncombe in 1761 Susanna Duncombe lived in Canterbury, where her husband was one of the Six Preachers at the Cathedral; she does not seem to have been able to make long visits to London, probably for financial and family reasons. She had four children, only one of whom survived childhood, and she actually wrote a poem explaining that she had given up poetry and painting in favour of motherhood (Mild, 382). None of the first bluestockings was required to make that choice.

# 5 · 'Feminist Consciousness' and the Bluestockings

THE lives of the bluestockings show an assertion of individual interests within or outside of marriage which seem to be related to what we can call a rise in 'feminist consciousness'. Gerda Lerner in *The Creation of Patriarchy* offers a useful analysis which helps to place the bluestockings. She finds that the development of understanding which she calls 'feminist consciousness' takes place in different stages: '(1) the awareness of a wrong; (2) the development of a sense of sisterhood; (3) the autonomous definition by women of their goals and strategies for changing their condition; and (4) the development of an alternate vision of the future' (242).

As young women the bluestockings were beginning to find their way to Stages 1 and 2. They were becoming aware of wrongs and were developing a sense of sisterhood—of sharing common problems with other women. But their perspectives on Stages 3 and 4 were necessarily incomplete. They did have goals—better opportunities for education and a more equal partnership with men in social and intellectual life. They hoped to change the attitudes of both men and women by advocating the cause of women. But they had no feeling for the political and legal changes which would eventually be necessary. As for the future, they did not really think in terms of long-term improvements for life on earth, but looked forward to eternal life in the hereafter, when they hoped all inequities would be redressed, and they would continue in pure friendships with those to whom they had been close on earth.

The bluestockings were finding their way slowly and individually because they were not close to feminists who had gone before, and did not regard themselves as inheritors of a 'feminist tradition'. The extent to which the bluestockings may have been influenced by bold and assertive writers like Margaret Cavendish (Duchess of Newcastle), Bathsua Makin, Sarah Fyge Field Egerton, or Mary Astell, portions of whose work appear in *First Feminists: British Women Writers, 1578–1799*, edited by Moira Ferguson, is difficult to assess. I have found no evidence in their letters that the bluestockings read any of the works of the women of the late seventeenth and early eighteenth centuries which Ferguson considers to be feminist, except for the poetry of Katherine Philips. In her case, Elizabeth Carter remarked that Philips's reputation in her own time was very great but that her poems were now very scarce. Elizabeth Carter had two or three 'little pieces in a miscellany . . .' which she offered to send to Catherine Talbot, who was asking about Philips (13 June 1761). I have found no references in their letters to Mary Astell. Ruth Perry has indicated that Mary Astell's fame as a writer dissipated very quickly after her death in 1731. 'The last sale of her books in 1743 was meant to dispose of surplus stock from the unsold printing of 1730' (Perry (1986), 324). A much less-well-known writer, Sarah Fyge Field Egerton, was forgotten after her death in 1723. There were some inquiries about her towards the end of the century, but then she was forgotten again. As Jeslyn Medoff says in 'New Light on Sarah Fyge (Field, Egerton)', her case was not unusual. 'She is only one of a number of women poets of the Restoration and early eighteenth century who published their work, achieved a measure of notoriety, and then, except for sporadic resurfacings, disappeared' (155).

In fact, the history of the women's movement has been characterized by the loss of works by previous generations of women writers. Dale Spender has shown in *Women of Ideas and what Men Have Done to Them* how works critical of the conditions of women's lives have so often disappeared, and have had to be rediscovered by later generations; furthermore, men have not regarded the literary contributions of women as worthy of being brought down in history. In *Intruders on the Rights of Men: Women's Unpublished Heritage*, Lynne Spender has shown how male 'gatekeeping' has functioned to diminish the reputations of literary women; she quotes Germaine Greer on the 'transience of literary fame', a phenomenon in which women who were known in their own times later become invisible because of male gatekeeping (51).

In addition, we need to recognize that the gap in the production of feminist works between about 1710 and 1739 which Ferguson found in her study (19), roughly covers the period of the childhood and youth of the bluestockings. I think we must conclude that the bluestockings did not have a clear awareness of a broad range of women writers of the past.

Although the bluestockings do not seem to have developed out of a feminist tradition, they were influenced by some writings which had come down to them, or which were contemporary. During this time they had access to the general periodicals which had been or were interested in raising questions about the condition of women: the *Tatler*, the *Spectator*, and the *Gentleman's Magazine*.

The *Tatler* and *Spectator* were among the most popular resources for educational reading for young women and had a very long life. The two series of the *Spectator* alone came to a total of eight volumes; the bound volumes went through eleven editions by 1729. Michael G. Ketcham, in *Transparent Designs: Reading, Performance, and Form in the Spectator Papers*, quotes Hugh Blair as saying that in the 1760s the *Spectator* was 'in the hands of everyone' (4).

Steele's work helped to arouse interest in aspects of women's lives. In 1929 Rae Blanchard in her article on 'Richard Steele and the Status of Women' argued that Steele's conservatism and superficiality kept him from being one of the reformers like Poullain de la Barre, Daniel Defoe, or Mary Astell. She added:

But probably for this very reason he had more influence and a far larger reading public than they. Tactful, sincere, avoiding over-earnestness, he continued for twenty years to disseminate ideas which contributed to the evolution of feminist thought in England. (355)

As I indicated in Chapter 4, marriage was being regarded less as an instrument for familial aggrandizement than as a means to personal satisfaction. In *Transparent Designs* Ketcham shows that the family was a central focus for the *Spectator* papers (105–8). The *Spectator* argued that marriage might be a source of joy, if based on mutual good will. In such a revaluation the ideal for women was changing from that of the obedient wife to the companionate wife. Although we now see that the arguments in favour of marriage still kept women within traditional bounds, yet the concept of the companionate wife makes greater demands on the female partner and adds dignity to her role. It is probably for this reason that Elizabeth Montagu believed that Joseph Addison had been especially helpful in encouraging women to be more forthright and independent:

The Women have infinite obligation to him; before his time, they used *to nickname Gods creatures, & make their ignorance their pride*, as Hamlet says. Mr. Addison has shown them, ignorance, false delicacy, affectation & childish fears, are disgraces to a female character, which should be soft not weak, gentle, but not timerous. He does all he can to cure our sex of their feminalities without making them masculine. (MO 3148, 16 July 1765, to Elizabeth Carter)

Mrs Montagu used the term 'feminalities' to denote those traits of women—ignorance, affectation, timidity—which were connected with the traditional constraints in which they had been held, and in effect was arguing for a concept of a stronger, more effective woman. The *Spectator* had also influenced Mrs Montagu's thinking as a girl. Her observation in her letter to William Freind quoted in Chapter 1 (MO 1000) about the Muhammadan view that women have no souls probably derives from a letter to the *Spectator*, No. 53.

*The Ladies Library*, which was compiled by the Revd George Berkeley and published by Steele (Parks), also disseminated writings which could contribute to analysis of women's condition. *The Ladies Library* is a *mélange* of unidentified philosophical and religious tracts. A section in the second volume (270–346) under the heading of *The Mother* was excerpted from John Locke's *Thoughts Concerning Education*; it contains the discussion which Locke wrote in favour of giving daughters 'an education almost as rigorous as their brothers' (280). Another unacknowledged contributor was Mary Astell. The compiler used two selections from *A Serious Proposal* for the chapter on 'Ignorance' in the first volume; he printed arguments for educating women to be rational beings but did not include Astell's more unsettling ideas about retreating from the world to lead an independent life (Dammers, 533).

In her important article, 'The Eighteenth-Century Englishwoman: According to the *Gentleman's Magazine*', Jean E. Hunter found that only one quarter of the articles in the *Gentleman's Magazine* supported the traditional ideas of women as the weaker sex who were to be kept from study and public activities. Usually such articles were reprinted from other publications which wrote against women, like *Common Sense*. In fact, Hunter found that most of the articles in the *Gentleman's Magazine* that dealt with the female sex were sympathetic to the problems of women. The articles and letters which appeared in the *Gentleman's Magazine* were concerned with lack of educational opportunities, lack of career opportunities outside of marriage, the inequities of marriage, and the need for equality between the sexes (Hunter, 80–1). Lack of educational opportunities headed the list of grievances, but there was also a concern with narrow opportunities. One article (*Gentleman's Magazine* (Oct. 1739), 525–6) advised parents to apprentice their daughters to a trade or craft in order to avoid the difficulties attendant on trying to marry them off with a small fortune (Hunter, 83–4). Other writers in the *Gentleman's Magazine* also argued for the equality of men and women, and sometimes suggested female superiority. Hunter points out that in 'The Female Sex not the Weakest' ((Oct. 1735), 588–9), a woman, Climene, argued that 'women were inferior to men in nothing but brute strength, and excelled the male sex in such attributes as beauty, constancy, friendship and love' (Hunter, 86). Climene also complained that women were deprived of learning because of the jealousy of men.

The prominence of the *Gentleman's Magazine*, its popularity among both men and women, meant that there existed a voice which spoke to the general public on issues involving the condition of women. Thus the periodicals of the early and mid-eighteenth century helped to sensitize some men and women to the difficulties inherent in women's lot.

There were other influences. The popularity of the name 'Elizabeth' would in and of itself promote awareness of that vigorous intellectual woman, Queen Elizabeth I. We know that Talbot and Carter admired Elizabeth Singer Rowe, the prominent religious woman poet of this period. During their youth and early maturity the prospective bluestockings were gradually bringing together ideas and works which gave them insight into their situation. We know that Elizabeth Carter read the anonymous Sophia, A Person of Quality's *Woman not Inferior to Man* (1739) when it was first published. The writer used the arguments of the seventeenth-century French author Poulain de la Barre but adapted them to English history and contemporary life (Bell and Offen, 24–5). Poulain de la Barre's treatise, *De l'égalité des deux sexes* appeared in Paris in 1673, 1676, 1679, and in English as *The Woman as Good as the Man* in London in 1677 (Seidel, 499). In *Woman not Inferior to Man* Sophia argued that equal education would enable women to enter all kinds of public work; they might even participate in military actions. As I mentioned in Chapter 2, Elizabeth Carter was curious about this work, presumably partly because it praised her learning and directed attention to Thomas Birch's account of her in the *History of the Works of the Learned*. But it also must have encouraged her thinking about the problem of equal education.

Elizabeth Carter and her friends also developed their views by turning to philosophers like John Locke and the Spanish philosopher Feijóo. They gained further awareness from their contemporary reading—Richardson's novels, Johnson's *Rambler* essays, the work of George Ballard, and the poems of Thomas Seward and John Duncombe.

As Hunter indicated, deprivation of education was very high on the list of grievances and became a subject of poems which reached the general public. An example of such poems which appeared in the *Gentleman's Magazine* is 'An Epistle to Mr. Pope. By a Lady. Occasioned by his Characters of Women', in the December 1736 issue (745). The poet argued that males and females are essentially alike:

> In education all the diff'rence lies;
> Women, if taught, would be as bold and wise
> As haughty man, improv'd by art and rules . . .

The author of the poem was Anne Ingram, Viscountess Irwin (*c*.1696–1764), who went on to plead with men to take an interest in educating women, in order to rescue them from 'this Gothic State'.

Another minor poet, Thomas Seward, expressed the view of a man encouraging women to educate themselves, in 'The Female Right to Literature, in a Letter to a young Lady, from Florence', published anonymously in Dodsley's *Collection of Poems by Several Hands* (London (1748), ii. 295–302). Seward had been tutor to the son of the Duke of Grafton, and travelled with him on the continent. The poem was sent to Miss Pratt, later Lady Camden, whom he addressed as Athenia. Seward later became a prominent clergyman in Lichfield. He also has a claim to fame as the father of the poet Anna Seward (1747–1809). But, although he followed his own recommendations and educated Anna very early, both parents became alarmed at her studiousness and versifying, and wished to repress her interest in poetry (Ashmun, 10).

Whatever happened in practice later, in theory at least he was speaking for the 'female right to literature'. In so doing, Seward was using the term 'literature' in its eighteenth-century sense as 'acquaintance with "letters" or books; polite or humane learning; literary culture'; this is the meaning the word had for Samuel Johnson (*OED*). Seward was essentially asking for advanced education for women.

The poet wished to encourage Athenia to continue her studies, but acknowledged that in encouraging her, he was going against custom. He reviewed the countries in which he believed man had been a tyrant over women: Assyria, Persia, the Muhammadan countries. Even Greece and Rome, which once treated women with respect, now had domestic tyrants. Then the poet questioned his native land, ostensibly a country of freedom:

> But say, Britannia, do thy sons, who claim
> A birth-right liberty, dispense the same
> In equal scales? Why then does Custom bind
> In chains of ignorance the female mind?

(299)

The poet wondered why science was hidden from women, and why 'each pedant' begged to be shielded from that 'supreme of plagues a *learned wife*'. To reassure his readers, the poet then provided an image of the acceptable educated young woman:

> Her sprightly wit no forward pertness spoils;
> No self-assuming air her judgment soils;
> Still prone to learn, tho' capable to teach,
> And lofty all her thoughts, but humble all her speech.

(301)

In stressing the importance of combining learning with virtue and the domestic skills Seward was responding to the growing emphasis on female virtue as the key to public acceptance of women who studied or published. Jane Spencer discusses this development in *The Rise of the Woman Novelist: From Aphra Behn to Jane Austen*. Chastity in life and morality in writing became essential for the woman writer (75). Gradually the idea that women are actually superior to men in spiritual qualities such as capacity for friendship and love gained ground. While this view was an improvement over the earlier treatment of women as the source of evil, the idea of women having special moral attributes of course had its own limiting effect.

In 1751 another minor poet, John Duncombe, the friend of Elizabeth Carter who later married Susanna Highmore, also set out to redress the injustices of 'lordly Man', who had usurped the Muse's 'tributary Bay', in *The Feminead; or, Female Genius, A Poem*. It circulated in manuscript before being published (London, 1754; 2nd edn. 1757). Duncombe felt that the condition of women was actually improving. He saw the 'British Nymphs', unlike their unfortunate eastern sisters who are condemned to slavery, roving in freedom 'thro' Wisdom's sacred Grove'. There is now a 'blooming, studious Band' in England:

> With various Arts our Rev'rence they engage,
> Some turn the tuneful, some the moral Page,
> These, led by Contemplation, soar on High,
> And range the Heavens with philosophic Eye;
> While those, surrounded by a vocal Choir,
> The canvas tinge, or touch the warbling Lyre.
>
> (2nd edn., ll. 57–62)

Like Seward, Duncombe was concerned to warn against the 'bad' learned woman, for 'husbands oft experience to their Cost | The prudent Housewife in the Scholar lost'. The 'good' learned woman is unassuming, though her mind is 'grac'd by Nature, and by Art refin'd'. She is 'pleas'd with domestic Excellence', and manages to spare some time from 'studious Ease' to 'social Care'.

In reviewing the literary work of a number of women whom he wished to praise, Duncombe took care to distinguish between

the virtuous and vicious ones. Among the virtuous ones were
Katherine Philips, 'the chaste Orinda', Anne Finch, Countess
of Winchelsea, Catherine Cockburn, Elizabeth Singer Rowe,
Hester Mulso, and Elizabeth Carter. The poet singled out
Delariviere Manley, Susanna Centlivre, and Aphra Behn as
'Vice's Friends and Virtue's Female Foes':

> Tho' Harmony thro' all their Numbers flowed,
> And genuine Wit its every Grace bestow'd,
> Nor genuine Wit, nor Harmony, excuse
> The dangerous Sallies of a wanton Muse.
>
> (2nd edn., ll. 145–8)

Duncombe was following what were becoming accepted judgements in placing these writers beyond the pale.

Finally, the 'Aonian Maid' appeared to the poet as he
wandered in the fields, and praised him for speaking in favour
of women. In her introduction to the Augustan Reprint Society
edition, Jocelyn Harris expresses the view that this section was
written by another hand (p. v). This person might have been
Elizabeth Carter, although the verse does not sound like hers.
Perhaps it was Susanna Highmore's. Susanna Highmore both
painted and wrote poetry. There are sixteen surviving poems
by her in various collections (Mild, 379). In any case, this
woman advised her 'Sister Choir' to follow 'The flowery Paths
of Fame, by Science led | Employ by Turns the Needle and the
Pen | And in their favourite Studies rival Men' (2nd edn.,
ll. 355–8). Competition was to be carried on without giving up
that domestic tool, the needle. The Aonian Maid assured
women that their studies would give them pleasure in youth,
consolation in old age, and immortality after death.

It was George Ballard's *Memoirs of Several Ladies of Great
Britain*, published by subscription in 1752, which attempted to
revive the fame of learned women of past centuries. It fits
appropriately into this period, coming just at the time when
women of the present age were being encouraged to pursue the
right to literature. Although the connection with the bluestockings was only tangential, it was a poignant one. Living in
the household of the Duchess of Portland as the children's
governess was Elizabeth Elstob (1683–1756), a linguist and
scholar whose life, after a period of study and publication, had

lapsed into obscurity. She had been educated by her brother William, a clergyman, linguist, and Saxon scholar. After her brother's death in 1715 and the death of their friend and mentor, Dr George Hickes, she had struggled to continue to publish her work by subscription. But her inherited funds had been used up during her brother's illness, and she fell into debt. The press on her book *Saxon Homilys* was stopped; she probably was unable to repay people who had subscribed. Elstob left London and lived in Worcestershire under an assumed name. She may have been a maid in the household of a great family (Green; Wallas, 152).

George Ballard, a self-taught antiquarian enthusiast, sought out Elizabeth Elstob some years after he had become acquainted with her *Homily on St. Gregory*, and her *English–Saxon Grammar*. At first he had been told she was dead, but he found her living in Evesham, five miles from his own home at Chipping Campden in Gloucestershire. She was the mistress of a school for poor children, and was struggling with hard work, a small income, and ill health. Twenty years had elapsed since the death of her brother, and she had been lost during that time to learned conversation. (Univ. of Nottingham Library, MS PC PwE 9 is a copy of Ballard's account of Elstob's life and of his seeking her out.) Ballard's correspondence, visits, and gifts restored her to some sense of what she had been. Sarah Kirkham Chapone had also known of her difficulties and had been trying since 1728 to help her. It may be that Mrs Chapone found the position at the school in Evesham (Wallas, 157). She also interested her old girlhood friends, Anne Dewes and Mary Pendarves, the former Anne and Mary Granville, on Mrs Elstob's behalf. It was Mrs Pendarves's efforts that led to Mrs Elstob's employment as the Portlands's governess in 1739. At that time the eldest girl was only four, there was another girl of three, and the boy was one. In a letter to Mrs Pendarves, probably also intended for the Duchess, Elizabeth Elstob explained that she saw as her programme teaching the little ones religion and virtue, reading, good use of English grammar, and history (Univ. of Nottingham Library, MS PC PwE 8).

The Duchess engaged Elizabeth Elstob in December 1738, and began paying her her stipend of £30 per annum at that

time, although she did not actually call on her to come to work
until November 1739. The Duchess began by showing Mrs
Elstob some of her natural curiosities and antique objects. But
if Mrs Elstob had hoped for some opportunity for conversation
or a return to some scholarly pursuits in her leisure, she was
disappointed. She found that the children took up almost all
her time; when they were not with the Duchess—which Mrs
Elstob said was not for long—they were with her (Bodleian
Library, MS Ballard 43, fo. 36). Eventually, her pupils consisted of three girls: Lady Elizabeth, Lady Harriet, and Lady
Margaret, and the two sons: William, Marquess of Tichfield
and Lord Edward. The boys began going to Mr Achard for
lessons at the age of five, and then to public school at nine. The
girls stayed with Mrs Elstob. She soon became absorbed in the
children, and seems to have felt strong affection for them. In
later years when she developed a painful contraction in her
hand which made it difficult for her to write, one of the young
ladies was her scribe for her letters to George Ballard. Her
affections were so engaged that when Lady Margaret died in
April 1756, Mrs Elstob was almost prostrate with grief. She
herself died two months later.

Ballard's *Memoirs* was really written with Elizabeth Elstob's
difficulties in mind, and was an attempt to change society's
treatment of learned women. Since Ballard was writing about
women not then living, he did not include a biographical
memoir of her, but he did mention the 'learned and ingenious
Mrs Elstob' as having supplied him with some materials. In
fact, Ballard was completing a work which she had attempted
much earlier. In the Ballard Collection at the Bodleian is a
bound blank book entitled 'Notes toward biographies of learned
ladies', signed and dated 'Elizabeth Elstob August 12, 1709'
(MS Ballard 64). It contains a list of references, and an alpha-
betical list carried on through the volume under which informa-
tion was to be entered. Elstob had entered details of the lives
and works of a number of women before she abandoned the
project. She had evidently sold the book, for Ballard noted
having bought it from 'Mr. Price Bookseller' in Gloucester,
18 June 1747.

In the bitterness engendered by her own experience, Elizabeth Elstob felt that Ballard had made the wrong choice of

subject. 'For you can come into no company of Ladies or Gentlemen, wh[ ] you shall not hear an open and Vehement exclamation against Learned Women.' Elstob herself hoped to see learning flourish in both men and women, but did not expect to see it in her lifetime (Bodleian Library, MS Ballard 43, fo. 89).

Ballard's *Memoirs* brought back into public notice the lives and works of learned women of previous generations. While the main method was to present in a simple biographical narrative the materials he had gathered from manuscripts, inscriptions, and his antiquarian friends, he also made some editorial comments, as when he pointed out that Sir Thomas More was not of that 'illiberal, narrow-sould way of thinking to make learning the property of men alone' (38). Ballard emphasized that conscientious fathers like Sir Thomas More obtained the best linguists and scholars for their daughters. Ruth Perry, who recently brought out an annotated edition of *Memoirs of Several Ladies*, shows that Ballard was actually a more vehement advocate of learning for women in the original manuscript than in the printed version. But criticism from men, not only those of the 'hunting tribe' but also academic and scholarly men, intimidated him, and he reduced the forcefulness of his advocacy of learned women (Perry (1985), 35–9).

In general the women Ballard presented were women of scholarship, religion, and piety. Many of Ballard's learned women knew Greek, Latin, Philosophy, Astronomy, Physic, Arithmetic, Logic, Rhetoric, Music. Some of them wrote in Latin and Greek, or did translations from those languages. Others translated French and Italian writings.

Ballard did not quite urge women of the present to follow the examples of the fifteenth- and sixteenth-century women whom he discussed in Part One of his work, but he thought posterity should praise, if it did not imitate, them. In his second part he presented seventeenth- and some eighteenth-century women, including Katherine Philips, Anne Wharton, Mary Astell, and Constantia Grierson. Since his purpose was to make learning respectable for women, he emphasized the close connection between learning and virtue. In fact, Sarah Chapone had urged him to say in his Preface that women of real learning and knowledge never applied their talents to evil principles. She thought Aphra Behn and Delariviere Manly were members of 'that Slight Sisterhood' who never were considered women of learning or had 'any pretense to be called women of Knowledge' (Perry (1980), 92). As a gatekeeper, Ballard was not a 'narrow soul'd' male, but of course he was interested in reviving the reputations of virtuous women only.

Ballard asked Elizabeth Elstob to help get subscriptions for his work. She felt that her position as governess had contracted her life to a narrow compass, but she promised to do what she could. She helped to circulate proposals and spoke of the work to visitors like Dr Shaw, who had not heard of it (Bodleian Library, MS Ballard 43, fo. 76). In the end she got subscriptions from her family—three Portland daughters, William, the elder son, and the Duchess herself. Mrs Delany subscribed for six copies, and her sister also subscribed. We do not know who else exerted themselves for Ballard, but the subscription list includes three copies for the Bishop of Oxford (Thomas Secker), and copies for Sir George Lyttelton, Dr Charles Lyttelton, Henry Chapone, Miss Chapone of Cheltenham, Samuel Richardson, Edward Gibbon, and other men connected with Oxford colleges. The Mrs Frances Smith who subscribed for two copies was Elizabeth Elstob herself.

This subscription list is suggestive, especially with regard to the Bishop of Oxford. His notebooks show that he was interested in the condition of women. He wrote brief commentaries about Helena Lucretia Cornara Piscopia, who received a Doctor of Philosophy degree in Padua in the seventeenth century, and about Laura Maria Catharina Bassi, who received a Doctor of Philosophy degree elsewhere in Italy in the eighteenth century. But he also noted about Cornara Piscopia that her published works were not valuable (Secker, Notebooks, Lambeth Palace Library, 2564, fos. 285, 461). Did the Bishop take his three copies? Did one go to Cuddesden, the other to the Deanery at St Paul's? Was there one perhaps for Elizabeth Carter, whose training closely resembled that of women of the earlier centuries? Did Talbot and Carter discuss Ballard? We have no evidence except for a remark made in regard to the possibility of Carter's appointment as a governess in the Princess of Wales's household which was being proposed about this time. Carter played down the suggestion as she had similar suggestions earlier; she did not feel suited for Court life, and would only accept such an appointment if her father absolutely required her to. She also pointed out that it was unlikely that she would be needed to teach Greek and Latin, for no one thought any longer of giving princesses the sort of education they had received in the past (Carter, *Memoirs*, i. 184). Perhaps she had been reading Ballard, who had reminded her of the difference between the Renaissance tradition of learning for women and the attitude of the present.

With the exception of hiring Elizabeth Elstob as governess for her children, subscribing to Ballard's work, and helping Mary Delany, the Duchess of Portland seems to have been above the battle; I have found no explicit concern with female advocacy in her letters. However, she lent her friend Mrs Delany money to buy a house, as I shall show in Chapter 10. The Duchess took her problems with her mother, and with formal society, as stemming from her particular family situation and high status; her bluestocking interests seem to have developed out of her father's collecting interests, and were supported by her financial resources, her friendship with Mary Delany, and her own determination. But the other women whose early lives I have discussed all expressed an awareness of female problems either in observations in letters, in efforts to help individual women, or in formal arguments in favour of equality.

Catherine Talbot's concern for women is shown in her letters to Elizabeth Carter. She complained of the treatment of women by Thucydides, whom she was reading in Hobbes's translation. She spoke

on behalf of all the Grecian ladies, of whom he does not think fit to mention one through his whole history; and indeed of all ladies in general, to whom he gives a very civil admonition in one of Pericles' speeches, to keep themselves quiet, and make themselves as little talked of as possible. (6 Jan. 1745)

Catherine added that she had asked some gentlemen to look into the Greek for her, but what they reported was even worse, for they explained that Pericles said that 'modesty is the only virtue that can belong to women, for they have neither prudence, justice, nor fortitude.'

In another letter she expresses anger at the way women are brought up. She is analysing the character of Harriet in *Sir Charles Grandison*. She defends Harriet against accusations that she is vain. Talbot sees a spice of this vanity in every female heart because

it is instilled into us from the very nursery, where we are told to *hold up our heads for there is money bid for us*, and partly, to own a mortifying truth, few girls can become of any consideration in the world, but from the proper regard paid to them by some one of *the condescending Lords of creation*. (Percy Lodge, 12 Nov. 1753)

We have seen that Elizabeth Montagu had a sharp awareness of the venality surrounding the choice of a husband. As she got older, and had the experience of becoming a partner in a distant marriage, and also a sympathetic observer of her sister Sarah's marital difficulties, her reactions in her letters become sharper, even bitter. But Mrs Montagu was also aware of the problems of other women. In fact much of the philanthropic efforts for which she was well known centred on helping women. She helped Sarah Fielding at several points in her career, either with a sum of money, or efforts to raise subscriptions for her work (MO 5281, 1760, Bath, Sarah Scott to Elizabeth Montagu). Mrs Montagu also tried to help girls in need. At one point she was trying to get a Miss Keith placed in the Newbury boarding-school, and hoped that the girl could pay some of her expenses by teaching drawing and drawing patterns for the school (MO 5761, 27 [Oct. 1756], to Sarah Scott). In another letter Mrs Montagu explained to her sister that Miss Keith had lost her mother, and she was trying to place her 'where she might get her bread by her genius & skill in drawing'. She thought Miss Keith might be capable of doing the drapery for Mr Hoare's pictures. 'I wanted to get her apprentice to those who draw for the Mercers, but they take only boys, & she is rather pretty, & I am afraid of her being ruin'd in this Town' (MO 5764, [1756]).

Mrs Montagu showed great concern for the welfare of a young woman who worked for her. She had taken Susan from poverty in a cottage to be her maidservant. The girl was seduced by a 'dangerous lover' (MO 3058, [c.21 Oct. 1761]). Mrs Montagu felt responsible for the girl's troubles, because she had taken her into a difficult situation, but Elizabeth Carter assured her that Susan might have been seduced by a ploughboy if she had stayed in the country (Carter, *Letters* (1817), i. 133). Mrs Montagu asked her friend if she could find a small family where she could board Susan (MO 3059). In subsequent letters Mrs Carter arranged Susan's care. She stayed with Mrs Green in Deal. Both Mrs Montagu and Mrs Carter were interested in lending her books; Mrs Carter's friends in Deal also taught her handiwork. Susan remained in Deal probably until December 1762. Comments in the correspondence about an anticipated improvement in Susan's depression suggest that she was pregnant but there are no direct references to such a condition and an eventual birth. Susan stayed in Deal for more than a year. Mrs Montagu paid her board bills and her apothecary bill (MO 3071; 3081; 3087).

Susan seems to have returned to work for Mrs Montagu in late 1762. Mrs Montagu was happy with her. Susan's handiwork was very pretty and she seemed to have gained moral principles from the friends at Deal (MO 3089; 3097). The relationship continued for life. In 1778 Susan married and left with her husband for an 'establishment in the North' which Mrs Montagu had arranged (MO 3447). Subsequent letters gave reports on Susan's excellent situation as a wife and eventually the mother of five children (MO 3454; 3552). On 20 October [1797], three years before her own death, Mrs Montagu wrote, 'Susan Woodhouse, to whom you were so good when at Deal, dyed of a decline a few days ago' (MO 3771).

Mrs Montagu became a strong advocate of her sister's cause after Sarah's separation from her husband. Sarah had married George Lewis Scott early in 1751, but had separated from him in April 1752. The separation was acrimonious. Evidently Mr Robinson and his sons removed Sarah from the house. At first, Sarah seems to have been at Hayes with Mrs Montagu. In a letter written 20 April [1752] to her husband, Elizabeth Montagu said that Sarah's spirits were so bad, and she was so ill, that she could not be alone.

Indeed poor Creature her situation is miserable; allied to the faults & infamy of a bad Man, subject to his aspersions, & liable to the

censures of his friends, for the worst have some, and in all disagreements in Wedlock blame falls even on the innocent. (MO 2249,
20 Apr. [1752])

Why the marriage disintegrated can probably not now be
ascertained. There has been speculation that Sarah's close
friendship with Lady Barbara Montagu, whom Sarah had met
at Bath in 1748 (after she had begun her friendship with George
Scott), interfered with the marriage. Sarah had felt that Lady
Bab's company and her goodness to her were the reasons why
she had agreed to stay on with her in Bath after their first
acquaintance. Writing to her sister she had said, 'I am of your
opinion that to stay on her account is right, & on her account
I determin'd to do it' (MO 5205, [13 June 1748]). Lady Bab
may have resided with the newly-weds. As we have seen by the
example of her sister, it was often usual for the bride to have a
female companion. Early in her marriage, when Sarah wrote to
her sister that she was planning to move into her house in
Leicester Fields, she reported on the health of both Lady Bab
and Mr Scott (MO 5221).

Eventually, after she separated from her husband, Sarah
retired to Bath. Although her estranged husband sent her a
stipend, she had financial problems. She wished to buy a
house, which she thought she could manage for £400, but her
father refused to advance the money on the grounds that Mr
Scott might claim it as part of her fortune of £1,500. Mrs
Montagu attempted to use strong argument with her father,
suggesting that Mr Scott might claim that Sarah had been
deceived by her family about her circumstances. Her father
claimed the match was not of his making, but she thought that
'what a Father permits he encourages, & that he had more to
do in it than any body . . .' (MO 5728, [Dec. 1752]). The
acrimony generated by the separation got into the public
sphere. On 21 January [1753] Elizabeth sent Gilbert West a
song written about her sister and Mr Scott (MO 6696). In a
letter to her sister Mrs Montagu expressed great anger at Scott's
behaviour; she thought he was telling lies about Sarah. Allud-
ing to the ghost in *Hamlet*, she expressed her wish to 'revenge
thy [i.e. Sarah's] foul & most unnatural M----ge with that
foul unnatural animal: but I will not hurt him with his weapons

lying & falsehood, he shall have truth armed like the porcu-
pine.' She exclaimed, 'Oh that we had had a divorce! I believe
his poor case is a plain case, & wd have given little trouble'
(MO 5731, 6 Feb. [1753]).

Eventually, Sarah shared a house in Bath with Lady Bab,
and a house in Batheaston in the summer. Another resident
seems to have been a Miss Arnold, who was an illegitimate
daughter of their brother Morris (MO 6018; 5380). Sarah
received a quarterly payment from her husband, but her father
was adamant about not helping her. In 1762 Mrs Montagu
described to her sister a terrible quarrel which she had had with
her father about her sister. Sarah and Lady Bab wanted to
move to a house in Bath which cost 60 guineas, but if they did
so, they would not be able to keep their summer house in Batheaston. Mrs Montagu asked her father to add £20 to Sarah's
allowance; Mr Montagu would do the same. These additions
would make it possible to keep both houses.

My Father flew into a passion, & said it was a monstrous proposal &
unreasonable, & he could not afford to comply with it. I told him you
had had but a thousand pound of him, & you could not have been
maintain'd for the interest of that sum if you had staid in his house,
that he had got back part of that thousand pound, & every one must
think you was hardly used . . .

(These statements indicate that the amount advanced for
Sarah's dowry was only £1,000 rather than the £1,500 originally
mentioned by her sister (MO 5728). One of the reasons for the
failure of the marriage may have been this discrepancy between
what Scott had been promised and what he received. In any
case Scott retained part of the dowry and returned the remainder
to Mr Robinson.) Mrs Montagu and her father then began to
quarrel about the younger children; Mr Robinson didn't think
he should have to help any of his children once they were
grown up. She asked him again to help Sarah:

he said he cared not a farthing for me or what I desired, & he did not
desire Mr M to trouble his head with his family & then got up & took
me by the hand & put me out of the room, I told him I did not expect
to be insulted in that manner, however I was not very sorry to find
myself on the other side the door where I shall remain till he pleases to

visit me, & thus ends the chapter of paternal love. (MO 5791, 16 June [1762], Sandleford)

During these years Mrs Montagu had begun to feel constraints in her own marriage, and her letters to her sister express her anger at the complacent assumption by a husband of his power over his wife. Mr Montagu's reluctance to join his wife at Tunbridge Wells was a point of contention. Mr Montagu complained that Tunbridge was as bad as a prison; Mrs Montagu fumed that she did not want to be his gaoler. Under any other circumstances they could have chosen to do as each wished, 'but Hymen is such a powerfull Deity that he changes the nature of all things . . . Indeed in all ye metamorphoses there is none so strange as changing two persons into one, & of two minds making one will' (MO 5756, 6 [July 1756], to Sarah Scott).

Some years later she wrote a burning description of the way in which she got permission to visit Mrs Boscawen at Hatchlands. Her husband said that she 'had rambled enough this summer'. She offered to write and explain that fact. Thereupon her husband said she could go for three days. She said that would not do; so he franked a cover for the letter in which she was to let Mrs Boscawen know that her husband did not wish her to come:

You wd have laughd if you had seen the gravity with which he frank'd a cover for ye letter which I said I was to write to acquaint her with his denial, he thought I shd repeat my request, point du tout, I took the cover with great indifference & was determined either to have my pleasure or give a signal mark of my obedience to his noble exertion of prerogative. Do not you admire these lovers of liberty! What do the generality of men mean by a love of liberty but the liberty to be saucy to their superiors, & arrogant to their inferiors, to resist the power of others over them, & to exert their power over others. I am not sure that Cato did not kick his wife. What inconvenience cd be to his honour that I shd be in Hillstreet, in the County of Middlesex rather than at Hatchlands in ye County of Surrey, he being all the while in Coun. Berks. and the pretence of my keeping order in the family is trifling, as I shall leave all the Servants here but my own Maid & footmen. But these Lords of the Creation must be lordly. Thanks to termagantism there are some Ladies of the creation who have them in due subjection. (MO 5829, 25 [Oct. 1765], to Sarah Scott)

Aside from the remarks and observations in their letters which alert us to their awareness of their difficulties, two of these women also made strong efforts to argue for improvements in the condition of women. Both of these efforts involve critiques of the work of Samuel Richardson.

In *The Feminead* Duncombe had called Samuel Richardson the friend and 'constant Patron' of women, 'who so oft with pleas'd, but anxious care, | Hast watch'd the dawning genius of the fair' (2nd edn., ll. 17–18). Richardson was in fact the important writer who was recommending learning and virtue to women in a most insinuating and effective way.

In 1747 and 1748 Richardson was publishing *Clarissa* in parts of two or three volumes each. His heroine's troubles with her family and the subsequent tragic events of her life were intensely interesting to his readers. As the work proceeded in parts, issues involving Clarissa became the subject of serious discussions among his friends. Richardson felt that all of these discussions were for the improvement of women. They probably were, but, above all, his creation of a heroine who was a reader and writer provided his readers with an image of woman alone, thoughtful, autonomous. In a letter to Susanna Highmore on 2 August 1748, from Tunbridge Wells, Richardson showed that he was aware of the kind of influence he was having. Complimenting her on the succinctness of her letters, in contrast to his own, he spoke of the 'beauties of contemplation which she enjoys in her Clarissa-closet (as she is pleased to call it) with pen, pencil, and books!' (Richardson, *Correspondence*, ii. 208). Richardson's portrayal of the 'beauties of contemplation' is a complete reversal of Tassoni's fearful anticipation of its dangers which I quoted in the Prologue. Now women were being encouraged to spend time alone, reading, drawing, or writing.

But while Richardson's friends were warmly admiring and sympathetic, some of them were critical of aspects of his views on women. They saw inherent contradictions in Richardson's attitudes: he was encouraging self-development for women at the same time that he clung to traditional views of women's frailty, especially their sexual vulnerability. His advice to Susanna Highmore is a case in point.

Susanna Highmore was evidently an active, gregarious,

straightforward person who believed in 'freely keeping company with both sexes'. Richardson considered this practice dangerous, especially during the years of sixteen, seventeen, and eighteen, when the 'seducer within them' was especially insidious. Girls would have to be morally prepared ahead of time to cope with such freedom. For he believed that women were always on the defensive, and that men always carry on 'an offensive war against them'. Girls in middle life, such as his own daughters, he would indulge with public diversions three times a season at the most (Richardson, *Correspondence*, ii. 211–14).

In another letter of advice to Susanna, Richardson compared girls to spiders who make webs to entangle insects. But the spider runs into her hole, 'when a powerful finger of some giant man brushes down or demolishes her cobweb!' (ii. 220–1). Richardson's simile makes a strong point about his view of the relative power of men and women. The novelist advised his young correspondent to stay in her father's home in Lincoln's Inn Fields, and let her friends and 'lovers' come to her there. He thought she should not visit so much. 'Domesticate yourself.' 'The lovers like to come *home* to a girl.' He advised her that spending six or seven months in Kent and long periods of time in other places would not do (ii. 222–3).

Susanna was one of Richardson's correspondents who objected to the novelist's stress on parental authority and filial obedience in *Clarissa*, and spoke for the importance of ties of gratitude and love. However, a stronger and more extensive attack on Richardson's treatment of the duties of a woman to her parents, and on his patronizing attitudes towards their capacities for independence, was made by Hester Mulso. Richardson and the young woman exchanged three letters of very great length, with Hester criticizing Richardson's treatment of Clarissa, and Richardson defending himself. Unfortunately, we do not have Richardson's side of the correspondence, but we have letters in which he talked about it.

Richardson felt proud to be helping to ease the taboo against learning for women. Writing to Lady Bradshaigh about his correspondence with Hester Mulso, Richardson assured Lady Bradshaigh that he believed that 'a woman who writes a book, breaks not thereby the rank she holds in the world' (vi. 118).

He thought Miss Mulso a 'charming writer, and an excellent child to an indulgent father; as affectionate a sister to three worthy brothers' (vi. 121). Richardson evidently planned to show Lady Bradshaigh the exchange of letters with Hester, for he apologized for the extreme length of his own: 'What care I for that, if I can but whet, but stimulate ladies, to show what they are able to do and how fit they are to be intellectual, as well as domestic companions to men of the best sense' (vi. 122). The letters, circulated privately, aroused a great deal of interest, and gave an audience to Hester's stronger views on the equality of the sexes. Hester's letters were first published in a two-volume edition of her *Posthumous Works* (London, 1807), and in a four-volume edition of her *Works* (London and Edinburgh, 1807).

Richardson had asked Hester to put into writing her beliefs on the subject of filial duty and parental authority. In her first letter, dated 12 October 1750, Hester wondered why Clarissa, who otherwise seemed to be so sensible, should be so 'superstitious' as to fear parental authority. Prejudice prevented her from using reason as her guide in this instance. Hester asked Richardson to mitigate her objections to this aspect of Clarissa's character.

Her second letter, dated 10 November 1750, takes up forty-nine printed pages; some of it is devoted to quotations from the work of John Locke. In this response, Hester wrote that the arguments Richardson had sent her had not convinced her. She used Locke's discussions of parental authority in his *Treatises on Government* as a source for her second round. Locke had agreed that children do not have the natural rights to freedom which adults have, because they must be cared for by others, but as they grow, the bonds drop off and leave men free. Hester insisted that Locke's arguments about a man and his liberty must apply to a woman also. Since natural liberty arises from reason, women must be considered reasonable creatures capable of liberty. Locke also argued that children are obliged to honour their parents out of gratitude, but such a duty is very far from granting parents absolute power over children when they are grown. From these points Hester deduced that Clarissa need not have submitted to her parents' commands to marry Solmes.

Evidently Richardson had also argued that a woman could

learn to love as her husband a man whom she had not cared for as a suitor; Hester thought it extremely unlikely. She pointed out that a married woman is in the power of her husband, and Clarissa married to Solmes would be in chains. In fact, marriage to Solmes would have made her guilty of perjury in promising to love and honour a man she hated.

Hester Mulso was a close reasoner and attempted to refute Richardson's specific assertions. She made it plain that she judged the actions of women as those of rational beings who could consider the consequences of their actions. Thus if Clarissa's parents wished to act according to their own mercenary values, they were free to do so. But Clarissa was free to act according to her own values: 'it is the *child's* happiness and the *child's* conscience only which are concerned' (Chapone, *Works* (1807), ii. 73).

Hester went on to assert that Clarissa had no other recourse but to leave her home, although this was a dangerous and finally a fatal step. She believed that a father who asked for divine vengeance on his child had very little right to be looked upon as a father. But she felt that Clarissa's concern for her father was worthy of her as a Christian.

In her third letter, of 3 January 1751, Hester was trying to reconcile the opposing parties. She expressed her sense of the value of having Richardson's attention, and her gratitude that he was willing to take seriously 'the rude essays of an ignorant girl, the unconnected sallies of a wild imagination with but little judgment to direct or control it' (Chapone, *Works* (1807), ii. 89–90). She was willing to suggest that their positions were not so far apart as they seemed. Locke was probably on the side of both. But she was still asking searching questions. What were children to do whose parents treated them in an unjust manner? Were they to pay the same obedience 'to cruel tyrants as they would do to kind and indulgent parents?' (Chapone, *Works* (1807), ii. 93). Then what was the advantage of living in a free country? Did the title of parent give the right to make a child miserable for life?

In particular, Hester questioned the mistreatment of women by their parents. She gave several instances: the Miss B---s, whose mother abused her daughters physically; Miss W., whose father denied her the common necessaries of life while she was living in his house at the age of thirty; Miss – – –, who was cruelly treated by her parents but was finally able to leave her home when she received an inheritance from a friend. In such cases Hester believed that the unfortunate women had the right, if finances made it possible, to separate from their parents. Richardson had given her a black catalogue of misbehaving children. Hester replied that if she knew as much of the world as he did, she probably could give as black a catalogue of misbehaving parents.

Hester's conclusion on the question of freedom of choice in marriage was that parents had no right to force a child to marry against its inclination, and that although parents might refuse to consent to a marriage, a negative when the child was between eighteen and thirty, or older, should be given only under exceptional circumstances. (Hester's view would have left Catherine Talbot emotionally free to marry George Berkeley.)

Hester's strongest points were made when she demanded for women the same rights as for men. Richardson had objected that women can never be in a 'state of independency' (Chapone, *Works* (1807), ii. 114). But Hester believed that although women in her society were actually seldom independent, the general truth was that '*women*, as rational and accountable beings, are free agents as well as *men*' (Chapone, *Works* (1807), ii. 115; emphasis in the text).

Hester recognized that it was the customs of the world that made the breach of filial duty more serious for the daughter than the son:

The rules of the world being made by *men* are always more severe on *women* than on themselves, insomuch that as you observe, 'perpetrated crimes in a man hurt not his reputation in the world's eye half so effectually as imprudences in a woman.' Indeed I don't know that any crimes except cowardice and stealing, (stealing of *money* I mean, stealing of daughters or wives is nothing;) disqualify a man from being received into all companies, and living with credit in the world. But though men's ways are unequal, the ways of God are equal, and with him *even women* shall find justice. (Chapone, *Works* (1807), ii. 115–16; emphasis in the text)

Richardson had evidently alluded to the heavier punishments which fell on women, and in reply Hester Mulso made a direct attack on the double standard.

Furthermore, Hester recognized that it was class which determined differences in the position of women:

But with regard to parents, I own I do not see that *God* and *nature* have made daughters *more* dependent on them than sons. Custom indeed allows not the daughters of people of fashion to leave their father's family to seek their own subsistence, and there is no way for them to gain a creditable livelihood, as gentlemen may. But amongst the lower ranks of people, daughters are so soon independent as sons. The girls and boys are alike sent out to provide for themselves. (Chapone, *Works* (1807), ii. 117)

Having written herself into an uncomfortable position as an assertive female, Hester realized that she seemed to be wanting in the 'characteristic graces of her sex', in *'meekness, patience, resignation, submission'*. She asked Richardson not to let the *'reading and writing Ladies* suffer for this; *I* never was a writing lady till *you* made me one'. She hoped that he would not because of her bring up the old question whether 'our fore-fathers were not in the right when they bestowed so little attention on the education of girls'. Hester went on to exclaim:

Forbid it science! Forbid it justice! that the sex, and the cause of learning, should thus suffer for the faults of *one ignorant girl*! For if I have erred, you should impute it rather to my *ignorance* than know-ledge. Miss Carter says, (and she is herself a proof of the truth of her assertion) 'tis certain that every accession of understanding, whether in man or woman, in its natural tendency, leads to the improvement of the heart. Be not then discouraged, good Sir, from your laudable design of 'making young ladies better than some of them think they need to be;' and let me obtain mercy, if not for myself, yet for the *reading and writing ladies.* (Chapone, *Works* (1807), ii. 132-3)

Hester's penetrating remarks had raised some open expression of prejudice against women. Hester herself thought that Richardson had responded unfairly by accusing her of having become the spokeswoman of impatient girls. It seemed to her that he was putting her at the head of a regiment of wilful daughters: 'for I think you have presented me with a set of Amazonian soldiers, all drest in flame-coloured taffety, expert in leaping windows, or scaling walls, but whose conduct is by no means equal to their courage . . .'. Hester denied her capacity to lead such a group of assertive women, and suggested that he find some veteran widow to put in charge (Chapone, *Works* (1807), ii. 103–4). Richardson had evidently tried to frighten her by suggesting that her position did put her into company with assertive women.

Her marriageability was also called into question; it was suggested that she might disqualify herself from marriage by putting herself forward in this way. Relaying this ultimate threat, her brother John reported to Gilbert White that 'Old Cibber swore to her Face She would never be married' (Mulso, 45).

But her position had also raised some sympathetic responses. Her friend Elizabeth Carter had evidently taken Hester's side in the controversy; she also dared to make fun of Richardson's prolixity (Chapone, *Posthumous Works*, i. 26; 29). John Mulso reported in a letter of 13 December 1750, 'Several great men as the Bp of London, the Speaker &c: have seen this Dispute & think Mr R – – hard pressed, & Heck has gained great Honour' (Mulso, 45).

The questions Hester Mulso raised were also of great interest to Elizabeth Carter. About this time she was reading *Defensa de las mugeres* (Defence of Women) by an important eighteenth-century Spanish writer, the Benedictine monk Benito Jeronimo Feijóo (1676–1764), which appeared in the first volume of his *Teatro crítico universal* (1726–39).[1] Elizabeth must have written to Hester about Feijóo's arguments in favour of women, for Hester expressed regret that she herself did not know Spanish:

> Will you in pity to us Ignoramuses, give us, in English, a few of those passages in which he speaks so honourably of our sex? Do, dear Miss Carter. We have not many patrons amongst the men; let us hear all that has been said by any of the ungenerous sex in our favour, since we are pretty sure to hear of their abuses. (Chapone, *Posthumous Works*, i. 35)

These were the years Elizabeth Carter was busy educating her brother, translating Epictetus, and making shirts, and she did not translate Feijóo. But she used some of his arguments for her defence of women which Richardson printed in *Sir Charles Grandison*.

Feijóo provided surprisingly thorough arguments for the equality of the sexes. He believed that women had the same abilities and moral capacities as men, and pointed out that one cannot claim women are not capable of doing things which they have not been trained to do. Furthermore, women of good abilities are deprived of the experience on the basis of which they could learn to reason. Men learn from their conversations with each other; women are primarily occupied with domestic affairs, and cannot get these benefits. Feijóo said he was unable to find any physical reasons for the supposed disparity of intellect between the sexes. He also provided some historical background, to prove 'by examples, that female intellects are equally capable of the most abstruse sciences, as those of men' (c.1765, 149). He cited a number of women who had distinguished themselves in recent times in literature and science in Spain and other countries. Feijóo also considered the question, why God chose man for mastery over woman; he suggested that God's motives were inscrutable. However, he believed that as a practical matter women would be better able to defend themselves from men if they thought they were as bright as men.

Elizabeth Carter probably felt greatly helped in her analysis of the problems of women by the work of the Benedictine monk. Although Carter recognized Richardson's power as a writer, she resented his condescending attitudes towards women. In particular Richardson's *Rambler*, No. 97 (19 Feb. 1751) irked her. The novelist had harked back nostalgically to earlier days when women were confined to home and church, and recommended going back to that custom. Writing to Catherine Talbot on 4 March 1751, Carter observed, 'I cannot see how some of his doctrines can be founded on any other supposition than that Providence designed one half of the human species for idiots and slaves' (Carter, *Letters* (1808), i. 254–5). Catherine went to the defence of her idol, and Elizabeth backed down, saying that perhaps she had misunderstood Richardson's meaning. But later she must have found an opportunity to express her views. Elizabeth Carter had now been brought into a personal relationship with Richardson. In May 1753 she visited North End with Mrs Talbot while Catherine was staying with the Duchess of Somerset; later in the summer Elizabeth Carter talked with and exchanged letters with Richardson (*Original Letters of Miss E. Carter and Mr. S. Richardson*). He was composing *Sir Charles Grandison* at this time. In fact, Richardson wrote to Lady Bradshaigh that a lady had showed him 'some pretty observations on the education of women, and their attainments'. He begged a copy, and made use of these remarks by staging in volume vi of *Sir Charles Grandison* a debate on 'the inferiority and superiority of the two sexes' (Richardson, *Correspondence*, i, pp. cxxxix–cxl).

The debate is touched off by some of uncle Selby's remarks against women. Then Lady G. argues for the superiority of the female sex. Finally, Mrs Shirley gives her considered opinion, which accepts the doctrine of separate spheres, but urges many more opportunities for women to develop their capacities. Mrs Shirley's speech was probably the work of Elizabeth Carter.[2]

I think . . . women are generally too much considered as a species apart. To be sure, in the duties and affairs of life, where they have different or opposite shares allotted them by Providence, they ought not to go out of their own sphere, or invade the men's province, any more than the men theirs . . . But in common intercourse and conversation, why are we to be perpetually considering the *Sex* of the person we are talking to? Why must women always be addressed in an appropriated language; and not treated on the common footing of reasonable creatures? And why must they, from a false notion of modesty, be afraid of shewing themselves to *be such*, and affect a childish ignorance? (iii. 243)

The speaker goes on to argue for permitting women to have knowledge 'compatible with their duties' to make them 'fit companions for men of sense'. She points out that if men made proper use of the educational advantages which they actually have, they would inevitably be superior. 'But then don't let them despise us for this, as if their superiority were entirely founded on a natural difference of capacity!' She asserts that women do not have opportunities for knowing science and polite literature because of their situation in life; there are many men in various professions (merchants, army, and navy officers) who suffer from the same disability. Furthermore, it is a waste of opportunity not to include women in conversation on any but very common subjects; if they were included, women might learn from such conversations. (This argument in particular is similar to Feijóo's.) In a straightforward way Elizabeth Carter was recommending that women be allowed a larger share in education and in ordinary social relations to improve their development. The bluestockings were especially interested in literature, and at various times their feminist consciousness made them female advocates for women writers, especially those who were respectable and had financial difficulties. Catherine Talbot wrote to Mrs Montagu to recommend *The Death of Abel*, a translation of Salomon Gessner's *Tod Abels*, by Mary Collyer (1716/?17–1763). Mrs Montagu responded that she knew that Mrs Collyer, 'a very good woman' with seven children, was working to support her family; Mrs Montagu planned to read the work and recommend it if possible (MO 3068, [19 Dec. 1761]). In fact, the translation was very popular and was reprinted many times after Mrs Collyer's death (Fullard and Jarvis).

Another woman writer whose problems aroused sympathy was Charlotte Turner Smith (1749–1806). Elizabeth Carter hoped that Smith's novel *Emmeline: The Orphan of the Castle* would be successful, to compensate her financially for having had to 'purchase her freedom from a vile husband, by giving up part of the little fortune she had left; so that she has at present little more than a hundred a year to support herself and six or seven children' (30 June 1788, *Letters* (1817), iii. 295). Mrs Montagu had been concerned about the difficulties of Sarah Fielding earlier; later she and Hannah More were prompted by their concern for Ann Yearsley's difficulties to help her, not with the hoped-for results (see Chapter 10).

Elizabeth Carter took a positive attitude towards women writers on principle. Montagu Pennington explained that because she thought 'men exercised too arbitrary a power over them [women], and considered them as too inferior to themselves', she had 'a decided bias in favour of female writers, and always read their works with a mind prepared to be pleased, if the principles contained in them were good, and the personal characters of the authors amiable' (*Memoirs*, i. 447–8).

The different strands of female advocacy, wider social opportunities, and female aspirations to a life of the mind came together in the late 1750s. Elizabeth Carter's translation of *Epictetus* was published. That publication inspired Elizabeth Montagu to seek out Elizabeth Carter and to form the friendship which was to lead to further publication. With the encouragement of male and female mentors and friends, the women later to be called bluestockings became essentially, if with much trepidation, women of letters. The shifting uses of the term 'bluestocking'—from reference to intellectual men to the needs of women for some intellectual life, and finally to women themselves who had intellectual interests and wrote and published—took place in the period from 1756 to 1775 and paralleled the emerging reputations of the first generation of bluestocking women writers.

# PART III

# The First Bluestockings as Women Writers
## (1758–1775)

# Introduction

FEMINIST analysis has shown us that the educational deprivation of women and the persistent denigration of their abilities under patriarchy has had a pervasive inhibiting influence on women with intellectual interests. Gerda Lerner has argued that women have been kept from creative thinking by the lack of education, the lack of contact with a group of educated people, and by the lack of private time (223). In *The Madwoman in the Attic: The Woman Writer and the Nineteenth-Century Literary Imagination*, Sandra M. Gilbert and Susan Gubar show that patriarchal culture of the western world sees literary creation as a male enterprise in which the 'text's author is a father, a progenitor, a procreator, an aesthetic patriarch whose pen is an instrument of generative power like his penis' (6). Hester Mulso's remarks calling her poems 'her half-starv'd brats' show her attempting to counter in a small way the overbearing masculinization of creative work. Thus, for women who wished to study and to write, there has always been an uncomfortable sense of going against the grain of their societies' attitudes, and of lacking a supportive structure which would give them authority to write.

As Gilbert and Gubar point out, the woman writer often begins her effort to become a creative person by seeking 'a *female* precursor who, far from representing a threatening force to be denied or killed, proves by example that a revolt against patriarchal literary authority is possible' (49). Thus, the first bluestockings, as they reached out in the direction of literary work, noticed and responded to a variety of women writers who had gone before them. To a certain extent these women became 'role-models'.

Probably the most important role-model for Elizabeth Carter and Catherine Talbot was Elizabeth Singer Rowe, about whom Carter had written in her youth, and whose manuscripts Talbot read when she visited the Duchess of Somerset. In her unpublished Clark Library lecture, 'Augustan *Women?*': Four Poets of the Eighteenth Century', Margaret Anne Doody shows that Mrs Rowe was able to find support for *her* work by her strong religious feelings. She was a mystic, and, as Doody points out, 'In choosing to be a religious poet, Mrs Rowe was able to find a medium in which private experience could be taken as universal and thus public' (23).[1] Catherine Talbot and Elizabeth Carter both tried to follow in Rowe's footsteps. But Mrs Rowe was probably too intense and other-worldly a religious poet to be entirely suitable for them. Both women were actually more interested in the personal pleasures and difficulties of everyday life than Mrs Rowe, so that Mrs Rowe's model as a religious poet could be only partly appropriate.

There were other women writers who provided partial models. The bluestockings read with pleasure the letters of Mme Marie de Rabutin-Chantal, Marquise de Sévigné (1626–96) in French. Thirty-one letters had been published in 1725 and much-enlarged editions in 1735–54. The bluestockings welcomed the appearance of new letters and anecdotes about Mme de Sévigné and her family. Here again the influence was partial. They enjoyed her wit and expressiveness, and considered her a model for their letters, but they were embarrassed by her emotionalism. None of the bluestockings approached Mme de Sévigné in controlled lightness of style and wit, although Catherine Talbot has some passages which are vivid and anecdotal. Elizabeth Carter used a prose of simple directness, which made it possible for her to reveal herself, but still remain in control. Elizabeth Montagu, who was influenced by Mme de Sévigné as a reader, was less affected by her writing. Mrs Montagu's own letters tend to become weighted down by sententiousness, but she occasionally produces vivid anecdotes. Certainly, Mme de Sévigné stimulated the bluestockings to write to each other in an intimate way, with regard to the particular person addressed.[2]

The first bluestockings were handicapped by the fact that some women writers who might have been role-models were not acceptable to them. In fact, Lady Mary Wortley Montagu might be considered an 'anti-model'. Writing to her sister on 27 August 1762 Elizabeth Montagu said, 'The papers would tell you the famed Lady Mary is dead; one use the world may make of her life, it fully exhibits that parts, riches, birth, and beauty, all combined, cannot rescue a character from contempt unless virtue and reason direct the use of them' (MO 5793). Some years later Elizabeth Carter wrote to Elizabeth Montagu, 'I lately met with Lady M. W. Montagu's Letters, they have certainly wit, knowledge, and observation; but there is such a defect of delicacy and of sentiment, that one could never wish such a writer either for a companion or for a friend' (Deal, 28 Oct. 1775).

The first bluestockings were naturally anxious about their own reception in a man's world. In his recent study of Hester Thrale Piozzi, William McCarthy found that Mrs Piozzi, who is actually of the second generation of bluestockings, suffered from an 'anxiety of competence' as a woman writer—an anxiety with which all women writers struggled, and which involved an awareness that male critics took a negative view of female abilities (54–5). There is certainly an underlying anxiety present in the first bluestocking writers, and a sense that they are intruding on male preserves. But their concern about their competence would not be unreasonable, given the generally unsystematic nature of their education; and fear of male animosity would also not be unrealistic, since they could perceive it all around them.

Their ambivalent attitudes towards writing for a livelihood also had a dampening effect. Although they were sympathetic to women writing to support themselves and their families, the first bluestockings preferred not to regard their own work as having been done for money. Montagu, Carter, and Chapone were all reluctant to seem to be writing for financial gain. When Mrs Montagu was told that rumour had it that the profits from her *Essay on Shakespear* had gone for charitable purposes, she replied that she could hardly expect to gain enough from the product of her brain to provide for her charities (MO 3312). Women who relied on the profit from their work were regarded as needy and dependent. The blue-stockings wished to feel that they were pursuing their intel-lectual interests because such activity gave them pleasure, self-respect, and a way of influencing others for good.

Thus, the creative powers of the bluestockings were dimin-ished not only by their realistic fears of the masculine world of letters but also by their own inner ambivalence. It is clear from their comments that they had all internalized society's injunctions against learned ladies, and in favour of modesty and self-abnegation; yet their own interests and ambitions, the example of other women writers, and the encouragement of their mentors and friends, pushed them against these admonitions. The outcome was intellectual work characterized by diffidence and uncertainty.

Given these pressures, we can be surprised that they wrote at all. But in the privacy of their closets, between domestic duties and social engagements, they read, considered, put pen to paper. For they were not really alone: they had a sense that their friends were interested in their work and supported it. In some cases flattery diligently applied helped ease the fear of self-exposure; in others straightforward demands were made on the writer's abilities. In the following four chapters, I will show how these women of some talent and ambition were impeded by their own inner conflicts, and how friendship helped them to do serious work.

# 6 · Elizabeth Carter: Essayist, Translator, Poet

AT a crucial time in her life, Elizabeth Carter met Samuel
Johnson, who seems to have provided her with an example of a
scholar and writer who lived and worked in close touch with the
real world but also with deep concern for ethical and religious
standards. Although Samuel Johnson is not usually considered
Elizabeth Carter's mentor, for there is insufficient documentary evidence to build a day-to-day picture of their contacts with
one another, he was clearly a writer whom Elizabeth Carter
admired deeply, and whom she always defended from criticism.
They had admired each other's learning from the old days on
the *Gentleman's Magazine*, when, as we have seen, they praised
each other in print (Chapter 2). They were colleagues. Johnson
gave advice about projects, and may have helped to correct the
press of her translation of Algarotti (BL Add. 4254, fos. 19–68;
Carter, *Memoirs*, i. 47 n.).

In the first few months after Miss Carter's return to Deal she
sent her compliments to Johnson in her letters to Cave. How
the friendship was kept up from that point on we do not know,
for the only letter we have from Samuel Johnson to Elizabeth
Carter dates from 14 January 1756, when he wrote to ask her
help with Anna Williams's benefit. The letter suggests that,
although they did not keep in close touch, he would know when
she was in London, for he explained that he had forgotten to
ask her help earlier because she had not been in town. His
feelings were tender. Edward Cave had died recently, and
Johnson wrote, 'Poor dear Cave I owed him much, for to him
I owe that I have known you', and he concluded with 'respect
which I neither owe nor pay to any other' (*Letters*, i. 84–5).

In the years preceding this letter, there must have been
contacts between Samuel Johnson and Elizabeth Carter when
she happened to be in London. While the *Rambler* was appearing in 1750 and 1751, Catherine Talbot and Elizabeth Carter
took a close interest in it. The women exchanged pieces which
they had written, and discussed the suitability of their work for

the *Rambler*. Evidently Miss Carter must have been seeing Johnson during this time, because Catherine Talbot suggested that Elizabeth was just the tactful person to tell Johnson that some of the words he used were too difficult. In any case, Carter's and Talbot's essays were among the very few pieces of writing not by himself which Johnson printed in the *Rambler*. Of particular interest is Carter's essay on religion versus superstition (No. 44) which states her personal philosophy that society should be considered as a training-ground for the discipline of the heart. Johnson also printed her satire of city life as No. 100, Talbot's essay on Sunday observances as No. 30, and some letters of Hester Mulso purporting to be from the fashionable world as No. 10. Richardson had felt that the modesty of women would prevent their appearing in the 'Commonwealth of Letters' (*Selected Letters*, 234). Johnson's attitude was more welcoming. He was willing to help a number of women who were seriously interested in literary work and has been considered a 'patron' of women (Gae Annette Brack; Gae Annette Holladay and O. M. Brack, jun.).

Boswell, relying on the comments of Francis Barber, Johnson's servant, listed Elizabeth Carter as one of the friends who visited Johnson after the death of his wife on 17 March 1752 (*Life* (1934), i. 241–2). Catherine Talbot wrote to Elizabeth Carter about his sorrow, 'he is in great affliction I hear, poor man, for the loss of his wife' (Carter, *Letters* (1808), i. 297, 22 Apr. 1752). But Elizabeth was in Deal during that period and did not come to London until February 1753. The letter in 1756 may hark back to some consolation offered by letter and afterwards in person during the days of his sorrow. In any case, Johnson's tender, respectful stance towards Elizabeth Carter seems to have continued unchanged throughout his lifetime. His remark that 'his old friend, Mrs Carter . . . could make a pudding, as well as translate Epictetus from the Greek, and work a handkerchief as well as compose a poem' (Hill, *Johnsonian Miscellanies*, ii. 11) shows Johnson's adherence to the recommended model of the literary woman who maintains her domestic skills. However, since Carter accepted this point of view (although she did describe her efforts at cake-making and sewing shirts with some wry humour) and did not seem to have found slights in Johnson's attitudes towards women in general, her allegiance to him continued throughout his life. His admiration of her must have given her some pleasure, and some reinforcement of her dedication to the world of learning.

When Johnson stopped issuing the *Rambler* papers, Elizabeth Carter felt very angry at the 'world', especially at great and powerful people, who would not applaud and support 'a genius who contributes all in his power to make them the rulers of reasonable creatures' (Carter, *Letters* (1808), i. 296). Later on she defended him from the attacks of her friends. She urged that his personal eccentricities were unimportant, and stressed his extensive learning, strength of character, and moral integrity. She admired his powers both as a critical thinker and an argumentative writer: 'I have lately been reading his notes on Shakespear. I will not undertake his defence as a commentator; but the work is valuable for many strokes of his own great, and refined, and delicate way of thinking.' Elizabeth Carter went on to remark that Johnson had treated Bishop Warburton's work on Shakespeare more severely than other critics had:

Some of them have scratched his face with their nails, and others have pelted him with stones and brickbats, till he was black and blue; but the pen of Dr. Johnson, like the ethereal stroke of lightening, without any external mark of violence, has penetrated to his vitals. (Deal, 30 Nov. 1770, *Letters* (1817), ii. 94)

ALTHOUGH Johnson was in a financially difficult situation during the 1750s, he subscribed to the work by which Elizabeth Carter achieved reputation, some financial stability, and status. This work, a translation from the Greek of *All the Works* of Epictetus, a Stoic philosopher of the first century AD, was begun in 1749 as a private act of friendship, and converted by the assistance and encouragement of her friends into a successful publishing venture. Epictetus was one of the Roman Stoics whom the *philosophes* of the Enlightenment admired. Peter Gay wrote that 'Epictetus touched minds as different as Frederick the Great, Immanuel Kant, and Jeremy Bentham' (120).

As we have seen, Catherine Talbot was the pupil and friend of bishops. The Bishop of Oxford usually participated in family readings with Mrs Secker, Catherine, and her mother. A frequent visitor was Martin Benson, Bishop of Gloucester, who was Mrs Secker's brother. Although the men had classical educations and knew many languages, the women did not. Catherine knew French but the older women probably did not. Catherine explained to Elizabeth that their family readings had to be done in English. On 29 July 1745 Catherine reported that they were reading translations of Greek authors. 'For our family book we are reading Dion Cassius translated from Xiphilin; it is surely a great pity we have no better translations of most of the Greek historians' (Carter, *Letters* (1808), i. 67). She added that they had recently read a translation of Arrian's life of Alexander, 'which was full of faults, and yet with all that disadvantage an admirable book, but few clever people will deign to employ themselves in making translations' (Carter, *Letters* (1808), i. 68). In 1747 she was reading Pliny's *Letters* in translation, and complimenting the public spirit of good translators. It was at this time that she made the observation that the 'common herd of translators are mere murderers' (Carter, *Letters* (1808), i. 126). She seems to have been working up to asking Elizabeth to translate a classical text.

As we have seen, the growth of greater intimacy in the friendship of Elizabeth and Catherine came in the spring of 1748, when Elizabeth stayed in London for a long visit with her friend. Catherine Secker died during this time. Elizabeth Carter tried to help her friend deal with her grief in person through the spring, and later by letter. Between November 1748 and April 1749 they were both in London again and some time before Elizabeth Carter went home she had promised to translate Epictetus for her friend.

Although Elizabeth Carter believed deeply that only Christianity offered true solace from life's unhappy events, she also believed that stoicism, though a pagan philosophy, helped people learn how to discipline themselves. Her willingness to translate Epictetus must have arisen from her feeling that she would be undertaking a task that would help her friend gain mental fortitude. On the other hand, Catherine, while appreciating the benefit the work might have for her, felt strongly that Elizabeth was wasting her life in the obscurity of Deal, and probably wished to encourage her to begin on a challenging project.

Young men were still being taught Latin and Greek in the universities. But many graduates did not retain their facility in using these languages, and translations of Greek and Latin works were much in demand by men and also by women interested in the classics. The teachings of Epictetus had been preserved by Arrian, his pupil, in two works: the *Discourses*, of which four books are extant, and the *Enchiridion* or *Manual*, a condensed aphoristic version of the main doctrines (*Micropaedia, Ency. Brit.*). As it happened, there was no translation in English of the complete works of Epictetus, although there were Latin and French translations, and there were English translations of the *Enchiridion*. Elizabeth Carter translated *All the Works*, consisting of the four books of *Discourses*, the *Enchiridion*, and *Fragments*. She worked with texts borrowed from Secker and James 'Hermes' Harris, a well-known classical scholar, who also helped her with scholarly queries about the text.

Thomas Secker certainly functioned as Elizabeth Carter's mentor, especially at the beginning of the project. Although John W. Draper, in his 'Theory of Translation in the Eighteenth Century', claimed that eighteenth-century translators in general were not concerned with accuracy, and adapted their texts to suit eighteenth-century tastes and attitudes, in this case both the translator and her mentor took the problems of translation seriously, debating in the course of her work how she could retain accuracy and yet transform the text into readable English. When Elizabeth Carter began her translation, she sent Secker a few samples of her work. Catherine Talbot replied:

The Bishop of Oxford says your translation is a very good one; and, if it has any fault, it is only that of being not close enough, and writ in too smooth and too ornamented a style. Epictetus was a plain man, and spoke plainly; a translation that should express this would, he thinks, preserve more the spirit of the original, and give an exacter notion of it. (Carter, *Memoirs*, i. 163-4)

Catherine Talbot then enclosed a few examples of a hasty translation which Secker had made, with the message that the Bishop had nothing more to say, 'except that he much hopes you go on in a work you are so well fitted for, and for which I hope to be much the wiser.'

But these criticisms discouraged Elizabeth Carter and for a while she did not continue working on the translation. She could not find a level of style she felt happy with, and thought the translation should have more 'ornaments'. But Talbot relayed the message that while the Bishop would be happy to hear her arguments, 'unless you can prove to him that Epictetus wore a laced coat, he will not allow you to dress him in one.' Then the Bishop added in his own handwriting: 'Let me speak a word for myself: why would you change a plain, home, awakening preacher into a fine, smooth, polite writer, of what nobody will mind? Answer me that, dear Miss Carter' (Carter, *Memoirs*, i. 165).

Elizabeth Carter continued to question how to maintain the sense of the author while presenting him in an easy and natural style. Secker replied with a general statement on translation:

Arrian is not a commentator on Epictetus, as Simplicius is; but professes to exhibit his very conversations and discourses, as Xenophon doth those of Socrates: and a translator should represent him in our tongue, such as he appears in his own: not indeed copying the peculiarities of the language he speaks in, but still preserving his genuine air and character, as far as ever is consistent with making him rightly understood. (Carter, *Memoirs*, i. 166-7)

He agreed that what was obscure should be cleared up, and what was unsuitable might be softened. 'But with proper exceptions of this kind, every ancient writer should, in common justice, be laid before the modern reader, if at all, such as he is.' Secker pointed out that Epictetus disapproved of the formal and professional style of philosophers of his own time. Therefore, it was important not to smooth his work:

And I am fully persuaded, that plain and home exhortations and reproofs, without studied periods and regular connections, in short, such as they might be supposed to come extempore from the fulness of the old man's good heart, will be more attended to and felt, and consequently give more pleasure, as well as do more good, than any thing sprucer that can be substituted in their room. I do not mean by all this to vindicate my own specimens. I confess myself to have bent the stick as strongly as I well could, the opposite way to yours. But I am content to divide the difference with you; which, perhaps, after we have both explained ourselves, will be no great one. Yet indeed, of the two, I think a rough and almost literal translation, if it doth but relish strongly of that warm and practical spirit, which to me is the characteristick of this book, infinitely preferable to the most elegant paraphrase, that lets it evaporate, and leaves the reader unmoved. (Carter, *Memoirs*, i. 168–9).

As Elizabeth proceeded with the translation, she sent portions up to London; both Catherine and her mother were enjoying the work, and Catherine wrote that 'we' copy them into a little book (Carter, *Letters* (1808), i. 209). Although Catherine was sharing the work with her mother, it is not clear who was doing the copying. Elizabeth was encouraged by Catherine's enthusiastic response. Catherine wrote:

What force, what life, what strength, and shortness of expression! What excellence of sentiment! What dignity and authority of reason, and common sense! And what an excellent reproof and lesson has the honest, plain old man given me, (thank you a thousand times for transmitting it.) Whenever I am seized with an impertinent, untimely fit of reformation, or with a splenetic dissatisfaction either with the company or tedious lowliness, methinks I hear his voice sounding in my ears—'But you are wretched and discontented; be pleased, and make the best of every thing. Call society an entertainment and a festival.' (Carter, *Memoirs*, i. 171–2)

At this point the Bishop said he had given Elizabeth all the advice he wished to, and left her to work on her own.

Elizabeth Carter carried on her translation during the next few years. She was living in Deal, and educating Henry in the classics for entry into university. In the spring of 1753 when she came to London, she stayed in lodgings near St Paul's, where the Talbots were now living, for Secker, while still Bishop of Oxford, was now also Dean of St Paul's. Elizabeth spent much time with Catherine and Mrs Talbot; it was during this period that publication of her translation of Epictetus was proposed.

Catherine Talbot had been aware of her friend's insecure financial status for some time. It was probably for this reason that she had earlier been urging Elizabeth to marry. But as Elizabeth refused to marry, and refused to consider taking a position as governess to a member of the Royal family, an arrangement which had once been held out to her as a possibility, and which was again coming up for discussion, Catherine was afraid Elizabeth's future was very precarious. Elizabeth could always have a home with her father while he was alive; after his death her situation would be difficult. A couple of years earlier Catherine had noted in her journal the difficulties of another woman of letters of an earlier generation, Catherine Trotter Cockburn (1679–1749). Mrs Cockburn had been a prodigy, writing poetry, plays, and philosophical tracts as a young woman. After her marriage she had given up literature for the tasks of raising her family. Her husband, a clergyman, was not well off, and at times their circumstances were very difficult. In later life she returned to intellectual activities, and a collected edition of her works was being planned for her benefit when she died in 1749. This edition, with a life by Thomas Birch, was published in two volumes in 1751. Among the subscribers to this edition were Ralph Allen of Bath, the Earl of Bath, the Archbishop of Canterbury, Miss Carter of Deal, Edward Cave, the Bishop of Durham, Marchioness Grey, the Bishop of Colchester, various members of colleges at Cambridge, Revd Dr Lynch, Dean of Canterbury, the Bishop of Oxford, the Duchess of Portland, Mrs Talbot, Miss Talbot, Philip Yorke, and Charles Yorke.

On 13 May 1751 Catherine noted that she had been dipping into books while in a dull and listless state. She must have been looking into her edition of Mrs Cockburn's works, for she noted that Mrs Cockburn's writings had amused her and that she thought her a very good woman:

She was a remarkable Genius, & Yet how Obscure her Lot in Life! It seems grievous at first, & such Straitness of Circumstances as perplexes & Cramps the Mind, is surely a Grievance, but on consideration what Signifies Distinction & Splendour in this very Transitory State? Hereafter Every Good Heart Shall be Distinguished in Honour & Happiness. But methinks those who knew Such Merit did not do their Duty in letting it remain so Obscure. E: C: is her Superiour—Alas will not she live & die perhaps as Obscurely, & What Alas can I do to prevent it? (BL Add. 46690, fo. 7$^{r-v}$)

What she did to prevent Elizabeth Carter's obscure fate was to set in motion the project to publish *All the Works* of Epictetus by subscription.

Subscription publishing was a popular form of publication at that time. The author wrote up and printed proposals; the proposals were circulated to friends, neighbours, and assorted prominent people with whom the author or his or her friends might have contact. When a reasonable number of subscribers had been signed up, with payment of part or all of the cost, the work could go to press.

On 11 January 1755 Elizabeth Carter reported that she had at last got through Epictetus, 'though not so free of blots and interlineations as I could have wished' (Carter, *Letters* (1808), i. 375). Now she needed to prepare a short account of the stoical philosophy which was to precede the translation. Catherine Talbot had also asked for a life of Epictetus. In her reply (Deal, 5 Mar. 1755) Elizabeth Carter remarked that 'whoever that somebody or other is who is to write the Life of Epictetus, seeing I have a dozen shirts to make, I do opine, dear Miss Talbot, it cannot be I' (Carter, *Letters* (1808), i. 382). But in fact she gathered together what materials she could and wrote it.

Preparation of the translation for publication did bring the friends into an intellectual dispute regarding what sort of notes and comments were to be included. As devout Christians, both Catherine Talbot and Elizabeth Carter were conscious of what they regarded as the limits of the pagan philosophy of Epictetus, which counselled emotional self-discipline and self-restraint, but of course did not provide Christian reliance based on the promise of a spiritual reward in the hereafter. Catherine pressed Elizabeth to disarm the possible pagan influences of Epictetus with notes on the superiority of the Christian religion. Elizabeth responded rather tartly that she did not think such a defence was necessary. However, Elizabeth was also corresponding with the Bishop about certain points in her translation (he had taken a month of his stay in the country while immobilized with gout to read it) and he too felt that the edition should be guarded with the 'proper notes and animadversions' that Catherine was asking for. Catherine felt that many might study Epictetus who would not look into the Bible, and, therefore, those readers should be directed to the Christian principles which were superior to stoicism, because they offered redemption (Carter, *Memoirs*, i. 195).

To Catherine Talbot's arguments for notes Elizabeth Carter replied that it had never occurred to her that so strict an author would be studied by 'bad people'. One of the things Catherine Talbot worried about was that Epictetus seemed to find suicide acceptable. Elizabeth Carter was not certain that he had actually argued that suicide was allowable; if he had argued that way, she agreed that she found that view difficult to understand. But she could not agree with her friend that Epictetus had read, but not believed, the New Testament:

> Though there is the utmost reason to think that Epictetus, as well as other philosophers since our Saviour, owed much more than they might be sensible of to the Gospel, I find a difficulty in persuading myself that he had ever seen the New Testament, or received any right amount of the Christian doctrine. The great number of Christians dispersed about the Roman empire might probably have rendered the New Testament phrases a kind of popular language; and a general illumination was diffused by the Gospel, by which many understandings might be enlightened which were ignorant of the source from whence it proceeded. (Carter, *Memoirs*, i. 201)

Miss Talbot reported that the Bishop thought this argument had much merit.

Elizabeth Carter respected the stoics because they believed in a supreme God and in a particular Providence, rejecting the idea of chance. She agreed that stoicism was inferior to Christianity because the stoics did not believe in personal existence in the hereafter, nor in rewards and punishments. They thought too highly of human nature, not perceiving the imperfect nature of man. Elizabeth Carter therefore acceded to the necessity for the notes which Catherine Talbot advocated. 'I am extremely obliged to the Bishop of Oxford and you for the admirable remarks you have been so good as to send me, and which, if the book is ever published, will make the most valuable part of it' (Carter, *Memoirs*, i. 202–3).

By May 1756 Elizabeth Carter was finishing the edition. She had transcribed Catherine Talbot's notes, except for one. She thought Catherine Talbot was too severe upon the 'poor heathen': Elizabeth Carter did not think it useful or appropriate to 'depreciate the heathen morality'. She believed that

> wise and good men in all ages, who sincerely applied their hearts to the discovery of their duty, cannot, I think be supposed in any very material instances to have failed, though they had neither a proper authority, nor could promise sufficient encouragements to qualify them for effectual instructors of the multitude of mankind. (Carter, *Letters* (1808), i. 400)

She believed that the case for Christianity could rest on its own advantages, without denigrating heathen morality.

When it appeared, therefore, the edition did have some of her friends' cautions which she originally argued against. She did provide an introduction which pointed out the shortcomings in the philosophy of Epictetus and other stoic philosophers compared to the superior truth and wisdom of Christianity. But she also defended Epictetus' work and viewpoint stoutly; that philosophy was very useful in the heathen world.

Their Doctrine of Evidence and fixed Principles, was an excellent Preservative from the Mischiefs, that might have arisen from the Scepticism of the Academics and Pyrrhonists, if unopposed: and their zealous Defence of a Particular Providence, a valuable Antidote to the atheistical Scheme of Epicurus.

The virtuous lives of some stoics helped to preserve their society from being absolutely dissolute, and strengthened the individuals who were subjects of arbitrary government (Epictetus, pp. xxv–xxvi). Despite her strong religious commitments, Elizabeth Carter's studies had taught her to look at cultures other than her own in a dispassionate way, and she managed to give an even-handed treatment of the value of Stoicism in the ancient world and its value in the present:

Even now, their Compositions may be read with great Advantage, as containing excellent Rules of Self-government, and of social Behaviour; of a noble Reliance on the Aid and Protection of Heaven, and of a perfect Resignation and Submission to the divine Will: Points, which are treated with great Clearness, and with admirable Spirit, in the Lessons of the Stoics; and though their Directions are seldom practicable on their Principles, in trying Cases, may be rendered highly useful in Subordination to Christian Reflexions. (Epictetus, p. xxvi)

As she finished her task, Elizabeth Carter expressed both awareness of the diversity of her duties, and relief at a new accession of freedom.

As soon as I have dispatched Epictetus to St. Paul's, Harry to the University, and finished my fifteen shirts, I comfort myself with the hopes of being at liberty to grow most delectably idle, to read what books I please, and run wild over hill and dale for the rest of the summer. (Carter, *Letters* (1808), i. 399)

For the next couple of years Elizabeth Carter was in London during the winter months while subscriptions were being solicited for the work. Although Elizabeth herself was very diffident about soliciting friends for subscriptions, they were evidently not deterred by such inhibitions. The Bishop of Oxford, the Bishop of Norwich, Sir George Oxenden, and other local dignitaries were all active on her behalf. Her father also pressed her, anxious that her name should be known as the translator, and urging her to think of the money: 'It is just that you should have some profit for your labor' (Carter, *Memoirs*, i. 209).

In the end Carter counted 1,031 subscriptions (*Memoirs*, i. 208). The subscription list reflected a variety of supporters; the presence of nobility and a large number of bishops suggest the influence of the Bishop of Oxford. But there were also men and women who were simply relatives or friends of Carter in London and Kent. The list was headed by the Prince of Wales and the Princess Dowager of Wales, and included the Earl of Bath, Mrs Boscawen, Revd Mr Berkeley (presumably George), Mrs Berkeley (presumably his mother, Anne), Revd Dr Birch, FRS, the Bishops of Carlisle, Chester, Chichester, and Clogher, the Archbishop of Canterbury, James Carter of Devonshire Street, Revd Dr Dalton, Revd Dr Delany, Mrs Delany, Mrs Donnellan, Marchioness Grey, Samuel Johnson, MA, Lord Lyttelton, Revd Dr Lynch, Dean of Canterbury, his wife and daughters, Revd W. Mason, Mrs Mary Masters of Norwich, George Montagu, Mrs Montagu (presumably Elizabeth), Miss Mulso, Sir George Oxenden, the Bishop of Oxford, the Duchess of Portland, Mr Theophilus Rowe, Miss Sawbridge and Miss Catherine Sawbridge of Olontigh, Kent, Mrs Talbot and Miss Talbot at the Deanery of St Paul's, Mrs Underdown of Deal, Kent, Mr James Vere of Bishopsgate Street, Merchant, the Archbishop of York, and Revd Dr Young, Rector of Welwyn. Several subscribers subscribed for more than one copy. The Bishop of Oxford subscribed for twelve copies; the Revd Dr Barnard, Master of Eton, for seven. There were also subscriptions from various Cambridge college libraries, as well as the libraries of St John's College, Oxford, and Eton College.

The venture turned out to be a profitable one. According to

Elizabeth Carter's nephew, Montagu Pennington, printing was begun in June 1757 and completed by April 1758. The first edition, printed by Samuel Richardson, was a one-volume quarto of 505 pages with 34 pages of preliminary matter. A total of 1,018 copies was printed, but as these were insufficient for the subscription, 250 more were printed in July. The cost of the subscription was one guinea, with one-half to be paid before, one-half after publication. Expenses for printing were £67. 7s. for the first 1,018 copies. Evidently the subscribers for multiple copies did not claim all their copies. Pennington believed that Elizabeth Carter made almost £1,000 from the translation (Carter, *Memoirs*, i. 207–8). The translation sold well, and kept up its price. Several years later Secker (by then Archbishop of Canterbury) complained jokingly that a bookseller's catalogue was listing his sermons at half-price, but that Epictetus was still being priced high at 18 shillings (Carter, *Memoirs*, i. 208).

A twentieth-century translator and bibliographer of Epictetus, W. A. Oldfather, in 1927 called Elizabeth Carter's translation 'a very respectable performance under any conditions, but for her sex and period truly remarkable' (Oldfather, 15). For her contemporary readers and reviewers Elizabeth Carter's sex had also been important. Pennington claimed that some people could not believe she had done the work; they attributed it to her father or the Bishop (Carter, *Memoirs*, i. 212). But the reviewers took a more enlightened attitude. The *Critical Review* of August 1758 remarked that

whilst the ladies and lady-like gentlemen of this age employ their leisure hours in the reading of plays and romances, and three parts of the fashionable world confine all their knowledge within the narrow limits of a Circulating Library, it is not a little extraordinary to find a woman mistress of the Greek language, sounding the depth of antient philosophy, and capable of giving a faithful and elegant translation of one of the most difficult authors of antiquity. (149)

And the critic in the *Monthly Review* (June 1758) found the publication a sign that if women had

the benefit of liberal instructions, if they were inured to study, and accustomed to learned conversation—in short, if they had the same opportunity of improvement with the men, there can be no doubt that they would be equally capable of reaching any intellectual attainment. (588)

Comparisons were made with the seventeenth-century French woman scholar, Anne Dacier. Elizabeth was called the 'English Dacier' but in fact Elizabeth Carter's career was spasmodic and unproductive compared with the determined and consistent output of the Frenchwoman, who had worked alongside a scholarly husband (Farnham).

The publication of Epictetus made it possible for Elizabeth Carter to buy a house in Deal with a view of the sea. (The house had originally been two houses; Elizabeth and her father lived in separate quarters and met for meals.) Her financial independence was a modest one. A few years later, Lord Bath inquired of Mrs Montagu, by then a close friend of Elizabeth Carter, whether she thought Elizabeth might be interested in becoming a companion-governess to Sir Robert Rich's granddaughter. Mrs Montagu replied that her friend had already turned down a similar offer 'from a Lady of the highest rank'. At that time Elizabeth had gently complained that her friends' esteem for her was prompting them to apply for a situation for her which 'no superiority of rank or fortune could justify'. She never complained of her circumstances, and thought it wrong of her friends 'to suppose she would enter into a state of dependency to mend them' (MO 4610, 11 Dec. 1763). In regarding Court life as involving much too great a degree of dependency, Carter was a clearer thinker than Fanny Burney, who accepted a dependent Court position a generation later. But Elizabeth Carter's father left her to her own judgement, while Burney's father urged her on.

This letter of Mrs Montagu to Lord Bath about a possible position for Carter gives us the clearest statement we have of Carter's financial situation. Mrs Montagu pointed out to Lord Bath that Revd Carter had 'decent' preferment, her brother had an estate of £500 a year, had married well, and was heir to his uncle, the merchant. Mrs Montagu explained that her friend 'has £800 of her own [presumably what was left of her earnings after she bought her house], & her uncle has, I believe, kind intentions towards her.' But her present income was small, and actually

was only enough to maintain her in clothes. Later, her circumstances were improved by an inheritance of £1,300 from her
uncle (MO 1438), an annuity of £100 from Mrs Montagu
(Carter, *Letters* (1817), ii. 314–15), and an annuity of £100
settled on Carter by Mr and Mrs Pulteney, heirs of Lord Bath
after his brother, General Putney (Carter, *Letters* (1817), i.
360–6; Montagu, ed. Blunt, i. 164).

As her nephew said, Elizabeth Carter's translation from the
Greek, as the work of a woman, 'made a great noise all over
Europe' (Carter, *Memoirs*, i. 212). In addition to greater
financial resources, which enabled Elizabeth Carter to improve
her living conditions and introduce some variety into her life,
the publication of Epictetus brought her the friendship of Elizabeth Montagu. Mrs Montagu seems to have been taken by
the composure and quiet dignity of this classically educated
woman. Mrs Montagu worked, as she well knew how to do, to
develop an intimate friendship with Elizabeth Carter. Her
strong influence brought Carter out into a social life among
people of literary interests and wealth. Lord Bath's letters to
Mrs Montagu show his interest in and concern for Elizabeth
Carter. It was he who insisted on the publication of her poems,
and supported the work.

This slim volume of *Poems on Several Occasions* (1762) was
Elizabeth Carter's last publication in her lifetime. After the first
flush of poetic effort in her youth, Carter seems to have found it
harder to write poetry. She had written poems to her women
friends of the 1740s somewhat in the style of another woman
poet, Katherine Philips. In 'To Miss Lynch: Occasioned by an
Ode Written by Mrs. Philips', Elizabeth Carter paid tribute to
Mrs Philips's writings on friendship:

> Sweet may her Fame to late Remembrance bloom,
> And everlasting Laurels shade her Tomb,
> Whose spotless Verse with genuine Force exprest
> The brightest Passion of the human Breast.
>
> (1762 edn., 16)

But while Philips had stressed her emotional ties to her friends,
Carter addressed her friends in moral terms, urging them to
detach themselves from the vanities of this world, and put their
minds on the life hereafter.

In addition to poems from the 1738 collection, and the poems to her women friends of Canterbury, Elizabeth Carter also included in the 1762 collection other poems which are characteristic of her interests. One was her 'Ode to Wisdom', a poem which Richardson had borrowed as a text for Clarissa to set to music, without knowing or consulting the author. (Carter's tart reproof is in *Original Letters of Miss E. Carter and Mr. Samuel Richardson*, 533–4.) Carter's tribute to mental beauty was considered as expressing her essential views. The poet finds Wisdom to be the gift of God:

> No more to fabled Names confin'd
> To Thee! Supreme, all-perfect Mind
> My Thoughts direct their Flight:
> *Wisdom's* thy Gift, and all her Force
> From Thee deriv'd, unchanging Source
> Of intellectual Light!
>
> (1762 edn., 89)

Another significant poem is that to her father, 'Thou by whose fondness and paternal care', in which she thanks him for encouraging her studies, and makes the point that he had left her free:

> Ne'er did thy Voice assume a Master's Pow'r,
>     Nor force Assent to what thy Precepts taught;
> But bid my independent Spirit soar,
>     In all the Freedom of unfetter'd Thought.
>
> (1762 edn., 63)

Elizabeth Carter had spent much of her life musing by the sea, and in two of her poems she uses the imagery of the sea to convey her feelings about human nature and about religious strivings. In 'Written Extempore on the Sea-Shore', she says:

> Thou restless fluctuating Deep,
>     Expressive of the human Mind
> In thy for ever varying form,
>     My own inconstant Self I find.
>
> How soft now flow thy peaceful Waves,
>     In just Gradations to the shore:
> While on thy Brow, unclouded shines
>     The Regent of the midnight Hour.

> Blest Emblem of that equal State,
>> Which I this Moment feel within:
> Where Thought to Thought succeeding rolls,
>> And all is placid and serene.

But the serenity of the ocean gives way to storms—those brought to the sea by Eurus, the god of the south-east wind, and to the breast of the poet by 'rising sorrows':

> Obscur'd thy *Cynthia's* Silver Ray
>> When Clouds opposing intervene:
> And ev'ry Joy that Friendship gives
>> Shall fade beneath the Gloom of Spleen.
>>>> (1762 edn., 38–9)

A poem to Miss Talbot also uses the imagery of the sea-shore:

> How sweet the Calm of this sequester'd Shore,
>> Where ebbing Waters musically roll:
> And Solitude, and silent Eve restore
>> The philosophic Temper of the soul.
>>>> (1762 edn., 70)

Here Carter anticipates the setting of Arnold's 'Dover Beach'. But in her poem the sunset and calm sea convey feelings of serenity which encourage the poet 'to chear the Soul with more than mortal Views'. She asks her friend to come and share with her the joys of anticipating heaven.

A poem addressed to her sister Margaret, 'Ah! why with restless, anxious search explore', deals with Margaret's anxious concern with death; the poet assures her that she must submit to God and let what must die, die.

Elizabeth Carter's view of friendship was that she and her friends were fellow-travellers on a journey through life, during which their most important mission was to follow virtue; for doing so, they would be rewarded in heaven. Above all she looked forward to a renewal of her friendships in the hereafter. She wrote several poems in which watches are emblems of fleeting time, as in 'To Miss Burton: On a Watch':

> While this gay Toy attracts thy Sight,
>> Thy Reason let it warn;

> And seize, my Dear, that rapid Time
> That never must return.

> (1762 edn., 56)

Several of Elizabeth Carter's poems are addressed to other close friends of the bluestocking circle. A poem to Mrs Montagu, 'Where are those Hours, on rosy Pinions borne', recalls the pleasure of past days of friendship; those days have been replaced by stormy ones. But the hours of friendship will live on in heaven. Her poem to the Earl of Bath reviews his days as a powerful statesman, but assures him that every stage of life has its task:

> With calm Severity, unpassion'd Age
> Detects the specious Fallacies of Youth:
> Reviews the Motives, which no more engage,
> And Weights each Action in the Scale of Truth.

> (1762 edn., 77)

After her death her nephew reprinted her poems from a manuscript corrected by the author; he presented them in chronological order with the names of the recipients of the poems, which had been left blank earlier, filled in.[1] Now published were a few poems Carter had left in manuscript, among them two poems from the 1740s in which she mourned the death of a male friend abroad, another to Miss Hill (1749) speaking of the collapse of all the poet's dreams, and poems written after 1762, mainly poems of friendship. Among these is a poem to Mrs Vesey (1766) in which Carter reassures her friend that life is eternal. Another poem to Mrs Montagu, 'No more my friend, pursue a distant theme', muses on Winchester Cathedral, which they visited together, and which becomes a symbol of the chaos of history:

> While pensive wandring o'er this equal scene,
> Where blended sleep the humble and the great,
> Let Wisdom whisper to our souls how vain
> The short distinctions of our mortal state.
> . . . . . . . .

> O blest with ev'ry talent, ev'ry grace,
> Which native fire, or happy art supplies,
> How short a period, how confin'd a space
> Must bound thy shining course below the skies!

For wider glories, for immortal fame,
  Were all those talents, all those graces giv'n:
And may thy life pursue that noblest aim,
  The final plaudit of approving heav'n.

(Carter, Memoirs, ii. 114–17)

Elizabeth Carter's poems are interesting as the work of a woman who wrote as a private person with deep religious feeling. Her moods and settings vary; she may speak of sadness at an oratorio, or serenity at the seaside. She wrote a few humorous poems. She tried a variety of metres and forms: four-stress lines, five-stress lines, couplets, and irregular odes. Her diction is sometimes imprecise; she uses the conventional phrases of eighteenth-century poetry without much care, and in some cases her sense of the sounds of her poems seems to be vague. But sometimes she expresses genuine personal feeling in vital language, and she conveys to her reader a sense of her joy and ease in friendship, her strong idealism, and her deep religious faith.

After the success of Epictetus, Elizabeth Carter established a pleasant kind of life within her financial constraints. In summer, autumn, and early winter she was usually in Deal, where she maintained those relationships with family members and neighbours which were important to her. She did a great deal of walking, reading, and study. She taught herself new languages, such as Portuguese and Arabic. In the London season (usually January to May) she was in town, in lodgings at Clarges Street. During some of those years her life was invested in giving others emotional support: Catherine Talbot during her illness in 1759; Mrs Montagu after the death of Lord Bath (1764). Elizabeth Carter had earlier accompanied Mr and Mrs Montagu and Lord Bath on a trip to Spa, but ill health had spoiled the trip for her. In later years Carter was very much a part of the bluestocking circle, the woman who lent it the aura of solid learning and religious piety. Sometimes the Duchess of Portland sent her coach for her, and Carter was a guest in company with the Duchess and other friends at Mrs Delany's. On 20 April 1781, James Boswell recorded a very happy occasion; it was the first dinner-party Mrs Garrick had given after her husband's death on 20 January 1779. In addition to Boswell, the guests were Hannah More, Frances

Boscawen, Sir Joshua Reynolds, Dr Burney, Dr Johnson, and Elizabeth Carter (*Life* (1934), iv. 96).

The translation had established Carter economically and socially, but it did not lead to any other large projects. Publication as a form of self-exposure made Carter uncomfortable, and she published nothing after her book of poems. She essentially had two periods of productivity which showed a similar pattern. During both periods, the one in London when she was a young woman, and the period of the 1750s and early 1760s, she became involved in intellectual activities and worked and published, but this involvement was followed by a period of withdrawal. Her virtues and her learning brought her reputation and respect, but praise did not build the sort of consistent confidence and determination which would have been necessary to overcome her personal scruples against putting herself into the public sphere more often by further publication.

# 7 · Elizabeth Montagu: The Making of a Female Critic

IN the late 1740s and early 1750s Elizabeth Montagu experienced ill health, the deaths of close relatives, the collapse of her sister's marriage, and an increasing awareness of the incompatibility underlying her relations with her husband. But these sorrows and concerns did not daunt her. Again and again she made the effort to manage her interests and her relationships with her friends and with her husband in such a way as to maintain a sense of control over her life.

The solution to some of the problems of health often seemed to be a summer spent at Tunbridge Wells. Tunbridge Wells was one of the eighteenth-century watering-places to which people came to seek health by drinking the waters, and to find amusement by becoming acquainted with their fellow visitors. Tunbridge Wells was small and rural; there were some general entertainments, but much time was taken up with walks, visits to local scenic spots and stately homes, picnics in the open air, and meals in the various houses which made up the rented residences of the place. Sometimes there were lectures in the Great Rooms (Barton, chap. 12).

Tunbridge Wells was visited by people from a wide range of backgrounds—from booksellers, actors, scholars, clergymen and their wives to bishops, politicians, statesmen, and members of the aristocracy and their wives. Unlike Bath, which had numerous social activities that tended to be forced on the visitors, the social life at Tunbridge Wells seemed to arise from the nature of the visitors in a particular season. Sometimes people rented houses together and formed an inner circle. In 1752 the Wests and the Montagus rented the Stone House; in later years the Wests and William Pitt shared a house together. Thus within the rural village small circles might form as people became acquainted with each other; Elizabeth Montagu developed many of her friendships from initial acquaintanceships at Tunbridge Wells. She first met Frances Boscawen and Elizabeth Vesey there.

*Elizabeth Montagu.* Drawn by W. Evans and engraved by T. Cheesman from
the original by Sir Joshua Reynolds. Witt Library,
Courtauld Institute, London.

Unfortunately, Mr Montagu did not care for Tunbridge Wells, and although she made arrangements for him to come on several visits, he came reluctantly, stayed only a few days, and after a few years admitted he did not like the place. His wife conceded that Tunbridge was not really the place for serious scholars like her husband and his mathematician friends. But, she argued, it was frequented by men of reading, whose society she preferred to that of more frivolous people (MO 2255). It was some of these men whom she made her friends, and who encouraged her to pursue her intellectual interests. The 'men of reading' with whom she developed lasting friendships included Gilbert West and Sir George Lyttelton, later Lord Lyttelton. The test of congeniality was in essence not only that they enjoyed each other's company at Tunbridge Wells, but also exchanged letters, saw each other in London, or occasionally visited each other at one or another country house. Thus, we first find the word 'bluestocking' being used by Samuel Torriano, a spa friend whom West mentions having met in 1750. Torriano used the term in 1756 when he wrote to Elizabeth Montagu from London about Benjamin Stillingfleet, another friend, who was then visiting at Sandleford (see Prologue).

The friendship with Gilbert West was most significant in encouraging Mrs Montagu to think seriously of religion. The deaths of her mother and of two of her brothers, as well as the earlier death of her own son, had shaken her sense of security. Further, she had discovered that her husband was not a believer in Christianity. In those days Elizabeth Montagu felt the need to turn to her religion for assurances of God's purpose here and in the life hereafter. West himself had questioned Christianity. But by 1747 he had come round to an acceptance of religion, and published his *Observations of the Resurrection*. West had been educated at Oxford, and originally intended for the clergy. Samuel Johnson remarked on West's piety in the *Life* he wrote to accompany West's poems. According to Johnson, West read prayers to his family every day and to his servants on Sunday evening. Serious conversations with West on the subject of religion seem to have helped Elizabeth Montagu to strengthen her religious faith.

Several times West and his wife Catherine came to Tunbridge

Wells in company with William Pitt. The amusements of the group of friends included visiting local sights such as Penshurst, picnicking in the country, or meeting for meals and conversation. Mrs Montagu's group read aloud as one form of entertainment. Their reputation for literature was so high that they were called the 'Muses' of Tunbridge Wells.

Elizabeth Montagu made her friendship with Gilbert West a family friendship. She was on cordial terms with Mrs West, and took an interest in their only child, a son Richard. Mrs Montagu invited the couple to use her house in London when the need arose. She herself spent periods of time in a cottage at Hayes near Wickham, where the Wests lived. The area was close enough to London for her to spend time there while in residence in London.

Gilbert West and Elizabeth Montagu also conversed about literature, in person and by letter. West encouraged her to use their correspondence to express her interests and ideas on a variety of subjects. In a letter of his from Wickham (MO 6642, 29 Nov. 1752) West assured her that he much admired her taste and judgement and encouraged her in her reading: Nathaniel Hooke's *Roman History* and Archibald Bower's *History of the Popes*. In 1753 she lent West Hooke's copy of the *Works* of Catherine Cockburn. Later Hooke wanted it back, but she told him that West still had the work, and she didn't know when he would part with it. She explained to West that Hooke was much pleased 'that his favourite author found favor in your sight' and she herself felt that West was 'so much a friend to the fair sex' that he would rejoice in Cockburn's argumentative triumphs (MO 6703).

On 14 November 1754 she wrote an analysis of the 'impieties' of Lord Bolingbroke, and of her dissatisfaction with the answers to Bolingbroke of William Warburton. West thought so highly of her letter that he showed it to Archbishop Thomas Herring, whom he was visiting. The Archbishop asked for a copy of the paragraph and promised not to divulge the name of the author (MO 6721; 6667).[1]

On 18 November 1755 Montagu wrote to West about Voltaire's 'chinese tragedy', *L'Orphelin de la Chine*. At this time she expressed the views on Voltaire versus Shakespeare which were to become the subject of her book:

I read it without any concern, when I compare this indifference with the interest, the admiration, the surprize with which I read what the saucy frenchman calls the farces monstreuses of Shakespeare I could burn him & his Tragedy. Foolish coxcomb, rules can no more make a poet than receipts a cook, there must be taste, there must be skill. Oh that we were as sure that our fleets & armies could drive the french out of America as that our Poets & Tragedians can drive them out of Parnassus. I hate to see these tame creatures taught to pace by art, attack *fancys sweetest child*. (MO 6733)

Her correspondence with West stimulated Mrs Montagu's critical faculties, although it had a stiffening effect on her prose. West's sentences were complex, with many dependent clauses; in her letters to him she tried to write with greater formality than she usually employed. In the passage she expressed a strong irritation with Voltaire's treatment of Shakespeare. Her aggravation eventually prompted her to write in freer and more idiomatic language than she used later in her *Essay*. The passage shows that her response to Shakespeare was personal; she stated her own view of him as dramatist long before she could have read Kames's *Elements of Criticism* (1761) or Johnson's Preface to his edition of Shakespeare (1765).

The death of the Wests' only child in January 1755 saddened the parents; writing from Tunbridge Wells on 9 July 1755, West spoke of the pain he felt when he remembered the past; 'adieu then, ye happy seasons of 1750—51—52—& 53' (MO 6672). He himself had had a long struggle with gout, and at times had been confined to an invalid's chair. After long seeking for preferment, he had finally been made paymaster to Chelsea Hospital with the help of William Pitt. But he did not benefit from this office long, for he died on 27 March 1756.

George Lyttelton, another scholar, poet, and an active politician, was a good friend of both West and William Pitt and inevitably Mrs Montagu was brought into contact with him. Young Elizabeth Robinson had seen him at Lady North's in London in 1740 when the guests came in Court dress prepared for a Royal birthday. She wrote to her sister that the women's clothes were very striking in fabric and workmanship. 'The men were not fine; Mr. Lyttelton, according to Polonius's instruction; his dress rich, not gaudy; costly, but not exprest in fancy.' (Montagu, *Letters* (1810), i. 126.) But that judgement was that of a youthful observer. Now Elizabeth Montagu renewed her acquaintance with Lyttelton, and it became an important friendship. He was a man with literary interests who had published some well-known poems (notably the *Monody* on the death of his first wife, Lucy). He knew the classics. Like West he had become more religious-minded as he grew older; in 1747 he published his *On the Conversion of St. Paul*, which he addressed to West. His *Persian Letters* were thought to show some satiric ability; his later *Dialogues of the Dead* to show taste and scholarship (Rao, 331–3).

In 1752 Lyttelton and his second wife were at Tunbridge Wells and Mrs Montagu complained that Mrs Lyttelton was distant and unsociable. In fact, the Lytteltons separated soon afterwards; Elizabeth Montagu became one of the friends who provided Lyttelton with a continuing relationship after the breakdown of his marriage.

Lyttelton's letters to Mrs Montagu breathed a spirit of admiration for her beauty and her intellect, considered as far beyond that of other women. Such a technique permitted men to reconcile their praise of a particular gifted woman with their sense of the incapacities of most women. In the postscript to a letter written by Archibald Bower to Elizabeth Montagu, Lyttelton raised the question:

> How are we to Maintain the Dignity of our Sex, and our Superiority over the Ladies, if they excell us in Eloquence as much as in Charms? We told you the Ocean resembled a Looking Glass: You consider it *as a Mirrour that represents Omnipotence.* Is This the Stile of a Woman? Shew me in Homer, in Pindar, in Milton, a nobler Idea, a bolder Expression. Longinus would have given it as an Instance of the truest and highest Sublime. Do you think then I will write Postscripts to you as I would to a Woman? There is as much Difference between your Genius and that of your Sex as between a murmuring Stream and the Ocean. (MO 639)

Eighteenth-century correspondence abounds in exaggerated flattery; West addressed Mrs Montagu as his 'dearest and most amiable Cousin'. But Lyttelton seems to have reached unusual heights in these efforts. Following the example of Archibald Bower, the historian with whom Mrs Montagu was corresponding in Italian, Lyttelton addressed her as 'Madonna'. In

No. 49 of his *Persian Letters* (1735) Lyttelton had advocated education for English women similar to that of men. He argued that it was important that their minds and hearts both be trained so that they could play their part in society well. But, in actuality, when he found a woman with intellectual interests, he responded with the kind of surprise which indicates, as his postscript also shows, that he thought very little of the capacities of most women.

There may have been a sense also that the sort of friendship he wished to have with Mrs Montagu was an uncommon one. His flattery of her intellect would indicate that this was not a worldly man–woman flirtation involving what the eighteenth century called 'gallantry', but a friendship based on intellectual values. Mrs Montagu herself must have taken his flattery with a grain of salt, because she always had the sense that talents were dangerous for women to have. In complimenting Lyttelton himself on the fact that he brought up his daughter for domestic life, she said:

Extraordinary talents may make a Woman admired, but they will never make her happy. Talents put a man above the World, & in a condition to be feared and worshippd, a Woman that possesses them must be always courting the World, and asking pardon, as it were, for uncommon excellence. (MO 1403, 21 Oct. [1760])

see p313

She, of course, was consistently drawn to the idea of female abilities, but she also feared the hostile reactions of the world.

When Lyttelton was dismissed from his post as Chancellor of the Exchequer he went back to working on the history of Henry II which had been his scholarly project for some time. A letter by Mrs Montagu written on 24 July 1759 shows the extravagant flattery in which she also could engage in encouraging him in his work. She suggested that history was preferable to fable, and that the tree which 'shaded Lord Lyttelton while he wrote his History' would be honoured by posterity. By contrast, since Chaucer's and Sidney's oaks grew in the light soil of fancy and fable, they flourished only a little while and then faded. Works that spring from fancy do not live on because they are affected by changes in taste and style, whereas 'the historical plants have their root in the Terra firma of truth & wisdom, & are for ever preserved with veneration' (MO 1386).

Mrs Montagu had, in fact, a strong interest in history because it brought her into contact with significant human affairs. She had confided to West that while in the country she read the accounts of people

whom superior parts & noble ambition led from the silent path of life, to its busiest & most turbulent scenes; if I can get some of their experience without any of their dangers, & a little of their knowledge witht any of their passions, I may keep my tranquillity without falling into that stupidity & insensibility which I think still more unworthy of the human mind than vain sollicitude, & idle perturbation. (MO 6704, 13 Oct. [1753])

She wanted knowledge and experience of the world—but at a distance.

Lyttelton's work on his history of Henry II became a strong link in their friendship. It figures in what seems to have been the only account we know of which raised a question about the propriety of Elizabeth Montagu's behaviour. Horace Walpole, who could be counted on to relay every bit of scurrilous gossip, repeated an incident in which a young servant supposedly expressed scepticism about what Lord Lyttelton and Mrs Montagu were doing when they closed the door and retired to 'write history'. But the humour of the anecdote was in the respectability of the people involved, compared to the suspicions and *naïveté* of the servant (Walpole, ix. 255).

As with West, Elizabeth Montagu's letters to Lyttelton provided her with opportunities for philosophical musings, descriptions of nature, and discussions of literature. One of the subjects of their correspondence was the Greek drama. In 1760, while at Tunbridge Wells, Montagu was reading Thomas Francklin's translation of the tragedies of Sophocles. She said that *Oedipus at Coloneus* in particular affected her extremely, but that the intensity of her response was diminished by the presence of the chorus. 'But after all, I envy the Athenians an entertainment, so noble in itself, so affecting to their State, so glorious to their Country, and honourable to their founder Theseus' (MO 1397, 7 Aug. 1760). She wished the play had ended with Oedipus' tragical and mystical death rather than with his daughter's lamentations. The circumstances of Oedipus' death 'leave the mind in a very peculiar situation: and I think I would defy the tragick muse to do anything greater.' Lyttelton responded with enthusiasm to Mrs Montagu's criticism and told her that he had read her comments to a friend, Sir James Macdonald, 'who declared at once that you were a Critic as much superiour to Brumoy, as he is to most others' (MO 1287, 14 Aug. 1760). In another letter praising her criticism, Lyttelton quoted a phrase from Horace in the original and suggested that she not lose the letter, because people would discover the secret that she knew Latin; in fact, considering the excellence of her criticism of Sophocles, they might begin to suspect that she also knew Greek, 'for no body will believe that without being a Mistress of the Original Language you could so perfectly judge of that author' (MO 1289). But Mrs Montagu responded that she deeply regretted that she could not read the plays in Greek (MO 1398).

In the course of the correspondence, the friends also discussed *Oedipus tyrannus*, *Philoctotes*, and *Ajax*. In a letter from Newcastle, she wrote at length on Lyttelton's favourite Sophoclean tragedy, *Philoctotes*. Mrs Montagu added that although she admired Athenian drama very much she had still not lost her esteem for Shakespeare. Her comment, 'he alone, like the Dervise in the arabian tales, can throw his soul into the body of another man; feel all his sentiments, perform his functions, & fill his place' (MO 1402, 10 [Oct.] 1760), reappeared in a slightly altered form in her *Essay on Shakespear* (37).

The letters continued to deal with literary questions in the mid-1760s, after Mrs Montagu had begun her serious study of Shakespeare and the drama. In July 1765 she was reading Euripides in Italian (MO 1438). On 24 September 1765 Lyttelton was urging her to continue her studies (MO 1335). In MO 1452 (*c*.1766) she reported to Lyttelton that she was reading Corneille and finding him most difficult of all to deal with. As a lover of nature she did not enjoy the unnatural.

Above all, Lyttelton encouraged her to publish, and provided her with an opportunity for publication. In 1760 when he published his *Dialogues of the Dead* he included in the volume three essays by another hand. These essays were Mrs Montagu's efforts at writing in the classical tradition of short dialogues on literary and moral themes. Later, when she was at Sandleford in May 1764, Lyttelton urged her to write something else for publication.

We will not be satisfied with a fine Letter to Ld. Bath or Sr. J. Macdonald, which you can write while Mrs. Jenny is combing your Hair: we will have something to be printed, something to be published, something to shew the whole World what a Woman we have among us! (MO 1321, 21 May 1764)

She replied to this urging that she had a dread of ink. He responded that 'The Epidemical Distemper of this Nation at present is *the Love of Ink*: even the Ladies daub their fingers with it much more than they should; it is very hard that you alone, who can use it so well, should be afraid to use it!' (MO 1322, 2 June 1764).

In the course of their friendship Lord Lyttelton clearly performed the function of a mentor. As we have seen, he discussed her ideas with her and encouraged her to further study. Mrs Montagu was drawn to the primitive imagery of the *Ossian* poems but when she debated the question of their authenticity with Lyttelton, Mrs Montagu said that his arguments had staggered her belief in the poems (MO 1404). In a letter of 13 October 1765, after her work on the *Essay* was under way, he warned her that she must consider Shakespeare's faults as well as his 'beauties' and also be just 'to those excellencies in other dramatic Writers, which are of a different kind from his, but yet admirable in their kind' (MO 1336). He compared plays to orderly versus disorderly gardens and city streets to explain his view of the difference between what he considered the disorder of *Hamlet* and the order of a play by Racine or Voltaire. She did not like the constraints of the rules of unity, and argued these points with him. In spite of his habitual flattery, his responses were often informative and honest. He was also careful not to hurt her feelings. He criticized the style of her letters but praised her essays; he told her that her witty sayings came too thick in the letters but were clear and controlled in her essays. Above all, he encouraged her to continue, and made it seem a reasonable action for her to publish.

During these years Elizabeth Montagu had begun to focus on study as a way of employing her energies during the gradual deterioration of her marriage, although she also found an absorbing interest in helping with the management of her husband's lands and coal-mines, finally doing much of the management herself. During the early years Mrs Montagu still felt grateful to her husband for having married her with a 'mean dowry' and she felt that she gained self-esteem by reflection from his reputation as a trustworthy and reliable man of business (MO 2255, [9 July ?1752] to Edward Montagu). But as time went on Mr Montagu seems to have withdrawn into his own interests—mathematics, business, and politics. In the summer of 1755, Montagu wrote to Gilbert West that her husband was 'studiously disposed' at Sandleford and that she was alone for seven or eight hours at a time (MO 6723). But she had Virgil and Milton for companions. The Montagus had occasional visitors—family and friends—at Sandleford, but it was too far from London for casual visits, and Mr Montagu seemed to enjoy his long, fairly solitary stays there. She was determined to be a dutiful wife, however, and to begin with made the effort to be flexible, although she grumbled sometimes in her letters to friends about having to accede to his schedule. One way to make her periods of enforced solitude profitable was serious study. Elizabeth Montagu, like Catherine Talbot and Elizabeth Carter, enjoyed the letters of Madame de Sévigné, who had found in country life a space for reading and reflection. Mrs Montagu began to order her life on this contrast—the city for sociability and friendships, the country for reading, study, and letter-writing.

Reading and study were interests Elizabeth could also share with her sister. Sarah Scott's separation from her husband had brought with it financial problems. In later life she had the benefit of several legacies.[2] But, especially during the first years after her separation, Sarah was interested in earning money. She began with romances and French translations. She asked her sister to send her French novels so that she could prepare translations before the novels became well known. She explained that she would like to earn £40 a year, but insisted on anonymity regarding her work (MO 5238, (?Jan. 1754)). By 1758 she had published a novel, several translations, and a series of romantic tales.

The letters of the sisters discuss their reading and Sarah

Scott's publishing efforts. Mrs Scott herself made a distinction between authors who write for profit and authors who write for fame. A visitor had mentioned that Mrs Montagu was supposed to be engaged in a literary work. Sarah Scott encouraged her to do such work. Mrs Scott thought that now that most authors wrote for bread, or at least for butter for their bread, that those who were not

hurried by necessity should write for the honour of the age, for certainly those who become Authors for the sake of profit can never produce what even their talents might afford, since their aim will make them hurry to an end, therefore it belongs to those who are rich in purse & parts to shew that there are Genius's as well as Writers in the Nation. (MO 5287, 28 Nov. [1761])

In fact, Sarah Scott spoke of her own significant novel, *Millenium Hall* (1762), which described the orderly, pious life led by a group of women, a life similar to that which Sarah and Lady Barbara had been leading themselves, in strictly pecuniary terms. She explained to her sister that she did not get much for the novel, but as it only took a month to write, it brought in a guinea a day, which she thought good (MO 5300, (31 Jan. 1763)). Sarah seems to have been hampered in her development by her lack of respect for her own work because she was writing for money.

The collapse of her sister's marriage had brought home to Mrs Montagu the powerlessness of women and, as we saw in Chapter 5, she took it upon herself to struggle with their father to try to get money for Sarah. But early in the controversy Mrs Scott had said she was willing to leave her father in possession of her fortune to achieve peace in the family (MO 5223). In the later years of her life, Sarah Scott chose to live at Catton near Norwich, far from London and Sandleford. It was evidently still necessary for Elizabeth Montagu to help her sister financially, for she wrote to Sarah, 'Talk not of being a burden on my purse while you lighten my heart' (Bodleian Library, MS Autogr b 10, no. 1059, 21 Aug. 1791, Newbury).

Sarah Scott's marriage had failed; it was only to her sister that Elizabeth Montagu could express her disappointments in her own marriage. She had an increasing sense of 'imprisonment'. She wondered why marriage should always require two people to think alike. It seemed monstrous to her that people should marry and then expect to retain a close affection over a long period of time. As I have shown in Chapter 5, she dealt with her emotional frustrations by venting her anger in her letters to her sister; she also carried on an independent social life, kept up with new publications, and read and studied during the summers.

By 1758, when Mrs Montagu met Elizabeth Carter, she was ready to admire, and to try to emulate, a serious scholar. Earlier, during one visit at Tunbridge Wells, she had expressed admiration for an educated woman she met there; this woman was learned in the classics, had 'a great deal of wit, vivacity, politeness', spoke French very well, had moved in French society, and had been a friend of Pope, Lord Bolingbroke, Lord Bath, '& all the most famous Wits and Politicians . . .'. Furthermore, 'what is uncommon in our Sex, [she] is free from Conceit, pedantry, or vanity of any sort' (MO 5724, 3 Sept. [?1752], to Sarah Scott). Now Elizabeth Montagu was very pleased with Elizabeth Carter's intellectual abilities, her religious convictions, and her modesty. She wrote to her sister:

I suppose you can have Miss Carters Epictetus at Mr Leake's, if not I will send it you. The introduction appears to me a piece of perfect good writing, the doctrine, the style, the order is admirable. The preference given to the Gospel morality above the philosophers is done with the greatest justice & an animated zeal, Parts & learning are never better employ'd than in setting forth their inability to discover the means of salvation which it has pleased almighty wisdom to hide from ye Wise & reveal to babes & sucklings. Epictetus's discourses & ye Enchiridion are allow d by all ye learned to be admirably translated, there is so much absurdity in ye Stoical doctrines one cannot read their works with intire pleasure but Epictetus is reckend one of ye best of them & I believe Miss Carter has done him ample justice. . . . Miss Carter is to dine with me to morrow, she is a most amiable modest gentle creature not herissé de Grec nor blown up with self opinion. (MO 5768, 3 May [1758])

The ways in which Elizabeth Montagu went about developing her friendship with Elizabeth Carter are revealed in the letters the women began to exchange after their meeting.[3]

How did an affluent woman with intellectual interests cement her relationship with a shy, independent scholar of modest means? First of all, Elizabeth Montagu simply asked for Elizabeth Carter's friendship. Then, gradual intimacy was developed by open discussion by Mrs Montagu of her financial situation, and of her feelings, with recurrent compliments to Miss Carter on her values, and much discussion of books.

There had evidently been an overture of some sort the preceding year to which Miss Carter had been distant, and Mrs Montagu admitted

I can perfectly understand why you was afraid of me last year, & I will tell you, for you wont tell me perhaps you have not told yourself; you had heard I set up for a wit, & people of real merit & sense hate to converse with witlings as Rich Merchant-ships dread to engage with Privateers; they may receive damage & can get nothing but dry blows. . . . If you will give affection for affection 'tout simple' I shall get it from you, & even if you wont part with it without other good qualities I hope to get them of you, if you will continue to me the happiness & advantage of your conversation. (MO 3019, 6 [July 1758, London])

Of course, Mrs Montagu was the one who made the over-tures. Miss Carter's humility was such that she would feel no surprise or make any effort to change the situation if Mrs Montagu dropped her. But Mrs Montagu kept up the corres-pondence (although sometimes some months elapsed between letters), expressing concern about Elizabeth Carter's health, complimenting her on her intellectual abilities, and holding her up as a pattern of morality.

Elizabeth Montagu openly discussed her own wealth. Early in the friendship she complained about the harassment involved in the increase in property Mr Montagu had recently inherited from his cousin. At that time Elizabeth Carter could assure her that use of her wealth for humane and charitable purposes would compensate her for her difficulties.

Unhappiness caused by the loss of family members was shared early in the friendship. Writing on 13 July 1758 Eliza-beth Carter spoke of the sorrow occasioned by the death of her brother's wife at the age of twenty-three (*Letters* (1817), i. 5–7). In replying, Mrs Montagu asserted that she was positive that Miss Carter's 'Christian fortitude' would soften her sorrow; but while her grief could not be blamed, Mrs Montagu urged her not to conceal it in order to spare others.

The following year Elizabeth Carter shared with her friend her sorrow at the death of her stepmother, who had always given her love and affection, and had never been from home. To this sadness Elizabeth Montagu could also respond, explaining that she too had regretted her own mother's death, which happened too soon after the children were grown for Mrs Robinson to enjoy any respite from family cares.

In the autumn of 1758 Elizabeth Montagu gave her friend a graphic account of her own horrifying experience—an accident in which her maids, attempting to deal with a fainting fit, dropped 'eau de luce' into her left eye and nostril and into her mouth. Since this remedy was a combination of sal ammoniac and quicklime, she was badly injured, and almost suffocated; it took several weeks of medical care and nursing before she began to recover (MO 3022, 20 Oct. 1758, [Carville]).

One of the pleasures of this friendship was the opportunities to exchange ideas about books the women were reading. Here they seem to have been sharing their efforts at continuing self-education; the writers discuss the works in which they are interested in a direct and personal way. Early in the friendship Mrs Montagu began to reread Antonio de Solis's *History of the Conquest of Mexico* in a French translation, because Miss Carter was reading it (probably in Spanish); Elizabeth Carter was outspoken in her disdain for the so-called advantages Europeans were supposed to have brought to other parts of the world. Her comments elicited from Mrs Montagu an exercise in criticism—she analysed the historian's work and wondered about the models he might have been following (MO 3021). Mrs Montagu regarded Miss Carter as a mentor as well as a friend. Miss Carter had hoped that she might visit her at Deal, and Mrs Montagu looked forward to such a possibility. 'You would give ballast to an imagination that carries too much Sail, & your judgment like a skilfull Pilot wd direct its course' (MO 3022).

In the first winter season after the friendship had begun, Mrs Montagu hoped for her friend's company in London. At first Elizabeth Carter resisted coming. (She was now over forty, and Mrs Montagu began to address her as 'Mrs'—a common form of address for older single women.) Mrs Carter felt that she could not enjoy London without a lodging, and at present she could not afford one; 'my spirit of liberty is strangely untractable and wild; I must have something like a home; somewhere to rest an aching head without giving any body any trouble; and some hours more absolutely at my own disposal than can be had in any other situation' (*Letters* (1817), i. 19-20). This independent stance in fact set the pattern for the friendship. That first winter Mrs Carter did manage to come to London, primarily because Catherine Talbot was ill. Mrs Montagu had suggested that Mrs Carter take a lodging near Hill Street; in reply Mrs Carter asked Mrs Montagu to have her housekeeper 'inquire for some sober quiet family where I may have one neat decent room besides a sleeping room . . .'. Mrs Montagu had evidently offered to provide Mrs Carter with dinners, but her friend replied that when she dined by herself, 'I revel in cake and tea, a kind of independent luxury in which one needs very little apparatus, and no attendants; and is mighty consistent with loitering over a book' (i. 23-4). The lodging found was with Mrs Norman on Clarges Street, which Elizabeth Carter used regularly during the season for many years. For that first season, however, Mrs Montagu had to relinquish her new friend to the Talbots, whom Mrs Carter joined for the long stay at Bristol. But before that time she must frequently have walked from her lodging the few blocks to Mrs Montagu's home on Hill Street at Berkeley Square to be with her, for Mrs Montagu remarked that they had spent every day of the month Mrs Carter was in London together. When Mrs Carter and the Talbots were on their way back from Bristol, she left the Talbots to return home by themselves and visited Mrs Montagu at Sandleford.

Authorship entered the picture about this time, for Mrs Montagu was writing her three dialogues which Lyttelton published anonymously in his *Dialogues of the Dead* (1760). Her authorship was supposed to be a secret, and her friend Edmund Burke was writing them over so that the handwriting of the manuscript would not be recognizable. She expected some amusement in hearing people criticize the unknown writer's work, but she also assured Mrs Carter that she was attempting to do 'that little good it was in my power to aim at'. In fact, Mrs Montagu was rather proud of her little essays, 'A Dialogue between Cadmus and Hercules', one between 'Mercury and a Modern Fine Lady', and one between 'Plutarch,

Charon and a Modern Bookseller'. Mrs Carter refuted criticism
of Mrs Montagu's work. There had evidently been complaints
that, in the dialogue between Cadmus and Hercules, Cadmus
had sounded like a pedant, but Mrs Carter believed that he
spoke with 'all the elegance of polite literature'. Furthermore, she argued that it was not true that Mrs Modish was not
amusing; Mrs Modish's definition of the *bon ton* was 'perfectly
original' (i. 83–4). Elizabeth Carter fortified her friend on the
value of her work.

In her reply Mrs Montagu announced her interest in pursuing
authorship:

I have just received my Dear Mrs Carters letter, & am very happy in
her approbation of ye dialogues. With her encouragement I do not
know but at last I may become an author in form. It enlarges ye
sphere of action, & lengthens ye short period of human life. To
become universal & lasting is an ambition which none but great
genius's should indulge; but to be read by a few, & for a few years,
may be aspired to. We see in Nature some birds are destined to range
the vast regions of ye air, others to fly & hop near the ground, & pick
up the worms. I shall think myself happy if I can do any thing towards
clearing society of their lowest & meanest follies. The dialogues,
I mean the three worst, have had a more favorable reception than
I expected. (MO 3034)

This curious metaphor of worm-eating birds suggests the diffidence at the heart of Mrs Montagu's literary ambitions.

In 1760, after the friendship with Mrs Carter was reasonably
well established, Mrs Montagu also formed a friendship with
William Pulteney, Lord Bath, but this was a friendship with
deeper emotional overtones. Her relationship with Lord Bath,
a close, seemingly platonic relationship with a much older
man, was as far as she dared to go in establishing an emotional
tie in opposition to her husband.

Mrs Montagu had once remarked that she would enjoy
knowing a great statesman in his hours of retirement from the
world. Bath was the answer to that wish. A politician and
office-holder of long experience, and a sharp political writer,
Bath, now in his eighties, took a detached view of society and
its foibles. He enjoyed Mrs Montagu's wit and vivacity. He
took the stance that he was no longer interested in (perhaps no
longer capable of) physical relationships—his letters with their

romantic trifling suggest a pseudo-courtship, which neither party was expected to take seriously. But there was a real emotional tie. They liked to see each other, and saw each other every day in London, as business, duties, and health allowed, or wrote notes and letters.

The pleasant compatibility of their spirits produced a great deal of correspondence and a trip to the German watering-place called Spa, for which Mrs Montagu and Lord Bath formed a large party which included Mr Montagu and Elizabeth Carter, for this friendship with Bath was conducted with great care on both sides so as not to damage the domestic reputation of the Montagus. There were times when Bath did not visit Mrs Montagu because her husband was not in town. But evidently she could be a dinner guest in his London home without concern. When a visit to Sandleford by Bath was projected, it had to be done when Mr Montagu was also in residence. When Bath's only son died in Portugal in 1763, Bath retired to his country residence to mourn. Mrs Montagu was anxious to visit him to try to console him; she went accompanied by Elizabeth Carter and stayed two days, but left early. Although both Lord Bath and Mrs Montagu claimed not to feel nervous about the opinion of the world, the visit was carried on with some circumspection.

This close friendship lasted from 1760 to 1764, when Bath died after a short illness. Although Mrs Montagu knew that her friend was of advanced age, she was not prepared for this loss and expressed great grief. She went to Sandleford to mourn, while her husband remained in London. Elizabeth Carter finally made a special trip to be with her in the summer at Sandleford to console her.

In such a time of grief, one of Mrs Montagu's resources was to turn to study. Her sister had been writing and publishing during these years, and *Millenium Hall*, the work for which she has retained a place in literary history, was published in 1762. Mrs Montagu had continued the interest in Shakespeare which she had had since youth, and about which she had written to Lyttelton in great detail. She was also interested in drama as a form and in its function in society. Mrs Montagu's own interest, the example of her sister's productivity, Lord Lyttelton's and Mrs Carter's urging now encouraged her to undertake a serious study of Shakespeare's plays with a view to publishing a critique of them. She began to read and reread Greek drama (in English, French, and sometimes in Italian translations), the dramas of Corneille, Racine, Voltaire, and works of Latin and French criticism. She read Horace's 'Art of Poetry', the works of Boileau, Le Bossu's *Traité du poème épique* (1675), Abbe Du Bos's *Réflexions critiques sur la poesie et sur la peinture* (1719), and Father Brumoy's *Le Théâtre des grecs* (1730). She had read Joseph Warton's *Essay on the Genius and Writing of Pope* soon after it was published. She also read several times, as she herself later told the author, *Elements of Criticism*, by Henry Home, Lord Kames, who used many examples from Shakespeare to illustrate his critical theories. When Samuel Johnson brought out his edition of Shakespeare's plays in 1765, she was rather intimidated, and wondered if she should continue. But by then she was strongly committed, and she decided that there was still room for her to provide some meaningful comment. She felt that Johnson had not dealt as fully with the dramatic form of the plays as he might have; she also felt that there were certain areas where she might have something to contribute.

The next few years were devoted to serious study and writing. When Lady Barbara died in Bath, Sarah Scott moved to a country place, Hitcham (Suffolk). In planning a visit there Mrs Montagu revealed her continuing interest in working on Shakespeare, and her uneasiness about having it known. She explained to her sister that she was planning to continue her work on Shakespeare during the visit, but she would do the work in her bedroom 'because shd I sit with my Shakespear & Brumoy in Publick,[4] I may appear in the light of Miss Biddy Syphion to any visitors not so used to see ye pen as ye needle in the hands of a Woman' (MO 5878, [8 ?Mar. 1768]). In referring to 'Miss Biddy Syphion' Mrs Montagu seems to be playing with the name of the heroine of Frances Sheridan's novel, *Memoirs of Miss Sidney Bidulph* (1761). She is probably thinking of the scene in which Miss Bidulph's suitor discovers her reading Horace in the drawing-room. He is surprised and makes her blush as he chides her with neglecting to finish the embroidery of a rose which is in a frame in front of her (Sheridan, *Memoirs*, i. 170–1).[5]

Mrs Montagu worked on her project slowly, sometimes in the country, sometimes in London, sometimes at Newcastle, when she was there to help her husband manage the coalmines. In the autumn of 1764, when her commitment to the project had essentially begun, her correspondence with Elizabeth Carter dealt with Plato and the critical issues aroused by his views on tragic poetry. Mrs Carter provided an abridgement of Plato's views, and suggested, probably as a jest, that her friend learn Greek in order to understand his ideas more clearly in the original. Another possibility would be to get a French translation by one of the Daciers. As a Platonist, Mrs Carter defended Plato's concepts of ideal perfection and explained why the tragic poet was excluded from a wellgoverned commonwealth. Mrs Montagu offered arguments against Plato's views in her letters, which Mrs Carter then attempted to refute. Mrs Carter explained that Plato wished human beings to moderate rather than heighten their passions, but Mrs Montagu did not agree with the relevance of such an attempt in tragedy. In fact, Mrs Montagu thought that the sympathy aroused by tragedy was a response to the distress of the situation rather than to the passion which occasioned it. 'Do King Lears misfortunes dispose one to give all one has to ones next heirs to subsist on their bounty?' However, she thought that in love tragedies the sympathy does go back to the original passion (Carter, *Letters* (1817), 9, 17, 25 Oct. 1764; MO 3132, [10 Oct. 1764]; MO 3133, 23 Oct. 1764).

In the winter of 1765 Mrs Montagu was still working on Shakespeare between social engagements. It was at this time that she used the term 'bluestocking philosophers' for her male friends (see Prologue) when she explained to Mrs Carter on 24 December 1765 that 'I expect to have a party of our bluestocking philosophers on Friday' (MO 3165). On 31 December she wrote,

I can now & then steal an evening for my favorite Shakespear, whose merits open as I consider him, & I think I have made Lord Lyttelton taste him more than he did [*Lyttelton defended the formal structure of the French dramatists in his letters*]. It is amazing to me how Johnson could read him with ye attention it required to write notes & yet understand his general merit so little.

She explained that she had just finished her criticism of 'the first and second parts of Henry ye 2nd' (an error for Henry IV); Lord Lyttelton thought she had done well, which gave her encouragement to proceed,

but I believe you will laugh to see such an ignorant animal talking continually of Sophocles & Euripides, who never spoke to me but by an Interpreter, but as I think I can enter into the scope & manner of their Dramas by such assistance, I believe it may be allow'd, tho to say ye truth I am almost ashamed of pretending to judge of them, yet as I greatly admire Sophocles, & all the World admires Euripides, I cannot help shewing how the french differ from them. My stomach loaths ye french plays to such a degree I know not how to read them, & I yawn most prodigiously over them. (MO 3166)

In the summer of 1766 Mrs Montagu made a tour of Scotland, accompanied by Dr John Gregory and his son and eldest daughter. She enjoyed the social life of the old town in Edinburgh, and responded with romantic enthusiasm to the Highland scenery. She met Lord Kames and began the friendship with him which was later kept up in letters. Back at Denton Hall in Northumberland, she continued to work on Shakespeare. She had Johnson's edition with her. She discussed with Elizabeth Carter the harsh criticism which Johnson had met with in his edition. Although she detested the 'ribbaldry' with which he was treated, she felt he had not really pointed out the

peculiar excellencies of Shakespeare as a *Dramatick* poet, this point I shall labour as I think he therein excells every one. I have been very busy in writing upon the tragedy of Macbeth, which opens a large field for criticism, as I have there taken notice how he employs his supernatural Beings who, by the by, other Poets have not made at all supernatural. I have compared the Manes of Darius with the Ghost of Hamlet, & have, asking yr pardon, spoken a little irreverently of Minerva in the Ajax of Sophocles. How larned must yr friend appear when she so familiarly criticises Aschylus & Sophocles. You give me ardor for my work when you encourage me. (MO 3176, 19 July 1766)

Mrs Montagu's progress on her *Essay* seems to have been delayed by the illness of her husband. In the summer of 1768 she was spending most of her time in attempts to amuse him. She had sent Mrs Carter her account of Fable and Allegory, and asked for Mrs Carter's vigorous criticism. Mrs Montagu discussed with Mrs Carter her views of Euripides. Mrs Montagu believed that 'Euripides understood the human heart, & knew it was to be touched by a certain simplicity which the ignorant presumption of lower genius is apt to disdain.' She thought it was 'pleasant enough in Voltaire to make such exclamations against Shakespear for being low & grossier, where Euripides, a polite writer, in the politest Æra of the Politest people in the World, is in some respects more so.' She finished lightly in a postscript: 'Pray communicate all yr remarks on Euripides *that I may steal them* the confession is honest whatever ye act may be' (MO 3220, 16 July 1768). Mrs Carter reassured Mrs Montagu about the validity of her view that Voltaire was wrong in his judgement of Shakespeare. Mrs Carter thought it unfair or absurd of Voltaire to blame Shakespeare for 'any faults arising merely from the manner of the times in which he lived'. She argued, 'The human heart is pretty much the same in all ages, as well as the occurrences of life, which produce its feelings; but manners perpetually vary' (Carter, *Letters* (1817), i. 392–3, 19 July 1768). This view of Mrs Carter, that Shakespeare's work rose out of a largely ignorant and barbaric age, was a common one in this period (Vickers, v. 3–4).

As she went on with her work, Mrs Montagu sent portions of it for Mrs Carter to read. In August 1767 she thanked Elizabeth Carter for her annotations, some, but not all, of which she agreed with (MO 3203, [13 Aug. 1767]). On 1 September 1768 she wrote from Sandleford, 'I thank you most kindly for ye corrections, all of which I perfectly approve' (MO 3225). Mrs Montagu consulted the original 'bluestocking'—Benjamin Stillingfleet—and also sent her work to Dr John Gregory for criticism. By October 1768 she was thinking of printing and wanted Mrs Carter to read her work before she sent it to the press (MO 3229, 24 Oct. [1768]). In December 1768 she was waiting to consult Mr Stillingfleet, and then she would go to press (MO 5909–10). But at the last minute she decided to alter the arrangements of a part of her work, and had to seize any moment she could to do the revision. In December she was also arranging to have a manuscript by Sarah Scott brought to Cadell (MO 5915). Stillingfleet had offered to correct the press for her (MO 5103, 26 July 1767). But he was delayed by floods (MO 5910, [1 Dec. 1768], to Sarah Scott). She wrote to her sister later, 'Mr. Stillingfleet is just arrived & I warrant Shakespear groans in his Tomb to think of more nonsense going to be printed about him' (MO 5916, [Dec. 1768]). Her work was finally published in May 1769 as *An Essay on the Writings and Genius of Shakespear, Compared with the Greek and French Dramatic Poets, with Some Remarks upon the Misrepresentations of Mons. de Voltaire.* The title-page indicated that the book had been printed for J. Dodsley, Baker and Leigh, J. Walter, T. Cadell, and J. Wilkie. Mrs Montagu probably contributed to the production costs.

This anonymous publication about Shakespeare came out very appropriately a few months before the Jubilee in honour of Shakespeare produced by David Garrick in Stratford on 6, 7, and 8 September 1769, and during a time when much was being written and published about Shakespeare. The friends who knew the work was hers wrote to congratulate her. Those who did not know it was hers naturally thought the author was a man. Mrs Montagu was especially pleased by the report that the painter Sir Joshua Reynolds had wagered that the *Essay* had been written by Joseph Warton, author of *Essay on the Genius and Writing of Pope.* Mrs Vesey sent Mrs Montagu some of her characteristically disjointed letters in which she recounted the guesswork that had gone on in attempts to determine who had written the *Essay* (MO 6287; 6288). Mrs Montagu clearly enjoyed reporting that the author had been referred to as 'a clever fellow' (MO 5129, [2 June 1769], to Benjamin Stillingfleet).

As her authorship became known, there were some who took the view that she was stepping out of her proper sphere. The Dowager Countess Gower wrote to Mrs Delany that 'M$^{rs}$. Montagu has comenc'd author in *vindication* of Shakespear, who *wants none*, therefore her performance must be deem'd a work of supererogation; some comend it. I'll have y$^t$, because I can throw it away w$^n$ I am tired' (Delany, 2nd ser., i. 236–7).

Mrs Montagu expressed some fear of the reviewers, but the early review in the *Critical Review* (May, 1769) was favourable; it provided extracts, and praised the treatment of dramatic poetry. The reviewer, who has been identified as William Guthrie (Vickers, v. xiii–xiv), quoted Mrs Montagu's comparison of Sophocles on filial disobedience with that of Shakespeare in *King Lear*, and concluded, 'the age has scarcely produced a more fair, judicious, and classical performance of its kind, than this Essay' (355). Although the *Monthly Review* (Aug. 1769) complained that the style was sometimes affected, and the use of language sometimes incorrect, it stated that the faults 'bear no proportion to the general excellence of the work' (142). This review was by John Hawkesworth (Nangle, 20; 98).

Writing in September to her husband, Mrs Montagu pointed out that

the Monthly Review is ye only periodical paper which has not treated my essay with indulgence, but I think they will not do the work much harm, for much of their cavilling is unintelligible. They say the language of ye Essay is affected, & in many places corrupt, & triumph over a sentence falsely printed. They write with peevishness & ill manners even to great Shakespear himself, so how can his poor little Critick hope to escape. My work has undoubtedly many defects & deficiences, but if it keeps its ground till these carping Pedants write a better Criticism it may flourish long. It is whisperd in Town that I am the Author of ye Essay, & perhaps with these Reviewers ye work has not met with more candid treatment for being a Ladys. (MO 2719, [10 and 11 Sept. 1769])

In fact, by December 1769 Mrs Carter was advising Mrs Montagu to admit to the authorship of the *Essay*. Elizabeth Carter had not found bias in the treatment the anonymous work had received.

It gives me great pleasure that it was at first a secret, as it helped you to that unprejudiced applause of the work, which it might have been difficult to separate from a regard to the author. But now I think one may lawfully speak out. (*Letters* (1817), ii. 61)

However, during Mrs Montagu's lifetime the reputation of the work did suffer—mainly from the alleged downgradings by Samuel Johnson reported by Boswell. In his *Journal of a Tour to the Hebrides*, published in 1785, Boswell reported that Johnson had said that 'neither I, nor Beauclerk, nor Mrs. Thrale, could get through it' (*Life* (1891), v. 279). This report then caused a quarrel between Boswell and Mrs Piozzi, who in her *Anecdotes of Samuel Johnson* (1786) denied the assertion, and claimed she had always commended the work. In a long note to the third edition of the *Tour to the Hebrides* (1786) Boswell repeated his insistence on Johnson's unfavourable opinion of Mrs Montagu's book and pointed out that Mrs Piozzi had read the *Tour* in manuscript before it was printed (*Life* (1891), v. 279 n. 1). In the *Life of Johnson* (1791) Boswell repeated the charge in a somewhat different form. He represented Johnson as saying that the work did Mrs Montagu honour, but would do nobody else honour. Johnson acknowledged that he had not read it all; he had looked at some of it but found 'packthread', not embroidery. He asserted further that 'there is no real criticism in it: none shewing the beauty of thought, as formed on the workings of the human heart' (*Life* (1891), ii. 101). Boswell himself, however, in a note to the *Life* remarked that he admired the *Essay* as a piece of secondary or comparative criticism, and thought that it was 'clearly and elegantly expressed', and actually did vindicate Shakespeare from the misrepresentations of Voltaire ((1891), ii. 101 n. 3). Boswell also raised the issue of prejudice, only to deny it. He pointed out that since Johnson did not know who had written the *Essay* when he first disliked it, Johnson could not be accused of being prejudiced, or feeling 'any proud jealousy of a woman intruding herself into the chair of criticism' ((1891), ii. 102). But the frequent returns to the issue of Mrs Montagu and her work seem to suggest some underlying, perhaps unconscious 'jealousy'.

In later years Johnsonian scholars have taken their cues from Boswell. George Birkbeck Hill, editor of Boswell's *Life of Johnson*, said, 'that this dull essay, which would not do credit to a clever school-girl of seventeen should have a fame, of which the echoes have not yet quite died out, can only be fully explained by Mrs. Montagu's great wealth and position in society' ((1891), ii. 101 n. 3). Thomas Lounsbury, in his work on *Shakespeare and Voltaire*, repeated this view: 'the number of editions and the way the work was spoken of by men of great and of little ability' show how social position and reputation can gain success for a book (290). In questioning the reasons for the success of the work, Lounsbury also took occasion to echo the assertion that her knowledge and powers were 'hardly more respectable than those of a highly intelligent school-girl' (301). The way the tag about school-girls persisted suggests a special irritant—that there was some prejudice about a woman intruding herself into the chair of criticism.

Other scholars have not been so scathing. René Huchon, in
*Mrs. Montagu and her Friends*, published in 1907, showed that
Mrs Montagu's criticism of Voltaire's treatment of Shakespeare
was astute and justified. Huchon pointed out that Mrs
Montagu's greater knowledge of French than Voltaire's of
English also enabled her to indict his translation of *Julius Caesar*
(138 ff.). Robert W. Babcock, in *The Genesis of Shakespeare
Idolatry, 1766–1799*, published in 1931, stressed that Mrs
Montagu was one of the significant contributors to Shakespeare
criticism during this period. She carried on the defence of
Shakespeare against the critics who insisted on the unities. She
stressed the flexibility of English blank verse and the beauties of
particular passages in Shakespeare. In some ways her views
reflect a continuation of older attitudes, but in presenting
Shakespeare as a genius of primitive powers, and in stressing
his power to create characters Mrs Montagu was participating
in the creation of a new view of Shakespeare. Babcock pointed
out that Mrs Montagu offered more arguments against Voltaire
than any other critic of her time. In many of the portions of his
analysis of late eighteenth-century Shakespearean criticism,
Babcock found something pertinent to which to refer in Mrs
Montagu's *Essay*; he concluded that contemporary approval of
her was not entirely 'misdirected' and that the *Essay* should be
rescued from the 'castigations of modern critics' (108–9).

In *Samuel Johnson and Neoclassical Dramatic Theory: The Intellectual Context of the Preface to Shakespeare* (1973), R. D. Stock saw
Mrs Montagu as in the forefront of changing criticism of the
drama. The interest in mid-century criticism, both English and
French, was changing from an interest in what the drama
represents to the sentiments which it arouses (42). In praising
Shakespeare's characters for their individuality, Mrs Montagu
is one of the new school. She is interested in realistic characters
who can win our sympathy.

In her long and remarkable defense of Shakespeare against Voltaire,
published four years after Johnson's *Preface* (but dismissed very
contemptuously by Johnson himself) the newer theories of dramatic
character are conspicuous; and they are skilfully argued as well. (45)

Finally, Brian Vickers, editor of *Shakespeare: The Critical
Heritage* (1979), included selections from the *Essay* in his work.

He pointed out that her *Essay* 'was perfectly adapted to the taste of the age, and went through further editions in 1770, 1772, 1773, 1778, 1785, and 1810, with a French translation in 1777 and an Italian in 1828.' He referred to Johnson's complaint that there was no true criticism in the book, but added that

it was praised by Boswell, Reynolds, and others, while Cowper admired its 'good sense, sound judgement', and wit; in the magazines and newspapers of the period it is treated with universal respect, and frequently plagiarized. Her introductory defence of Shakespeare against Voltaire owes much to Johnson, and many sections are commonplaces of the age; but the response to *Macbeth* is personal, and perceptive. (v. 328)[6]

In fact, Mrs Montagu's authorship of a critical work on Shakespeare was a logical outcome of her literary and theatrical interests. She had read Shakespeare over the years, and attended performances by Quinn, Garrick, and other actors. She had kept up her knowledge of French critical writing, and read Rousseau's and Voltaire's works as they came out. She was an admirer of Macpherson's version of the poems of Ossian, as conveying a taste of the imagery of primitive times. She had delved as well as she could into Greek poetics and drama, always with a sense of regret that she could not read these writers in the original. As she felt that Johnson had covered much of the ground of Shakespearean scholarship, she chose to emphasize certain aspects of Shakespeare which especially interested her. She discussed the drama, Shakespeare as a dramatist, the special genre of the historical plays, and *Macbeth* and *Julius Caesar*. Some of her criticism was comparative, as she wished to compare Greek drama with Shakespeare's and some French drama with his. She compared *Julius Caesar* with Corneille's *Cinna*.

Elizabeth Montagu had a special interest in the drama as something akin to a religious institution, which conveyed to audiences an understanding of themselves, their actions, and their gods. She recognized that when religion dies, the audience no longer believes in the same way. Shakespeare's theatre was not a religious institution, but in Shakespeare a sense of national identity supplied something of a similar purpose. Mrs Montagu saw the history plays as arising out of that awareness, and of supplying some self-knowledge. In a similar way, by his use of preternatural beings, Shakespeare was tapping a native source of popular superstitions, the Celtic traditions. She also recognized that Shakespeare's drama dealt with walks of life which the learned did not know about. The knowledge of 'connoisseurs' is formed in the library, not in the streets, camp, or village. Shakespeare's dramas deal with life outside the library and give an air of reality to everything.

She thus argued her preference for the active, vibrant plays of Shakespeare over the formal, measured drama of the French, and expressed her anger at Voltaire, who had denigrated Shakespeare's work over a period of years, and whose dismissal of the tragedies as monstrous farces had originally stung her.

Shakespeare had for Mrs Montagu a particular appeal. She lived in the world. She knew the venality of much of the politics of her time. She knew the venality of many marriages, and the adulteries which often accompanied these marriages. She was aware of the poverty of the people who lived in her country neighbourhood; in her time in the North she had come to know the hardships of the coal-miners of her district. The emotions evoked by the experiences which she had had were given expression when she read or saw Shakespeare's plays. The histories told her of the complex and confused course of human political affairs, the tragedies of the ways in which men and women struggle against their characters and fates. Mrs Montagu was a person of some sensitivity, idealism, and emotional capacity. To the actual realities of the life of her time she was not blind, nor to some of her own less worthy characteristics. But she felt that she was obliged to keep a close rein on her emotions, in fact to repress them. At one time she wrote, probably to Mrs Carter, of a person who alternately neglected and showed concern for her. In response to the discovery of faults in others, she had taught her heart to be numb; she felt, she said, as if she were gradually turning into a marble statue (MO 3096, [?1762]). Shakespeare offered her an outlet for her emotions. It is not surprising, therefore, that she found the restrained and declamatory style of the French drama unpleasant. The complex portraits of life which Shakespeare created permitted her to escape imaginatively from the repressions which she felt obliged to sustain.

Furthermore, in her production of the *Essay* there was a sense of moral duty or obligation. She always considered her husband a disinterested man, a just and upright politician. (In fact, his cousin, the fourth Earl of Sandwich, for whose family borough of Huntington Mr Montagu held a seat in Parliament from 1734–68, complained that Mr Montagu, 'though a very honest man . . . will always be an opposer of all Administrations' (Sedgwick, ii. 266–7). We can surmise that Mr Montagu saw himself as an independent patriot, and Mrs Montagu seems to have shared some of his attitude in matters where literature and patriotism touched. Her attack on Voltaire evidently stemmed from this need to right a wrong being done to England's greatest dramatist.

Mrs Montagu had not entered the arena of authorship without trepidation. She had spent several years working on the *Essay* and had consulted a number of people. Probably her greatest error was to ask too much advice. Her divisions of her work are logical and easy to follow. But the discussions themselves within the sections are disjointed. She seems to have worked very hard to write individual formal sentences. But on the whole her prose lacks internal transitions and is therefore difficult to read. Thus the *Essay*'s greatest fault is the lack of a strong, controlling prose style. Here timidity may have been the underlying cause, or a misguided effort to polish separate sentences. But in spite of her trepidations, both as a woman entering the public arena of literary criticism which was tacitly forbidden to her, and as a woman ignorant of Greek (in fact some critics specifically held this against her), she accepted the challenge of the project, carried it out, and fulfilled in so doing some of her own emotional and intellectual needs.

Buoyed up by the praises of her *Essay*, Mrs Montagu thought of doing something of a more serious nature. She was evidently debating doing a critique of Voltaire on moral grounds, but abandoned the idea. Later she wrote to Elizabeth Carter of her interest in doing a work on Queen Elizabeth I and contrasting her with Catherine de Medici (MO 3444, 24 Apr. 1778). In her letter of 28 April 1778 Elizabeth Carter encouraged her to give a 'general and particular history' of Elizabeth I and to rescue her from the nonsense later historians have talked about her. 'They seem to think they have quite annihilated the superiority of her talents, by saying she was assisted by a fortunate concurrence of circumstances' (*Letters* (1817), iii. 61).

But Mrs Montagu felt her incapacity to undertake such a work. In her earlier letter she had explained, 'I have only had such a dream after supping upon Litterary Lambs Wool when some of ye Learned & ingenious Persons had flatterd me. The moment I awoke I perceived my incapacity, inability, insufficiency &c.' (MO 3444). To Mrs Carter's complaint about the short shrift historians had given Elizabeth's talents, Mrs Montagu retorted with an outspoken comment about male chauvinism in scholarly matters:

As to what the Men say of Elizabeth's being assisted by a fortunate concurrence of circumstance, & by that means her Government was the best & her Reign ye happiest of any of our Princes, they mean no more than that as a Woman cannot be as Wise as a Man, it was not owing to her, but to incidents that she appears the Wisest of our Sovereigns. For the same reason, were I capable of doing justice to her character, & setting it in a true light, the Lords of the Creation wd only say, that I got a good goose quill, had good paper, & sat in a Bow window; by which means I had both ye morning & evening Sun to give me ye assistance of good light, so I leave their high Mightinesses to write about it, & about it. (MO 3445, 30 Apr. [1778])

Elizabeth Montagu reaped much social benefit from her critical work, but she published no more.

# 8 · 'A Buried Talent': The Writings of Catherine Talbot

CATHERINE Talbot was a naturally gifted writer, whose works began to circulate in manuscript when she was very young. Both her poetry and prose were admired; there are a number of her pieces scattered in manuscript archives. Thomas Birch, who, as we have already seen, was an indefatigable collector of letters and manuscripts, had in his possession a copy of her 'Letter to a New-born Child, daughter of Mr. John Talbot, a son of the Lord Chancellor'. He dated his copy November 1742, but the letter must have been written as early as 1734, or earlier (BL Add. 4291, fos. 271–272; there is another copy in the Bodleian Library, MS Add. c. 243, p. 395).[1] This letter is the first example of the kind of writing to and for young people which Catherine enjoyed doing. The letter offered her infant cousin a hearty welcome 'into this unquiet world . . .'. One of Catherine's wishes for her was that the infant would have 'a nurse with a tuneable voice, that may not talk an immoderate deal of nonsense to you.' Catherine spoke amusingly of the present 'philosophical disposition' of the child, for whom the gaieties and follies of life have no attraction; she does not worry about dress, and she observes the Bishop of Bristol's first rule of conversation, 'Silence'. The writer suggested that her aunts and mother would increase in loving her, and warned her cousin not to be so much like her mother in preferring to be much at home. The writer also reminded the child that she might soon be supplanted by a little brother. All the little girl will be able to do is to be good, and therefore

prove what, believe me, admits of very little dispute, (tho' it has occasioned abundance) that we girls, however people give themselves airs of being disappointed, are by no means to be despised: Let the men unenvied shine in public, it is we must make their homes delightful to them; and, if they provoke us, no less uncomfortable.

This piece of delicate raillery, which touches the universal optimism that a new-born child brings out, with some attention

*Catherine Talbot*. Engraved by C. Heath. British Museum, London.

to redressing the low esteem in which girls are held, had a long life. In August 1750 her friend Jemima, Marchioness Grey, consoled her over the fact that the letter had appeared in a collection. Jemima thought that if people were born to be famous, they might as well submit to their fate (Bedfordshire County Record Office, Lucas Papers L 30/21/3/9). Even in the 1760s it was evidently still circulating, for to Catherine Talbot's great chagrin Eliza Berkeley sent her a copy of it. Catherine explained that the child and her mother and father, in fact all the persons spoken of, were long since dead, and she herself felt the pain of finding that her own situation and attitudes were very much altered. Lady Mary Gregory, who was the only one who saw her letter before it was sealed, was also dead. 'How many recollections does this Ghost of my former Vivacity bring with it from the Regions of Silence?' And she added that 'All my ideas of those days, my projects, imaginative pursuits—all are vanished as a dream—the days themselves' (BL Add. 39312, fo. 319). The 'Letter to a New-born Child' appeared in the February 1770 issue of the *Gentleman's Magazine* soon after her death; I have quoted from that issue (76).

Thomas Birch also copied letters which Catherine wrote to Lady Mary Grey and to Jemima Campbell. Among these papers is a letter to Jemima, dated 25 April 1738, describing a visit of Browne Willis and his daughters to the metropolis (BL Add. 4291, fos. 267–8; 265–6—folio nos. out of sequence). Willis was an antiquarian enthusiast and a coin collector, whose four 'wild girls' lived in a 'great rambling mansion-house in a country-village', without a 'female directress to polish their behaviour'. Willis brought his daughters to town in pairs—the two good and insipid girls, whom he called the 'Lambs', he brought first, and their visit evidently passed without incident. But Catherine and her family found the other two girls, the 'Lions', very amusing, because they had 'a little spirit of rebellion, that makes them infinitely more agreeable than their sober sisters'. Catherine explained that although the Lambs went with their father to every church to which he wanted to go on the day he wished to do it, the Lions differed with him in their choice of when to go to particular churches.

The Lambs dined here one day, were thought good awkward girls, and then were laid out of our thoughts for ever. The Lions dined with

us on Sunday, and were so extremely diverting, that we spent all
yesterday morning, and are engaged to spend all this in entertaining
them . . .

The writer then recounted several examples of the naïve but
amusing behaviour of the Lions:

As they sat in the drawing room before dinner, one of them called to
Mr. Secker [a visitor], *I wish you would give me a Glass of Sack!* The
Bishop of Oxford [Secker] came in; and one of them broke out very
abruptly, *But we heard every word of the Sermon where we sate; and a very
good Sermon it was* added she with a decisive nod. The Bishop of
Gloucester gave them tickets to go to a play; and one of them took
great pains to repeat to him, till he heard it, *I would not rob you; but I
would not rob you; but I know you are very rich, & can afford it; for I ben't
covetous, indeed I an't covetous.*

The girls were to be sent home the next day; they had begged
to be allowed to stay as long as their sisters had done (a fort-
night) but all entreaties were in vain, 'and tomorrow the poor
Lions return to their den in the stage-coach'. The girls begged
the Talbots and Mrs Secker to come to breakfast in their tiny
lodgings in Chapel Street at eight o'clock in the morning, and
'bring a stay-maker and the Bishop of Gloucester with us'. The
guests put off the invitation until eleven, sent the stay-maker
at nine, and when Mrs Secker and Catherine came, they found
the ladies

quite undressed; so that instead of taking them to Kensington Gardens,
as we promised, we were forced, for want of time, to content ourselves wth carrying them round Grosvenor Square into the Ring,
where, for want of better amusement, they were fain to fall upon the
basket of dirty sweetmeats and cakes that an old woman is always
teizing you with there, which they had nearly dispatched in a couple
of rounds.

This letter, written when Catherine was seventeen, was not
published in her lifetime. It appeared as a note in *Literary Anecdotes of the Eighteenth Century*, by John Nichols (1812). I have
quoted from this printed version (vi. 204–7). In *The Learned
Lady in England, 1650–1760* Myra Reynolds called attention to
the letter's 'gay spirit and a talent for minute observation and
social satire of the Jane Austen type' (243).

Catherine was also writing poetry in those days. One of her

poems, written in 1742, was 'On reading the Love-Elegies of James Hammond'. Hammond, a friend of Lyttelton, Cobham, Chesterfield, and Pope, wrote his Elegies before he was twenty-two; the love poems were addressed to Miss Dashwood, who refused him, evidently for financial reasons. Hammond died in 1742; the Elegies were published in 1743 with a preface by Lord Chesterfield (Hammond, *Poetical Works* (1787)). Catherine read the poems in manuscript before their publication (Talbot, *Works* (1809), 410 n.). Her poem strikes a soft and plaintive note, mourning the death of the writer who in vain 'Trac'd the fair Scenes of dear domestic Life'. She ends with a classical allusion:

> O luckless Lover! form'd for better days,
>     For golden Years, and Ages long ago,
> For Thee Persephone impatient stays,
>     For Thee, the Willow and the Cypress grow.
>             (Talbot, *Works* (1780), 323–4)[2]

The friends of Catherine's first circle were literary. For Jemima, Lady Grey, and her husband Philip Yorke, reading the literature of various times and places was a favourite activity of country life. Once when Catherine was visiting Wrest, she noted that they were teaching her to like the French poet and critic Boileau. While at Cambridge, Philip and his brother Charles had participated in the production of a work called *Athenian Letters; or, The Epistolary Correspondence of an Agent of the King of Persia, Residing at Athens During the Peloponnesian War*. This work, privately printed in an edition of 12 copies, volumes 1 and 2 in 1741, volumes 3 and 4 in 1743, attempted to recreate the writing of Thucydides in a series of letters between Cleander and his friends and associates. Catherine also took part. She contributed Letter XCVI, Cleander to Orsames, a detailed description of the ceremonies of the Eleusinian mysteries; the writer suggests that in the rites that were kept most secret the worshippers were celebrating one god, the 'supreme director of the world' (1798 edn., i. 413). She also wrote Letter CLII, Smerdes to Cleander, a letter in response to Cleander's uneasiness at having taken an unethical action. Smerdes's advice to Cleander was to preserve his integrity by leaving his position and seeking security in retreat. This is the only penance that can be at all effectual towards thy passing the eternal bridge in safety, and arriving in those regions of the blessed, the certain, though distant, contemplation of which is the fragrant oil, that keeps alive the sacred flame in the bosom of every true believer, with a brightness, to which the splendors of all earthly greatness are more dim than twilight, outvying even the radiance of the Persian throne. (1798 edn., ii. 270–1)

The society of friends led by Philip and Charles Yorke seems to have assigned to Catherine letters in which her sense of the importance of religious faith could be expressed. In addition, there are two letters, CLXXVII and CLXXVIII, Sappho to Cleander, which refer to Cleander's relationship with a certain Athenian lady named Sappho in a rather obscure way. The first letter compliments Cleander on an ode which he has written upon her. She desires, however, to be distinguished by the domestic virtues, rather than by the external charms which shine so much in poetry. In the next letter she cuts off all connection with him and places herself in the chaste service of Minerva. In the 1741 edition Letter CLXXVI was signed merely 'A later Sappho' but in the Key to the authors which appeared in the 1792 and 1798 editions both were assigned to 'T' for Catherine Talbot. Sappho's letters may reflect some private meaning among the friends. The position of women, and the way women should be treated, had come up earlier in the correspondence. In Letter CXXVI, Cleander to Hydaspes, by Revd Dr Green, Aspasia was presented as an example of the intellectual abilities of which all women might be capable. In Letter CXXXVII, Cleander to Hippias, written by Charles Yorke, Cleander related conversations with Aspasia about the influence of various forms of government on the manners of women, and ended by praising most highly the matrons of Athens, who have been diligent in the education of their families and are respected when old. As the *Athenian Letters* show, Catherine Talbot, the Yorkes, and their friends shared an awareness of the need for improvements in the condition of women.[3]

In 1741 another literary project was also afoot, a scheme of writing a 'Set of Oriental Tales to be called African Tales' by Mr Yorke, Lady Mary Gregory, and Miss Talbot. On 25 July 1741 Mr Yorke sent a paper about the scheme and asked

Catherine and Lady Mary to supply a story, jointly or separately, about the Adventures of the Caliph Mansoul Ebn Laïr or any other of the stories. On 30 July 1742 Jemima relayed Mr Yorke's recommendation of the use of Eastern books as aids to expression. Mr Yorke himself had been working on Arabian Tales. On 24 September 1741 Lady Grey thanked Catherine for her African Tale, but in 1744 Lady Mary Gregory was asking Lady Grey about the Africans. Jemima thought either Lady Mary or Miss Talbot had them (Bedfordshire County Record Office, Lucas Papers L 30/9A/3, pp. 69–73). This project seems to have been abandoned.

Along with her capacity for bright, playful observations, Catherine had a tendency to merciless introspection. In the middle 1740s she became increasingly concerned about what she thought were her inclinations to frivolity and to excessive indulgence in fancy and imagination. She was especially unhappy because her reputation for youthful compositions still dogged her. While on a visit to Wrest in May 1745, she was still writing teasing poems to Philip's brother Charles, and noting them down in her journal. But she was upset when other people, coming to dine, treated her as the memorable Miss Talbot. She regretted that the world regarded her as a Phoebe Clinket; in fact she detested the 'idle Character, the Malicious Commendation'. Catherine added: 'She [a guest] struck me down at once with talking of Verses of Mine forsooth that she had seen at Bath 14 Years ago. Well if she did then see some follies of a Child are they to be reproached her on to Fourscore.' Still worse, her host teased her with the fact that another guest had asked, 'What is that the famous M? I expected to have heard her say fifty ingenious things.' Her friends indulged themselves in teasing her. 'They make themselves vastly merry with the numberless Persecutions I undergo, & my hatred to this detestable *Fame*' (Bedfordshire County Record Office, Lucas Papers, 11 June [1745], L 31/106).

But despite her reluctance to be known as a writer, she continued to compose. Essays, meditations, poems, dialogues, allegories, and prose pastorals all went into what she called her 'green book', which then went into what she called her 'considering drawer'. Elizabeth Carter urged Catherine to publish, but Catherine complained that she found little order or connection, and returned the green book to the 'considering drawer'. The only piece of writing she willingly let go into print was her essay signed 'Sunday' which Samuel Johnson made *Rambler*, No. 30, dated 30 June 1750. Speaking in the voice of the spirit of the day, Catherine attempted a reform of Sunday habits. She indicated the kind of affronts people gave Sunday, such as travelling, or staying in bed. 'Sunday' wishes to be received at an early hour with good humour and gratitude. He expects people to attend him to church, but does not require finery. He hopes for cheerful meals, pleasant walks, and reading of appropriate books. Catherine clearly indicated her wish for an easy, friendly observance of the day set aside for religious worship, with neither neglect nor cold ceremony.

Most of her remaining work was published from her green book after her death without any dates. Therefore, we cannot be certain when some of these pieces were written. Although light and humorous touches occur in what are probably later pieces, there seems to be an increasing concern with moral teaching, and a rising tendency to religious striving. During the late 1740s and early 1750s, as we have seen, Catherine Talbot was much in contact with Samuel Richardson, and was discussing his work with him and others. She was also reading Johnson's *Rambler* essays, and sharing her interest in his work with Elizabeth Carter. Catherine enjoyed the *Rambler* essays very much, although she thought Johnson's style was too complex and difficult. Some of the twenty-six essays that appeared in her posthumous works were probably written under Johnson's influence. They deal with moral and social issues in behaviour and provide examples of individual conduct as Johnson does.

The loss in the late 1740s and early 1750s of several people who were very important to her had a chastening effect, and deepened her sobriety and religious tendencies. When Mrs Secker died, Catherine wrote a poem of loss—'To the Memory of Mrs. Secker, who died in the Spring of the Year 1748'— published by Revd Weedon Butler in 1799 in *Memoirs of Mark Hildesley* (588–9). She remembered Mrs Secker's companionship in every room and walk; she felt she owed her the preservation of her infant life:

> Thy memory, still for ever dear,
> I, as a parent's, will revere!

Thine image ever in my mind
Shall the most tender welcome find.
    And when this mortal scene is past,
And our glad spirits meet at last,
Such shalt thou find my faithful heart,
As when, alas! compell'd to part,
With bleeding agonizing pains,
It left entomb'd thy loved remains!


A few years later, during 1752 and 1753, the deaths of her family friends, Bishops Butler, Benson, and Berkeley, represented a series of shocks. Catherine had the friendship of Elizabeth Carter to support her, and during that time she made a new friend, Frances Seymour, the Duchess of Somerset; her close relationship with George Berkeley also developed at that time.

The Duchess of Somerset (1699–1754) is more commonly known by her earlier title as Countess of Hertford; in her younger days she was the friend and patron of Elizabeth Singer Rowe. She was now a widow living mainly at Percy Lodge. In November 1752, Bishop Secker, Catherine, and Mrs Talbot came to visit the Duchess at Percy Lodge and Catherine remained there for a longer stay. There were several subsequent visits which seem to have stimulated Catherine's interest in composition. The Duchess could talk about Mrs Rowe, whom Catherine admired, and show her manuscript copies of some of Mrs Rowe's poems. We are not certain of all that Catherine wrote under this influence, but we know from the Talbot–Somerset letters that Talbot's 'Fairy Tale' was written for the young grandson of the Duchess and his cousin, who made the Duchess long visits, and whom Catherine met at Percy Lodge. The grandson, Algernon, Lord Warkworth, was a good, amiable child of four, but George, Lord Greville, the cousin, was eight, and a bad boy. The Duchess said that although he looked cherubic, he lied and pilfered; weekly spankings did not seem to help (Hughes, 414). Catherine probably wrote the tale in an attempt to reform the boy by gentle means. After her visit to Percy Lodge in the spring of 1754 she sent it to Lord Greville, who shared it with Lord Warkworth. The Duchess was permitted to see a portion of the tale and asked for more. But

Catherine refused. She had taken a resolution against circulating her work (BL Add. 19689, fos. 7–10; 11–15).

With George Berkeley, Catherine Talbot shared her literary and religious interests. Some time in the mid-1750s she fashioned a series of instructions for living a truly Christian life. *The Reflections on the Seven Days of the Week* is a document which promotes self-examination in regard to correct behaviour but also stresses the enjoyment which can be a part of life. She is concerned with the ways in which members of her society both high and low may try to lead a Christian life as preparation for salvation. Each day is devoted to an aspect of life as it relates to religion, concluding with self-questioning on Saturday. How has she employed herself in the preceding week? If she has honestly tried to do good, behave correctly and with consideration for others, then she may take communion on the following day. Catherine must have discussed this work with George Berkeley. A manuscript of the *Reflections* (there called 'meditations') in George's handwriting is in the British Library (Add. 46689, fos. 137–171ᵛ). On the manuscript are several notations in which George reminded himself to use some of her observations in her sermons or speeches (fo. 142ᵛ; fo. 139). Since the transcript is dated 1754 the work was probably in his possession at that time and afterwards.

In late 1758, as I have shown in Chapter 4, Catherine Talbot refused George Berkeley's proposal of marriage. Catherine wished above all to remain Berkeley's friend; she must have repressed any marital desires in favour of this friendship. Catherine was granted her wish. She remained George's friend and became a friend of his wife, and a sharer in news about their family. From the psychological point of view it does seem to have been something of a *ménage à trois*, with Catherine clearly asserting her claims to George's attention, as his old friend, and even writing rather archly to Mrs Berkeley of her first-born as 'our son' (BL Add. 39312, fo. 325). Eventually, it was George's bride who felt the grievance. Although George was her husband, Eliza sensed the strength of the bond with Catherine. At one point she discovered that when they visited Lambeth her husband was always talking to Catherine Talbot in her dressing-room. She thought the best thing to do was to join them there. There seems to have developed a pattern of resentment which she expressed much later in life.

After his death, in 1795 Eliza Berkeley went through her husband's manuscripts. Some of these papers must have confirmed her old feelings of alienation. She discovered that her husband had copies of Catherine Talbot's love poems. Even though almost thirty-five years had passed, Mrs Berkeley's feelings were still fresh and she wrote bitter, defensive remarks on the manuscripts. From these remarks we get a vivid sense of the stresses involved. Mrs Berkeley complained that George Berkeley had avoided introducing her to the 'divine' Catherine before the marriage. When she saw them together, Eliza knew at once that 'a tender attachment' had existed between them. When Catherine asked her how she knew, Eliza explained that she perceived it the first time she saw them together. According to Eliza's account, Catherine said that at that first meeting, 'I thought I must have fainted at your feet when saluting you as his bride.' Eliza claimed that Catherine 'used frequently to say —that from the day She was obliged by *Parental* Authority to give him up for herself—she never ceased to Pray that God wd vouchsafe to send him the woman in the world the most calculated to render him happy' (BL Add. 39316, fo. 42). Although Catherine assured Eliza that she was that woman, Eliza noted that her husband had often scolded her. In fact, the marriage seems to have developed severe strains.[4]

Mrs Berkeley must have felt that at last she could tell what had happened. In particular, two poems which she believed Catherine Talbot had written just before the Berkeleys married, seemed to her to epitomize the unhappy story. She sent the poems to the *Gentleman's Magazine* with an account of the friendship which the two women had evolved in sharing the love of her husband. Of course, she claimed, she knew it was a platonic attachment, because both the man and the woman had feared God ('Singular Tale of Love in High Life', Aug. 1796, 631–2). Elizabeth Carter was still alive at the time; it is to be wondered whether she recognized the situation or the poems and shared her knowledge with her nephew, who later felt obliged to deny that Catherine had had any proposals in mature life. In fact, Elizabeth Carter was probably George Berkeley's source for the love poems. When Elizabeth received Talbot's manuscripts after her death, the original love poems could have been among her papers. It is probable that she sent them to Berkeley, who made copies and returned them to her. Of course she would not publish them because of their personal nature; she probably destroyed her copies.

Of the two poems Eliza Berkeley selected to publish, the first acknowledges the loss of the beloved and asks to be remembered:

Song

1.
Now Summers gaudy charms are gone,
    How does my . . . pass ye day?
Dost thou not mourn the distant Sun,
    And grieve at his diminish'd ray?
When languid drooping plants you See,
Oh think of Absence—Think of me.

2.
When tedious evening shades prevail
    do the long hours unheeded waste?
Perhaps oe'r some poetic tale,
    In pleas'd attention are they past:
When tenderest Woes described you See,
Oh think of Absence—think of me.

3.
When rosy morning cheers ye plains
    After a cold unjoyous night,
Oh think how long a Space remains
    E'er thou must cheer thy Sylvia's Sight;
When boundless Joyless plains you see,
Oh think of Absence—think of me.

4.
If Social mirth & sprightly joy,
    The ever Smiling moments drown;
If Sports the healthful morn employ,
    And evening wears a rosy Crown,
Whatever gay You round You See,
*Yet* think of Absence—think of me.

5.
But should kind leisure with it bring
    *Reflection*, I were blest indeed:
No genuine Sentiment could Spring
    From thence, but must for Sylvia plead:
If Truth, if Faith can plead with thee
Thou wilt in Absence think of me.

(BL Add. 39316, fos. 55–56; 41)

The second poem has a note on the manuscript by Eliza Berkeley, in which she states that the poem was written in February 1761, 'just before her only Love as she told me married me—in March 1761'. Eliza took this poem as a recognition of her own benevolent part in the relationship; it was to explain the mention of the person in stanza 3 who is to be blessed that she wrote the very long footnote explaining the history of Catherine's love and loss, and of Catherine's conviction that Eliza was the wife for George in answer to Catherine's prayer:

> Song
>
> 1.
>
> In vain fond Tyrant hast thou
>     To dip *in gall* thy dart:
> Thy poisons all to cordials change
>     Where *Wisdom* guards ye Heart.
>
> 2.
>
> If black despair be in *thy* train
>     In *hers* fair patience Smiles;
> And cheerfulness from *duty* Sprung
>     The tedious time beguiles.
>
> 3.
>
> For jealous hate & envy, See
>     *Benevolence* appears—
> —Who e'er + she be, ye powers prolong
>     And doubly bless her Years!
>
> 4.
>
> Thinks't thou blind boy my stubborn heart
>     Will e'er of Thee Complain?
> Or *own* it *drags in reasons Spite*
>     an Heavy, Hopeless Chain.
>
> (BL Add. 39316, fos. 41–42)

The emphasis on certain words as shown above seems to be George Berkeley's. His is also the hand which wrote 'this' and 'this' and 'another' before the poems, and at some of the conclusions made heavy underscorings. Eliza Berkeley's long note about discovering the 'tender attachment' after her marriage is squeezed in between these black marks, as a footnote to the 'plus' mark before 'she' in stanza 3, which presumably refers to Eliza herself as the bride. Although Catherine Talbot admitted that she still loved in despite of reason, she seems to have been trying to convince herself that all could still be well, especially if George's bride would be benevolent.

There are actually ten poems preserved in George Berkeley's handwriting among his papers. Most of the unpublished ones also deal with Catherine's feelings at this crucial time. They show that Catherine discovered she could not escape a severe conflict between reason and feeling. Mrs Berkeley left in manuscript poems which convey the sense of struggle and a wilder grief, such as this sonnet, 'La Disperata':

> I yeild, I yeild, I every prize resign,
> Each hope of every joy that once was mine;
> I have no right, I have alas no claim,
> To pleasure, Honor, Love, esteem or Fame;
> Mean is my path of life, chimaeras all
> That once, Vain Fancy, *Hopes* & *joys* could call;
> despised, Neglected, thro' ye World I stray,
> To me a Wild, deserted joyless way;
> Shut out from every Scene of gay delight,
> The Sun, the Stars grow painful to my Sight;
> No heart partakes my grief, I weep alone,
> Or to ye Silent groves repeat my Moan:
> Weep on Sad eyes, till creeping age has brought
> A dull Lethargic truce from Anxious Thought.
>
> (BL Add. 39316, fo. 49)

Other poems which speak of a hidden grief made more painful because it cannot be expressed are, 'Sonnet—In ye Manner of Petrarch', 'Il Silenzio', 'To Delia, on her going to the Opera'. A 'Song' beginning, 'Fear not proud reason Says; & eyes | With Stedfast look ye Sky Serene', ends, 'Vainly we Natures power defy', a line heavily marked by George Berkeley. I think we can judge by his underlinings that George Berkeley felt that Catherine Talbot's renunciation of love had been against nature.

We do not know whether Catherine Talbot confided in Elizabeth Carter about her proposal, although it would be surprising if she had not during the time of her illness. On 6 June 1760 Catherine Talbot wrote casually that the Berkeleys (presumably George and his mother) were coming to visit. In general Elizabeth Carter believed that people who wished to marry should be permitted to do so, and not be harassed by family considerations, but of course we do not know how she felt about this broken love-affair. She did express herself as concerned about the confined life her friend lived at Lambeth Palace. Several times she visited Lambeth and stayed in the River Tower. She thought Catherine's life was too monotonous and that Catherine and her mother should make attempts to get away for various periods of time.

Catherine Talbot eventually resolved the conflict between love and reason by achieving a pious resignation that looked to a future state which would compensate for the sorrows of the past. In her life at Lambeth Palace she had many duties which devolved on her in helping to manage the household of forty people; there was a housekeeper, but still Catherine's time was taken up on a daily basis dealing with servants, clerical, and other visitors. Some of the visitors she enjoyed, but the routine also involved many dull 'dinnerings'. Once she lingered in the hall of the Palace to see two Christian American Indians who were visiting the Archbishop (BL Add. 39312, fo. 326). She became a sort of confidential secretary to him as gout in his hand often made it difficult for him to write.

As an aftermath of her renunciation of George Berkeley she became a powerful friend of Berkeley and his family—she had the ear of the Archbishop. The letters of George and Catherine written after his marriage show the easy intimacy of two people who knew each other well. Catherine heard from George the details of various clerical preferments, discussed them with the Archbishop, and let George know what could or could not be done for him or friends of his. She still cared about George and enjoyed his visits to Lambeth. But there was only a limited amount she could do for him. She seems to have thought him something of a complainer, and on several occasions she wrote him letters in which she essentially told him to buck up. She was also open about her own feelings of depression. She was aware that her depression was related to an inability to take a forceful part in life. In a letter written probably in 1763 she conveys her sense of restlessness; she wishes she could go to France, because she has become too stiffly English. She indicates ironically that only the most powerful and important tasks would really satisfy her (BL Add. 39312, fos. 304–306). But she was confined, or had confined herself, to Lambeth Palace.

The truth of the matter seems to be that Catherine's emotional life was now invested in the welfare of the Archbishop. She had always tended to centre her interests in him, and enjoyed her life either in town or country when he was there to share horseback rides, walks, or readings. Her letters show affection and a deep concern for his well-being. She worried when he went without his dinner because of long attendance at the House of Lords. Elizabeth Carter had brought her in touch with Elizabeth Montagu, and Catherine sent some 'covers' for Mr Montagu to sign as a Member of Parliament, to save the Archbishop's hand. Although suffering occasional illnesses, Secker continued to carry on his numerous and varied duties (he was of course the cleric who conducted the coronation ceremonies of George III, married King George and Queen Charlotte, and went to the Palace to baptize their children). He died in 1768 after a short illness.

After his death the two women who had been so integral a part of Secker's life experienced a period of painful uncertainty because the Archbishop's will could not be found. They moved from Lambeth to the house of a relative in the country. After some weeks the will was found, with other papers, in an open cupboard where they had been overlooked, and it was ascertained that Secker had actually left Catherine and her mother the income from the investment of £13,000—a sum which brought about £400 per annum ((Photostat) Lambeth Palace Library, Arch P/A Secker, Bundle 25). Catherine and her mother moved to Grosvenor Street. Catherine was already ill with cancer; neither she nor her mother had been told the cause of her illness, but the Archbishop, Catherine's maid, and Elizabeth Carter had been told. For the summer and part of the autumn Catherine was at a house in Richmond lent to her by Lady Grey; she came home in October and died in January 1770. Mrs Berkeley had come to help care for her but went home before the end; Elizabeth Carter saw her not long before she died. In a draft of a letter written after Catherine's death, George noted that he wanted everyone who knew him to know 'how dearly I valued so inestimable a friend, How affectionately I loved her.' He wished he could hear her pleasing voice again; he looked forward to a reunion in the hereafter (BL Add. 39316, fo. 40).

After her daughter's death, Mrs Talbot gave Elizabeth Carter the manuscripts from Catherine's 'considering drawer'. Elizabeth decided to publish them at her own expense; her friend's reputation as a writer is therefore a posthumous one.

The first book, the series of 'meditations' of which George Berkeley had had a copy, appeared in 1770 as *Reflections on the Seven Days of the Week*. It went through several editions during the first year. In this work Catherine conveyed her sense of both the serious introspection and the striving for proper action necessary to live a Christian life and achieve the life everlasting. *Reflections* was reprinted many times, and distributed by the Society for the Promotion of Christian Knowledge. More than 25,000 copies were sold between 1770 and 1809 (Robbie, 114).

In 1772 a volume of essays, dialogues, pastorals, allegories, imitations of Ossian, the fairy-tale, and some poems appeared. The essays on moral subjects are varied in theme and style. Some of them show the sparkling diction and incisive comments of which the writer was capable. In Essay I she compares the hard life of a poor person who is tied to necessity with that of a rich one who may be idle, but she admits that she envied a man who was hard at work mending the roof of a church.

I, who had been seeking out the coolest Shade, and reclining on the greenest Turf, amid the Fragrance of a thousand Flowers: I, who had Leisure to attend to the Warbling of Birds around me, or in Peace and Safety might amuse myself with the liveliest Wit and Eloquence of *Greece* and *Rome*—would have resigned all these Delights with Joy, to sit whistling at the Top of a high Ladder suffering both Heat and Hunger. (*Works* (1780), 51–2)

In other essays she considers the qualities which make for appropriate social behaviour. In Essay III she coins a word 'accommodableness' to define the flexibility of mind which would permit a person to adjust her mood to the circumstances in which she found herself. In Essay V she advocates that wealthy people use their wealth to improve country estates and encourage manufactures rather than for self-indulgent displays. Essay VII, on literary composition, speaks for the plainest and least ornamented style. In Essay XIV she argues the value to young people of studying the history and manners of people around the world. Studying geography would make people look on all the inhabitants on the earth as fellow-creatures. Essay XVIII deals with the joys and difficulties of friendships; she looks forward to friendship in eternity. Essay XIX is an allegory of the moral life, as shown in a dream that includes a visit to a fair. Essay XX advises people to be content with the limitations of the present world, because the higher experiences are to come. Pleasure was created to lead man through the world, but we need to resist attachments to particular things. We should make an effort to share in pleasures such as the botanist, astronomer, painter, and antiquarian feel in their pursuits.

These later essays deal with the differences between the experiences of life and the eternity which religion promises in the future. In Essay XXII she discusses the human tendency to find dissatisfaction in everyday life. The cause is a striving for a higher life in eternity. Every stage of life has its employments, but in the end all employments come to nothingness: 'The strongest Monuments of human Art and Industry, Obelisks, Temples, Pyramids are mouldered into Dust, and the brittle Monuments of Female Diligence in Pye-Crust, are not more totally lost to the World' (*Works* (1780), 188). She thought that even noble employments were not entirely answerable to our ideas. What we can do is poor compared to our capacities in our original state.

The dialogues attempt to juxtapose two different views of life. In Dialogue II, in a humorous interrogation, an eighteen-year-old girl is interviewed, or essentially asks herself, what she has done this summer. She replies: 'Rode, and laughed, and fretted.' But what did she intend to do? Her intentions were an amusing *mélange* of ambitious reading, 'work', and personal improvement. She intended to have learned

Geography, Mathematics, Decimal Fractions and good Humour: to work a Screen, draw Copies of two or three fine Prints, and read Abundance of History: to improve my Memory, and restrain my Fancy: to lay out my Time to the Best Advantage: to be happy myself, and make every Body else so. To read Voltaire's Newton, Whiston's Euclid and Tillotson's Sermons. (212–13)

Dialogue IV considers the problem of vanity and reliance on the praise of other people. One voice speaks of the joys of the cloistered life, 'where the World is quite shut out'. The other replies: 'That sure is an Extreme, the Extreme, of the buried talent' (223). The speaker advises the other person to do her duty, but without any interest in the slightest praise. Avoid 'shining' in any company (226). Dialogue V is a conversation between Lisaura and Paulina. Lisaura complains that she can find happiness nowhere. Paulina counsels her not to look for that impossible ideal of perfect happiness, but to recognize that happiness in this world is bound to be imperfect. 'Our Business, in this World, was not to sit down, and be satisfied, but to rub on through many Difficulties, and through many Duties, with just Accommodations enough to support us among them, in a cheerful Frame of Mind . . .' (*Works* (1780), 235).

Talbot's 'Fable' is a children's story that tells of the experiences of two young schoolboys who visit the castle of instruction. This tale, which, as I have already indicated, was written for the young visitors of the Duchess of Somerset, instructed two young boys, Henry and George. It features a nosegay of violets, which preserves against flattery, a mirror which shows falsehoods by conveying an image of an ass's ears, and a key which has to be kept bright to help the possessor to a proper education. After some difficulties the boys learn to follow truth and avoid pride, and become happy visitors to the castle. Catherine Talbot had probably read Sarah Fielding's *Governess* (1749), an early children's book which taught moral lessons.

Allegory I presents life as a series of play rehearsals. Allegory II tells the story of a person brought by Imagination to Parnassus. She thinks she is seeing Apollo and the nine muses. Then two men come up who tell her not to eat the fruit she has been offered, because it is called 'obstinacy'. One of the men then pushes her off what seems to be a precipice, as Mentor did Telemachus when he wished to rescue him from Calypso in Fenelon's *Télémaque* (i. 178–9, Smollett trans.). She becomes aware that the place she had visited was Folly. The men, who turn out to be 'Good Advice' and 'Good Sense', tell her they have rescued her from bombast, romance, etc. She sees a scene of horror, unhappy mortals, mostly young women, who have been run away with by romance.

The volume contains three prose-poems written in imitation of Ossian. Imitation I is a poem about loneliness. She seems to be speaking of the Coronation day of George III, 'when the Voice of Joy was in the Hall of Kings'.[5] But the poet goes on to say that

Therina past the Day silent and solitary. When a thousand Oaks flamed beyond the Stream, she saw the distant Blaze, like the red Streaks of the setting Sun. She heard the Murmur of the distant Shouts; and at last through the dark Air, she saw the approaching Torch, that lighted back her Friends, from the Feast of empty Shells. She ran to meet them through the lonely Hall: and the Wind lifted her Cloke. (*Works* (1780), 294)

The collection contains nine poems, some of which were written when she was young. There is a poem probably addressed to Lady Mary in youth, for Talbot uses the name 'Laura' by which she addressed her in her journals. There is a poem on Cheerfulness, who 'all Nymphs dost excel'. But there are also poems on the contrast between present life and eternity. The following 'Stanzas' give Talbot's acceptance of the mixed nature of human life; they contain a traditional religious image of 'sliding feet' which conveys her sense of the transience of human existence:

I.
Welcome the real State of Things
   Ideal World adieu,
Where Clouds pil'd up by Fancy's Hand
   Hang lou'ring o'er each View.

II.
Here the gay Sunshine of Content
   Shall gild each humble Scene:
And Life steal on, with gentle Pace,
   Beneath a Sky serene.

III.
Hesperian Trees amidst my Grove
   I ask not to behold,
Since ev'n from Ovid's Song I know,
   That Dragons guard the Gold.

IV.
Nor would I have the Phoenix build
   In my poor Elms his Nest,
For where shall odorous Gums be found
   To treat the beauteous Guest?

V.
Henceforth no Pleasure I desire
   In any wild Extreme,
Such as should lull the captiv'd Mind
   In a bewitching Dream.

VI.
Friendship I ask, without Caprice,
   When Faults are over seen:
Errors on both Sides mix'd with Truth
   And kind Good-will between.

VII.
Health, that may best its Value prove
   By slight Returns of Pain:
Amusements to enliven Life,
   Crosses to prove it vain.

VIII.
Thus would I pass my Hours away
   Extracting Good from all:
Till Time shall from my sliding Feet
   Push this uncertain Ball.

           (*Works* (1780), 329–31)

   Talbot had strong literary gifts: to write prose in an easy, graceful style, to describe what she saw with vivid details, and to write poetry which expressed strong feeling in a female voice. Her unpublished letters to Lady 'Belle' and Lady 'Mouse', the young daughters of Jemima, Lady Grey, are bright and amusing and show a gift for writing for children. Her well-known letters to Elizabeth Carter have an easy prose style and often present sharply realized vignettes. Her obscurely published and unpublished love poems are surprisingly direct and powerful for a mid-eighteenth-century woman writer. Yet, seemingly because she had absorbed lessons which taught her to regard the effects of literary aspiration as 'that detestable Fame', she never learned to develop and fully to use her powers. Of all the bluestockings she seems to be the one whose cleverness and talent were most dampened by her own discomfort at being known as a person who wrote, and by the peculiar stresses of her own life, which did not give her space to develop, or the emotional and intellectual support she needed.

   Some of her friends perceived part of the problem. In 1772

Susanna Highmore Duncombe published a 'Sketch of the Character of the Author of "Reflections on the Seven Days of the Week", and "Essays on Various Subjects"', which appeared as 'by a Lady' but also gave the initials 'S.D.' Mrs Duncombe spoke of Catherine's exquisite sensibilities and her quick discernment of individual characteristics. Catherine's mind was improved by education and she had the benefit of conversation with people of high rank and distinguished abilities. Her love for the Muses and for literature brought her into so close an acquaintance with the classics that she was able to bring into her familiar writings appropriate allusions.

She had a luxuriant imagination, when she ventured to indulge her genius in the fields of Fancy; but so sincere was her humility, so diffident was she of her own powers, so awed by the deference she paid to the respectable friend with whom she constantly resided, that her elegant and refined taste was sometimes nipped in the bud; and many sweet flowers were often stripped away by the pruning hand of too severe a judgment. (*Gentleman's Magazine*, June 1772)

Mrs Duncombe was a good friend of Elizabeth Carter, and it may be that this perceptive analysis of the way in which Secker inhibited Catherine Talbot's creative powers owes its authority to Elizabeth Carter.

If Catherine had married George, would she have found the release from the Archbishop which she needed? George Berkeley and his wife travelled; such experiences might have stimulated her creative powers. George's respect for her abilities might have encouraged her to express herself more fully. In any case, her deep piety made it impossible for her to assert herself in this way; ironically enough, in the eyes of her contemporaries she became a sort of saint, whose example showed the fortitude of a life lived without self-assertion, according to Christian principles. There is a painful impression of lost potential; hers really is a 'buried talent'.

# 9 · Life after Fifteen: Hester Mulso Chapone on the Education of Women

AS a girl Hester Mulso had been the friend and companion of her brothers. The sense of their interest must have helped to nurture her independent spirit, and to develop in her an assertive attitude to a variety of things—education, travel, and the position of women. As a young woman she wrote poetry and fiction, and, as I have indicated in Chapter 5, engaged in a long and significant controversy with Samuel Richardson on women's rights. She met her husband, John Chapone, through her social contacts with Richardson and his friends. The engagement seems to have come about not by family arrangements but by their own choice. Financial restrictions delayed the marriage for several years, but Hester endured the long wait with spirit, and at last was able to marry. Chapone's death after a short illness towards the end of their first year of marriage was a shock from which it took her a long time to recover. After the death of her husband, Hester Chapone's suffering took the form of both mental and physical illness. Mrs Chapone gradually regained her resilience, but the young woman who had looked forward with impatience to wearing her 'wedding shoes' was a much chastened person.

Her widowhood determined the pattern of Hester's later life. Her husband had left his affairs in disarray (we do not know whether there were debts, or simply a lack of money for his widow's financial support). Her uncle, Bishop Thomas, allowed her a stipend of £20 a year. Her life after her husband's death seems to have been divided between long visits to relatives in the country, such as Revd John Mulso or Bishop Thomas, in spring, summer, and autumn. She helped nurse John's wife through a breast infection after the birth of her first child; she stayed through 'horrible' scenes of childbirth, and she attended the dying Mrs Thomas, wife of the Bishop. In his letters to Gilbert White her brother John stressed her welcome presence in households in trouble. In the winter seasons Hester Chapone was generally in lodgings in London.

One of the ways a single woman or a widow who needed to support herself could earn a reputable living was to become a governess in a great family. Friends had agitated about a position at Court for Elizabeth Carter on several occasions, but she had firmly rejected such possibilities. Similar efforts were made for Hester Chapone. The first suggestion was that she become a companion of the Duchess of Beaufort, but Mrs Montagu did not think the post suitable for her (Montagu, ed. Blunt, i. 129). A similar offer was made by Edward Bridgen to Mrs Chapone through Mrs Montagu as mediator: that Mrs Chapone become a governess in the household of a German prince.[1] Mrs Montagu had evidently been impressed with Hester Chapone's abilities and thought that such a position might be suitable for her. But Mrs Chapone refused. As Mrs Montagu explained:

Our incomparable Friend Mrs. Chapone, after all I have urged to put courage into her, finds her spirits unequal to the task. I gave her time to consider of it, hoping she might familiarize herself with the Idea, & find out that Bavaria was not in any region of the Moon, but I have her final determination not to venture, deterrd by a weak state of health & spirits. I am not the less obliged to you Dear Sir for your great goodness in making me this offer, which I heartily wish Mrs. Chapone had had the courage to accept. Her mind makes her fit to converse with a great Princess she speaks the language of virtue as she does her Mother tongue in the greatest purity & elegance. (MO 675, 7 Jan. 1768, Hill Street to Edward Bridgen)

Presumably Hester's job would have been to teach English to a young princess. But if she consulted her friend Elizabeth Carter, Carter would probably have counselled the inadvisability of attempting to make a life in a Court position. Mrs Montagu spoke of Hester Chapone's lack of courage; I think what Mrs Montagu was referring to was Mrs Chapone's loss of courage after the death of her husband. Hester Chapone had been an energetic, outgoing person; the sudden fatal event reduced her confidence in herself and made the challenge of a new country and new duties seem impossibly difficult.

During her visit in 1765 to her brother John and his family, then living in Yorkshire, Hester had had the idea of writing a series of letters on self-education for the benefit of her eldest niece, and in the ensuing years must have done so. In the summer of 1770 Hester accompanied Mrs Montagu on one of her northern trips and visited Hagley, Yorkshire, and Scotland with her. Presumably, some time afterwards, Mrs Montagu began to urge the publication of the letters. The *Letters on the Improvement of the Mind: Addressed to a Young Lady* was published in 1773. Her niece, born in 1758, was fifteen in 1773, the age she is when her aunt addresses her in the *Letters*. Hester must have revised the letters just before publication. Hester sold the copyright to this work for £50. The book was dedicated to Mrs Montagu. Its success far exceeded Hester's expectations, and soon a second edition was in press. Her friends scolded her for having sold the copyright 'and grudge poor Walter his profits'. But Hester insisted that the book would not have done so well in her hands as in his (Farnham Castle, 20 July (?1773), to Elizabeth Carter, *Posthumous Works*, i. 162–3).

John Mulso was proud of his sister and her work. On 5 July 1773, he wrote to Gilbert White that he had not seen her

since ye great Harvest of her Fame: She is much gratified by ye Praises that resound on all Sides; & indeed I fairly think that She deserves them. The critical Reviewers have confined their Plaudit chiefly to ye religious Turn of the Book, wherein indeed it shines, but I wonder that they took no Notice of some elegant & very judicious Observations in it, that are very much out of ye Common way of Writing. (Mulso, 244)

Later he remarked that *Letters on the Improvement of the Mind* gained its charm from having been written to an actual niece. While urging Gilbert White to publish his own work, he used his sister as an example: 'How was it with Mrs. Chapone? it was the genuine Affetuoso, the con amore of her Book that gave it it's Run: Had She wrote to an imaginary Niece the most animated Traits would have escap'd her Pen' (Mulso, 284).

As it turned out, *Letters on the Improvement of the Mind* was the most widely read work of the first generation of bluestockings. It was reprinted at least sixteen times in the eighteenth century in separate editions, and appeared in a 1776 Dublin edition of Chapone's *Works*. There were at least fifteen editions of the *Letters* between 1800 and 1829, with many of these used in schools. There was a French translation in 1829. *Letters on the Improvement of the Mind* gained wider circulation with the publication of Mrs Chapone's *Works* in 1807. This edition contained

both her works and letters, including the letters to Samuel
Richardson and to Elizabeth Carter, as well as her 'Matrimonial
Creed' addressed to Richardson. This set was also reprinted
several times. The *Letters* also became part of a mixed repertoire
of books of advice to young women which were popular well into
the middle of the nineteenth century. They were reprinted with
such works as Dr John Gregory's *Legacy to his Daughters*, and
Catherine Talbot's *Reflections*.

The heaviness and sobriety of some of the didactic works
addressed to women towards the last part of the eighteenth
century, with which Mrs Chapone's work has been grouped,
have led to an over-emphasis on her religious zeal and a mis-
understanding of her attitudes towards women. She was not
the sanctimonious person that Taylor presents her as in *The
Angel-Makers*, where he mentions her with Mrs Sherwood, Mrs
Opie, Mrs Trimmer, Hannah More, and Mrs Sandford as
didactic women writers who 'emphasise, with almost sadistic—
and quite certainly obsessive—iteration, that women must submit themselves to men, that they must eschew learning,
abandon all idea of a career, and so on' (287). In fact, she
addresses her niece without censoriousness, as a thoughtful,
capable person. She points out that her niece is now in her fifteenth year, and must soon act for herself. She should begin
now to strive for virtue and happiness. When she understands
the true duties of life, her 'chief delight will be in those persons,
and those books, from which you can learn true wisdom'
(Chapone, *Letters* (1773), i. 9). Mrs Chapone gives her advice
in separate essays which cover moral, social, and educational
topics.

Religion was of central importance and Mrs Chapone gave
her niece instructions on how to read the Bible, explaining
which parts of the Old Testament should be read for a connected narrative with the help of the index, and which parts
might be omitted. She urged reading the Psalms for their poetic
qualities. In reading the New Testament she recommended the
four Gospels, the Acts, as well as selected Epistles. She pointed
out which parts are difficult and can be postponed until later.
She mentioned supplementary works, such as Lyttelton's book
on the conversion of St Paul (Chapone, *Letters* (1773), i. 93).

In later letters Mrs Chapone recommended reading history

and literature. She provided specific instructions for a regular plan of historical studies. She suggested techniques for understanding the chronology of the ancient world; she counted the age of the world in the traditional way as 4,000 years. She gave advice on the reading of ancient and medieval history, and offered lists of works on English and European history. She called attention to the development of the British Empire, and recommended that her pupil read of the discovery and conquest of America. She pointed out that the conquerors were unjust and cruel and that 'the history of the world is little else than a shocking account of the wickedness and folly of the ambitious' (Chapone, *Letters* (1773), ii. 200). She recommended poetry as a way of developing the imagination, 'the faculty, in which women usually most excel' (Chapone, *Letters* (1773), ii. 127). She urged her niece to know the best English poets, especially Shakespeare and Milton. She praised Mrs Montagu's *Essay* as an introduction to Shakespeare's work. She suggested the reading of *Paradise Lost* and Addison's criticism of Milton in the *Spectator*. She provided for learning French and Italian but thought that the classical languages should be studied only by women who had a call for such instruction. Classical works were available in translation in various European languages, and by not learning Greek and Latin a young woman would avoid the envy of both men and women.

Mrs Chapone was well aware that what she was instructing her niece in was a substitute for the regular course of education which boys received. For example, her niece should learn mythology, which, she pointed out, boys were taught routinely and therefore learned more easily (Chapone, *Letters* (1773), ii. 135-6). She also advocated the study of nature as bringing the student into touch with objects made by the 'Almighty Hand . . .' (Chapone, *Letters* (1773), ii. 136-7). Perhaps in her interest in close observation of nature she was influenced by her long friendship with Gilbert White the naturalist, who sometimes sent her his poems to criticize and was preparing his studies of nature later published as *The Natural History and Antiquities of Selborne* (1789). Mrs Chapone was also interested in methods of learning. She urged her niece to recount what she had been reading in a letter to a friend or in conversation, as an aid to learning. Above all she recommended that her niece not spend

the crucial next few years in trivial activities. It is not from lack
of abilities that so many women are insipid companions: they
neglect to cultivate a taste for intellectual improvement (ii. 224).

Mrs Chapone was interested in helping to form a woman
capable of independent judgement in personal life. She disliked
affectations of tender feelings in women, and believed women
were capable of 'passive courage' (Chapone, *Letters* (1773), i.
124–5). She stressed care in the choice of female friends, and
recommended against intimacy 'with those of low birth and
education' (i. 166–7)—advice which Jane Austen may be
reflecting in her narrative of the friendship of Emma and
Harriet. Mrs Chapone advised her niece against superficial
friendships with girls her own age, but recommended having a
woman friend eight or ten years older than herself who could
act as a mentor. Hester saw the conjugal relationship as the
highest form of friendship. In her 'Matrimonial Creed',
written when she was young, she had acceded to the institu-
tionalized superiority of men, but required an equality of
friendship between husbands and wives (*Works* (1807), ii.
146–56). Now she claimed that each individual could have a
great variety of friendships; she did not believe in trying to
possess her friends exclusively, but in sharing them with others.
In her recommendations on a choice of a husband, she does
seem to have retreated from her earlier action in having chosen
a husband for herself. She advised her niece to consult her
family before giving 'a "lover" any encouragement' (Chapone,
*Letters* (1773), i. 196–7). If women could know men as well as
they do each other, a woman could choose a husband for herself, but as this is not possible, she advised her niece to rely on
her parents' views (Chapone, *Letters* (1773), i. 190–1). But she
would not advise her niece to marry where she did not love: 'a
mercenary marriage is a detestable prostitution' (i. 193). She
also reassured her niece that a single life has its own rewards:

But if this happy lot [marriage] should be denied you, do not be
afraid of a single life.—A worthy woman is never destitute of
valuable friends, who in a great measure supply to her the want of
nearer connections.—She can never be slighted or disesteemed, while
her good temper and benevolence render her a blessing to her
companions.—Nay, she must be honoured by all persons of sense
and virtue, for preferring the single state to an union unworthy of

her.—The calamities of an unhappy marriage are so much greater
than can befal a single person that, the unmarried woman may find
abundant argument to be contented with her condition, when pointed
out to her by Providence. (Chapone, *Letters* (1773), i. 199-200)

Mrs Chapone's positive remarks on how a single woman can
form a satisfying life are actually a form of female advocacy.

Mrs Chapone gave a rational and careful treatment of household economy in letter 7. She recommended that her niece keep
a notebook and learn to manage a household while still in her
mother's house. Mrs Chapone's definition of economy was a
life lived in accordance with one's fortune and rank; but if
fortune is weak, rank must give way.

She stressed rational understanding and control, but left
some leeway for feeling. In remarks on reading, Mrs Chapone
claimed not to be excluding fiction, but she stressed careful
selection, because of the possible corruption of female hearts by
most novels and romances (Chapone, *Letters* (1773), i. 144-5).
She preferred young people to read moral essays in periodical
papers like the *Spectator*. In dealing with deportment, she urged
ease and politeness in social behaviour and advised her niece to
treat men as directly and simply as she treats women (Chapone,
*Letters* (1773), ii. 112-13). In her advice on the government of
the temper, letter 6, she stated that women can and should
learn to govern their tempers. Yet she allowed for anger, when
it is a reaction to real injuries (Chapone, *Letters* (1773), ii. 15).

Chapone's work was immensely popular. Its directness, simplicity, social conservatism, and piety made it an acceptable
tool to help women educate themselves. Thirty years after the
publication of Thomas Seward's 'Female Right to Literature',
which, as I pointed out in Chapter 5, argued for a more extensive
education for women, Mrs Chapone was offering a practical way
to achieve this end. She was not an innovator who would demand
a regular education for girls after fifteen. But she encouraged
girls to make that effort for themselves. Mrs Chapone was not
content, furthermore, with slight, or 'potted' knowledge. She
wished her niece to study thoughtfully and critically on her own.
A young woman should use her time creatively, rather than
simply engaging in trivial activities while waiting to marry.

In 1775 Hester Chapone published a collection of her previous writings under the title of *Miscellanies in Prose and Verse.* This work was dedicated to Elizabeth Carter. Brother John reported happily that she had made a much better bargain. She received £250, and her brother calculated that she had therefore been compensated for selling the first work so cheaply (Mulso, 254). Although her *Miscellanies in Prose and Verse* did not gain the popularity of her earlier work, this volume kept in public attention her work as a poet and as a writer of serious moral essays. Mrs Chapone's poems, most of which were written when she was young, deal with the difficulties of sustaining health, the horrors of war (her earliest poem was written on the rebellion of '45), and the pleasure and pains of friendship. She uses the device of personification to develop contrasts and conflicts that she finds within herself. Her poem 'To Solitude' reflects a wish to escape from life by withdrawing into solitude and fancy; this impulse is countermanded by the wish to find wisdom and resignation. She invokes Wisdom,

> from the sea-beat shore
> Where, list'ning to the solemn roar,
> Thy lov'd Eliza strays
>
> (159–60)

referring of course to Elizabeth Carter at Deal. Similarly the 'Irregular Ode', which appeared in Elizabeth Carter's translation of Epictetus, praises Carter's knowledge of the classics, but stresses Hester's belief that stoicism relies too much on flawed human nature, and that true help is to be found only in Christ. Another poem, 'To Winter', describes the other seasons, but praises the difficult season as the friend of 'sweet Society'. Furthermore, Winter is part of the pattern established by 'great Nature's King', and deserves the homage of Devotion (165). Hester found it easy to write poetry, but as she explained to Elizabeth Carter, she did not like to revise. Miss Carter would understand, 'for you, who are a work-woman as well as a writer, know well that it is much pleasanter to make than to mend' (*Posthumous Works*, i. 21–2). She seems to have preferred to think of her poems as easy and spontaneous. They are interesting because they show her attempts to grope towards a philosophy to regulate her feelings and conduct. That regulation she found in Christianity.

The second volume also contained her moral essays, and the story of Fidelia, which appeared originally in *The Adventurer* (Nos. 77–9, July–Aug. 1753). The short narrative called 'The Story of Fidelia' dramatizes the unhappy fate of a young woman raised on rational principles, but without religion. After her father's death and her refusal to marry a merchant who is her uncle's choice, Fidelia leaves home. She is unhappy because her difficulties have arisen from her virtuous refusals, and she is easily seduced by Sir George Freelove. When her lover is to be married to a wealthy woman, she leaves the house and drives into the country, planning to commit suicide. She is about to jump into the river when an elderly clergyman calls to her. He takes her to his wife, who has lost her children and is dying of cancer. But she has equanimity. When Fidelia asks its source, the wife hands her a Bible. The older woman knows they will be happy in a future state. Fidelia stays with the couple and the clergyman teaches her religion. The lady dies an exalted death. Christianity changes Fidelia; she is now willing to go into service to support herself. She concludes, 'Though Vice is constantly attended by misery, Virtue itself cannot confer happiness in this world, except it is animated with the hopes of eternal bliss in the world to come' (136).

The essays, 'On Affectation and Simplicity', 'On Conversation', 'On Enthusiasm, and Indifference in Religion', give examples of rational behaviour based on the principles of revealed religion. In Essay 3 on religion Chapone explains that when she was young she was attracted to mystical ideas of religion; as she grew up she realized they were the effects of imagination, and as insubstantial as dreams. We sometimes try to love God with excessive feelings. God is the choice and object of reason rather than emotions. She objects to the Mystics who borrow their devotion from images of desire. But enthusiasm is less pernicious to the mind than coldness in religion. She concludes with an example of a couple who follow the rational pleasures of life which are conformable to religion and virtue. Sir Charles and Lady Worthy have a quiet social life in town without cards. In the country they visit the poor.

After the publication of her works, Mrs Chapone continued her social life with a reputation as a literary woman. She wrote some poems, but published no more. Although she felt that she had to limit her participation in society because of her narrow means, she had a circle of male and female bluestocking friends of various ages and status, including Mary Delany, Fanny Burney, and other members of the Burney family. When Mrs Chapone's uncle, Dr John Thomas, Bishop of Winchester, died in 1781, Mrs Delany was indignant that he had added only £30 a year for life to the stipend of £20 he had given her during his lifetime out of his income of £6,000. Mrs Delany felt that he had provided amply for all his relations while he was alive, 'and if he would *not* distinguish her *as a relation* it would have done him honour to have placed such an uncommon and estimable *woman*, whose talents have been so nobly employed at least in an easy state of life . . .'. The figures specified are very small to have provided Mrs Chapone with an adequate subsistence, but as Mrs Delany added, 'Providence, who has enriched her mind with useful as well as elegant sentiments, will give her the best support—that of *contentment*!' (Delany, 2nd. ser., iii. 19).

Mrs Chapone continued an active reader and astute critic. At one time (probably after 1792) she was reading Erasmus Darwin's 'strange, but beautiful poem "The Loves of the Plants", Mrs. Piozzi's travels, the poems of Mrs. Smith, and Gibbon's six volumes' (*Works* (1807), ii. 197–9). Her reception of Mary Wollstonecraft's work was mixed:

I have seen nothing of Mrs. Wolstonecroft's except her Rights of Women,—in which I discerned some strong sense, amidst many absurdities, improprieties, and odious indelicasies. The desire of distinction is, I believe, the grand spring that sets so many pens at work, to shake and overturn every principle of order and happiness, and makes so many foolish people depart from the good they have been taught, to become their disciples, and affect a libertinism which their hearts disavow. Humility is indeed our great preservative: Mrs. Wolstonecroft is so good as to attribute it to *me*; and I have at least enough to be not ashamed of it, and earnestly to wish I had more. (*Works* (1807), ii. 202–3).

She had long been aware of the difficulties in the position of women, and had attempted to express those grievances within the framework of her Christian principles and the need for Christian fortitude. Her principles would keep her from reacting with enthusiasm to Mary Wollstonecraft's revolutionary doctrines. Still, Hester Chapone felt she herself had done something, and that satisfied her. As she explained to Elizabeth Carter not long after the appearance of her works, publication has its effect:

It appeases, in some measure, that uneasy sense of helplessness and insignificancy in society, which has so often depressed and afflicted me; and gives me some comfort with respect to the poor account I can give of 'That one talent which is death to hide.' (15 June 1777, *Posthumous Works*, i. 171–2)

In quoting Milton's sonnet on his blindness she was expressing  a sense of the disabilities which in fact made it so difficult for women to accomplish anything in the intellectual world. But Mrs Chapone could not foresee what her influence would be. The numerous editions of her work must have had some effect in encouraging young women to strive for continuing education.

# PART IV

Bluestocking Fame (1775–1800)

# Introduction

THE women of the first generation of the bluestocking circle all seem to have had in common supportive mentors and friends, their own intellectual interests and energies, and the inhibitions that came from feeling that it was not quite ethical to write for money. Hester Chapone was embarrassed to find that her publisher, Walter, had advertised a second edition of the *Letters* 'with a *Puff*, which mortifies me much'. If the book was succeeding, she saw no reason for such an action (MO 707, 15 Sept. 1773, to Mrs Montagu). It was the mention of sales which seems to have upset her. Walter's 'puff' consisted of a statement that the fifteen hundred copies of the first edition sold out in six weeks, which 'has fully testified the Public's very high approbation of these letters' (*London Chronicle*, 34 (7–9 Sept. 1773), 247; *Daily Advertiser* (11 Sept. 1773)).

Perhaps extreme necessity might have pushed the first bluestockings further; however, their hesitations suggest that the inhibitions were very strong. As it was, they did not move beyond limited publication prompted by friendship. In a tentative way they were approaching professional authorship—a pursuit which includes a concern with making a living by writing, if possible, and a long-term commitment to productive work—but they could not and did not reach that stage, because of their own internal constraints and the lack of support of their society. The process of restructuring both women's and society's attitudes has been a long one. Elaine Showalter has shown in *A Literature of their Own* that it was only in the 1840s that the work of women novelists began to be recognized as a profession (19).

However, even in the generation of the bluestockings, women like Catherine Macaulay (1731–91), Sarah Scott (1723–95), and Charlotte Lennox (?1729–1804) felt less trepidation or more urgency. Macaulay was ambitious and politically radical. The first volume of her *History of England from the Accession of James I to that of the Brunswick Line* appeared in 1763. The second volume followed in 1767 and further volumes in 1768, 1771, 1781, and

1783. She published political pamphlets, other histories, and in 1790, *Letters on Education* (Schnorrenberg). The first bluestockings were not in favour of her political views. In 1775 Elizabeth Montagu announced that she would not read one of Mrs Macaulay's books; Elizabeth Carter replied that she would, as she had a 'higher opinion of her [Mrs Macaulay's] talents' than Mrs Montagu had. Elizabeth Carter explained that she had spent two or three hours in a tête-à-tête with Mrs Macaulay, and found that she had 'a very considerable share both of sense and knowledge' (Carter, *Letters* (1817), ii. 309).

As we have seen, Sarah Scott was interested in adding to her income; she wrote five novels and three histories between 1750 and 1772. Charlotte Lennox needed to write for a living; during most of her life she was writing and translating to support herself, her children, and her husband. She wrote five or six novels, translated at least six works from the French, published poems and plays, a translation of Shakespeare's sources called *Shakespeare Illustrated* (1753-4), and in 1760-1 she edited a magazine, the *Lady's Museum*. But she spent her last years in extreme poverty (Shevelow).

After 1775, when the term 'bluestocking' began to focus on women as learned ladies and writers rather than on the men who had been called bluestockings in the early days, the term also widened to include both writers like Macaulay, Lennox, and Scott, who were not members of the bluestocking circle, and women of the younger generation like Hester Salusbury Thrale, Fanny Burney, and Hannah More, who became members of the circle. Later all of these women would be called 'bluestockings' as the word itself became an umbrella covering the activities of intellectual women. And, of course, the term was also used to refer to the social gatherings of women with literary interests. This broadening of the use of the term 'bluestocking' was the result of the intense interest focused both by the participants and their friends and by commentators in newspapers and periodicals on this new phenomenon—women writing, publishing, and taking a public role in the life of the mind.

# 10 · The Observed and their Observers

THE members of the bluestocking circle were self-conscious observers who noted in their letters and journals the nature and significance of their activities. Their comments show their awareness of the fact that learning for women was beginning to come into its own. While observers like Fanny Burney and Horace Walpole had their own inimitable ways of describing the personal traits of their friends and acquaintances, they were also making implied judgements as to the extent to which learned women were measuring up to bluestocking ideals of learning and virtue. For example, uneasiness about Mrs Montagu's ostentation derived from a sense that her literary interests did not properly go with such display.

During these years, furthermore, the social life of the blue-stocking circle became a persistent topic of comment by the participants themselves. Literary quarrels, such as that of Mrs Montagu and Samuel Johnson about Johnson's treatment of Lord Lyttelton in his *Lives of the Poets*, were played out in the drawing-rooms of the circle, and reported in personal letters and private diaries. Gossip about the drama of these events tended to dominate in the observations of the friends them-selves, but underneath the accounts of these events there also existed a sense of a new stage in the progress of women towards the 'female right to literature'. It was the perception of this new phenomenon which shifted the gender of the term 'bluestocking' to the women. The change stemmed partly from the attitudes of the circle itself, and partly, as I shall show in Chapter 11, from the bright light of publicity which was placed on this new development.

Early on, the unique capacities of Elizabeth Carter had become material for self-conscious assertions. In 1763, when Mrs Montagu and her friends were travelling to Spa, she described to Mrs Vesey an incident during a visit the party made to the Jesuit College at St Omer's. They asked for Greek manuscripts for the amusement of Mrs Carter, to the great amazement of the Librarian, who imagined her to be possess'd, & would fain have exorcised her, but we assured him her learning could not lye more quietly in the red sea than it did in her head, such was the depth of her capacity. (MO 6370)

Hearing about the trip, King George III was curious about these 'learned ladies'. After the travellers had returned, the King asked Lord Bath which of the ladies he had travelled with was the most learned. To Mrs Montagu's mock chagrin, his reply was 'Miss Carter' (MO 3101, 27 [Sept. 1763]). Lord Bath himself was ambivalent about Elizabeth Carter's learning. He enjoyed her knowledge of Greek and sent messages to her in Greek via Mrs Montagu. But he also felt that her learning must be in some way responsible for her headaches, and if she gave up her learning, and acquired a gentleman friend, her health would improve (MO 4246, 10 Jan. 1762).

With Mrs Carter as an example, Mrs Montagu wished to be one of the learned ladies. In 1765 Catherine Read, the Scottish woman painter then working in London, asked to paint Mrs Montagu's picture. Although she respected Mrs Read and admired her talents, Mrs Montagu hesitated. She felt she hardly deserved to be considered one of the 'select & sacred number nine, when to be sure they are in this Land nine thousand such sort of good women as I.' She felt that even Elizabeth Carter would only distinguish her for making good marmalade. Unless she should be drawn with a pot of marmalade, and labelled 'in ye stile of receipts, *Orange Marmelade the best way*', Mrs Montagu did not see what other claim she had to being included with these women (MO 3146, 30 June 1765, Sandleford). Since she was working on her *Essay on Shakespear* at the time, we can surmise that one of her motives for pursuing her work was to try to achieve such literary distinction. (Catherine Read did the portrait of Elizabeth Carter which is now in the Johnson Museum at Gough Square, London; I have not found a portrait of Elizabeth Montagu by her.)

Although Mrs Montagu felt an estrangement from her husband in the later years of her marriage, she remained a dutiful wife to the end of his life. As she nursed him during his last illness his condition fluctuated, and she said that if it were not for the fact that he was eighty-four and that his constitution

*Elizabeth Carter.* Painted by Catherine Read, *c.*1765. Her arm is resting on a copy of her translation of Epictetus. Dr Johnson's House Trust, Gough Square, London.

was 'so worn' he might yet recover. She told her sister that their father, 'not liking ye last act of ye Human Drama' did not even call at her door, although her brothers Morris and Charles visited. She saw no one of her friends but Mrs Vesey and Mrs Carter (MO 970, (13 May 1775)).

Mr Montagu had made his religious views clear in a private conversation he had in 1773 with James Beattie, author of the *Essay on Truth*. Although Mr Montagu professed to regard himself as a firm believer in a Deity, he seemed incredulous in regard to a future state. When Beattie pressed him on the subject, he proposed to discuss it again at another time (Beattie, *London Diary*, 58). As far as I can judge, that time never came, and on his deathbed Mr Montagu was not reconciled to the truths of Christianity in which his wife believed. During the last few days Mr Montagu had a period of delirium in which he was pained by an impression that he had hurt his wife in some way. He repeatedly spoke of her merits and felt sad that he had shortened her life. Mrs Montagu was upset by these outbursts. Her husband still recognized everyone; she felt she could not bring Mrs Carter into the room, evidently in fear that Mrs Carter might hear him say these things (MO 5971, (16 May 1775), to Sarah Scott).

When Edward Montagu died on 20 May 1775, he left his wife his entire fortune, with the exception of some legacies. His will, originally written on 12 July 1752, amended on 16 April 1759, and again on 17 March 1774, was consistently concerned to secure to her all his real and personal estate, as well as property he had inherited successively from his cousin John Rogers, and later from his sister Lady Meadows (MO 1700). In the late 1760s he had been very ill and difficult to deal with. Mrs Scott, who took a rather grim view of life, feared that Mr Montagu might disinherit his wife, but Mrs Montagu was certain that that would not happen.

Despite his loyalty to his wife, he had not been generous while he was alive, for Mrs Montagu had on occasion complained that her private purse was not very heavy. But she was a very prudent manager, and probably those sums which she used for small charities and to assist deserving women writers like Sarah Fielding, she saved by her careful expenditure in household funds. When she became a widow, she was free to spend as she wished. She established legacies for her sister, for Elizabeth Carter, and for Dr Johnson's friend Anna Williams. She adopted her nephew Matthew Robinson as her heir, and received permission to change his name to Matthew Montagu. (Mr Montagu had been very fond of Matthew when he was a child, and had enjoyed having him for long visits at Sandleford, and it may be that Mrs Montagu's action in making Matthew her heir had been discussed with her husband earlier.)

After her husband's death Mrs Montagu determinedly made herself an independent woman. Some years after she was widowed, she was writing to Elizabeth Carter that 'we are not so perfectly ye rib of Man as Woman ought to be. We can think for ourselves, & also act for ourselves.' The past was softened in her memory.

When a Wife, I was obedient because it was my duty, & being married to a Man of sense & integrity, obedience was not painful or irksome, [ ] in early Youth a director perhaps is necessary if the sphere of action is extensive; but it seems to me that a new Master & new lessons, after ones opinions & habits were form'd, must be a little awkward, & with all due respect to ye superior Sex, I do not see how they can be necessary to a Woman unless she were to defend her Lands & Tenements by Sword or gun. (MO 3530, 11 July [17]82)

The last part of her life shows this active, independent woman. In addition to her reputation as a woman of letters, her extensive social life, varied literary patronage, business management, and charity to the poor made her a leading figure in the bluestocking circle of the 1770s and early 1780s, and did much to spread the idea of the bluestockings to a wider social group.[1]

In 1776 Mrs Montagu travelled to France in a party including Matthew, Elizabeth Carter's nephew Montagu Pennington, and Dorothy Gregory, Dr John Gregory's daughter, who had lived with her since Dr Gregory's death in 1773. Mrs Montagu also had a tutor for the boys. Her travelling equipage consisted of a coach, a chaise, and a complement of between twelve and fourteen horses. She rented a house in Chaillot, then a suburb of Paris, furnished it, and participated actively in the social and literary life of Paris. She was warmly received and lionized as a woman of letters. Mrs Montagu thought that celebrity was the object in France rather than riches and power as in England

and therefore talents made a greater show. 'My very Coiffeuse while she curls my hair flatters me on my reputation as an author' (MO 5991, 16 July 1776, (Paris), to Sarah Scott).

Mrs Montagu had the experience of being present at a ceremonious meeting of the French Academy at which, among other things, a paper of Voltaire's against Shakespeare was read in which Voltaire expressed fear that translations of Shakespeare into French would spoil the taste of the nation. Mrs Montagu wrote to Mrs Vesey that she considered the paper a 'most blackguard abusive invective'. But when she was asked by an academician if she would answer it, she thought that, although she could have done it very well, it was more politic to say that she thought Mr L'Abbé Arnauld had done it better than she could with his praise of original genius (MO 6486, 7 Sept. 1776, (Chaillot)).

In later years Mrs Montagu occupied herself in building a grand house in Portman Square. Her income was at least £7,000 a year, and she could pay for the expenses of building her house from ready income without borrowing. She moved into this house in December 1781; it is with its elegant appointments that her later extensive entertaining is associated. The years between 1757 and 1775 had been those in which one might speak of the bluestockings as a relatively small group of close friends. After 1775, and especially after the completion of Mrs Montagu's new house, the circle widened. The parties became larger, there was a heavy complement of the aristocracy, and there were interlocking circles of the observed and their observers. A number of women became prominent hostesses. Fanny Burney noted of the Hon. Miss Monckton in 1782 that she was 'one of those who stand foremost in collecting all extraordinary or curious people to her London conversaziones, which like those of Mrs. Vesey, mix the rank and the literature, and exclude all beside' (*Diary*, ii. 123).

In *Life in the English Country House* Mark Girouard has shown that towards the end of the eighteenth century English social life was becoming more informal, and that upper-class people were including books and art as well as gardens in their lives. He finds the change reflected in the changing styles of country houses (Girouard, chap. 8). The informal style seems to have originated in the less rigid social life of the spas; as we have

seen in Chapter 7, Mrs Montagu developed some of her friendships with male intellectuals at Tunbridge Wells. The new style
was also reflected rather early in the country house life of the
Duchess of Portland at Bulstrode; she pursued her interests in
art, gardening, and nature, and had people with academic or
intellectual backgrounds to stay. But Mrs Montagu's country
house, Sandleford, was limited in its accommodations, and
Mrs Montagu focused her larger social ambitions on the season
in London, partly out of necessity and partly out of preference.
She and the other women who became known as bluestocking
hostesses thus transplanted the informal style of the spas and
country houses to London. In the bluestocking assemblies a
variety of people known for intellectual, artistic, or musical
achievement, or of high rank, met and mingled.

It was the bluestocking assemblies of Elizabeth Vesey
(?1715–1791) which aroused much comment. She was the wife
of Agmondesham Vesey of Lucan near Dublin, who was for
many years a member of the Irish Parliament. The daughter of
an Irish Bishop, Mrs Vesey was well educated; the bookseller's
catalogue prepared for the sale of her library in 1926 shows an
extensive collection of literary, political, and classical works
(William H. Robinson Ltd.). In the Prologue I showed that
Mrs Vesey's use of the term 'bluestocking' in her letters of the
sixties made her especially influential in using and preserving
the term. In fact, she probably invented the term, and had a
proprietary interest in keeping it alive. Fanny Burney claimed
that Mrs Vesey had originated the term when *she* told Benjamin
Stillingfleet that he need not worry about coming to a party in
his blue stockings (Charles Burney, *Memoirs*, ii. 262–3). The
teasing of Stillingfleet which I quoted in the Prologue probably
originated then.

The friendship between Mrs Vesey and Mrs Montagu probably began as a spa friendship. Mrs Montagu seems to have
met Mrs Vesey as early as 1749. In July 1755 Gilbert West was
at Tunbridge Wells, and mentioned meeting Mrs Vesey there.
Mrs Montagu was enthusiastic about Mrs Vesey's good
manners, good sense, and improved mind (MO 6725). In June
1762 Mrs Montagu and her husband went on a tour of Oxford
and Blenheim, then on to Hagley to visit Lord Lyttelton, where
Lord Bath, Mr and Mrs Vesey, and Dr Monsey met them.

During this visit Mrs Montagu felt that she had experienced a delightful interlude, somewhat like the visits to Bulstrode years earlier. About two years afterwards, in a letter to the Duchess of Portland, Mrs Montagu described Mrs Vesey's abstractions from everyday realities. Ordinarily, Mrs Handcock, the sister of Mrs Vesey's first husband, and Mrs Vesey's companion, took care of the affairs 'of the body', and left Mrs Vesey to mental pursuits. But Mrs Handcock was not present at Hagley, and Mrs Vesey was left to indulge her ethereal fancies. Mrs Montagu explained that Mrs Vesey was never where she was expected to be, and had always to be searched for (MO 434, 12 Nov. [1764]).

During the late 1760s and early 1770s the friendship of Mrs Montagu and Mrs Vesey seems to have been especially close. When Mrs Montagu's book was published, Mrs Vesey took a great interest in its success. She invited people to her drawing-room so that they might talk about the book; she especially enjoyed hearing speculation about which male writer the author might be. Mrs Vesey even went round to a bookseller where she was not known and asked about the *Essay*. She was happy to hear that her friend's work was judged by the bookseller to be a sensible book, and was doing well (MO 6288).

Mrs Vesey's letters to Mrs Montagu reveal Mrs Vesey's romantic tendencies—her love of the rural countryside, her interest in Gothic buildings, in the poetry of 'Ossian', and in the idea of primitive culture. She was romantic about the estate at Lucan; she described a cottage on the banks of the Liffey where she had tea and indulged in reveries. During part of the time her husband spent at Dublin, Mrs Vesey was 'alone' at Lucan (although presumably Mrs Handcock was actually there as her companion); at other periods Mrs Vesey had to participate in Dublin society, which she thought too busy and superficial. The qualities Mrs Vesey demonstrated suggest a deliberate repression of assertive tendencies. She was not happy in Ireland, but she felt absolute loyalty to her husband, and took the position that when she travelled and where she stayed were to be determined by him. Her airiness and withdrawal from practical realities seem to have been the way she dealt with conflicts she could not resolve.

One of Mrs Vesey's difficulties was that she was not con-

vinced of the existence of the life hereafter, in which all the
friends were to meet; Mrs Montagu tried to reassure her on the
grounds of the reverence all people pay to their dead, which
must arise from an internal sense of the future state (MO 6433,
24 Oct. 1773, Sandleford). Mrs Vesey often expressed melancholy and depressed thoughts when she was at home at Lucan.
Mrs Montagu wrote her many letters urging perseverance,
and encouraging her to come to London, where she would be
happier when she was doing the honours of her blue drawing-
room. Mrs Vesey's diffidence and selflessness were part of her
charm as a hostess. Unlike Mrs Montagu, who imposed a
circle on her guests, and who also could not help wishing to
'shine', Mrs Vesey concentrated on the needs and interests of
her guests, and encouraged them to form small groups. Mrs
Vesey's techniques as hostess became the subject of comment
by private observers, and of two poems, 'Modern Manners' by
Charles Hoole, and 'Bas Bleu' by Hannah More.

Elizabeth Carter was also a good friend; she saw Mrs Vesey
sometimes twice a day when they were in London, and wrote
her encouraging letters when they were apart. Mrs Vesey
confided in her her religious uncertainties, her fears of memory
loss and of insanity. Elizabeth Carter tried to help her by discussing the imperfect state of human nature and the need to
strive for virtue. It was best to concern oneself only with one's
duties. Later she advised Mrs Vesey not to listen to the French
philosophers, 'who would persuade you it is best to wander
over a wide stormy ocean without a pilot, and without a
leading star' (*Letters to Catherine Talbot*, ii. 312). Interestingly
enough, Elizabeth Carter confided in Mrs Vesey her own
negative feelings about Elizabeth Montagu. She disapproved of
Mrs Montagu's incessant social activities. 'Fashionable life is
a hard service, and when once people are engaged in it, the
dismission I suppose is not very easily procured' (ii. 202). Yet
she was forgiving. Mrs Montagu was a busy person and Elizabeth Carter asked Mrs Vesey to write directly to herself. If she
encloses 'to our dear careless friend, they sometimes lie several
days quietly in her dressing room, before she thinks of giving
them to me' (ii. 203).

By 1775 women of the younger generation were taking their
places as 'bluestocking hostesses'. One of the most prominent

*Thrale*

was Mrs Thrale. Hester Lynch Salusbury was born in 1741. She was an only child, the 'joint plaything' of her parents, who encouraged their clever daughter. There was no very consistent plan of education, but she was taught several modern languages, and had special tutors, in particular Dr Arthur Collier, who taught her Latin and with whom she formed a close friendship. But, because of financial difficulties, she was married off in 1763 to a brewer, Henry Thrale. Thrale was an educated man and a bon vivant, but as a suitor and husband he showed no concern with Hester's special qualities. Thus, as I have shown in my article 'The Ironies of Education', her education had essentially involved her in a double bind. She had been encouraged to read widely in several languages, and to write poetry, but her early married life was very circumscribed. She was restrained from social diversions by her mother and husband and from some ordinary domestic duties by her husband's dictum that he did not wish her to supervise the kitchen (Hayward, i. 257). Her winters were spent at the house next to the Brewery in Southwark; at other times of the year she was in their country place at Streatham, south of London.

During the years of her marriage, she was bearing, rearing, and also burying many children. In the 'Children's Book', which she began in 1766, she entered details about her children and her feelings about them, her efforts at educating them, and the painful details of their serious illnesses. By the end of the 'Children's Book' in 1778 she had noted the deaths of two new-born infants, four young children, and her schoolboy son. Of the twelve children she eventually had, four daughters lived to maturity. (Mary Hyde has published the 'Children's Book' in *The Thrales of Streatham Park*.)

Not long after their first child was born, Mr and Mrs Thrale formed a friendship with Samuel Johnson. Arthur Murphy, a friend of Mr Thrale, made them acquainted with each other by bringing Johnson to dine at the Brewery house on 9 January 1765. In the ensuing months Johnson often stayed at the Brewery house, or at the country place in Streatham. When they discovered that Johnson was suffering from severe emotional illness, they brought him to Streatham, and Mrs Thrale undertook to help him (Hyde, 19–20). The friendship, thus begun, developed into an easy familial intimacy. For Mrs

Thrale, in particular, this long-lasting friendship with Dr Johnson filled a variety of needs. She had the extraordinary pleasure of sharing the intellectual life of the man whom she regarded as a great moralist and philosopher. She had the solace of sharing with him the burdens of life—his illnesses and depressions in exchange for her domestic and maternal anxieties and struggles. She gradually evolved a life which was similar to that of the first bluestockings. She read the classics, wrote poetry, talked with and wrote to Johnson, and cultivated a circle of literary friends. Finally, her friendship with Mrs Montagu brought the older and the younger generation of bluestockings in touch.

Hester and Henry Thrale first met Elizabeth Montagu at a dinner-party given by Sir Joshua Reynolds in January 1775. The friendship which ensued between Mrs Montagu (then fifty-five) and Mrs Thrale (then thirty-four) was carried on by visits by Mrs Thrale to Mrs Montagu in London and visits by Mrs Montagu to Streatham, with periods of time when both women were at Bath. Mrs Montagu was much impressed with Mrs Thrale's abilities. Writing to Mrs Vesey, she spoke of visiting Streatham, where she had had a fine dinner, '& ye best of all feasts, sense, & witt, & good humour. Mrs Thrale is a Woman of very superior understanding, & very respectable as a Wife, a Mother, a Friend, and a Mistress of a Family' (MO 6505, 12 Aug. 1777).

During the difficult years of Henry Thrale's illness and eventual death, Mrs Montagu expressed sympathy and concern. When the question of the fate of the Brewery was being discussed after Mr Thrale's death, Mrs Montagu at first counselled holding on, because, as she explained later, she was not sure that anyone would be able to make such a great purchase. This advice aroused Mrs Thrale's anger and led to the outburst in *Thraliana* about the 'Wits and the Blues' which I quoted in the Prologue. This entry, dated 17 May 1781, is followed by another remark in which Mrs Thrale expressed anger at Mrs Montagu's praise of her. Mrs Montagu had said that 'Such . . . is the Dignity of Mrs Thrales Virtue, and such her Superiority in all Situations of Life, that nothing is now wanting but an Earthquake to show how She will behave on *that* Occasion: Oh brave Mrs Montagu!'

Observers have sometimes hinted that Mrs Montagu's interest in Mrs Thrale was prompted by Mrs Thrale's close friendship with Samuel Johnson. Johnson had called on Mrs Montagu years earlier, when she had found him proud and distant. But as Johnson was living with the Thrales for long periods, especially at Streatham, it was natural for Mrs Montagu to ask about him or mention him in her letters to Mrs Thrale, as she took an interest in the children and the Thrale family affairs. At one point Mrs Montagu did admit to a feeling of jealousy, adding in a PS to a letter to Mrs Thrale, 'I dare not trust a Rival with what I wd say to Dr. Johnson' (John Rylands Library, Eng. MS 551, no. 6). The outbursts against Mrs Montagu and the 'blues' may be due to Mrs Thrale's sense that Mrs Montagu was attempting to intrude on her relationship with Dr Johnson. In the early days of her friendship with Mrs Montagu, Mrs Thrale probably felt possessive about her intimacy with Johnson. Later, after her own break with him, Mrs Thrale added a note to her *Anecdotes of Samuel Johnson* denying that she had made the negative comments about Mrs Montagu's *Essay* attributed to her by Boswell in his *Journal of a Tour to the Hebrides* (chap. 7).

But by that time Mrs Thrale was Hester Lynch Piozzi, wife of the Italian musician who had given lessons to her eldest daughter, and to whom she had turned after her husband's death; in fact before she was widowed she had found Piozzi a sympathetic person who reminded her of her own father. The second marriage had been a shock not only to Johnson, but also to the bluestocking circle. They prided themselves on their virtue and seriousness. In 1778 they had expressed their shock at the second marriage of Catherine Macaulay to the young Mr Graham. Ironically enough, Mrs Montagu wrote to Mrs Thrale at the time, exclaiming that Mrs Macaulay had substituted Venus for the chaste Minerva by her choice of a 'surgeons mate aged 22, ah! it is both passing strange & wondrous pittiful!' (John Rylands Library, Eng. MS 551, no. 30). Mrs Montagu thought the marriage came about 'from Mrs. Macaulay's adopting Masculine opinions, & masculine manners' (John Rylands Library, Eng. MS 551, no. 29).

The bluestockings were upset at what they took to be Mrs Piozzi's unbridled passion. The comments of her contemporaries echoed Hamlet's savage indictment of Gertrude's second marriage. Hester Chapone wrote to her friend Mrs Pepys:

surely there must be really some degree of *Insanity* in that case. for such mighty overbearing Passions are not natural in a 'Matron's bones.' The 4 daughters render it a most frightful instance of human wretchedness indeed! it has given great occasion to the Enemy to blaspheme and to triumph over the Bas Bleu Ladies. (Gaussen, i. 408)

Her comment indicates that she was aware of the kinds of scathing remarks that could be made about women who were known to participate in the life of the mind. There was the old underlying suspicion that women who shared the wider knowledge of men might also share their freer tendencies in sexual behaviour (see Prologue).

Another member of the younger generation, Fanny Burney, was a careful and astute observer, and the later years of the bluestocking circle are well documented in her journals. Frances Burney (1752–1840) was the daughter of the musician Charles Burney; in 1795 she married General Alexander d'Arblay. She was a prolific early diarist and secret fiction-writer whose novel, *Evelina*, was published anonymously in 1778. After its publication, however, the secret of her authorship of the novel was divulged in the Streatham circle, and Fanny became something of a protégée of Mrs Thrale. At least she spent periods of time in Mrs Thrale's company at Streatham and on visits to Bath.

Unlike Mrs Thrale, Fanny Burney's responses to the bluestocking ladies show a positive feeling and even a sense of solidarity with women who had been singled out for their abilities. In 1778 while Fanny was at Streatham, Mrs Thrale asked her if she would like to see Mrs Montagu. 'I truly said, I should be the most insensible of all animals not to like to see our sex's glory' (*Diary*, i. 109). Mrs Thrale then wrote to invite Mrs Montagu to Streatham. Lady Ladd, Mr Thrale's sister, expressed her belief that Mrs Montagu would not be interested in 'girl acquaintance' because she cultivated only people of consequence, so Fanny decided to lie low and keep out of the way. Johnson's response was to 'see-saw'; he was amused at the prospect of rivalry between the two women. Mrs Montagu was now the top wit and Fanny Burney was a rising one. He incited Fanny to put her down.

Both Mrs Thrale and Dr Johnson agreed that Mrs Montagu diffused more knowledge in her conversation than any other woman Samuel Johnson knew, and almost any man. Mrs Thrale pointed out, however, that Johnson would not quarrel with her, 'as everybody else does, for her love of finery' (*Diary*, i. 116).

Fanny Burney described Mrs Montagu as 'middle-sized, very thin, and looks infirm; she has a sensible and penetrating countenance and the air and manner of a woman accustomed to being distinguished, and of great parts' (*Diary*, i. 120). Mrs Montagu had heard of *Evelina*, whose authorship had not yet been publicly acknowledged. She expressed herself as pleased to hear it had been written by a woman. Finally Mrs Thrale burst out with the secret of the novel's authorship, and Fanny in intense embarrassment rushed from the room. While she was out of the room Mrs Montagu asked what else Fanny might write. Mrs Thrale explained she had suggested a comedy, to which Mrs Montagu responded that she hoped Fanny would let her see it; 'and all my influence is at her service' (*Diary*, i. 126).

In 1780 while on a visit to Bath with the Thrales, Fanny Burney had the opportunity of seeing much of Mrs Montagu. Fanny concluded that, although Mrs Montagu reasoned well and 'haranged' well, she had no wit, while Mrs Thrale had almost too much (*Diary*, i. 352). During that visit Fanny also had the opportunity of meeting Elizabeth Carter. She

received me with a smiling air of benevolence that more than answered all my expectations of her. She is really a noble-looking woman; I never saw age so graceful in the female sex yet; her whole face seems to beam with goodness, piety, and philanthropy. (*Diary*, i. 390–1)

At the last ball of the Bath season Fanny met an acquaintance, a Capt. Bouchier, who stayed to talk with her after she had refused to dance with him.

He told me that he had very lately met with Hannah More, and then mentioned Mrs. Montagu and Mrs. Carter, whence he took occasion to say most high and fine things of the ladies of the present age,—

their writings, and talents; and I soon found he had no small reverence for us blue-stockings. (*Diary*, i. 403)

Although Fanny had reservations about women learning classical languages, because it might expose them to criticism (see her conversation with Mr Fairly, *Diary*, iv. 222–3), she still evidently enjoyed a sense of identification with other women whose abilities had brought them into notice. Dorothy Gregory told her of Hester Chapone's praise of *Evelina*, to which she responded, 'Who would not be a blue-stockinger at this rate?' (*Diary*, i. 359).

Fanny Burney soon circulated in bluestocking social circles. She met Mrs Vesey, who she thought had 'the most wrinkled, sallow, time-beaten face I ever saw'. But she admitted that Mrs Vesey's abilities as a hostess must involve some special talent (*Diary*, i. 253–4). On 30 December 1782 Fanny went by appointment to Mrs Chapone, where she met Mr and Mrs Pepys, Mr and Mrs Mulso, Mr Burrows, and his sister. Mrs Chapone offered to introduce her to Mrs Delany (*Diary*, ii. 167). She soon became an intimate friend of Mrs Delany, whom she described as gentle and benevolent, and reminding her of her maternal grandmother, Mrs Sleepe (Hemlow, 5). On 7 July 1783 she reported spending the whole day with 'sweet Mrs. Delany, whom I love most tenderly'. Mrs Sandford (the late John Chapone's sister), who had been a protégée of Mrs Delany, was there. The network of those days offered ties of friendship to a range of women who varied in social status, financial resources, and age. The bringing together of women of various ages seems to have been especially characteristic of the later bluestocking circle.

At Mrs Delany's party, Horace Walpole came in; Fanny Burney described him as bright but caustic, and noted that although she admired she could not love or trust him (*Diary*, ii. 216). In fact, at the time of the Montagu–Johnson quarrel about Lyttelton, Horace Walpole's private letters to William Mason contained scathing references to Mrs Montagu 'and all her Maenads, [who] intend to tear him [Samuel Johnson] limb from limb for despising their moppet Lord Lyttelton' (xxix. 97). Since 'Maenad' meant 'mad woman', referring to the female votaries who celebrated the orgiastic rites of Dionysus, or more generally any frenzied unnaturally excited woman, Walpole's use of this term suggests a judgement on his part that Mrs Montagu and her friends were intruding in an unpleasantly feminine way in the business of literature.

Fanny Burney, who was extremely conscious of every comment or puff made about her and those with whom she was connected, began now to note in her journal items about her and other bluestocking ladies which appeared in print. These references belong to my discussion of 'Bluestockings in Print and on Canvas' in Chapter 11.

In the following years, after Fanny Burney went into the service of Queen Charlotte as Second Keeper of the Robes (1786), she retained her interest in her bluestocking friends, although the friendships were attenuated by the close confinement involved in her service to the queen. After she retired from the queen's service in 1791, she was free to take up old friendships. There was still a great deal of interest in her work. When *Camilla* was in process of publication, the bluestocking ladies participated in building up the subscription list. Mrs Montagu gave a large sum for one copy; both Mrs Crewe and Mrs Boscawen received and kept lists of subscriptions (Burney, *Journals*, iii. 118–19 and n. 8).

Of the members of the younger generation who came to prominence as bluestockings, Hannah More (1745–1833) was probably the most regressive in her attitudes towards the advancement of women. The situation is ironic, because she herself had benefited by the changes in life-style instituted by the bluestockings. Born the same year as Hester Salusbury, Hannah More had a career which in some ways paralleled and in other ways diverged extremely from that of Mrs Thrale. Daughter of a schoolmaster, Hannah had had an early education in Latin and mathematics. Later educated in the school her sisters set up in Bristol, Hannah also learned Italian and Spanish. Her father, worried that she was making too much progress for a girl, discontinued her study of mathematics. She began to write and publish in 1762. Her play, *The Inflexible Captive*, a translation from Metastasio, was well received in Bath.

Hannah More's first visit to London in the winter of 1774–5 brought her into bluestocking circles. She became a close friend of David and Eva Marie Garrick. Her tragedy *Percy*, staged in

1777 with assistance from Garrick, was very successful. She wrote and published other plays, poetry, and prose. She thus became a prominent woman writer, a position she was to retain throughout life. After Garrick's death she spent much time with Mrs Garrick. There were friendships with Mrs Montagu and with Horace Walpole. Hannah More visited Sandleford and Mrs Montagu visited Cowslip Green.

In 1784 Hannah More and Elizabeth Montagu became involved in helping Ann Yearsley, the milkwoman poet. The project was Hannah More's but Mrs Montagu collaborated with her in bringing out by subscription in 1785 Yearsley's *Poems, on Several Occasions*. Their feminist consciousness impelled them to try to protect Ann Yearsley from her husband by investing the money she earned by her publication in a trust fund and acting as her trustees, so he would not have access to the money (MO 3990). But Mrs Yearsley soon felt she had been unjustly treated and created a public fuss. She included in her fourth edition of her *Poems* (1786) a 'Narrative' to the subscribers which detailed what she regarded as Hannah More's high-handed and unfair treatment. Mrs Yearsley thought she should be admitted as a joint trustee. She was willing that she and her husband should have no claim to the principal, but thought the parents should receive the interest, and asked that the money might be divided among their children when they reached the age of twenty-one. In her next volume, *Poems, on Various Subjects* (1787), she printed the offending 'Deed of Trust' which she and her husband had signed on 10 June 1785; it explicitly stated that the money in the trust fund would be used for the benefit of Ann Yearsley and her children, and that John Yearsley or any future husband would not be able to touch the contents of the trust (Yearsley (1787), pp. xxvii–xxix). Mrs Yearsley's very public rejection stung Hannah More; she and Mrs Montagu resigned the trust, which eventually went to Mrs Yearsley (Tompkins, 71–6). Miss More and Mrs Montagu were attempting to provide protection to a woman they regarded as likely to be taken advantage of by her husband. They obviously were not sensitive to the problem of Mrs Yearsley's relationship with her husband, to her wish to control her earnings, and to her prickly self-respect as a woman of the working class.

Hannah More's poem on the bluestockings, *The Bas-Bleu; or Conversation*, brought into public notice her view of bluestocking social life. It also introduced the term 'bas-bleu', which had been used by the French Ambassadress for the bluestockings (Carter, *Letters* (1817), ii. 202–3). This poem, which 'wandered about in manuscript', in Samuel Johnson's phrase (*Letters*, iii. 157), was very popular in the circle itself. Mrs Boscawen spoke of having a copy written for Mrs Delany; Mary Hamilton read it in manuscript, and King George wished to have a copy written by Hannah More herself.

With the publication of *Bas-Bleu* in 1786, More's view of the bluestockings as conversationalists became prominent. In actuality, her treatment was somewhat misleading. More spoke of the bluestockings as reformers, who had instituted conversation-parties in opposition to whist. We know that as young women Elizabeth Montagu and the Duchess of Portland had objected to the time taken up by cards. Hester Mulso had written against cards in *Rambler*, No. 10. But Hannah More, who herself had a great deal of reforming zeal, which later led to her absorption in evangelical work, was making a rather superficial estimate of the significance of the bluestockings without going deeper into the original motives of the older women. Elizabeth Carter's position, that it was unfair to women to keep them from rational conversation with men because it kept them from developing their intellectual capacities, was probably closer to the underlying purpose of the bluestocking social life which had grown out of the intellectual interests of these women.

Ironically enough, in her own advice to women, Hannah More was more conservative than the women of the earlier generation. Catherine Talbot had objected to the passage from Thucydides in which Pericles is quoted as advising women to be silent (see Chapter 5). Hannah More used that very passage as an epigraph on the title-page of her *Essays on Various Subjects* (1777), a book which essentially stressed a separate way of life for women. Even in her *Strictures on Female Education*, published in 1799, More was advising a limited education for women, although at that point she had to admit that whether women were capable of tackling difficult subjects was unknown, because it had not been tried.

On the other hand, in this period the personal example of the bluestockings must have encouraged some young women to work at improving their minds by study. Mary Hamilton (1756–1816) was a younger woman of the bluestocking circle who strove for education. When she was sixteen, she asked her guardian, William Napier, later Lord Napier, to buy the poems of Elizabeth Carter for her. Mary studied Latin; when she wrote to her guardian about this project, he expressed dismay. He permitted her to continue, but cautioned her to keep it a secret. Later he pleaded with her not to send him any more Latin or Greek letters (Anson, 17–18). Mary moved to London with her widowed mother in 1775, and in 1777 she received a Court appointment as an assistant in the establishment of the princesses. During her period of service at Court, she formed a close friendship with Elizabeth Carter. The queen was evidently interested in Elizabeth Carter, and, through Mary Hamilton, lent Mrs Carter books and sent her medicine. After Mary Hamilton resigned her appointment in 1782, she shared a house in Clarges Street with two other young women, for her mother had died in the interim. She visited and was friendly with many of the people of the bluestocking circle: the Duchess of Portland, Mrs Delany, Elizabeth Carter, Hannah More, the Veseys, and Dr and Miss Burney.

The term 'bas-bleu' as an alternative for bluestocking caught on quickly. In her journal Mary Hamilton noted various occasions at which she heard literary talk. She went with Mrs Boscawen to a 'bas-bleu' party given by Miss Burrows (Anson, 171). On 12 April 1784 she went to a 'bas-bleu' party at which Mrs Montagu, Mr Walpole, Mr and Mrs Pepys and Sir L. Pepys, Lady Rothes, Mrs Garrick, Miss H. More, Dr and Miss Burney, Sir Joshua Reynolds, Miss Palmer, Lord Monboddo, and Mrs Carter were present. 'The chief thing I heard was a difference of opinion respecting *Dryden*, Mr Walpole & Dr. Burney extolled him above all our Poets' (Anson, 174). On 23 May she heard Mr Pepys read aloud a 'dedication to Mrs. Montagu, prefix'd to a Poem just published by Miss Williams . . .'. Later that day Mary Hamilton went to Mrs Montagu's. She had 'a large Assembly of People of fashion . . .'. Miss Hamilton told Mrs Montagu how much she had enjoyed the poem; Mrs Montagu replied, ' "You know Poets are said to excel in *fiction*." . . .' (Anson, 187). Mary Hamilton's bluestocking life shows her trying to educate herself by listening.

But, like Lady Grey forty years earlier, Mary Hamilton used the term *femmes-savantes* as a term of opprobrium. She thought such women were in general pretenders to learning, but believed that there were exceptions: Mrs Carter was learned, wise, and good. Mary Hamilton also included Miss More, Mrs Chapone, and one or two others as exceptions (Anson, 217). It was these exceptions who influenced her. In the winter of 1785 she wrote to her fiancé John Dickenson that she was reading Blair's *Sermons*, and recommended Dr Warton's works to him. 'As I wish to occupy my mind as much as I can, I shall begin to learn Italian, but as I cannot afford a Master, I shall make slow progress I fear . . .' (Anson, 262). After their marriage, the couple divided their time between houses in the country and visits to London. Mrs Dickenson seems to have kept up her intellectual interests, and carefully watched over the education of her only child, a daughter. Music in particular was an interest she shared with her husband. A selection of her correspondence and diaries was published in 1925 by her great-granddaughters, Elizabeth and Florence Anson. In these letters and diaries Mary Hamilton gives her own fresh views of the bluestockings. I have not determined if the correspondence from which the book was culled still exists.

Marianne Francis (1790–1832) was another member of a still younger generation who had personal ties to the bluestocking circle. She was the daughter of Charlotte Burney and Clement Francis, and the niece of Fanny Burney. She learned many languages and seems to have followed Elizabeth Carter's example in reading in every language every day to keep them up (Menagh, 325). She carried on a correspondence with Mrs Piozzi from 1806 to 1820. But the bluestocking circle had already fallen into decline when she was a young woman, and she lacked the support of like-minded friends. She thought nostalgically of the earlier world of the bluestockings; in 1812 she met Arthur Young and William Wilberforce, and turned to the world of evangelical Christianity (Menagh, 337). As Diane Menagh says, 'having abandoned hope for a renewed golden age of literary society, Marianne found her only solace in faith in an afterlife according to the Evangelicals' (340). Marianne Francis was a late observer of the bluestockings. She left a mass

of manuscript materials: diaries, musical compositions, a fragment of a novel, her letters to Mrs Piozzi (1806–20) and to her
sister Charlotte Barrett, who edited Fanny Burney's *Diary and
Letters*. There are also correspondences with Arthur Young and
with William Wilberforce, for whom she worked. Nothing has
been published except for a few hymns. In her article, 'The
Life of Marianne Francis', Menagh provides a bio-biblio-
graphical note on the location of the manuscripts (Menagh,
143–4).

   Marianne Francis was of the generation too late for the bluestocking circle. The late 1780s and early 1790s showed a
change in the bluestocking life-style. The older women were
dying or retiring from active social life. One of the first to drop
out was Mrs Vesey. During the late 1770s and early 1780s Mrs
Vesey had been under pressure to spend time in Ireland, where
her husband had built an elegant Georgian house and was still
serving as a Member of Parliament. Mr and Mrs Vesey both
suffered from bad health. Her deafness was increasing. She
feared loss of memory. On a couple of occasions Mrs Vesey
went to watering-places with Mrs Handcock and a friend,
Lady Primrose. Once her husband was at Spa, amusing
himself, as his wife said, with fat German countesses. She did
not know when he would be willing to return to a lean wife.
Down through the years there have been rumours of a flirtation
Mrs Vesey carried on with Laurence Sterne. Arthur H. Cash,
whose *Laurence Sterne: The Later Years* appeared in 1986, concludes
that the sentimental friendship and walk through Ranelagh
which have been reported, were actually a fiction—the invention
of William Combe, who forged many letters of Sterne (25–7).
Sterne and Mrs Vesey probably knew each other. A letter to
Mrs Vesey from Mrs Montagu invited Mrs Vesey to join her to
see Sterne entertain Lord Bath, while Sir Joshua Reynolds was
making some alterations on Bath's portrait (116). But Cash
thinks they were neither at Bath nor Scarborough at the same
time (307).

   It is ironical that these rumours should have persisted, for
during the course of her marriage Mrs Vesey seems to have
maintained the role of the self-abnegating wife. She claimed to
rely on her husband's decisions as to when and where they were
to be. At one point the couple planned a visit to Sandleford.

Sarah Scott conveyed their request from Bath that Mr Vesey was ill and Mrs Vesey wanted a 'field bed', presumably so that she could sleep in his room, and care for him. Mrs Scott added acidly that she knew Mrs Montagu would 'not mortify her [i.e. Mrs. Vesey's] conjugal tenderness; but afford her all possible means of being as near the Dear Man both night & day as her fondness or *his* can desire' (MO 5395, (Aug. 1779)).

Although Mrs Vesey's reputation for etherealness and impracticality was widespread, her friends cherished the few instances when she showed an assertive character. On one occasion she was at Scarborough when the bathing-machine she was in began to drift out to sea. With quick presence of mind, she broke out of her reverie to hail the man in charge of the horse, who had to go out to bring her back in (MO 6392, 10 Sept. 1767). Another time, on a trip to Ireland, Mrs Vesey and her companions were being taken to shore from their sailing-ship in a small boat, when the boat started to sink. It was Mrs Vesey who gained help from another boat by waving a handkerchief, and shouting 'drowning, drowning'. Mrs Montagu celebrated her 'undaunted courage & presence of mind' in a letter to her sister (MO 6011, 12 Sept. 1777), to Elizabeth Carter (MO 3426, 2 Sept. 1777) and to Mrs Vesey herself (MO 6507, 2 Sept. 1777).

In his last years Mr Vesey's physical decline kept them in England more of the time, and Mrs Vesey's social activities continued. The death of her husband in 1785 provoked a long period of mourning. His death-bed seemed to her a tender parting, but since Mr Vesey had not stipulated an income for her in his will and she had married 'romantically' without a settlement, her income did not seem adequate to maintain her in her present style of life. Mrs Montagu thought Mrs Vesey had £350 a year as a jointure from her first husband, which Mr Vesey had always received. Furthermore, Mr Vesey had allowed her so little that Lady Primrose helped her with clothes. Although in earlier times Mrs Montagu had carried on some light verbal flirtation with Mr Vesey, now she was very angry:

Mr. Vesey has left £1000 to his kept Mistress, poor recompence to be sure for mortal sin, & loathsome habits, but he has shewn more regard to his companion in iniquity than to his tender faithfull friend. I will say no more of the Monster, for I cannot think of him with patience. (MO 6108, 26 [June 1785], to Sarah Scott)

Hannah More also wrote scathingly of Mr Vesey:

We have just learnt that that execrable Vesey has left that dear Woman *nothing* but that hole of a house, and the old Coach! The Plate to Ld Lucan after the death of the heir / what an absurd fellow! and £1000 to his W – – – – He was determined to make his memory hated as well as despised. (MO 3990)

Dorothy Gregory, who had married a poor Scottish clergyman, Archibald Alison, against Mrs Montagu's wishes, thought that despite the inconveniences of being reduced to £500 a year Mrs Vesey would be a richer and happier woman than she had been when she was living with her husband.

I'm not Surprised at his continuing that preference at his death, which he always shewed in his life, to the Woman he kept or that any other Man kept, for he was more likely to understand her merits than the Merit of his Wife. (MO 42)

Mrs Vesey herself felt that she would have about £900 a year and thought she and Mrs Handcock would have enough to be comfortable and keep a carriage. She was preparing an apartment for Vesey's heir, his nephew. Mrs Vesey discussed her financial difficulties as a widow in a perfectly calm and rational manner; yet in this letter she said, 'I have had such incessant Tears of late I believe the Mind has been warp'd . . .' (MO 6358, [16 July 1785], to Mrs Montagu). As it happened, the nephew was a man of good will, and seems to have arranged a somewhat larger income for her, so that she was able to continue to live in some degree of comfort. After a long period of intense mourning, which her friends thought the man not worthy of, Mrs Vesey gradually declined into senility. Her friends noted that she did not remember when they had visited, and, finally, did not recognize them. Mrs Handcock predeceased her in 1787; Mrs Vesey died in 1791.

The deaths of the Duchess of Portland in 1785 and of her close friend Mary Delany in 1788 can also be seen as a diminution of the bluestocking circle. Mrs Montagu had revived her friendship with the Duchess in the 1760s; there were at least two visits to Bulstrode, and a visit to Tunbridge Wells, in which the Duchess graciously shared Mrs Montagu's Tunbridge lodging. The Duchess had spent the years of her widowhood studying botany, collecting *objets d'art*, and subsidizing scientific expeditions, such as the botanizing of her clergyman assistant and teacher of botany, the Revd John Lightfoot, and some of the explorations of Sir Joseph Banks. Her bluestocking social activities generally consisted of attending small dinners given by Mrs Delany for her and some friends, or occasional visits to hostesses like Mrs Montagu. But the Duchess thought her friend's parties had become too crowded and ostentatious.

In the later years, when the Duchess and Mrs Delany spent long periods of time together at Bulstrode, King George and Queen Charlotte took a strong interest in them, their collections, and their work. The royal couple and some of their many children would drive from Windsor to Bulstrode in a procession of carriages; the visits would have to be returned within a few days by the two ladies. Queen Charlotte was especially interested in seeing the Duchess's collections and Mrs Delany's work. Mary Delany, who had done embroidery and other kinds of needlework and shell work as well as painting for many years, had begun to do botanical studies from life, using bits of coloured paper to create flower mosaics. Her work was done with precision to show botanical details. She had undoubtedly been influenced by her friend's botanizing, and by the flower paintings by George Ehret, which the Duchess commissioned. The albums of Mrs Delany's work are contained in nine volumes of one hundred pictures each, and a tenth with seventy-two. Mrs Delany indexed each volume with botanical and common names (Hayden, 157). The volumes are now in the British Museum. In *Mrs. Delany, Her Life and her Flowers*, Ruth Hayden provides illustrations of Mrs Delany's work in both black-and-white photographs and colour plates.

After the death of the Duchess, her collections, like her father's before her, were dispersed in a sale that went on for thirty-eight days. Horace Walpole noted the purchase of several choice items for his own collection and bound into his copy of the sale catalogue an account of the Duchess and her varied interests (Walpole, *The Duchess of Portland's Museum*). Not long before her death she had purchased from Sir William Hamilton the Barberini vase, now known as the Portland vase, which is in the British Museum. The herbarium which the Revd Lightfoot created with the assistance of the Duchess was bought after his death in 1788 by King George and presented to the Queen. It is now in the Royal Botanic Gardens at Kew (Hedley, 179).

When the Duchess died, there was great surprise that she had not left Mrs Delany, her friend of many years, a legacy. The explanation is contained in a portion of Mrs Delany's will, as quoted in the Hemlow edition of the Burney *Journals*. The reason, which no one then knew, was that the Duchess had made Mrs Delany an interest-free loan of £400 at the time of the death of the Revd Delany, when she had thus been enabled to buy the London house she called the Thatched Cottage (Burney, *Journal*, iv. 158 n. 3). The death of the Duchess meant that Mrs Delany no longer had a pleasant summer residence, for she had visited Bulstrode regularly for years. The King provided a house at Windsor, and Mrs Delany's last few years were spent as a sort of favourite grandmother to the royal couple.

As late as 1792 Mrs Montagu was still giving grand public breakfasts in her palatial house, where Fanny Burney thought about 400 and 500 people had been assembled—a Ranelagh by daylight. By 1798 Dr Burney was writing to his daughter (10 Dec.) that although he had had a 'bit of blue' at Mrs Matthew Montagu's, the elder Mrs Montagu was sadly broken, blind, and unable to go out (*Diary and Letters* (1905), v. 430). The death of Mrs Montagu in August 1800 seemed the end of an era. Mrs Chapone died in 1801. At that time Fanny Burney, now Madame d'Arblay, wrote: 'How is our Blue Club cut up! But Sir William Pepys told me it was dead while living; all such society as that we formerly belonged to, and enjoyed, being positively over' (*Diary*, v. 481). Elizabeth Carter outlived the friends of her own generation, but she made younger ones. She continued to go up to London for the winter season, and died there in 1806 in her eighty-eighth year.

William Pepys was correct. The bluestocking circle was disappearing as a discernible phenomenon. In a period of social instability, with the turmoil of the French Revolution and the intensities of the evangelical revival, the idea of the bluestockings as it had evolved—a network of friendships supporting the literary and social activities of a group of men and women—was probably no longer viable. It had served the interests of the first generation of bluestockings who wrote, but published reluctantly and with trepidation. Once the limits of public exposure by publication were reached, Mrs Montagu and Mrs Carter could continue their intellectual activities with the support of friends, and without much risk. The bluestocking circle probably also helped the younger women to develop more professional attitudes, and stimulated them to be more ambitious, and to write and publish for money. Hester Lynch Piozzi profited by her experiences in bluestocking circles, but she can also be seen as breaking away from the inhibitions of the earlier generation both in her attitudes towards second marriages and to publication. Her publications after her second marriage of *Anecdotes of the Late Samuel Johnson* (1786), *Letters to and from the Late Samuel Johnson, LL D* (1788), *Observations and Reflections Made in the Course of a Journey Through France, Italy, and Germany* (1789), *British Synonymy* (1794), and *Retrospection* (1801), demonstrate a perseverance in her work and the interest in gaining an income from it which made her essentially a professional writer. Fanny Burney and Hannah More were also more productive than the women of the first generation had been.

Did the bluestockings have any influence beyond the personal changes in individuals affected by their example and friendships? Considering the nature of what we may call their 'bluestocking fame', I think they did. At this point we need to begin to consider the power of publicity. When journalists and satirists focused on the lives and work of learned and creative women, and artists chose to draw and paint them, the public at large inevitably became aware of the phenomenon of the bluestockings. Of course, there was still negative comment. But there were also positive responses as well. Between 1773 and 1800 we can trace a surprising number of public references to the members of the bluestocking circle which kept the idea of the bluestockings in public view.

# 11 · Bluestockings in Print and on Canvas

THE bluestocking phenomenon inevitably became a matter for public discussion. By the 1770s these women were being observed not only by their friends, but by various poets, journalists, even painters, who would make bluestockings part of their work. These commentaries varied in attitude. Some showed a positive awareness of the fact that bluestockings were making learning respectable for women. Men of good will used some of the bluestockings as touchstones of learning and virtue —they became token women who had demonstrated that learning for women was not dangerous, and did not unsettle society. Others made the idea of the bluestockings a subject for satiric attacks. These men betrayed anger that women had stepped into the masculine sphere.

The *Westminster Magazine* printed in its July 1773 issue a long account of the March celebrations in Oxford, Encaenia, with the installation of the Prime Minister, Lord North, as its Vice-Chancellor. Numerous honorary degrees were awarded and the recipients of Doctor of Civil Law degrees included Sir Joshua Reynolds, James Beattie, and Henry Thrale (Hyde, 72). This account was followed by an article 'On the Propriety of Bestowing Academical Honours on the Ladies', signed by 'L.P.'. The writer claimed that the 'wits of the town' had made themselves merry about an incident supposed to have happened at the ceremonies, in which a woman disguised as a man received an honorary degree. The writer stated categorically that 'Learning is not confined to Sex; nor have the men, in my opinion, any exclusive right to those honorary distinctions in Literature, which they so insolently arrogate to themselves.' The writer felt that the ladies present at the Encaenia would have done better in their English speeches than the 'aukward young Orators' who actually spoke, and had the young ladies had the same opportunities of becoming acquainted with the dead languages, they would have been more animated in their orations. Not that the writer thought it 'prudent' for the different sexes to study in the same college or university.

But the writer saw no reason why a woman who had achieved distinctions similar to those of a man should not be honoured on such an occasion. He (or perhaps she?) thought the names of 'several of the simple Baronets, Knights, and 'Squires' could have been supplanted by some of the literary ladies. Then the writer named names. He asked if the names of Doctor Elizabeth Carter and Doctor Montagu would not have done as well as those of certain baronets or esquires. He asked if Doctor Thrale, the wife, would not have sounded as well as Doctor Thrale, the husband. He then suggested that, if there was no wish to award doctor's degrees to women, a number of MAs might be suitable. These maids or mistresses of the arts could include 'Catherine Macaulay, A.M., [Anna Laetitia] Aikin, A.M., [Elizabeth] Griffith, A.M., [Charlotte] Lennox, A.M., [Frances] Brooke, A.M., etc.'; Mrs [Elizabeth] Sheridan and her sister could be awarded degrees as mistresses of music.

The writer took the occasion to point out that in foreign universities women have been honoured. He cited Father Feijóo's account of Dorothy Bucca of Bologna, Lucretia Helena Cornaro of Padua, and Isabella de Joya of Spain. (Feijóo's work on women had been translated into English in 1765.) The writer's final point was that he was aware that the heads of colleges at Oxford and Cambridge

affect to undervalue the Graduates of other Universities; but it would do them more credit to invite men of genius and letters indiscriminately *ad eundem*, from any College, than to prostitute their academical honours indiscriminately on those who have studied at no College at all. If, at the same time, they would make an innovation in their academical Laws in favour of such ingenious and learned Ladies, whom custom excludes from a College education, they would at least do as much honour to themselves as they bestow on others. (408–9)

The article had evidently amused Mrs Montagu, for she wrote to Elizabeth Carter on 6 August, asking, 'How do you do Brother Doctor?' She could not help feeling that the learning was all her friend's, but Mrs Montagu confessed she was 'always delighted with this enormous flattery' (MO 3317). At first Mrs Carter was puzzled by the salutation as 'Doctor', but when she figured it out she was calm. She claimed to feel little elevation by her appointment to the cap and gown. She was happy to be united with Mrs Montagu, 'even in a couplet of Tunbridge poetry, or a University degree', although she expressed her urgent hope that the ambitions of her friend and herself would be fulfilled in heaven rather than on earth (Carter, *Letters* (1817), ii. 210).

The various attributes of women who were becoming prominent for their learning, their writing, or their public participation in art and music now became a favourite topic in the press, in prints, and in painting, as well as in epilogues to plays. The general tendency was to praise a group of women together. The precise number of women praised varied, and their names sometimes differed. Hannah More added an epilogue to the third edition of her early play, *The Search after Happiness*, in which two young ladies review the complaints against women who read and write: they may be slatterns, and make 'sad *Mothers*, and still sadder *Wives*'. Such criticism may have been correct when Sappho and Corinna wrote; now times have changed:

> But in our *chaster* times 'tis no offence,
> When female *virtue* joins with female *sense*;
> When moral Carter breathes the strain divine,
> And Aikin's *life* flows faultless as her *line*;
> When all-accomplish'd Montagu can spread
> Fresh-gathered laurels round her Shakespeare's head
> When *wit* and *worth* in polish'd Brookes unite,
> And fair Macaulay claims a Livy's *right*.

(44)

The reviewer in the *Monthly Review* (Feb. 1774) was so taken by Hannah More's addition to this 'spirited' epilogue that he printed the lines given above, and added, *Bravissimo! Encore! Encore!* (156). A couple of months later, the reviewer of More's *Inflexible Captive* in the *Monthly Review* (Apr. 1774) was himself inspired to laudatory verse by his 'fair countrywomen':

> To Greece no more the tuneful maids belong,
> Nor the high honours of immortal song;
> To More, Brooks, Lenox, Aikin, Carter due,
> To Greville, Griffith, Whateley, Montagu!

> Theirs the strong genius, theirs the voice divine;
> And favouring Phoebus owns the British Nine.

(243, quoted by Lerenbaum, 26 n. 16)

In 1774 an obscure woman poet, Mary Scott, published with Joseph Johnson, later to be Mary Wollstonecraft's publisher, and publisher for other liberal causes, a poem called *The Female Advocate*. Miss Scott wished to amplify John Duncombe's work in his *Feminiad*, adding women whom he had omitted or who had come to prominence after he wrote. Although she thought the attitudes of men to female education were much improved from previous times, she still felt strongly the injustices of keeping women from the liberal studies. She hoped that in future men would give up their prejudices about women. She saw some changes already, 'for facts have a powerful tendency to convince the understanding; and of late, Female authors have appeared with honour, in almost every walk of literature' (p. vii).

After rehearsing the praises of some of the outstanding English women of the Renaissance, and celebrating the poets Anne Killigrew and Katherine Philips, she mentioned some other prominent women: Lady Rachel Russell, Mrs [Mary] Monck, Lady [Mary] Chudleigh, a 'zealous asserter of the *female right to literature*', Mrs Constantia Grierson, a self-educated learned woman of Ireland, and her friend Mrs Mary Barber of Dublin, writer of virtuous poetry. Miss Scott also mentioned Mrs [Mary] Chandler, Miss [Mary] Jones of Oxford, Mrs [Elizabeth] Cooper, Sarah Fielding, Elizabeth Tollett, Charlotte Lennox, Elizabeth Griffith [incorrectly called Frances], Mrs [Anna] Steele, Mrs [Frances] Greville, Phillis Wheatley, Catherine Macaulay, Anna Williams, and Lady Pennington.

Lines 357–70 of *The Female Advocate* are devoted to Elizabeth Montagu. The poet asks whether 'this unartful verse' can 'Thy Genius, Learning, or thy Worth rehearse?' Mrs Montagu's pen has traced Shakespeare's powers 'with nice discernment' and shown 'his various beauties', proving 'thy soul congenial to his own'. The poet, charmed with Mrs Montagu's work, wishes to go on to tell her 'nobler Fame':

> Dear to Religion, as to Learning dear,

Candid, obliging, modest, mild, sincere,
Still prone to soften at another's woe,
Still fond to bless, still ready to bestow.

(367–70)

After writing a tribute to Philanthropy inspired by Mrs
Montagu, the poet turns her attention to Catherine Talbot, the
'delightful moralist' who will 'please, correct, and mend the
rising age':

Genius and Wit were but thy second praise,
Thou knew'st to win by still sublimer ways;
Thy Angel-goodness, all who knew approv'd
Honour'd, admir'd, applauded too; and lov'd!
Fair shall thy fame to latest ages bloom,
And ev'ry Muse with tears bedew thy tomb.

(401–6)

The writer also praises Anna Laetitia [Aikin] Barbauld for her
taste, spirit, wit, and learning. Expressing the hope that there
would be equal education for both sexes in the future, the poet
concludes with a tribute to male helpers, John Duncombe, an
'able Advocate for Female Worth', Mr Seward, author of 'The
Female Right to Literature', her friend Philander, and another
encouraging male friend. To these 'generous pleaders of the
female cause' the Muse raises her 'drooping wing . . .'
(ll. 501–11).

Whether Mrs Montagu actually bought a copy of *The Female
Advocate* is unknown; she probably did because she recommended it to Elizabeth Carter, who said she could not get a
copy in Deal and would have to wait until she came to London
to read it (*Letters* (1817), ii. 233). Mrs Montagu certainly read
the review in the *Gentleman's Magazine* of August 1774. The
reviewer listed the women whom Miss Scott had singled out to
supplement *The Feminiad*, and then quoted from the tributes
to Mrs Montagu and to Miss Talbot offered by the poet. The
reviewer also had a candidate to add: another Scott, Mrs Scott,
sister of Mrs Montagu, and author of *Millenium Hall*, *The
History of Sir George Ellison*, and the *Life of Theodore Agrippa
d'Aubigné*.

Mrs Montagu was pleased with the mention of Mrs Scott.

On 7 September 1774 she wrote to her sister to urge her to buy the issue for August, 'in which we are made honourable mention of. I love we should be join'd in every thing. Have you met with yr names sakes poem which gave occasion to what is said of us in ye Magazine' (MO 5960). Sarah replied that she 'ought to purchase a whole Edition of it in gratitude for being joined with You . . .'. Sarah added that one author, Mr Court de Gebelin, had identified her in a new manner in his list of subscribers as 'Madame Scott, Sœur de Madame Montagu, a distinction in my opinion more honourable than any title in his list, tho there are some very splendid ones' (MO 5374, 12 (Sept. 1774)).

The *Westminster Magazine* returned to the subject of women's education with a leading article, 'Observations on Female Literature in General, including some Particulars Relating to Mrs. Montagu and Mrs. Barbauld, [Embellished with an Elegant Engraving of these Ladies]', in the June 1776 issue. The author begins with a long quotation from Duncombe's *Feminiad*, in which the poet contrasts the slavery of women in seraglios with the freedom of 'British Nymphs' to pursue all kinds of intellectual and artistic activities.

The writer then goes on to discuss specifically the two Ladies singled out from the number of ingenious Females: Mrs Montagu and Mrs Barbauld. Mrs Montagu is honoured for her polished mind and classical writings, the three *Dialogues of the Dead*, and the *Essay on Shakespear*. Anna Laetitia Barbauld (1743–1825), who had come into prominence a few years earlier with her poems, is complimented both for her appearance and for her intellectual conversation. Furthermore, the writer finds a masculine force in her poetical compositions, as well as a certain feminine grace of expression. She has also written some elegant prose essays.

Such repeated praise of groups of celebrated women must have inspired the painter Richard Samuel, a little-known Royal Academy member, to paint some of these women as the 'Nine Living Muses of Great Britain'. He chose to depict Elizabeth Montagu, Elizabeth Carter, Charlotte Lennox, Catherine Macaulay, Anna Barbauld, Elizabeth Griffith, Angelica Kauffman, Elizabeth Sheridan, and Hannah More. He first

*Nine Living Muses of Great Britain.* Engraved by Page from the painting by Richard Samuel, *c.*1775. British Museum, London.

did a print of his work from a preparatory drawing; the print was distributed in *Johnson's Ladies New and Polite Pocket Memorandum for 1778*, published by Joseph Johnson, and advertised in the *London Chronicle* for 8–11 November 1777 and other issues. Later he exhibited a finished Painting in the Royal Academy exhibition of 1779.[1] The portrait of the *Nine Living Muses of Great Britain* 'captures the moment when English women as a group first gained acceptance as natural and important contributors to the cultural and artistic world' (11).

During this period there were numerous paintings of Apollo and the Muses. Samuel seems to have adapted this theme to his group portrait of a number of literary and artistic women. In some ways this portrait resembles a 'Conversation Piece' or portrait of a family group or group of friends, such as Gavin Hamilton's *Group of Vertuosi* (1735), in which Matthew Robinson, Mrs Montagu's father, is a central figure (see Chapter 1). But Samuel's work is classical in theme and setting. Both the painting and the print show the nine women gathered before the temple of Apollo. They are wearing simple robes reminiscent of Grecian attire, and sandals. Although the reason for the gathering is not clear, the presence of these women certainly demonstrates the accomplishments of English women in learned languages, criticism, history, poetry, drama, art, and music.

In the print two groups of women sit or stand on either side of the central figure, Elizabeth Linley Sheridan, a well-known singer; she stands holding a lyre and looking up at the figure of a god on a pedestal who is holding a crown over a seated female figure. On the right, Angelica Kauffman, the painter, is seated at an easel; behind her (l. to r.) Mrs Carter is speaking to Mrs Barbauld, and gesturing at Mrs Sheridan. On the left hand is a group of five ladies less easily identified. In the print the names of Mrs Lennox, Mrs Macaulay, Miss More, Mrs Griffith, and Mrs Montagu are given under the group, but it is difficult to tell who is who. Leranbaum argued that the central seated figure on the left hand was Mrs Montagu, represented as Calliope, the leader of the muses, and wearing a gold band on her forehead. Mrs Lennox may be the figure holding a writing-pad and pen and seated to the left of Mrs Montagu; Mrs Macaulay is probably the woman seated to the right of Mrs Montagu, and holding a scroll to represent Clio, the muse of history. In that case Mrs Griffith may be the figure holding a writing-pad who is standing to the left behind this group. Elizabeth Griffith was a playwright and author, known for *A Series of Genuine Letters between Henry and Frances* (1757; 1767; 1770). She had also been an actress at various periods in her life. The last of this group, Hannah More, may be the figure standing to the right of Mrs Griffith.

In the final painting, now in the National Portrait Gallery, the pedestal shows the single figure of a god. The painter has given the temple more depth and visibility and expanded the drapery around the Greek columns. As Samuel probably worked from the preparatory drawing, the groups are reversed from their positions in the print. On the left hand Mrs Barbauld stands (l. to r.) with Elizabeth Carter behind Angelica Kauffman; Mrs Carter is still gesturing towards Mrs Sheridan. On the right hand Mrs Macaulay with her scroll still sits to the left of Mrs Montagu, with Mrs Lennox to the right. The figures behind them seem to be (l. to r.) Hannah More, holding a cup, and Elizabeth Griffith, holding a stringed instrument. Miriam Leranbaum explained the addition of the cup to More's representation as referring to her great success with *Percy* between the publication of the print and the completion of the painting; the cup is an iconographical emblem of Melpomene, the muse of tragedy (9–10). Mrs Griffith's connection with the musical instrument is not clear.

The great flaw in Samuel's work is that he does not seem to have worked from life, and that his figures are not, as Elizabeth Carter complained, recognizable as individuals. We do not know what the bluestockings thought of the painting, but we do know that Elizabeth Carter wrote to Mrs Montagu about the print on 23 November 1777,

O Dear, O dear, how pretty we look and what brave things has Mr. Johnson said of us! Indeed, my dear friend, I am just as sensible to present fame as can be. Your Virgils and your Horaces may talk what they will of posterity, but I think it is much better to be celebrated by the men, women, and children, among whom one is actually living and looking.

Mrs Carter was especially happy that she and Mrs Montagu seemed always to appear in the literary world together.

I am mortified, however, that we do not in this last display of our person and talents stand in the same corner. As I am told we do not, for to say truth, by the mere testimony of my own eyes, I cannot very exactly tell which is you, and which is I, and which is any body else. (Carter, *Letters* (1817), iii. 47–8)

Elizabeth Carter was beginning to be accustomed to publicity. In 1775 she had reported to her friend about a dream or vision of female authors which she had read. It involved a contest among them for a silver standish—that is, a stand containing ink, pens, and other writing materials and accessories (*OED*), and peacock feathers. Among the contestants were Mrs Macaulay and Carter herself. She reported that 'after the candidates have put in their several claims the standish is adjudged to Mrs. Macaulay, and all the other ladies dismissed with peacock's feathers' (Carter, *Letters* (1817), ii. 316).

I have not been able to find this contest, but a similar one was published as one of the *Six Odes*, presented to Mrs Macaulay on her birthday, and read to an audience assembled at Alfred House, Bath, on that occasion in 1777. 'Britannia's Reward: A Vision' depicts a contest in which Barbauld, Chapone, Montagu, Carter, and Macaulay appear before Britannia, who sits ready to award a laurel wreath to the most deserving. In this case Macaulay takes the crown, but there are no supplementary prizes for the others. The extravagance of the celebration aroused detractors; the *European Magazine* for 1777 commented that ' "the folly of it beggars description" ' (Quoted by Donnelly (1949), 185–6).

Another painting in which Mrs Montagu alone of the bluestockings took an important public role was produced by James Barry between 1777 and 1784 as part of the six murals he painted for the Royal Society of the Arts on *The Progress of Human Culture*. The mural in which Mrs Montagu appears is *The Distribution of Premiums in the Society of the Arts*. The London Society for the Encouragement of Arts, Manufactures and Commerce was founded in 1754. The object of the society was to make awards for discoveries, inventions, and advances in arts, manufactures, and commerce. The first membership list issued in October 1755 contained 110 names. Members included William, second Duke of Portland; Philip, second Earl of Hardwicke (then Viscount Royston), the husband of Jemima, Marchioness Grey; George, first Baron Lyttelton, vice-president of the Society; and Sir Joseph Banks, Charles Burney, Benjamin Franklin, David Garrick, Samuel Johnson, Sir Joshua Reynolds, Samuel Richardson, Henry Thrale, Horace Walpole, and John Wilkes. Ladies were eligible from the very beginning; Mrs Montagu became a member in 1758, and remained one until her death.[2]

The Society wanted its women members shown in this painting, as well as the founder, the presidents, and some prominent men. There are thirty-six individuals in the picture, of whom only eight are unnamed (Allan, 99). There were several women members. Barry chose to honour Mrs Montagu, 'a distinguished example of female excellence', with a central role in the picture as a patron of young people (Barry, 77). Among the numerous awards the Society regularly made were medals, prizes, and financial awards to both girls and boys for various categories of the 'polite arts', including drawings and different kinds of craft work such as ornaments, original designs for weavers, calico printers, or any other art or manufacture.[3] In the crowded scene before Somerset House, Mrs Montagu, dressed in yellow silk, stands left of centre, presenting to the Duchess of Northumberland one of two girls—the taller one in yellow and white stripes. This girl holds a length of fabric under her arm, while Mrs Montagu presents the upper part of it to the Duchess. The fabric appears to be a fine silk in mauve. The poses are informal. Mrs Montagu has her left arm around the taller girl; the younger girl stands a little to the right, displaying a medal in her left hand. To the right of centre Samuel Johnson stands behind the Duchesses of Rutland and Devonshire, and points to Mrs Montagu as an example for their edification. The duchesses were not members of the Society.

Barry worked from life and from portraits in cases when the subject was not living. The unfinished portrait of Dr Johnson by James Barry now in the National Portrait Gallery is a preparatory study for the mural; Barry did many studies of this kind, but Johnson's is the only one to have survived unaltered (Pressly (1983), 97–8). In an earlier work William Pressly indicated that a sale in 1807 mentioned a portrait, probably unfinished, of Mrs Montagu. It does not seem to have been located (Pressly (1981), 240).

The painting, 15 feet 2 inches by 11 feet 10 inches, still hangs in the Great Room of the Society of Arts in London. Moved from London during World War II, the painting narrowly escaped destruction in its hiding-place. In his catalogue for an exhibition of Barry's work at the Tate Gallery, William Pressly said of the *Distribution of Premiums*, 'With its grand, even if implausible, setting, its animated heads and poses, and its brilliant orchestration of colour, this work is a highly distinguished group portrait with few peers in the British School' (84).

Clearly the bluestockings had become prominent; as a consequence, not only honourable mention but also gossip inevitably pursued them in print. Fanny Burney noted references to her and the other 'bluestockings' in the *Morning Herald and Daily Advertiser*. Mrs Montagu was upset by a short report in the 10 December 1783 issue that there had been a dispute among the bluestockings at Mrs Vesey's which might have been serious, 'but for the timely interposition of some unlettered auditors'.

More seriously, in 1786 Richard Cumberland, the playwright, who had been introduced to the circle, harshly satirized Mrs Montagu as Vanessa in the *Observer*, No. 25. The writer is invited to a 'Feast of Reason'. He sees Vanessa as a person who is self-important about promoting literature among men and women. Cumberland observes that she teaches young ladies to write poetry and to train their Pegasuses 'to ride side-saddle'. In her drawing-room are displayed books she does not read, but whose authors come to honour her. Among her visitors are a man who is planning to go down in the sea in a diving-bell, an experimental philosopher, a lady novelist, and an actress whose performances are highly praised. Later Cumberland treated Mrs Montagu more gently, but still critically, in No. 70. In this piece he presents the view that Vanessa is a thoughtful, admirable person when she is a member of a small group at her own fireside. Vanessa herself says that 'the art of being agreeable, frequently miscarries through the ambition which accompanies it' (243).

Queen Charlotte read these pieces and asked Fanny Burney for the keys to the characters, about whom she was curious.

Fanny Burney thought the criticism of Mrs Montagu very severe. 'I think it a very injurious attack in Mr. Cumberland; for whatever may be Mrs. Montagu's foibles, she is free, I believe, from all vice, and as a member of society she is magnificently useful.' Fanny said all this to the queen, and defended Mrs Montagu as well as she was able from 'this illiberal assault. The Queen was very ready to hear me, and to concur in thinking such usage very cruel' (*Diary*, iii. 71).

In *Modern Manners* (1782), Revd Samuel Hoole (*c*.1758–1839), son of John Hoole, the translator of Ariosto, and a friend of the Burneys, told in four-stress couplets of a visit of Northern relatives to a fine London lady. Through the eyes of Ralph Rusty, one of the visitors, Hoole satirized the manners of society. In Letter 10, dated Portland Place, 1780, Rusty explains that he has been invited to a 'Conversatione' where the 'gay, and the grave, and the learned will meet'. He finds the refreshments scanty, and is surprised by the way the company arrange their chairs back to back; this is a direct hit at Mrs Vesey. Ralph explains:

> Then they got into parties, as suited them best,
> Each set by themselves, turn'd their backs on the rest;
> To be sure, such gay people well knew what was right,
> But *I* should have thought it not quite so polite.
>
> (84)

Ralph joins various groups: a party of beauties and beaux, then a group which talks about music, and then a group which discusses politics. Finally he joins a party of critics and authors, which he thinks will suit him. But the conversation consists of abuse of a book, which someone else's pamphlet will certainly demolish. The talkers get into a controversy about Samuel Johnson. One speaker likes his *Milton*. Another detests his religious and civil opinions. Finally, a Scot appears who denigrates Milton in favour of Ossian. After traducing Johnson for having accepted a pension, they conclude by discussing Johnson's hatred of Scots. The Scot complains of Johnson's *Tour*. How can Johnson claim that the Scots have no trees, since he cannot see? '

In *Aurelia; or, The Contest* (1783) Samuel Hoole wrote a mock-heroic poem in imitation of 'The Rape of the Lock'. His heroine learns by sad experience not to 'paint' and not to engage in superficial rivalries with other women, but to follow the examples of Carter, Chapone, Burney, Montagu in seeking worth and wisdom.

As with More's Epilogue to *The Search after Happiness*, such praise of women could become part of a public occasion. In 1787 Fanny Burney went to a performance of Thomas Holcroft's *Seduction*; she was seated in a Royal Box with the Royal Family 'and their suite' immediately opposite her. The Epilogue, which was spoken by Miss Farren, complimented those women whose taste combines with wit to grace 'the female mind'. Among the women mentioned were the female critic of Shakespeare and the author of *Cecilia*. Much to Fanny's embarrassment, the King raised his opera-glass and laughed at her; soon the entire party smiled in her direction. The King later explained that he was curious to know how she looked when her father discovered that she wrote; now he knew (*Diary*, iii. 238–9).

In his *Essays Moral and Literary* Vicesimus Knox, master of Tonbridge School, dealt with questions of female education in two essays first published in 1779 in the second edition of his work. The first of these, Essay 33, 'On Female Education' praises the bluestocking women. The essay is in the form of a letter written by a young lady who describes her education by her clergyman father. He has given her a thorough grounding in the Greek and Latin classics, and in the French and Italian languages and literature. She was then permitted to range freely in English literature, and found that her training in classical and European languages was invaluable because she could understand the allusions the writers used. She also read history, and learned a little science.

But she also learned the more usual female accomplishments of music and dancing. She was instructed to behave carefully so as not to offend those not as learned as she. But she finds she is not popular. The ladies are in awe of her, and the men think her too learned to become a wife. The writer argues that learning is in fact needed to form a companion and a teacher of her children. Nor does having advanced education mean that the woman will not be able, or will not be willing, to supervise her household. Writing in the character of the young woman,

Knox offers Montagu, Chapone, and Carter as examples of the right kind of intellectual woman:

That learning belongs not to the female character, and that the female mind is not capable of a degree of improvement equal to that of the other sex, are narrow and unphilosophical prejudices. The present times exhibit most honourable instances of female learning and genius in a Montagu, a Chapone, and a Carter. The superior advantages of boys education is, perhaps, the sole reason of their subsequent superiority. Learning is equally attainable, and, I think, equally valuable, to the woman as the man. For my own part, I would not lose the little I possess, to avoid all those disagreeable consequences of which I have just now complained. (334)

But Knox also showed the other side of the question in Essay 36, in which he presents women who reflect the consequences of superficial and ill-directed reading. Sempronia is a woman who is proud of having published an article or two. She is too confident, and she is also slovenly. Corinna has been influenced by sceptical works. She is dreaded by her own sex; she herself prefers the company of men, and some associate with her, but only to ridicule her. Fulvia lives near a circulating library and has read so many sentimental novels that she is inclined to fall in love with every man she meets. Lesbia has written poetry and considers herself a second Sappho. But her poetry sent her only suitor away; she spouted so fervently that he thought she was mad. Cornelia is a female politician. When she should be with the ladies she tries to engage in political discourse with the men. She speaks like a Billingsgate orator. A 'treaty' for marriage was delayed by political considerations.

Thus Knox offered arguments on both sides of the question— he demonstrated the qualities of the virtuous learned woman versus those of superficial and affected ones. However, there is a significant threat indicated in both cases. It seems that being either a good or bad learned woman may keep the woman from getting married.

In addition to the laudatory comments on the bluestockings which continued to appear, there was a rising current of satiric comment sparked by the conflict between those who supported the ideas of the French Revolution, and conservatives who clung to order and religion. In attacking pro-revolutionary women Richard Polwhele continued the custom of making the bluestockings his touchstone of learning and virtue. In *The Unsex'd Females: A Poem Addressed to the Author of* The Pursuits of Literature (1798), Polwhele attacked the new generation of women writers, especially Mary Wollstonecraft, who advocated such indelicate topics as the study of the sexual system of plants, and open discussion of the facts of human reproduction. Polwhele believed that Wollstonecraft's advocacy of muscular exercise at female boarding-schools would unfortunately reduce the delicacy of women. Others of the new generation of women whom he attacked are Mary Hays, Mrs [Mary] Robinson, Charlotte Smith, and Ann Yearsley. It seemed to the poet that talk about reproduction and physical exercise would undoubtedly lead to libertinism. In contrast to these 'unsexed females', he pointed out that a critic like Montagu, a scholar like Carter, a moralist like Chapone, contribute a great deal to society. Polwhele also mentioned favourably Mrs Barbauld, Miss [Anna] Seward, Mrs Piozzi, Fanny Burney, and Hannah More.

Among the satirists, Thomas Mathis in *The Pursuits of Literature* included Mrs Montagu in the pack of critics pursuing Shakespeare as the hounds pursued Actæon; 'her yelp was feeble and her sandal blue'. John Wolcot, using the pen-name 'Peter Pindar', also found the bluestockings fair game. In 'Bozzi and Piozzi, or The British Biographers, A Town Eclogue', Wolcot has Sir John Hawkins sit in judgement on Boswell's *Tour* and Mrs Piozzi's *Anecdotes*. Sir John disdains the titbits they include in their work. Part II opens with a dream in which Sir John imagines Johnson growling at him; Wolcot has Johnson ask Mrs Piozzi to 'Give up her *anecdotical* inditing, | And study *housewifery* instead of *writing:*' (i. 269). In 'Ode upon Ode' Wolcot satirizes Mrs Walsingham, 'A dame who dances, paints, and plays, and sings . . .'. Although not much bigger than a cat, she is a 'giant as to *fame*' compared to the other 'Bas Bleus' (i. 307). He reserved his harshest bluestocking satire for Hannah More. In 'Nil Admirari; or, A Smile at a Bishop . . .', he attacked her because Bishop Porteus had praised her Christianity. Peter thought her powers were scanty. He predicted that time would destroy her reputation, which has been created by flattery (iii. 444). In his 'Ode to the Blue-stocking Club' Peter tells the Club that Hannah is a 'little bit of an *imposter*'.

He accuses her of plagiarism, and asks the ladies 'To sift this *pretty* larceny of the pen!' (iii. 464–5).

The harshest satire was that of Charles Pigott in his *Female Jockey Club* (1794). Pigott offered a scurrilous treatment of various women. In writing about Hester Lynch Piozzi, he raised the familiar fear about sexual licence, giving sexual passion as the reason for her second marriage (171). In attacking the bluestockings as a whole, the writer claimed that the bluestockings wished to establish an 'aristocracy in the republic of letters' (257). The attack on Mrs Montagu stressed the greatness of her fortune, of which she gave only a small portion to the poor; her annual dinners for the chimney-sweeps were only a token effort to help these poor children (259–60).

Pigott had it both ways. In his attack on Mrs Piozzi he was harking back to the old tradition of equating female learning with sexual licence. But he also attacked the bluestockings for prudery. Wondering at the origin of the term 'bluestocking', Pigott says he thought talking about blue stockings seemed to bring up light and lascivious ideas.

But the *fair* members of this *Lyceum* are, in general, chaste even to a fault; most of them preferring to let their charms be withered by time, than submit them to the *rude mercy* of that *odious monster, man*; we must, therefore, imagine, that the name originated in some happy and sudden flash of wit, which fortunately found a resemblance between things so seemingly unlike, as *genius* and *coloured stockings*. (262)

There is a slashing attack on Hannah More, 'a *downright* Bishop Horsley in petticoats', who is a self-serving patroness, and a conservative defender of religion and monarchy (263). 'Lady' Horace Walpole is singled out in the final group of aristocrats for having been the cause of Thomas Chatterton's suicide, and the author concludes with a plea to these 'titled bookworms' to turn from literature to charity (263).

Finally, the spurious letters of Thomas Lyttelton (written by William Combe, author of the verses written to accompany Rowlandson's drawings of Dr Syntax) created a picture of Mrs Montagu as a woman who bribed and flattered, and whose literary circle was lacking in vivacity (80–1). Many years later Chauncey B. Tinker was to claim this portrait to have been an authentic one by her friend George, Lord Lyttelton (139).

What would be the coming pattern in the nineteenth century, and even into the twentieth, can be seen in the contrasting attitudes of applauders and satirists. To some extent the bluestocking ladies would continue to be called upon to illustrate the values of learning and virtue in women; on the other hand their names as 'bluestockings' would be associated with pedantry, prudery, assertiveness or any other quality the beholder felt served to indict those women who had dared to try to participate in the sphere of literature.

Some of the attention given the bluestockings in print was due to the way in which their social lives became public. Therefore, scholars have sometimes treated the members of the bluestocking circle as women interested primarily in having *salons*. The French offer a familiar model of the *salonière* and the English bluestockings are evaluated in terms of that model. As a consequence of the view that the bluestockings are significant essentially as *salonières*, the bluestocking circle is often seen as a special, discontinuous group that had no influence.

Certainly, because of their internal inhibitions and the pressures of their situation, the bluestockings did not, in the early stages, find their way to a committed professional literary life, but they did demonstrate their devotion to the cause of the 'female right to literature' by their own writings, by their personal friendships and letters, and by their wider social activities bringing together men and women interested in literature. I do not believe that the influence of the bluestockings passed with the decline of the circle itself. The amount of comment in print about the bluestockings must have had its effect. The power of publicity must have brought their example to many men and women in England and in other countries. The figure of the intellectual woman, called a 'bluestocking', did not vanish with the passing of the bluestocking circle itself. As I indicated in the Prologue, the term passed into usage in France, Germany, and the United States, and women in these countries as well as in England became adherents to the cause.

Margaret Fuller knew of Elizabeth Carter and pointed to her as an example of the learned woman author who was being accepted (48–9). It seemed to Fuller that the successes of female authors pointed out the path female education was to take towards equality (93-4). Furthermore, Fuller's own *conversations*, which she held from 1839-44, were designed to bring women out of their passivity into an active intellectual life (Cross, 112-22). They seem an adaptation of bluestocking aims and practices suited to Fuller's own needs and situation. In fact, Vernon Louis Parrington, writing about her in *The Romantic Revolution in America (1800-1860)* (1927, 1930), said Fuller was 'commonly looked upon as an intellectual monstrosity, the most fearful of Yankee bluestockings . . .' (427). The concept of the intellectual woman had attained an independent existence, and the idea of the 'bluestocking' stimulated or continued to bother the imaginations of many.

# Epilogue

## The Term 'Bluestocking' and The Bluestocking Legacy (1800–1986)

AS collections of letters, biographies, memoirs, and works of the bluestockings continued to appear in the years after the members of the bluestocking circle had died, the term itself became a shorthand sign for personal attitudes towards women with intellectual aspirations. Amid the struggles which have marked the feminist movement in the nineteenth and twentieth centuries, the term 'bluestocking' has persisted as a gathering-point for attitudes both for and against women in intellectual life.

A number of journals kept by prominent literary figures in the early nineteenth century reveal such usage. Byron was sensitive to the idea of the 'bluestocking'. In his journals Byron referred to certain women as 'blue'. On 1 December 1813 he wondered whether to go to a 'party of *purple* at the "blue" Miss *** [Berry]'s. Shall I go? um!—I don't much affect your blue-bottles;—but one ought to be civil.' He speculates that perhaps 'that blue-winged Kashmirian butterfly of book-learning, Lady **** [Charlemont] will be there. I hope so; it is a pleasure to look upon that most beautiful of faces' (*Journals*, iii. 228).[1]

Sir Walter Scott was more analytical about the phenomenon of the intellectual woman, and inclined to defend her from what he regarded as slighting comments. On 10 August 1826 he noted in his journal that visiting Minto he missed

my facetious and lively friend, Lady A[nna] M[aria]. It is the fashion for women and silly men to abuse her as a blue-stocking. If to have wit, good sense, and good humour, mixd with a strong power of observing, and an equally strong one of expressing the result, be *blue*, she shall be as blue as they will.

Scott remarked that 'such cant' was prompted by fear of blue-stocking ridicule (i. 213–14). On 13 July 1829 he wrote of meeting the poet Felicia Hemans. He thought she had taste and spirit in her conversation. 'My daughters are critical, and call her *blue*, but I think they are hypercritical' (iii. 95).

It is hardly surprising that the idea of the bluestocking should become a staple of comedy and satire. Byron sent his work, *The Blues: A Literary Eclogue*, to his publisher Murray from Ravenna, on 7 August 1821. Byron called this slight drama 'a mere buffoonery' . . . 'to quiz "The Blues"' (*Works*, iv. 569). He probably had some contemporary blues in mind for his satire, but it may be that the publication of Elizabeth Montagu's letters by her nephew (1810) or the publication of Elizabeth Carter's letters to Mrs Montagu (1817) had reminded him of the original bluestockings.

The First Eclogue of *The Blues* takes place before the door of a lecture room in London. The benches are crowded with women who have made learning the fashion. The audience is addressed by an absurd lecturer, Scamp. Tracy, one of the observers, is interested in the 'Blue', Miss Lilac. He is, however, advised by Inkel not to think of marrying Miss Lilac. Inkel doesn't know of any alliance with science which has been happy, and Miss Lilac is very learned. Then Inkel and Tracy go to Lady Bluebottle's collation.

Now Sir Richard Bluebottle is shown in the Second Eclogue regretting his marriage, because his wife keeps him busy with literary and social activities. The text indicates that Lady Bluebottle seems to have been drawn with Elizabeth Montagu in mind. Byron has Lady Bluebottle say:

> Come, a truce with all tartness;—the joy of my heart
> Is to see Nature's triumph o'er all that is art.
> Wild Nature!—Grand Shakespeare! . . .
>
> (iv. 585)

Of course, the reference to Shakespeare points to Mrs Montagu. Byron also has Lady Bluebottle use a phrase which appears in Mrs Montagu's letters (see Prologue):

> A truce with remark, and let nothing control
> This 'feast of our reason, and flow of the soul.'
>
> (iv. 586)

This phrase (from Pope) appears in Elizabeth Robinson's letter to Sarah from Bulstrode (MO 5557) which Matthew Montagu printed in his edition (Montagu (1810), ii. 62–4).

Byron's resentment of literary ladies appears in a number of stanzas of *Don Juan* (1821). He complains of the meaningless-ness of literary success:

> That taste is gone, that fame is but a lottery,
> Drawn by the blue-coat misses of a coterie.
>
> (IV. cix)

He explains that he does not know why learned ladies are called bluestockings, but wishes he could use the instrument Humboldt invented to measure the intensity of blue in the sky to measure Lady Daphne's depth of blue (IV. cx–cxii). As Steffan and Pratt, editors of *Don Juan*, point out,

Byron kept up a running fire against the bluestockings from the period of his introduction to the group of literary ladies in London to which belonged the Misses Berry, Miss Lydia White . . . Lady Beaumont, Mrs. Wilmot . . . Lady Charlemont, and others. In spite of his ridicule, it might be noted that Byron was always drawn to women who were well read . . .'. (iv. 26)

John G. Lockhart, Scottish writer and novelist, describes an Edinburgh *conversazione* which has something of a bluestocking appearance about it in his *Peter's Letters to his Kinfolk*. The gathering gives Peter a view of Mr Jeffrey, the critic, Lord Buchan, and Professor Leslie. Peter discovers Mr Jeffrey trapped 'by a skilful party of blue-stocking *tirailleures* [rifle-women]' (307). The women ply Jeffrey with literary questions. Peter concludes that 'I was never a lover of Blue-stockings either at home or abroad; but of all that I have met with, I think the French are most tolerable, the Scotch the most tormenting' (311). Peter thinks at least French ladies talk about things they understand, but Scottish bluestockings insist on discussing social and political questions which are really beyond them.

At another party Peter meets Mrs Grant, author of *Letters from the Mountains*. However, she is not at all a 'Blue-Stocking' but a modest, unassuming woman who is happy to talk with a stranger about the Highlands. 'The sound and rational enjoy-ment I derived from my conversation with this excellent person, would, indeed, atone for much more than all the Blue-Stocking sisterhood have ever been able to inflict on my patience' (314).

In 1818 Susan Ferrier included a scene of bluestockings in action in her novel *Marriage*; affected literary conversations are carried on at a tea-party given by Lady Bluemitts in Bath. The ladies spout poetry to show their learning and taste. Mary, the heroine, is much disappointed by her introduction to the circle at Mrs Bluemitts; 'they were mere pretenders' to literary distinction (ii. 251). The author contrasts these women with the women praised by Hannah More in her novel *Coelebs*; Ferrier quotes the passage from the novel in which Elizabeth Carter and Elizabeth Smith are held up to young women as shining examples.

'In them let our young ladies contemplate profound and various learning, chastised by true Christian humility. In them let them venerate acquirements, which would have been distinguished in an university, meekly softened, and beautifully shaded by the exertion of every domestic virtue, the unaffected exercise of every feminine employment.' (ii. 251; More, ii. 292-3)

Thus Ferrier, like Vicesimus Knox, addressed both sides, attacking affected learned women and praising those who seemed to be truly virtuous and domestic.

Henrietta Maria Bowdler had quoted the same passage from *Coelebs* in the Preface to her edition of Elizabeth Smith's *Fragments in Prose and Verse* (1810). Bowdler included the observations for the benefit of 'the younger part of my own sex, who admire the talents of my lamented friend, and wish to follow her steps in the paths of science . . .' (pp. vii–viii). Bluestockings were still being pointed to as models for young women to follow.

At the same time the satire of women with intellectual aspirations, which had such a long history before the bluestockings, now amalgamated with satire of the bluestockings themselves. In his comic opera, *M. P.; or, The Bluestocking*, Thomas Moore satirized the bluestocking in the character of Lady Bab Blue. Mr Hartington says that Lady Bab's father had no son, and was determined to pass on his learning to his daughter. Therefore, he 'stuffed her head with all that was legible and *illegible*, without once considering that the female intellect may possibly be too weak for such an experiment . . .'. Miss Selwyn asks if Mr Hartington would shut women out from learning. He replies, 'No—no—learn as much as you please, but learn also to conceal it.—I could even bear a little peep at the blue-stockings, but save me from the woman who shews them up to her knees!' (I. ii).

Lady Bab Blue carries a telescope, uses chemical terms, and is writing a poem on the Loves of Ammonia. Her literary ambitions become a motive for the plot, when Leatherhead, whom Lady Bab has chosen as the publisher of her poem, mis-understands her intentions, and thinks she is arranging for him to marry her niece.

The idea of the bluestocking had therefore linked up with the long-standing animosity towards the intellectual woman which, as I have shown, had intimidated women with intellectual interests in the eighteenth century. I quoted in the Prologue the fear of Jemima, Marchioness Grey, at being considered a *femme savante*. Catherine Talbot hated the idea of being thought a Phoebe Clinket. Into the nineteenth century, the suggestions that when women took an interest in intellectual affairs they were almost bound to display affectation and incompetence, continued as inhibiting factors. It was this image which William Pitt Scargill attempted to alter in *Blue-Stocking Hall*, because, as he indicated, the stereotype of the foolish blue-stocking was being used against the education of women.

Scargill (1787–1836) was a Unitarian minister who held the ministry of Churchgate Street Chapel, Bury St Edmunds, for twenty years. He attempted to improve his livelihood by writing for periodicals and publishing novels. Among his numerous works was *Blue-Stocking Hall* (1827), a three-decker novel set in Glenalta, Ireland. The work consists of a four-year corres-pondence between Arthur Howard and others about his aunt's family whom he is visiting. After his arrival Arthur soon discovers by examining the books in the library that he is among 'a batch of *Blues*' (i. 23). He finds the initials of Emily and Charlotte, two of the young ladies of the family, in at least a dozen volumes, among them Sallust, Virgil, Sowerby on Minerals, a book on Botany, etc. Arthur, who has come from fashionable society in London, is very upset. He doesn't wish to be with pedantic people and have to 'talk science all day to a set of *precieuses ridicules*!' (i. 24). Arthur imagines that Fanny, the youngest daughter at fifteen, will not have been tainted, and that the son Frederick will join him when he wishes to laugh at learned ladies. Arthur refers disparagingly to his aunt and her 'Aspasias'. But the first meal he participates in is in surprisingly good style, and there is not the slightest hint of *aspire*. The family speaks surprisingly well—without a brogue. But Arthur is apprehensive of being overwhelmed by this 'cursed blue' tomorrow. The girls write music, play the harp, and sing. It is all right for them to be musical, but he wishes they would leave Latin, Greek, botany, and chemistry alone.

Arthur speculates that the girls have been educated because their brother Frederick's tutor had time to spare. Since Arthur believes 'that men of the *present* day dread a *blue* more than a scorpion' (i. 30), he takes the position that although the girls cannot unlearn what they have learned, they should be frightened into concealment. However, he thinks that after they are married, their education will be useful to teach their boys Latin grammar.

In the course of the novel Arthur sees the errors in his way of thinking. He begins to see that his fashionable attitudes are not always correct. At one family discussion, Arthur, the Douglases, and Mr Otway, their philosopher friend, canvass the meanings of the term 'bluestocking' and its implications for women. Mr Otway explains that the term is one of ridicule for a 'learned lady'. Arthur speaks for the worldly view that women should not be educated beyond music, drawing, etc. But Otway argues eloquently that women were made by the Creator with minds and that it is not right for men to deny all women learning. Both sexes should strive for intellectual perfection. Arthur does admit that he regards women as guardians of morality. Otway points out that a fashionable education will not prepare women for that role.

Otway makes a strong statement for a thorough education for girls from five to fifteen. He argues for studying classical languages and the Scriptures. He views the male sex as a group of people who use their physical strength to determine what women do: they require physical servitude from lower-class women and ignorance from upper-class women. Otway is not asking for any particular regimen for educating women: Latin,

Greek, Hebrew, chemistry, botany, mathematics. But he
hopes to reduce the ridicule of learned women and to open
education to all women everywhere who want it (i. 79–108).

The disputants discuss whether the ridicule of learned
women is caused by the tendency of some women to display
their learning, or by the jealousy of men who do not wish
women to share their knowledge. Otway argues that the
'motive for denying, or, at least, *grudging* to women the
advantages of a sound and a literary education' is probably
owing to the negative attitudes of men, for he believes that the
best-informed men encourage women and 'delight in superior
talents' (i. 89).

Arthur then questions, 'what is the *use* of learning in a
woman?' He asks whether she is 'handsomer, more lively,
more attractive, for having her head crammed with strange
languages' (i. 94). To this argument Otway replies with
another question: 'have men *a right* to consider women as
objects merely of gratification to their eyes and ears? Are not
women endowed with sense and feeling; with high powers of
intellectual energy, and immortal spirits like men?' (i. 95).
Otway believes that intellectual companionship can be the
highest good on earth and a portent of future felicity.

Do you believe that the distinguishing, the ennobling boon of reason
is granted to *both* sexes, to be only exercised by a very limited number
of *one* sex, and lavished in thoughtless waste by all the rest? Never
entertain such an idea of the Creator, who has made nothing without
its end, purpose, and design. (i. 97)

In *Bluestocking Hall* Scargill made a strong case for educated
women and against the use of the term 'bluestocking' to ridicule
them. Did this work die upon publication? I have not been able
to find reviews of it, so its influence must be considered un-
proved.

Writing in 1852, Thomas de Quincey suggested in his 'Autobiography' that it was time to put the term 'bluestocking' to
rest. Reminiscing about a charming Irish woman he had met
as a boy, he himself first referred to her as an 'odious bluestocking' but immediately afterwards withdrew the term. He
thought that the 'order of ladies called *Blue-stockings* by way of
reproach' had become extinct. He recognized that for earlier

generations any intellectual interest by women 'carried with it an air of something unsexual, mannish, and (as it was treated by the sycophantish satirists that ever humour the prevailing folly) of something ludicrous.' But he felt that such a treatment had been possible only when literary ladies formed a 'feeble minority'. Now the vast increase in the number of educated men and women had rendered the term 'not simply obsolete, but even unintelligible to our juniors' (i. 322 n. 1). He evidently believed that since so many women were being educated, the attempt to stigmatize them as different had become meaningless. And yet the use of the term continued.

In nineteenth-century France the case of the bluestockings was much in the public mind. Honoré Daumier published a series of forty plates on 'Les Bas-Bleus' from January to August 1844 in *Le Charivari*. He had probably been influenced by Frédéric Soulie's *Physiologie du Bas-Bleu*, published in 1841–2 with sketches by Jules Vernier; 'The Bluestockings', a light comedy by Ferdinand Langlé and F. Devilleneuve, had been put on in 1842 (Daumier, 125). Daumier's lithographs concentrate on women who aspire to be writers. He shows them in various scenes which emphasize their literary infatuations and their physical ugliness. While they are involved in the search for fame, they fob off on their husbands domestic duties such as taking care of the children and even sewing on trouser buttons.

For Jules-Amédée Barbey d'Aurevilly (1808–89), novelist and critic, the term meant professional woman writer, a phenomenon he abhorred. In his work *Les Bas-bleus* (1878), published as part of his series *Les Œuvres et les hommes*, Barbey d'Aurevilly provided harsh criticism of the idea of the bluestocking as woman writer. For he believed that women who wrote were no longer women, but men—at least by pretence—and therefore failures.

Barbey believed, mistakenly of course, that the term bluestocking began in England in the time of Pope to indicate women who did not keep up their appearance because of intellectual preoccupations, and also wore stockings typical of all the English pedants of that time (!). It is curious how the association between neglected attire and intellectual interests in women has persisted. In this case Barbey was employing the term 'bluestocking' for the traditional stereotype of the slipshod woman intellectual—a stereotype which, as we have seen, antedated the development of the bluestocking circle.

Barbey recognized that there were bluestockings in all countries. But he did not believe that the 'précieuses' whom Molière satirized were really bluestockings. They approached 'bas-bleuism' but their stockings were always white or rosé. Neither Mme de Sévigné, writer of charming gossip, nor Mme d'Aulnoy, writer of delightful books for children, was a blue-stocking. For him the bas-bleu is the literary woman, who makes literature her profession and livelihood. She believes herself the equal of man in mental capacities, and wishes to share in the publicity and glory of literature: 'Le Bas-bleu, c'est la femme littéraire. C'est la femme quit fait métier et marchandise de littérature. C'est la femme qui se croit cerveau d'homme et demande sa part dans la publicité et dans la gloire' (xii).

Barbey blamed the successive pressures of the various stages of the French Revolution for having led men to accept the demands of women for intellectual equality. Thus, in the final analysis, Barbey equated 'bas-bleuism' with a demand for equality between men and women. He made it clear that he did not believe in such equality. He felt that women differed from men in spirit as they did in body. Women had been poets, writers, artists in all civilizations, but their work showed their femininity, and furthermore, was inevitably of an inferior order.

In a conference held on 11 April 1870, Mme Olympe Audouard refuted his arguments. She found him extremely conservative not only in attitudes towards women, but also in politics and religion. She took the opportunity to call for more extended, and more analytical education for women, who suffered from instruction which emphasized memorization. 'Les hommes, de sept à dix-huit ans, apprennent à connaître les diverses branches des connaissances humaines. Les femmes perdent ces mêmes années à végéter dans des horizons bornés' (24). She claimed that women were beginning to comprehend the insufficiency of their education and were aspiring to intel-lectual influence. She pointed out that women remained inferior to men at that time because of the denial of classical education: 'Aujourd'hui, en littérature, la femme reste inférieure à l'homme, car il lui manque l'instruction première. L'étude du grec, du latin est indispensable à tout homme qui écrit, et la femme, sauf de rares exceptions, n'en sait pas le premier mot' (26). She added that the literature of women was in its early stages. 'Si l'égalité devant l'instruction était proclamée de droit commun, il suffirait d'une ou de deux générations pour se faire une idée just de l'intellect féminin.' Furthermore, the profession of literature should be considered suitable for many kinds of women—women whose children have left home and who are isolated, women who are married and have no children, women who are poor, women who do not marry. She hoped she had influenced both men and women, although she feared she had not been a good pleader for the cause. But she didn't really expect to win over M. Barbey-d'Aurévilly, because his prejudices against the bas-bleus were too deeply rooted for him to give reason a chance.

Barbey's intemperate blast and Audouard's reply show that the issue had been joined. Resentment against women intellectuals was dying hard. Women were publishing in large numbers, feminist movements had come to the fore, and women were beginning to make progress in gaining higher education. As institutions of higher education for women began to be established in the United States and England, the idea of the bluestocking began to be associated with dedicated women intellectuals who were making academic life a career. Lucy Martin Donnelly (1870–1948) was professor and head of the English Department at Bryn Mawr College from 1911 to 1936. In 'The Heart of a Bluestocking' in the *Atlantic Monthly* for October 1908 she celebrates the joys of an academic life. She feels that because as a woman she has been 'permitted very late in the ages to partake of "the sweet food of academic tuition"', her joy in learning is probably greater than that of men (536). She sees herself in a tradition of 'Blue Stockings'. She thinks of the legendary little girl in an old library teaching herself difficult languages; she thinks of the queen who rose early to read Greek tragedies, and of other learned women. But these women were 'Reading Ladies'; the 'Lady Collegiate' loves a university. The 'Lady Collegiate' devotes her days to learned discourse and her evenings to solitary meditation. She is actually a 'militant Blue Stocking'. Donnelly defends the value of spending one's life dealing with study—of history, literature, geography, etc. She has been called to a collegiate life, which has its special qualities, different from the life of the outside world. But although she recognizes the limitations of the cloistered life, and does venture outside, she always comes back. 'While the old Strongholds of the World of Ideas, the "Homes of Wisdom", are to be maintained against the assaults of the World of Affairs, it is not for a militant Bluestocking, faint though her strength may be, to surrender an antique loyalty' (539).

Donnelly's clear use of the term to define the dedicated woman academic is probably a meaning the word acquired as the world of women professors developed its own characteristics. These women were usually unmarried, and living an independent life. The term also began to be used to refer to college-educated women as a group. The South African Association of University Women calls its Journal 'The Bluestocking'. I have also found the word used to refer to American college women and their teachers in a recent review by Lyle York in the *San Francisco Chronicle Datebook* (1 June 1986). The article discusses a documentary movie, 'The Women of Summer', made about a reunion of the 'factory girls' and teachers who attended the Bryn Mawr Summer School for Women Workers in Industry between 1921 and 1938. The school had been established by M. Carey Thomas to bring women workers to Bryn Mawr for a summer. The headline for the article is, appropriately, 'When Bluestockings Met Blue Collars'.

An unusual use of the term is seen in *A Bluestocking in India: Her Medical Wards and Messages Home*, by Winifred Heston MD (1910). This series of letters describes the experiences of a woman medical missionary in India. She is not an academic but a hard-working doctor and surgeon; the writer uses the term 'bluestocking' to refer to her career as a dedicated professional (9). But after two years in India she becomes ill, and gives up her work for love and marriage.

The term 'bluestocking' continues to appear in translations, in journalistic pieces, in novels, and in autobiography.

Translators working from French into English have used the term to refer back to the idea of the intellectual woman which developed in France before the use of the term 'bas-bleu' began. For example, Richard Wilbur, in the introduction to his translation of Molière's *The Learned Ladies* (1977), refers to the would-be *femmes savantes* as bluestockings (p. ix). H. C. Barnard, translator of Fénélon's *On Education* (1966), also uses the word 'bluestocking' as a translation for Fénélon's use of *précieuse* (1;5).

The term 'bluestocking' persists in reviews both in England and America. Anthony Holden, writing in the *Times Literary Supplement* (17 May 1982) about Diana Trilling's *Mrs. Harris, the Death of the Scarsdale Diet Doctor*, expressed the thought that the trial of Mrs Harris for the murder of her lover gained special interest because Mrs Harris was 'a bluestocking headmistress, symbol of chaste community propriety . . .'. In the *Observer* (15 July 1984) D. J. Enright, reviewing Sarah Lloyd's *An Indian Attachment*, refers to the author, who is describing her life in an Indian village, as 'this brisk bluestocking'. It seems that the woman's relationship with her Sikh lover was an unequal one, a reversal of the traditional gender-roles: 'an active, emancipated, analytic and strong-minded female and a passive, innocent, irrational and emotional male'. The heading for this review is 'A Bluestocking's Sikh'.

Although the term seems most at home in England, it also appears in American reviews. In a review by Emily Leider of the poems of Carolyn Kizer, 'Poetic Mermaids' (*San Francisco Chronicle*, 28 Oct. 1984), Leider remarks that 'Kizer excels in costume, clad in either the no-nonsense garb of a bluestocking or the patterned silk robe which is often Chinese.' In a profile of Marietta Tree (*Architectural Digest*, Mar. 1984), Arthur Schlesinger, jun., wonders how this socialite and social benefactor reconciles her worldliness and social purpose. The answer is that Marietta Tree comes from a long line of Puritans; their wives and daughters were bluestockings and reformers.

Novelists also use the term. In *The Honourable Schoolboy*, John Le Carré uses the term to characterize an agent. 'Molly Meakin was a prim, pretty graduate, a little blue-stocking perhaps, a little inward, but already with a modest name as a capable desk officer . . .'. (90). In *Some Tame Gazelle* (1950), Barbara Pym uses the term as part of her characterization of Olivia Berridge, a kind of 'female Don'. Archdeacon Hoccleve describes her as 'a very forceful young woman . . . and rather a bluestocking in appearance' (68). Olivia has been working on variant readings of a medieval poem, and another character says of her work, 'I believe some of those old poems are very *coarse*, so she may not be such a blue stocking as we think' (91). Pym has brought together the ideas that a bluestocking has a grim appearance and a primness of attitude which seem to have persisted in the modern view.

In 1986 Pandora Press published the unfinished autobiography of the British film critic, Helen Fletcher (1910–1947), which she wrote between 1943 and 1947. Fletcher's own title was *A Gay Goodnight*, but the book was issued with the title *Bluestocking*. Fletcher had had an unhappy childhood, with strong conflicts with her mother, who disliked the fact that her daughter read a great deal; mother threatened daughter with the idea that she might become a bluestocking whom nobody would want to marry.

The term 'bluestocking' has also been used in relation to a stereotypical treatment of a woman colleague by a scientist— the descriptions of Rosalind Franklin by James Watson in his book *The Double Helix* (1968), which was recently quoted in Jane Roland Martin's *Reclaiming a Conversation: The Ideal of the Educated Woman* (1985). Franklin, whom Watson refers to as 'Rosy', although that was not how anyone addressed her, is presented as difficult to work with, and so aggressive that the men were afraid she might strike them. During a seminar which she gives, Watson muses momentarily about how taking off her glasses and doing something novel with her hair might improve her appearance (Watson, 68–9; quot. Martin, 32). Watson belittles Franklin's seriousness of purpose. He also judges her to be unfeminine. And, not surprisingly, the term 'bluestocking' comes in at the end:

By choice she did not emphasize her feminine qualities. Though her features were strong, she was not unattractive and might have been quite stunning had she taken even a mild interest in clothes. This she did not. There was never lipstick to contrast with her straight black hair, while at the age of thirty-one her dresses showed all the imagination of English blue-stocking adolescents. (Watson, 17; quot. Martin, 32)

But in his Epilogue to the book, written some years after

Rosalind Franklin's death at thirty-seven, Watson apologized for his treatment of her. He praised her dedication and her intelligence in her scientific work, and indicated his realization of the difficulties she faced as a woman in trying to get equal and considerate treatment for her work.

Thus the legacy of the bluestockings was curiously mixed. By their efforts as female advocates who asserted the female right to literature, the bluestockings created a public image of the respectable, sensible woman with intellectual interests. Their published works and later published correspondence documented their activities and generated enough interest to fix the term 'bluestocking' as a name around which associations with and feelings about intellectual women could cluster. We have seen that they do cluster suggestively—sometimes in a positive way, when women are seen as self-directed and committed to intellectual work, but often in a negative way, when the image of the woman intellectual is associated with ideas that go back several centuries: that women whose interests are intellectual must be rather out of touch with reality, and that they are probably slipshod and unkempt in appearance. That successive generations of women have carried on the struggle is indicated by the continual carping of those prejudiced against education for women.

In these days of post-feminism we need to ask if one important goal has been achieved: are women as free as men to study and to take up active careers in the fields which involve intellectual endeavour? On the surface it would seem so. Barriers to equal education have fallen; women are less likely to be programmed internally against intellectual pursuits. But the fact that the word 'bluestocking' continues to surface, in a casual or in a pejorative way, suggests that the hostility—overt or hidden—to permitting women to share in the pursuit of knowledge—still has some power. Probably, like De Quincey more than a hundred and thirty years ago, we need to advocate putting the term 'bluestocking' to rest.

# NOTES TO THE TEXT

## PROLOGUE

1  The passage is from Guarini, *De pensieri diversi*, 227–8. Bayle quoted this passage in the original Italian in the article on Guarini in the *Dictionaire historique et critique* (Rotterdam, 1697). The passage appeared in Italian in the 1710 English edition of the *Dictionary*. In the English version, Bayle's *General Dictionary*, the passage appeared both in Italian and in the English version quoted in the text. The index of this edition contains an entry, 'Women, why several learned women among the ancients were very lustful'.

2  Wherever possible, I have quoted from the original letters in the Elizabeth (Robinson) Montagu Collection in the Henry E. Huntington Library, San Marino, Calif. Comparison with the letters printed by Matthew Montagu, Emily Climenson, and Reginald Blunt show significant alterations and omissions in the published versions. Many letters are unpublished.

3  I have not found this letter to Dr Monsey in the Montagu Collection in the Huntington Library.

4  MO 6387 is dated by the Huntington Library, 4 Feb. [1766]; Vesey's letter (MO 6276), which is the reply, is dated 11 Feb. [?1765].

5  The etymological dictionaries I consulted give somewhat different accounts of the rise of the term 'bluestocking'. Dauzat, *Nouveau dictionnaire étymologique et historique* (4th edn.), lists the term *bas-bleu* as follows: '1801, chez Mackenzie, calque de l'angl. *blue-stocking*, d'après les bas bleus que portait Stillingfleet, causeur brillant du salon de lady Montagu vers 1781. *bas-bleuisme* 1866, Barbey d'Aurevilly.' I wish to thank Prof. J. H. Davis for this reference. Kluge–Mitzka, *Etymologisches Wörterbuch der deutschen Sprache*, lists the term as follows under *Blaustrump*: 'Ein anderes B. ist (wie frz. *bas-bleu* seit 1820, nl. *blauwkous*, dän. *blaastrømpe*, schwed. *blåstrumpe*) Lehnübers. des engl. *blue-stocking*. Im Londoner Haus der Lady Elis. Montague versammelte sich seit etwa 1750 ein schöngeistiger Kreis, in dem Benj. Stillingfleet mit blauen Wollgarnstrümpfen (statt der sonst üblichen schwarzen Seidenstrümpfe) erschien, weshalb Admiral Boscawen *The blue stocking society* verspottete. Blaustrumpf 'gelehrtes Frauenzimmer' begegnet zuerst in der Jenaer Allg. Lit.-Ztg. 1797 Nr. 384 u. wird in der Dt. Monatsschr. 1798, 2, 284ff. erläutert. Eingebürgert erst vom Jungen Deutschland seit Börne 1830 Pariser Briefe 47.' Kluge–Mitzka makes the common error of thinking that the stockings were supposed to be black.

The spread of the word in western and northern Europe raises questions of international influence which it would be interesting to address.

CHAPTER 1

1   In 1740 Lord Oxford was forced to sell Wimpole because of his un-
    restrained expenditure on his collection, and after his death his widow sold
    the books and pamphlets belonging to the library. Samuel Johnson wrote
    'An Account of the Harleian Library' in 1742 as part of the bookseller
    Thomas Osborne's preparations for the sale. Osborne himself bought the
    works in a single lot for £13,000, and later resold the items separately at
    great profit. Lady Oxford did not sell her husband's manuscript collection
    because she wished it to be kept intact. In 1753 she gave her daughter and
    son-in-law authority to negotiate with the government for the sale of the
    manuscripts for the nominal sum of £10,000, provided that the collection
    was kept together in a proper repository, and called by the name of the
    Harleian collection of manuscripts. The government raised £20,000 by
    lottery for the purchase of the manuscripts and of Montagu House as a
    repository. The Harleian collection of manuscripts in 7,693 volumes thus
    became one of the important holdings of the British Museum (Lees-
    Milne, 184–5).
2   The Portland children were Lady Elizabeth (Oct. 1735), Lady Henrietta
    (Feb. 1737), William, Marquis of Titchfield (Apr. 1738), Lady Margaret
    (July 1739), Lady Frances (Apr. 1741), and Lord Edward (Mar. 1744).
    Emily J. Climenson, editor of two volumes of her correspondence,
    *Elizabeth Montagu, The Queen of the Blue-Stockings*, thought that Elizabeth
    stayed with the Portlands in 1737 (i. 23), but actually that year Elizabeth
    wrote from Kent on 5 Mar. to congratulate the Duchess on the birth of her
    second daughter. Most probably Elizabeth was in London when William
    was born (16 Apr. 1738); the next child, Lady Margaret, was born in July
    1739, again after Elizabeth had returned to Kent.
3   The dates assigned to these letters in the Huntington Library are not in
    sequence. MO 4756, Elizabeth Robinson to Matthew Robinson (her
    request for money), is dated by HEH ?1740. Her letter from Whitehall
    thanking him for the money is MO 4752, dated by HEH 1737. The letter
    to her mother, MO 4707, quoted above, is also assigned to 1737. In
    MO 4752, Elizabeth's request for money, she says that Pope has recently
    written an epitaph on himself. She would send it but hasn't got a copy of
    it. Climenson thought the epitaph was 'Under this Marble, or over this
    Sill', which was, however, published in 1741 (Montagu (1906), i. 24). An
    earlier epitaph, 'Heroes, and Kings! your Distance Keep:' with the
    heading 'For One who would not be Buried in Westminster Abbey', was
    published in 1738. Elizabeth may be referring to this poem. See Pope,
    *Minor Poems*, 376; 386.
4   Portland Loan 29/325 in the British Library is a bound book in the hand-
    writing of the Duchess of Portland. It contains copies of some letters by
    Elizabeth Robinson to Anne Donnellan. Letter quoted is not in HEH.
    Capitals are the Duchess's writing.
5   MO 812 is a fragment incorrectly dated by HEH 1740. The passage
    appears in BL, Portland Loan 29/325, p. 51. I have followed the text of
    the fragment, and the dating on the copy.

6   Nicolas Boileau Despreaux, 'Satire IV', ll. 5–6: 'Un pedant enivre de sa
    vaine science, | Tout herisee de grec, tout bouffi d'arrogance . . .'
    (*Œuvres* (Paris: Garnier-Flammarion, 1969), i. 67).
7   This letter was probably misdated. Elizabeth Robinson mentioned that
    she had not yet begun to drink the waters. She was in Bath in Dec.

CHAPTER 2

1   Nicolas Carter to Elizabeth, Bath, 8 Oct. 1729, copy in Stebbing/Ruther-
    ford extracts. The originals of Nicolas Carter's letters to his daughter and
    some of her letters to various correspondents survived in Deal in the
    possession of Mrs Gladys Brown. The late William P. D. Stebbing of Deal
    made a transcript of extracts from these letters. Copies of some of these
    extracts are among the Miscellaneous Papers from the Stebbing Collection
    in Deal County Library. Barbara Rutherford, retired headmistress of the
    Elizabeth Carter School, had a typed copy of a larger number of the
    extracts, which she very kindly permitted me to duplicate. Further
    references to the Stebbing/Rutherford and Stebbing/Deal County Library
    extracts are in the text. Some of the autograph letters are now in the
    possession of Gwen Hampshire, who kindly permitted me to see them.
    Quotations transcribed from these letters are indicated as being in the
    Hampshire collection.
2   For Wright see 'Biographical History of Mr. Thomas Wright'. For
    Desaguliers see Delany, 1st ser., i. 461 n. 1. Both are in *DNB*, and Wright
    is in *Dictionary of Scientific Biography*.
3   For pen-name identification in the *Gentleman's Magazine* see Albert Pailler,
    *Edward Cave et le* Gentleman's Magazine *(1731–1754)*.
4   At one time the ascription to Johnson was considered uncertain.
    However, Hampshire quotes from a letter of Nicolas Carter to Elizabeth
    in which he says that her sister Peggy sent him 'Johnson's Epigram' while
    he was in Scarborough and said she could 'construe' it (222). The refer-
    ence seems to be to the Latin epigram in the July issue, which would have
    been available at the beginning of Aug. Revd Carter's letter was dated
    13 Aug. 1738.
5   The British Library has an autograph copy of this poem with alterations
    that seem to be in Elizabeth Carter's hand in a different ink (Add. 4456,
    fos. 60–1). The date on the verso of fo. 61 may be in Birch's hand. This
    transcript differs from the *Gentleman's Magazine* copy in some small ways.
    One line has a different noun: 'As fancy various, and as Beauty sweet',
    rather than 'as bounty sweet'. The presence of the word 'beauty' in the
    version in Rowe, *Miscellaneous Works* and in Bayle's *General Dictionary*
    suggests that the British Library copy was probably used for the version in
    those works.

CHAPTER 3

1   This biographical history, written by George Allan of Darlington, was
    largely based on the 'Early Journal' kept by Wright. A more accurate

presentation of the contents of this journal (Edward Hughes, 'The Early Journal of Thomas Wright of Durham') was prepared as part of the bicentenary of the publication of Wright's major scientific work. Wright's actual words are quoted by Hughes and the phrase is, 'to teach ye Young Ladies Geometry etc' (13). More details of Wright's travels are given, and in Aug. 1741 Wright stayed three weeks in Deal with Revd Dr Carter (16). Lists of Wright's students are also given, and in one document it is noted that his correspondence included 100 letters to Miss E. Carter. This was the largest number written to any of his students (22).

## CHAPTER 4

1   Later in life Elizabeth Carter seems to have been hurt when her friend Miss Sharpe married. This friendship began about 1777. Elizabeth Carter's letters to Mrs Vesey mention Miss Sharpe. In 1778 she wrote to Mrs Vesey about Miss Sharpe's kind behaviour after the deaths of Elizabeth's nephew and sister-in-law (24 Jan. 1778). Miss Sharpe came back to Deal when she heard of these events and gave her 'all the care and attention which a parent could expect from the most affectionate child . . .'. Miss Sharpe was an orphan and had an uncle as a guardian. Elizabeth felt that the young woman had been over-protected as a child. 'She is but a poor creature at best, and all unfortunately owing to wrong treatment, or more properly speaking, too too much care having been taken of her in her childhood, when the wind of heaven was not suffered to blow on her, for fear she should catch cold' (7 Oct. 1780). Earlier Elizabeth Carter had reported on Miss Sharpe's excitement at having been caught in a rainstorm with her: 'to Miss Sharpe it is quite an adventure to talk of, never, I believe, having been wet by a shower of rain before' (30 Sept. 1779). Elizabeth Carter and Miss Sharpe made several tours in England together, and Elizabeth was grateful for her friend's attention to her health. In 1782 Miss Sharpe became engaged to Dr Osmond Beauvoir, late master of Canterbury school, a man much older than herself. There seems to have been a temporary estrangement between the two women. Although Elizabeth Carter obviously thought there were benefits to being young, wealthy, and unmarried, she could see that Miss Sharpe's decision to marry was her own, and something she should be free to do. 'By all accounts, as our friend chose to change her situation, she has made a respectable choice. One would think it was scarcely possible to find a condition more eligible than that she has quitted. But that odd kind of thing, which passes for happiness in this world, is made up of circumstances so peculiar to every individual mind, that provided, as in this case, no injury is done to any one, no objection ought to be made' (8 July 1782 to Elizabeth Vesey, in Carter, *Letters* (1808)).

After the death of her first husband, Mrs Beauvoir married the widower Dr Andrew Douglas, who had been married to Elizabeth Carter's half-sister. After Elizabeth Carter's death her friend wrote a *Sketch of the Character of Mrs. Elizabeth Carter*. She explained that they had been estranged for a 'season' because of a decision which she had made. But they were reconciled and remained so, and the disagreement was never mentioned again (18). Pennington verified that Miss Sharpe was the author of this piece (Carter, *Memoirs*, i. 457 n.).

2   The manuscript of Thomas Secker's Autobiography is in the Lambeth Palace Library. It is being edited for publication by Prof. John S. Macauley. In a private communication the editor indicated that Secker made some notes about the financial arrangements between the Talbots and himself. The Talbots had been living with Catherine Benson before his marriage; after his marriage Mrs Talbot paid about two-fifths of the family's expenses for herself and her daughter and two servants. Afterwards that was reduced to £100 a year for everything. After his wife died, he refused any payment. In 1748 he arranged for Mr John Talbot to give £100, part of a fee, to Miss Talbot and also gave her £100. Secker noted that while the Talbots were in Bristol in 1759 during Catherine's illness, they had a coach and a pair of horses at his expense. After Catherine's illness Secker made Mrs Talbot a present of £200. He noted that he had given her a present of £100 every year afterwards. The evidence suggests that the Talbots were short of money, and that Secker was supporting them.

3   According to Prof. Macauley, these dates for Catherine's illness are noted in Secker's Autobiography.

4   Faderman argues that great animosity developed between Chapone and her husband early in the marriage and that she met his death 'with apparent relief' (100). The original source of this canard is probably the anonymous biographical memoir which appeared in an early edition of Chapone's *Works* printed by James Ballantyne (see Bibliog.). The biographer devotes most of his memoir to arguing that Chapone's marriage was not happy. Since the writer admits that he does not know when the Chapones married or how long they were married before Mr Chapone died (he puts the date vaguely as some time before 1775) his discussion has only rumour as its basis. His argument is that Mrs Chapone may have been unfit for the 'cultivation of domestic tranquillity' by her 'want of temper'. Furthermore, the writer thinks that acquiring knowledge may in itself handicap both men and women in private life (p. xi). In other words, learning and matrimony do not go together. The biographer also uses Chapone's advice to her niece to avoid matrimonial bickering as evidence that her own marriage must have been unhappy (p. xii). But the observation of long-term marital unhappiness could not have been Mrs Chapone's from her own example, as she was simply not married long enough.

5   In 'Steele's "Ladies" Library', George A. Aitken identified the source of this passage as Taylor's *Holy Living*.

CHAPTER 5

1   A translation of *Defensa de las mugeres* was published as *An Essay on Woman, or Physiological and Historical Defence of the Fair Sex from the Spanish of* El teatro

crítico (London: Printed for W. Bingley, n.d. (but British Library cat. dates as c.1765)). There was a subsequent edition printed for D. Steel in 1774, and a further translation by John Brett, *Essays or Discourses Selected from the Works of Feijóo*, 4 vols. (London: Printed for the translator, 1780).

2  Jocelyn Harris, editor of the OUP edn. of *Sir Charles Grandison*, believes Elizabeth Carter was the author of this defence of women (iii. 243; 480 n.).

### INTRODUCTION TO PART III

1  I wish to thank Prof. Margaret Anne Doody for sharing with me her unpublished lecture, 'Augustan *Women?*: Four Poets of the Eighteenth Century', presented at the William Andrews Clark Memorial Library, Univ. California, Los Angeles, 1980.

2  In *The Converse of the Pen: Acts of Intimacy in the Eighteenth-Century Familiar Letter* (Chicago: Univ. of Chicago Press, 1986), Bruce Redford analyses the ways in which the 'great' letter writers—including Lady Mary Wortley Montagu, Horace Walpole, and Samuel Johnson—achieved the effects of intimacy. The first bluestockings did not produce letters which were performances, but they wrote openly about their lives. The fact that Mme de Sévigné was a woman writing about maternal relationships, as well as an observer of her society, and a lover of nature, must have helped the bluestockings to gain some sense of validation of their own interests—in books, nature, people, and their own feelings.

### CHAPTER 6

1  I have quoted from the 1762 edition of the *Poems*, and used the identifications Montagu Pennington gives in his edition of the poems in the *Memoirs*.

### CHAPTER 7

1  MO 6721, 14 Nov. [1754], Elizabeth Montagu to Gilbert West, has the critique of Bolingbroke. MO 6667, in which West tells her he has shown the letter to the Archbishop, is dated 18 Nov. 1754, Croydon. But Mrs Montagu's reply to this news is incorrectly dated by HEH as MO 6707, 23 Nov. [1753], Hill Street.

2  When Lady Barbara died in 1765 she left Sarah a legacy of about £2,200 plus her half of the furnishings of the house (MO 2575, 31 [Aug.] 1765, Elizabeth Montagu to Edward Montagu). When her brother the sea captain had died in 1756, he had left Sarah a legacy of £1,500 which she was to receive at her father's death. At that time, 1778, she inherited £1,900; it may have been the sum of the legacy from her brother plus £400 remaining to her from the part of the dowry returned to her father (MO 6042).

3  A great many of Mrs Montagu's original letters are in the Huntington Library Collection. These letters can be read in conjunction with

Montagu Pennington's edition of Elizabeth Carter's *Letters* . . . *to Elizabeth Montagu* (1817). The originals of Mrs Carter's letters have not been found. Although Pennington misplaced some passages and mistook some dates, the general interchange of letters can be followed and the course of the friendship can be clearly seen.

4  Father Peter Brumoy's *Théâtre des grecs* was originally published in a handsome quarto edition in 1730. He brought out another edition in six volumes duodecimo in 1763. Since Charlotte Lennox brought out her translation in 1759, she must have used the first edition as her text. I suspect that Elizabeth Montagu also worked with Brumoy's first edition. I have found no references by her to the Lennox translation.

5  Prof. Margaret Anne Doody discusses this scene in 'Frances Sheridan: Morality and Annihilated Time', 333.

6  In 1981 Marjorie Hanson provided an annotated text of the *Essay* in her Ph.D. thesis, 'Elizabeth Montagu: A Biographical Sketch and a Critical Edition of her Writings'.

CHAPTER 8

1  Thomas Secker was consecrated Bishop of Bristol on 19 Jan. 1734/5 and became Bishop of Oxford on 14 May 1737. The *Gentleman's Magazine* thought that the Bishop of Bristol mentioned in the letter was Dr Secker. However, in her letter to Elizabeth Berkeley which I quote from here, Catherine said that all the persons she referred to in the letter were now dead (BL Add. 39312, fo. 319). But this number did not include Secker, for in the same letter she speaks of the Archbishop 'riding out today in a storm of snow, hail & thunder'. So the Bishop of Bristol to whom she referred must have been Secker's predecessor in that office, and the letter thus dates from 1734 at the latest.

2  I am using the 1780 edition of Talbot's *Works* for quotation. When Montagu Pennington brought out the seventh edition of her *Works* in 1809 he made numerous editorial changes, such as giving headings to the sections of the *Reflections*, explanatory subtitles to the essays, and altering the titles of some of the poems.

3  In his *Life and Correspondence of Philip Yorke, Earl of Hardwicke, Lord High Chancellor of Great Britain*, Philip C. Yorke gave the list of contributors in addition to Philip and Charles Yorke and Catherine Talbot, as Thomas Birch, Henry Coventry, John Green, afterwards Bishop of Lincoln, Samuel Salter, their tutor and afterwards Master of the Charterhouse, Daniel Wray, G. H. Rooke, afterwards Master of Christ's College, John Heaton of Bene't College, John Lawry, afterwards Prebendary of Rochester, and W. Heberden. He added that the 1781 edition consisted of 100 copies. The book was reprinted in 1792, in 1798, and again in 1810. In 1800 an edition was published at Basle; there were two French translations in 1803 (i. 207–8).

4  Among the Berkeley papers in the British Library there is a letter from Eliza to her husband written in 1777 in which she complained of mistreatment by his mother, who had deprived her of her husband's love, and

others written at the same time in which she expressed anger at a scandal involving her husband and another woman. She also complained that not much money was left them except her settlement, which had not been equal to her fortune. But, she noted, she had married her husband because of his character, not his own small fortune (BL Add. 39312, fos. 1–8).

5  In his 1809 edition of Talbot's *Works* Pennington explained that Talbot wrote the first imitation in 1760, after some specimens of Macpherson's Ossian poems had been published (376 n.).

CHAPTER 9

1  The position seems to have been with the Duchess of Bavaria. In MO 625, his reply to Mrs Montagu's letter, Bridgen regrets that he will not be able to recommend Mrs Chapone 'to so genteel a situation at the Bavarian Court . . .'. Bridgen speaks of the special honour Mrs Chapone would have received in having been made a Lady of Honour to the Duchess, and that Mrs Chapone's menservants would have worn the Elector's livery. This letter is incorrectly dated *c.*1771 by HEH.

CHAPTER 10

1  Mrs Montagu carried on a remarkably full and diverse life. Aside from functioning as an estate and coal-mine manager, she also carried on charitable activities for individuals and for the people who lived on her estates. She was both a tough-minded business woman, and a provider of Sunday schools and charitable feasts. For her benevolent activities see Edith Sedgwick Larson, 'A Measure of Power: The Personal Charity of Elizabeth Montagu'.

Her literary patronage was also diverse. She helped women like Sarah Fielding and Anna Williams. She was supportive of James Beattie when attempts were being made to get him a pension from the King. She encouraged Robert Potter, translator of the Greek tragedies. He provided a set of notes to his translation of Aeschylus at her suggestion. The notes were sent to the University Press at Cambridge, with the hope that that press could produce a correct version of the many Greek quotations (MO 4158, 14 July 1778, Robert Potter to Mrs Montagu). On 5 Oct. 1778 he sent her the bill (MO 4159). He dedicated the work to her.

Mrs Montagu did not accept all the requests for dedications which were made to her; she was careful not to seem to lend her prestige to works of whose value she was not certain. However, her most unhappy experience as a literary patron was probably her long personal relationship with James Woodhouse, the shoemaker poet. She brought him and his family to Sandleford to run her farm. He was evidently an earnest, hard-working farm manager, but Mrs Montagu resented what she believed to be his pride and his wife's extravagance. In 1778 he left Sandleford, but three years later he came back to work as the steward of her London house and Sandleford. But in 1788 there was a final rupture. Later he wrote a long poem attacking her pride, vanity, and greed, which was not, however, published until 1896. See Katherine G. Hornbeak, 'New Light on Mrs. Montagu'.

CHAPTER 11

1  I owe these details to the late Miriam Leranbaum, who traced the history of the print and painting in her unpublished 1977 paper.
2  The subscription books are at the Royal Society of Arts, John Adam St., London; Mrs Montagu's fees are entered year by year until her death. I wish to thank Mr David Allan for his cordial help during my visit to the Society.
3  The Society of Arts published reports of the *Premiums by the Society* which contained lists of categories and lists of awards during successive years. See also Derek Hudson and Kenneth W. Luckhurst, *The Royal Society of the Arts, 1754-1954*, 15.

EPILOGUE

1  In her thesis, 'Discovering the Bluestockings', Mary L. Robbie traced pejorative uses of the term in such nineteenth-century writers as Barbey d'Aurevilly, Byron, de Quincey, Ferrier, Lockhart, and Scott. I found other references to the use of the term 'bluestocking' by reviewing library catalogues, publishers' catalogues, and standard bibliographies; I gathered some references by noting usage in the *Times Literary Supplement*, my local newspaper (the *San Francisco Chronicle*), and anything else I read during the last five years. Unlike Robbie, I concluded that there were both negative and positive uses of the term 'bluestocking'.

# BIBLIOGRAPHY

## A. MANUSCRIPT SOURCES

BERKELEY, GEORGE, jun., Berkeley Papers: Letters of Catherine Talbot to Anne, Eliza, and George Berkeley; Letter of George Berkeley to Thomas Secker (BL Add. 39311).
—— Correspondence of Anne, Eliza, and George Berkeley; Letters of Catherine Talbot to George Berkeley and to Eliza Berkeley (BL Add. 39312).
—— Journal (1754) (BL Add. 46689).
BIRCH, THOMAS, Correspondence (BL Add. 4320; 4321).
—— Diary: Latin and English (BL Add. 4478c).
CARTER, ELIZABETH, Letters to Edward Cave (BL Stowe 748).
—— Latin Letters, probably copied by Thomas Birch (BL Add. 4456).
—— MS and copies of Poems (BL Add. 4456).
CARTER, NICHOLAS, Letters to Elizabeth Carter, MS (private collection, Gwen Hampshire).
—— TS: Extracts (Barbara Rutherford, Deal).
—— TS: Extracts (Stebbing Collection, Deal County Library).
CHAPONE, HESTER, Letters to Frances D'Arblay (Fanny Burney) (BL Egerton 3698).
ELSTOB, ELIZABETH, Letters to George Ballard (Bodleian Library, MS Ballard 43).
—— MS: 'Notes toward biography of learned ladies' (Bodleian Library, MS Ballard 64).
—— Letter to Mrs Mary Pendarves (1738) (Univ. of Nottingham Library, MS Portland Collection PwE 8); unsigned letter about Elstob (MS PwE 9).
GREY, JEMIMA, March., Copies of Correspondence to Catherine Talbot (Bedfordshire County Record Office, Lucas Papers L 30/9a/3-9). See also *Catherine Talbot*.
MONTAGU, ELIZABETH (ROBINSON), Correspondence (Henry E. Huntington Library, 6,923 pieces, designated MO).
—— Berkeley Papers: Letters to Eliza Berkeley (BL Add. 39312).
—— Letters to Anne Donnellan: copies by Margaret, Duchess of Portland (BL, Portland Loan 29/325).
—— Letters to Duchess of Portland (Univ. of Nottingham Library, MSS Portland Collection PwE 35-57).
—— Letters to Hester Thrale (John Rylands Library, Eng. MS 551).

MONTAGU, ELIZABETH (ROBINSON), Letter to her Sister (Bodleian Library, MS Autograph b 10, no. 1059).

PIOZZI, HESTER THRALE, Poems on Several Occasions with Anecdotes, &c., Introductory to the Poems, Piozziana, and Scrap and Trifle Book, 1810–14, 5 MS vols. (Houghton Library, MS Eng. 1280).

Portland Papers, Letters and Papers of Margaret, second Duchess of Portland, and William, second Duke of Portland (Univ. of Nottingham Library, MSS Portland Collection PwE, D).

—— Marriage Settlement of the second Duke and Duchess of Portland, 10 July 1734 (Pl D). See also *Elizabeth Montagu.*

SECKER, THOMAS, Notebooks (Lambeth Palace Library, No. 2564).

—— Will (Photostat) (Lambeth Palace Library, Arch P/A Secker, Bundle 25).

SOMERSET, FRANCES, Duchess of, Letters to Catherine Talbot (BL Add. 19689).

TALBOT, CATHERINE, Journal at Wrest, Lucas Papers (Bedfordshire County Record Office, L 31/106).

—— Journals (partly French) (BL Add. 46688; 46690).

—— Letters to Miss Campbell, later March. Grey, and Lady Mary Grey: copies, probably by Thomas Birch (BL Add. 4291).

—— Berkeley Papers: Letters to George, Anne, and Elizabeth Berkeley (BL Add. 39311; 39312; 39316).

—— Miscellaneous Letters (Lambeth Palace Library, MSS 1719; 1349).

—— Reflections on the Seven Days of the Week (*MS Copy*, 1754) (BL Add. 46689).

—— Verses, etc., partly autograph (BL Add. 39316).

## B.  LIST OF WORKS CITED

ADAM, ROBERT B., *The R. B. Adam Library Relating to Dr. Samuel Johnson and his Era*, 3 vols. (London: OUP, 1929).

AITKEN, GEORGE A., 'Steele's "Ladies" Library', *Athenaeum*, No. 2958 (5 July 1884), 16.

ALGAROTTI, FRANCISCO, *Il Newtonianismo per le dame, ovvero dialoghi sopra la luce e i colori* (Naples, 1737).

—— *Sir Isaac Newton's Philosophy Explain'd for the Use of the Ladies, in Six Dialogues on Light and Colours*, trans. Elizabeth Carter (London: E. Cave, 1739).

*All the Works of Epictetus*, trans. Elizabeth Carter (Review), *Critical Review*, 6 (Aug. 1758), 149–58.

—— (Review), *Monthly Review*, 18 (June 1758), 588–97.

ALLAN, DAVID, 'The Progress of Human Culture and Knowledge: James Barry's Paintings for the Royal Society of the Arts at the Adelphi in London, 1777–1801', Pt. II: 'The Fifth and Sixth Pictures', *Connoisseur*, 188 (Feb. 1975), 98–107.

ANSON, ELIZABETH, and ANSON, FLORENCE (eds.), *Mary Hamilton Afterwards Mrs. John Dickenson at Court and at Home, from Letters and Diaries 1756 to 1816* (London: John Murray, 1925).

ASHMUN, MARGARET, *The Singing Swan: An Account of Anna Seward and her Acquaintance with Dr. Johnson, Boswell, and Others of their Time*, with Pref. by Frederick A. Pottle (New Haven, Conn.: Yale UP, 1931).

ASPINALL-OGLANDER, CECIL, *Admiral's Wife: Being the Life and Letters of the Hon. Mrs. Edward Boscawen from 1719 to 1761* (London: Longmans, Green, 1940).

—— *Admiral's Widow: Being the Life and Letters of the Hon. Mrs. Edward Boscawen from 1761 to 1805* (London: Hogarth Press, 1942).

ASTELL, MARY, *A Serious Proposal for the Ladies, for the Advancement of their True and Greatest Interest*, Pt. I, 3rd edn., corr. (London: Printed for R. Wilkin, 1696).

—— *A Serious Proposal to the Ladies, Wherein a Method is Offer'd for the Improvement of their Minds* (London: Printed for Richard Wilkin, 1697).

AUBREY, JOHN, *Aubrey's Brief Lives*, ed. Oliver Lawson Dick, with Foreword by Edmund Wilson, 2nd edn. (Ann Arbor, Mich.: Univ. of Mich. Press, 1957).

AUDOUARD, OLYMPE, *M. Barbey-D'Aurévilly: Réponse à ses réquisitoires contre les bas-bleus*, ed. E. Dentu, Conférence du 11 avr. 1870 (Paris: Libraire de La Société des Gens de Lettres, 1870).

AUSTEN, JANE, *Letters to her Sister Cassandra and Others*, ed. R. W. Chapman, 2nd edn. (London: OUP, 1952; repr. with corr. 1959).

BABCOCK, ROBERT WITBECK, *The Genesis of Shakespeare Idolatry, 1766–1799: A Study in English Criticism of the Late Eighteenth Century* (Chapel Hill, NC: Univ. of North Carolina Press, 1931).

BALLARD, GEORGE, *Memoirs of Several Ladies of Great Britain, who have been Celebrated for their Writings or Skill in the Learned Languages, Arts and Sciences* (Oxford: Printed for the author, 1752).

BARBAULD, ANNA LAETITIA AIKIN, *Works* (with a memoir by Lucy Aikin), 2 vols. (London: Printed for Longman *et al.*, 1825).

BARBEY D'AUREVILLY, JULES-AMÉDÉE, *Les Bas-bleus, Xix$^e$ siècle*, vol. v *Les Œuvres et les hommes*, Société Générale de Librairie Catholique (Paris: Victor Palmé; Brussels: G. Lebrocquy, 1878).

BARTON, MARGARET, *Tunbridge Wells* (London: Faber and Faber, 1937).

[BAYLE, PIERRE], *General Dictionary*, ed. Thomas Birch, *et al.*, 10 vols. (London, 1734–41).

BEATTIE, JAMES, *James Beattie's London Diary 1773*, ed. Ralph S. Walker, *Aberdeen University Studies*, 122 (Aberdeen: Aberdeen UP, 1946).

BELL, SUSAN GROAG, and OFFEN, KAREN M., *Women, the Family, and Freedom: The Debate in Documents*, 2 vols. (Stanford, Calif.: Stanford UP, 1983), i.

[BERKELEY, ELIZA], 'Singular Tale of Love in High Life', *Gentleman's Magazine*, 66 (Aug. 1796), 631–2.

'BERKELEY, GEORGE [jun.]', *General Biographical Dictionary*, new edn., rev. and enl. (Alexander Chalmers: London, 1812).

BERKELEY, GEORGE, *Works: with Prefaces, Annotations, his Life and Letters, and an Account of his Philosophy*, ed. Alexander C. Fraser, 4 vols. (Oxford: Clarendon Press, 1871), iv.

'Biographical History of Mr. Thomas Wright', *Gentleman's Magazine*, 63 (Jan.–Mar. 1793), 9–12; 126–7; 213–16.

BIRCH, THOMAS, 'Article XXXI, Sir Isaac Newton's Philosophy Explain'd for the Use of the Ladies', *History of the Works of the Learned* (June 1739), 392–408.

—— 'Rowe, Elizabeth Singer', in *Bayle's General Dictionary*.

BLANCHARD, RAE, 'Richard Steele and the Status of Women', *Studies in Philology*, 26 (July 1929), 325–55.

BODEK, EVELYN GORDON, 'Salonières and Bluestockings: Educated Obsolescence and Germinating Feminism', *Feminist Studies*, 3 (spring–summer 1976), 185–99.

BOSWELL, JAMES, *The Life of Samuel Johnson including Boswell's Journal of a Tour to the Hebrides and Johnson's Diary of a Journey into North Wales*, ed. George Birkbeck Hill, 6 vols. (New York: Harper, 1891).

—— *Boswell's Life of Johnson, together with Boswell's Journal of a Tour to the Hebrides and Johnson's Diary of a Journal into North Wales*, ed. George Birkbeck Hill, rev. and enl. L. F. Powell, 6 vols. (Oxford: Clarendon Press, 1934).

BRACK, GAE ANNETTE, 'Samuel Johnson and Four Literary Women', thesis (Arizona State Univ., 1979).

BRINK, J. R. (Introd.), *Female Scholars: A Tradition of Learned Women before 1800*, ed. J. R. Brink (Montreal: Eden Press Women's Publications, 1980).

BROWN, IRENE Q., 'Domesticity, Feminism, and Friendship: Female Aristocratic Culture and Marriage in England, 1660-1760', *Journal of Family History*, 7 (1982), 406–24.

BRUMOY, R. P., *Le Théâtre des grecs* (Paris: Rollin Pere, Jean-Baptiste Coignard, Rollin Fils, 1730).

—— *The Greek Theatre of Father Brumoy*, trans. Charlotte Lennox, 3 vols. (London, 1759).

BUCK, ANNE, *Dress in Eighteenth-Century England* (New York: Holmes and Meier, 1979).

BURNEY, CHARLES, *Memoirs*, ed. Mme D'Arblay, 3 vols. (London: Edward Moxon, 1832).

BURNEY, FANNY, *Diary and Letters of Madame D'Arblay (1778–1840)*, ed. Charlotte Barrett, Preface and notes by Austin Dobson, 6 vols. (London: Macmillan, 1905).

—— *The Early Diary of Frances Burney, 1768–1778, with a Selection from her Correspondence, and from the Journals of her Sisters Susan and Charlotte Burney*, ed. Annie Raine Ellis, 2 vols. (London: Bell and Sons, 1889).

—— *The Journals and Letters of Fanny Burney (Madame D'Arblay)*, ed. Joyce Hemlow and Althea Douglas, 12 vols. (Oxford: Clarendon Press, 1972–84).

BUTLER, WEEDEN, *Memoirs of Mark Hildesley, DD* (London: Printed by J. Nichols, 1799).

BYRON, GEORGE GORDON, Lord, *The Blues: A Literary Eclogue*, in *Works*, ed. Ernest Hartley Coleridge, Vol. iv (London: John Murray, 1901), 567–88.

—— *Byron's Don Juan: A Variorum Edition*, ed. Truman Guy Steffan and Willis W. Pratt, 4 vols. (Austin, Tex.: Univ. of Texas Press, 1957).

—— *Byron's Letters and Journals*, ed. Leslie A. Marchand, iii, *1813–1814* (Cambridge, Mass.: Belknap Press, Harvard UP, 1974).

CARTER, ELIZABETH, *Letters from Mrs. Elizabeth Carter to Mrs. Montagu between the Years 1755 and 1800*, ed. Montagu Pennington, 3 vols. (London: Printed for F. C. and J. Rivington, 1817).

—— *Memoirs of the Life of Mrs. Elizabeth Carter, with a New Edition of her Poems*, ed. Montagu Pennington, 2 vols, 2nd edn. (London: Printed for F. C. and J. Rivington, 1808).

—— *Poems on Several Occasions* (London: Printed for John Rivington, 1762).

—— *Poems upon Particular Occasions* (London, 1738).

—— *A Series of Letters between Mrs. Elizabeth Carter and Miss Catherine Talbot, from the Year 1741 to 1770: to which are added, Letters from Mrs. Elizabeth Carter to Mrs. Vesey, between the Years 1763 and 1787*, ed. Montagu Pennington, 2 vols. (London: Printed for F. C. and J. Rivington, 1808).

CASH, ARTHUR H., *Laurence Sterne: The Later Years* (London: Methuen, 1986).

CENTLIVRE, SUSANNA, *The Basset-Table: A Comedy: by the Author of the Gamester* (London: Printed for William Turner, 1706).

CHALMERS, ALEXANDER, *The General Biographical Dictionary*, new edn., 17 vols. (London: J. Nichols and Son, 1812-   ).

CHAPONE, HESTER, *Letters on the Improvement of the Mind: Addressed to a Young Lady*, 2 vols. (London, 1773).

—— *Miscellanies in Prose and Verse*, 2nd edn. (London: Printed for E. and C. Dilly, 1775).

—— *The Posthumous Works of Mrs Chapone, Containing her Correspondence with Mr. Richardson, a Series of Letters to Mrs. Elizabeth Carter, and some Fugitive Pieces, Never Before Published, together with an Account of her Life and Character, Drawn up by her Family*, 2 vols. (London: Printed for John Murray, 1807).

—— *The Works of Mrs. Chapone: Now First Collected, Containing, I. Letters on the Improvement of the Mind; II. Miscellanies; III. Correspondence with Mr. Richardson; IV. Letters to Miss Carter; V. Fugitive Pieces. to which is Prefixed an Account of her Life and Character, Drawn up by her own Family*, 4 vols. (London: Printed for John Murray, 1807).

—— *Works* (Edinburgh: Printed by James Ballantyne, 18--). A copy is in the Lewis Walpole Library, but its title-page is wanting. Published after 1801.

CLAY, CHRISTOPHER, 'Marriage, Inheritance, and the Rise of Large Estates in England, 1660-1815', *Economic History Review*, 2nd ser., 38 (1968), 503-18.

CLIFFORD, JAMES L., *Young Sam Johnson* (New York: McGraw, 1955).

COCKBURN, CATHERINE TROTTER, *The Works; Theological, Moral, Dramatic, and Poetical . . . with an Account of the Life of the Author*, ed. Thomas Birch, 2 vols. (London: Printed for J. and P. Knapton, 1751).

COLE, JOHN, *Memoirs of Mrs. Chapone* (London, 1839).

COLLINS, BARBARA, 'Letters to a Famous Daughter', *Deal and its Place in European Architectural Heritage* (Deal Society, n.d.), 7-9.

[COMBE, WILLIAM], *Letters of the Late Lord Lyttleton, Only Son of the Venerable George, Lord Lyttleton, and Chief Justice in Eyre, etc. First American Edition to which is Now Added, a Memoir Concerning the Author, Including an Account of Some Extraordinary Circumstances Attending his Death* (Troy, NY: Printed and Sold by Wright, Goodenow, & Stockwell, 1807).

COZENS, L. W., 'The Downs' (Deal Maritime and Local History Museum, n.d.).

CROSS, BARBARA M. (ed.), *The Educated Woman in America: Selected Writings of Catharine Beecher, Margaret Fuller, and M. Carey Thomas,*

*Classics in Education*, 25 (New York: Teachers College Press, 1965).

CROUSAZ, JEAN PIERRE DE, *An Examination of Mr. Pope's Essay on Man: Translated from the French of M. Crousaz . . .* , trans. Elizabeth Carter (London: Printed for A. Dodd, 1739).

CUMBERLAND, RICHARD, *The Observer: Being a Collection of Moral, Literary and Familiar Essays*, 4 vols. (Dublin, 1791).

DAMMERS, RICHARD H., 'Richard Steele and *The Ladies Library*', *Philological Quarterly*, 62 (1983), 530-6.

DAUMIER, *Liberated Women (Bluestockings and Socialist Women)*, Pref. Françoise Parturier, Catalogue and notes by Jacqueline Armingeat (New York: Vilo, 1982).

DAUZAT, ALBERT, *et al.*, *Nouveau dictionnaire étymologique et historique*, 4th edn., rev. et corr. (Paris, *c.*1964).

DELANY, MARY, *The Autobiography and Correspondence of Mary Granville, Mrs. Delany: With Interesting Reminiscences of King George the Third and Queen Charlotte*, ed. Lady Llanover, 1st ser., 3 vols. (London: Bentley, 1861); 2nd ser., 3 vols. (London: Bentley, 1862).

DE QUINCEY, THOMAS, 'Autobiography from 1785 to 1803', *Collected Writings*, ed. David Masson, i (London: A. & C. Black, 1896).

DONNELLY, LUCY MARTIN, 'The Celebrated Mrs. Macaulay', *William and Mary Quarterly*, 3rd ser., 6 (1949), 173-207.

—— 'The Heart of a Blue Stocking', *Atlantic Monthly*, 102 (Oct. 1908), 536-9.

DOODY, MARGARET ANNE, 'Augustan *Women?*: Four Poets of the Eighteenth Century', Unpub. William Andrews Clark Memorial Library Lecture, Univ. of California, Los Angeles, 1980.

—— 'Frances Sheridan: Morality and Annihilated Time', in *Fetter'd or Free? British Women Novelists, 1670-1815*, ed. Mary Anne Schofield and Cecilia Macheski (Athens, Ohio, Ohio UP, 1986), 324-58.

DORAN, JOHN, *A Lady of the Last Century (Mrs. Elizabeth Montagu): Illustrated in her Unpublished Letters; Collected and Arranged, with a Biographical Sketch, and a Chapter on Blue Stockings*, 2nd edn. (London, 1873).

DRAPER, JOHN W., 'The Theory of Translation in the Eighteenth Century', *Neophilologus*, 6 (1921), 241-54.

[DUNCOMBE, JOHN], *The Feminead; or, Female Genius, A Poem*, 2nd edn. (London: Printed for R. and J. Dodsley, 1757).

[DUNCOMBE, SUSANNA], 'A Sketch of the Character of the Author of "Reflections on the Seven Days of the Week" and "Essays on Various Subjects", by a Lady' (Signed S.D.), *Gentleman's Magazine*, 42 (June 1772), 257-8.

EAVES, T. C. DUNCAN, and KIMPEL, BEN D., *Samuel Richardson: A Biography* (Oxford: Clarendon Press, 1971).

ELSTOB, ELIZABETH, *The Rudiments of Grammar for the English-Saxon Tongue, First Given in English: With an Apology for the Study of Northern Antiquities. Being Very Useful Towards the Understanding our Ancient English Poets, and Other Writers* (London: Printed by W. Bowyer, 1715).

ENRIGHT, D. J., 'A Bluestocking's Sikh', Review of Sarah Lloyd, *An Indian Attachment*, *Observer* (15 July 1984), 21.

EPICTETUS, *All the Works*, trans. Elizabeth Carter (London: Printed by Samuel Richardson, 1758).

'Epictetus', *The New Encyclopaedia Britannica: Micropaedia* (Wallington, 1987).

*An Essay on the Writings and Genius of Shakespeare* (Review), *Critical Review*, 27 (May 1769), 350–4.

—— (Review), *Monthly Review*, 41 (Aug. 1769), 130–44.

EWING, ELIZABETH, *History of Children's Costume* (New York: Scribner's, 1977).

FADERMAN, LILLIAN, *Surpassing the Love of Men: Romantic Friendship and Love between Women from the Renaissance to the Present* (New York: Morrow, 1981).

FARNHAM, FERN, *Madame Dacier: Scholar and Humanist* (Monterey, Calif.: Angel Press, 1976).

FEIJÓO, BENITO J., *Teatro Crítico universal*, 8 vols. (Madrid, 1726–39).

—— *The Female Advocate; A Poem*, by Mary Scott (Review), *Gentleman's Magazine*, 44 (Aug. 1774), 375–7.

FÉNÉLON (François Salignac de la Mothe-Fénélon), *The Adventures of Telemachus, the Son of Ulysses*, trans. Tobias Smollett, 2 vols. (London, 1776).

—— *On Education: A Translation of the 'Traité de l'éducation des filles' and Other Documents Illustrating Fénélon's Educational Theories and Practice, Together with an Introduction and Notes*, trans. H. C. Barnard (Cambridge: CUP, 1966).

FERGUSON, MOIRA (ed.), *First Feminists: British Women Writers, 1578–1799* (Bloomington, Ind.: Indiana UP; Old Westbury, NY: Feminist, 1985).

[FERRIER, SUSAN], *Marriage, A Novel*, 3 vols. (Edinburgh: William Blackwood; London: John Murray, 1818).

FLETCHER, HELEN, *Bluestocking*, Introd. Dilys Powell, 1985; Letter of introd. C. V. Wedgwood, 1947 (London: Pandora, 1986).

FULLARD, JOYCE, and JARVIS, ROBIN, 'Mary Collyer (?–1763)', *A Dictionary of British and American Women Writers, 1660–1800*, ed. Janet Todd (Totowa, NJ: Rowman & Allanheld, 1985).

FULLER, MARGARET [OSSOLI], *Woman in the Nineteenth Century, and Kindred Papers Relating to the Sphere, Condition, and Duties of Woman*, ed. Arthur B. Fuller, Introd. Horace Greeley (Boston, Mass., 1855).

GAUSSEN, ALICE C. C. (ed.), *A Later Pepys: The Correspondence of Sir William Weller Pepys, Bart., Master in Chancery, 1758–1825, with Mrs. Chapone, Mrs. Hartley, Mrs. Montagu, Hannah More . . .*, 2 vols. (London: John Lane, The Bodley Head, 1904).

GAY, JOHN, POPE, ALEXANDER, and ARBUTHNOT, JOHN, *Three Hours After Marriage*, ed. Richard Morton and William M. Peterson, Lake Erie College Studies, 1 (Painesville, Ohio: Lake Erie College Press, 1961).

GAY, PETER, *The Enlightenment: An Interpretation, The Rise of Modern Paganism* (New York: Knopf, 1967).

*Gentleman's Magazine* (London, 1731–    ).

GILBERT, SANDRA M., and GUBAR, SUSAN, *The Madwoman in the Attic: The Woman Writer and the Nineteenth-Century Literary Imagination* (New Haven, Conn.: Yale UP, 1979).

—— and —— (eds.), *The Norton Anthology of Literature by Women: The Tradition in English* (New York: Norton, 1985).

GILLIGAN, CAROL, *In a Different Voice: Psychological Theory and Women's Development* (Cambridge, Mass.: Harvard UP, 1982).

GILPIN, WILLIAM, *Observations Relative Chiefly to Picturesque Beauty, Made in the Year 1776, on Several Parts of Great Britain; Particularly the High-lands of Scotland*, ii (London: Printed for R. Blamire, 1789).

GIROUARD, MARK, *Life in the English Country House: A Social and Architectural History* (New Haven, Conn.: Yale UP, 1978; Harmondsworth: Penguin, 1980).

GODBER, JOYCE, *The Marchioness Grey of Wrest Park*, Publications of the Bedfordshire Historical Record Society, 47 (Luton: White Crescent Press, 1968).

GOULDING, RICHARD W., *Henrietta Countess of Oxford* (Nottingham: Thoroton Press, 1924).

GREEN, MARY ELIZABETH, 'Elizabeth Elstob: "The Saxon Nymph" (1683–1756)', *Female Scholars: A Tradition of Learned Women Before 1800*, ed. J. R. Brink (Montreal: Eden Press Women's Publications, 1980), 137–60.

GUARINI, BAPTISTE, *De pensieri diversi* (Venice: il Barezzi, 1646).

GUNTHER, A. E., *An Introduction to the Life of the Rev. Thomas Birch D.D., F.R.S., 1705–1766: Leading Editor of the General Dictionary . . . 1741, Secretary of the Royal Society and Trustee of the British Museum* (Suffolk, England: Halesworth Press, 1984).

HAGELMAN, CHARLES, jun., and BARNES, ROBERT J. (eds.), *A Concordance to Byron's Don Juan* (Ithaca, NY, 1967).

HALSBAND, ROBERT, *The Life of Lady Mary Wortley Montagu* (Oxford: Clarendon Press, 1956).

[HAMMOND, JAMES], *Love Elegies: Written in the Year 1732* (London: Printed for G. Hawkins, 1743).

—— *Poetical Works* (Glasgow: Printed by Andrew Foulis, 1787).

HAMPSHIRE, G[WEN], 'Johnson, Elizabeth Carter and Pope's Garden', *Notes and Queries*, NS 19 (1972), 221–2.

*The Hamwood Papers of The Ladies of Llangollen and Caroline Hamilton*, ed. Mrs G. H. Bell (John Travers) (London: Macmillan, 1930).

HANSON, MARJORIE, 'Elizabeth Montagu: A Biographical Sketch and a Critical Edition of her Writings', thesis (Univ. of Southern California, 1981).

HARRIS, JOCELYN (Introd.), *The Feminiad, A Poem*, by John Duncombe, Augustan Reprint Society, No. 207 (William Andrews Clark Memorial Library, Univ. of California, Los Angeles, 1981).

HAYDEN, RUTH, *Mrs. Delany, Her Life and her Flowers* (London: British Museum Publications, 1980).

HEARNE, THOMAS, *Remarks and Collections, 27 Mar. 1728–8 Dec. 1731*, x, ed. H. E. Salter (Oxford: Clarendon Press, 1915).

—— *Remarks and Collections, 9 Dec. 1731–10 June 1735*, xi, ed. H. E. Salter (Oxford: Clarendon Press, 1921).

HEMLOW, JOYCE, *The History of Fanny Burney* (Oxford: Clarendon Press, 1958).

HESTON, WINIFRED, *A Bluestocking in India: Her Medical Wards and Messages Home* (New York: Fleming H. Revell, 1910).

HOLCROFT, THOMAS, *Seducation: A Comedy*, *The Plays of Thomas Holcroft*, ed. Joseph Rosenblum, i (New York: Garland, 1980).

HOLDEN, ANTHONY, 'The Homicidal Headmistress', Review of Diana Trilling, *Mrs Harris, The Death of the Scarsdale Diet Doctor*, *Times Literary Supplement* (14 May 1982), 526.

HOLLADAY, GAE ANNETTE, and BRACK, O. M., jun., 'Johnson as Patron', *Greene Centennial Studies: Essays Presented to Donald Greene in the Centennial Year of the University of Southern California*, ed. Paul J. Korshin and Robert R. Allen (Charlottesville, Va.: Univ. of Virginia Press, 1984).

[HOOLE, SAMUEL], *Aurelia; or, The Contest: An Heroi-Comic Poem; in Four Cantos, by the Author of Modern Manners* (London: Printed for J. Dodsley, 1783).

—— *Modern Manners; or, The Country Cousins: In a Series of Poetical Epistles*, 2nd edn., corr. and enlar. (London: Printed for J. Dodsley, 1782).

HORNBEAK, KATHERINE G., 'New Light on Mrs. Montagu', *The Age of Johnson: Essays Presented to Chauncey Brewster Tinker* (New Haven, Conn.: Yale UP, 1949), 351–61.

HUCHON, R[ENÉ], *Mrs. Montagu and her Friends, 1720–1800: A Sketch* (London: John Murray, 1907).

HUDSON, DEREK, and LUCKHURST, KENNETH W., *The Royal Society of Arts, 1754–1954*, Foreword by Duke of Edinburgh, Introd. Earl of Radnor (London: John Murray, 1954).

HUGHES, EDWARD, 'The Early Journal of Thomas Wright of Durham', *Annals of Science*, 7 (1951), 1–24.

HUGHES, HELEN SARD, *The Gentle Hertford: Her Life and Letters* (New York: Macmillan, 1940).

HUNTER, JEAN E., 'The Eighteenth-Century Englishwoman: According to the *Gentleman's Magazine*', *Woman in the Eighteenth Century and Other Essays*, ed. Paul Fritz and Richard Morton (Toronto and Sarasota: Samuel Stevens, Hakkert, 1976), 73–88.

HYDE, MARY, *The Thrales of Streatham Park* (Cambridge, Mass.: Harvard UP, 1977).

*The Inflexible Captive*, by Hannah More (Review), *Monthly Review*, 1st ser., 50 (Apr. 1774), 243–51.

[JOHNSON, CHARLES], *Caelia; or, The Perjur'd Lover*, 1st edn. (London: Printed for J. Watts, 1733).

JOHNSON, SAMUEL, *The Letters of Samuel Johnson with Mrs. Thrale's Genuine Letters to Him*, coll. and ed. R. W. Chapman, 3 vols. (Oxford: Clarendon Press, 1952, repr. 1963).

—— *Lives of the English Poets*, Introd. Arthur Waugh (World's Classics, 1906; repr. London: OUP, 1972–3).

—— *Poems*, ed. David Nichol Smith and Edward L. McAdam, 2nd edn. (Oxford: Clarendon Press, 1974).

—— *Proposals for Printing, by Subscription, the Two First Volumes of Bibliotheca Harleiana: or, A Catalogue of the Library of the Late Earl of Oxford, Purchased by Thomas Osborne, Bookseller, in Gray's Inn* (fac. repr., Oxford: OUP, 1926).

—— *The Rambler*, ed. W. J. Bate and Albrecht B. Strauss, 3 vols. (New Haven, Conn.: Yale UP, 1969).

—— *The Yale Edition of the Works of Samuel Johnson*, gen. ed. Allen T. Hazen; from 1966, John H. Middendorf, 15 vols. (New Haven, Conn.: Yale UP, 1958– ).

KETCHAM, MICHAEL G., *Transparent Designs: Reading, Performance, and Form in the Spectator Papers* (Athens, Ohio: Univ. of Georgia Press, 1985).

KING, MARGARET L., 'Book-Lined Cells: Women and Humanism in the Early Italian Renaissance', in Patricia H. Labalme (ed.), *Beyond Their Sex: Learned Women of the European Past* (New York: New York UP, 1984).

KLUGE, FRIEDRICH, *Etymologisches Wörterbuch der deutschen Sprache*,

19th edn., rev. von Walther Mitzka (Berlin: W. de Gruyter, 1963).

KNOX, VICESIMUS, *Essays, Moral and Literary*, 2nd edn., corr. and enlar., 2 vols. (London: Printed for Edward and Charles Dilly, 1779; repr. New York: Garland, 1972).

LABALME, PATRICIA H. (ed.), *Beyond Their Sex: Learned Women of the European Past* (New York: New York UP, 1984).

*The Ladies Library, Written by a Lady, Published by Mr. Steele*, 3 vols. (London: Printed for Jacob Tonson, 1714).

LARSON, EDITH SEDGWICK, 'A Measure of Power: The Personal Charity of Elizabeth Montagu', ed. O. M. Brack, jun., *Studies in Eighteenth-Century Culture*, 16 (Madison, Wis.: Univ. of Wisconsin Press, 1986), 197–210.

LE CARRÉ, JOHN, *The Honourable Schoolboy* (London: Hodder and Stoughton, 1977; repr. London: Pan Books, 1978).

LEES-MILNE, JAMES, *Earls of Creation: Five Great Patrons of Eighteenth-Century Art* (New York: London House and Maxwell, 1963).

LEIDER, EMILY, 'Poetic Mermaids', Review of Carolyn Kizer, *Mermaids in the Basement: Poems for Women* and *Yin: New Poems*, San Francisco Chronicle Review, 28 (Oct. 1984), 1; 10.

LERANBAUM, MIRIAM, 'The Nine Living Muses of Great Britain', unpub. paper presented to the American Society of Eighteenth-Century Studies, Victoria, BC (May 1977).

LERNER, GERDA, *The Creation of Patriarchy* (New York: OUP, 1986).

*Letters on the Improvement of the Mind*, by Hester Chapone (Advt.), *Daily Advertiser*, No. 13330 (11 Sept. 1773).

—— (Advt.), *London Chronicle*, 34 (7–9 Sept. 1773), 247.

—— (Review), *Gentleman's Magazine*, 43 (May 1773), 240–1.

LEWIS, JUDITH SCHNEID, *In the Family Way: Childbearing in the British Aristocracy, 1760–1860* (New Brunswick, NJ: Rutgers UP, 1986).

LOCKHART, JOHN G., *Peter's Letters to his Kinfolk*, 3rd edn., 3 vols. (Edinburgh, 1819).

LOUNSBURY, THOMAS R., *Shakespeare and Voltaire* (New York: Scribner's, 1902).

LUCE, A[RTHUR] A[STON], *The Life of George Berkeley, Bishop of Cloyne* (London: Thomas Nelson and Sons, 1940, 1949; repr. New York: Greenwood Press, 1968).

LURIA, GINA, 'Book Review', *Signs*, 4 (1978), 374–80.

[LYTTELTON, GEORGE], *Dialogues of the Dead* (London: Printed for W. Sandby, 1760).

—— *Letters from a Persian in England to his Friend at Ispahan*, 3rd edn. (London: Printed for J. Millan, 1735).

—— *Observations on the Conversion and Apostleship of St. Paul in a Letter to*

*Gilbert West, Esq.* (London: Printed for R. Dodsley, and sold by M. Cooper, 1748).

MCCARTHY, WILLIAM, *Hester Thrale Piozzi: Portrait of a Literary Woman* (Chapel Hill, NC: Univ. of North Carolina Press, 1985).

MCGOWAN, WILLIAM H., 'Anne Donnellan: The Critic as Friend', unpublished paper presented to the *American Society for Eighteenth Century Studies* (Houston, Tex., Mar., 1982).

MARTIN, JANE ROLAND, *Reclaiming a Conversation: The Ideal of the Educated Woman* (New Haven, Conn.: Yale UP, 1985).

MAVOR, ELIZABETH (ed.), *Life with the Ladies of Llangollen* (Harmondsworth: Penguin; New York: Viking Penguin, 1984).

MEDOFF, JESLYN, 'New Light on Sarah Fyge (Field, Egerton)', *Tulsa Studies in Women's Literature*, 1 (1982), 155–75.

MENAGH, DIANE, 'The Life of Marianne Francis: With an Account of her Letters to Mrs. Piozzi, an Old Friend of the Family', *Bulletin of the New York Public Library*, 80 (spring 1977), 318–44.

MEYER, GERALD DENNIS, *The Scientific Lady in England, 1650–1760: An Account of her Rise, with Emphasis on the Major Roles of the Telescope and Microscope*, University of California Publications English Studies, 12 (Berkeley, Calif.: Univ. of California Press, 1955).

MIDDLETON, CONYERS, *The History of the Life of Marcus Tullius Cicero*, 2 vols. (London: Printed for the Author, 1741).

[MIDDLETON, CONYERS], *A Letter to Dr. Waterland . . .* (London: Printed for J. Peele, 1731).

MILD, WARREN, 'Susanna Highmore's Literary Reputation', *Proceedings of the American Philosophical Society*, 122 (1978), 377–84.

MONTAGU, ELIZABETH, 'Dialogue XXVI: Cadmus—Hercules'; 'Dialogue XXVII: Mercury—And a Modern Fine Lady'; 'Dialogue XXVIII: Plutarch—Charon—And a Modern Bookseller', *Dialogues of the Dead*, by George Lyttelton (London: Printed for W. Sandby, 1760), 291–320.

—— *Elizabeth Montagu, The Queen of the Blue-Stockings: Her Correspondence from 1720 to 1761*, ed. Emily J. Climenson, 2 vols. (London: John Murray, 1906).

[——], *An Essay on the Writings and Genius of Shakespear, Compared with the Greek and French Dramatic Poets, with Some Remarks upon the Misrepresentations of Mons. de Voltaire* (London: Printed for J. Dodsley et al., 1769).

—— *The Letters of Mrs. Elizabeth Montagu, with Some of the Letters of her Correspondents*, ed. Matthew Montagu, 4 vols., 3rd edn. (London: Printed for T. Cadell and W. Davies, 1810–13).

—— *Letters of Elizabeth Montagu to the Duchess of Portland, Calendar of the Manuscripts of the Marquis of Bath Preserved at Longleat, Wiltshire,*

Historical Manuscripts Commission (London, 1904), i. 330–58.

—— Mrs. Montagu, 'Queen of the Blues': Her Letters and Friendships from 1762 to 1800, ed. Reginald Blunt, 2 vols. (London: Constable, n.d.).

MONTAGU, LADY MARY WORTLEY, The Complete Letters, ed. Robert Halsband, 3 vols. (Oxford: Clarendon Press, 1965).

MOORE, THOMAS, M. P.; or, The Blue-stocking, A Comic Opera, in Three Acts, First Performed at the English Opera, Lyceum, on Monday, Sept. 9, 1811 (London: Printed by W. Clowes, 1811).

[MORE, HANNAH], Coelebs in search of a Wife: Comprehending Observations on Domestic Habits and Manners, Religion and Morals, 2 vols. (London: Printed for T. Cadell and W. Davies, 1808).

—— Essays on Various Subjects, Principally Designed for Young Ladies (London: Printed for J. Wilkie and T. Cadell, 1777).

[——], Florio: A Tale, for Fine Gentlemen and Fine Ladies: and, The Bas-Bleu; or, Conversation: Two Poems (London: Printed for T. Cadell, 1786).

—— The Inflexible Captive: A Tragedy (Bristol: S. Farley, 1774).

—— Percy, A Tragedy, 3rd edn. (London: Printed for T. Cadell, 1780).

—— The Search after Happiness: A Pastoral Drama, 3rd edn. (Bristol. S. Farley, 1774).

—— Strictures on the Modern System of Female Education, 2 vols. (London: 1799; repr. with Introd. by Gina Luria, New York: Garland, 1974).

Morning Herald (and Daily Advertiser), No. 973 (10 Dec. 1783).

MORRIS, JOHN, A Practical Treatise Concerning Humility: Design'd for the Furtherance and Improvement of that Great Christian Vertue, bothe in the Minds and Lives of Men (London: Printed for S. Manship, 1707).

MULSO, JOHN, The Letters to Gilbert White of Selborne from his Intimate Friend and Contemporary The Rev. John Mulso, ed. Rashleigh Holt-White (London: R. H. Porter, 1906).

MYERS, SYLVIA H., 'The Ironies of Education', Aphra, 4 (spring 1973), 61–72.

NANGLE, BENJAMIN CHRISTIE, The Monthly Review, First Series, 1749–1789: Index of Contributors and Articles (Oxford: Clarendon Press, 1934).

National Trust, Wimpole Hall, Cambridgeshire, rev. edn. (London: National Trust, 1981).

NICHOLS, JOHN, Literary Anecdotes of the Eighteenth Century, 9 vols. (London: 1812–15).

NULLE, STEBELTON H., Thomas Pelham-Holles, Duke of Newcastle: His Early Political Career, 1693–1724 (Philadelphia, Pa.: Univ. of Pennsylvania Press, 1931).

'Observations on Female Literature in General, including some Particulars Relating to Mrs. Montagu and Mrs. Barbauld [Embellished with an Elegant Engraving of those Ladies]', *Westminster Magazine* (June 1776), 283–5.

OLDFATHER, W[ILLIAM] A[BBOTT], *Contributions to a Bibliography of Epictetus* (Univ. of Ill., 1927).

'On the Propriety of Bestowing Academical Honours on the Ladies', *Westminster Magazine* (July 1773), 408–9.

OSBORN, JAMES M., 'Thomas Birch and the *General Dictionary* (1734–41)', *Modern Philology*, 36 (Aug. 1938), 25–46.

'Original Letters of Miss E. Carter and Mr. Samuel Richardson', *Monthly Magazine*, 33 (1812), 533–43.

[OXFORD, EDWARD HARLEY, 2nd Earl], 'An Account of a Journey Made Through Part of the Counties of Suffolk, Norfolk, and Cambridgeshire in the Month of September, 1732', *Report on the Manuscripts of his Grace, the Duke of Portland, Preserved at Welbeck Abbey*, Historical Manuscripts Commission (London, 1901), vi. 148–68.

PAILLER, ALBERT, *Edward Cave et le* Gentleman's Magazine *(1731–1754)*, thesis, 2 vols. (Univ. of Paris, 1972; Lille: Atelier Reproduction des Thèses, University of Lille III; Paris: Librairie Honore Champion, 1975).

PARKS, STEPHEN, 'George Berkeley, Sir Richard Steele and *The Ladies Library*', *Scriblerian*, 13 (1980), 1–2.

PARRINGTON, VERNON LOUIS, *The Romantic Revolution in America (1800–1860), Main Currents in American Thought*, ii (New York: Harcourt, Brace, 1927, 1930).

PERRY, RUTH, 'George Ballard's Biographies of Learned Ladies', *Biography in the Eighteenth Century*, ed. J. D. Browning, *Publications of the McMaster University Association for Eighteenth-Century Studies*, 8 (New York: Garland, 1980).

—— (ed.), George Ballard, *Memoirs of Several Ladies of Great Britain who have been Celebrated for their Writings or Skill in the Learned Languages Arts and Sciences* (Detroit, Mich.: Wayne State UP, 1985).

—— *The Celebrated Mary Astell: An Early English Feminist* (Chicago, Ill.: Univ. of Chicago Press, 1986).

[PIGOTT, CHARLES], *The Female Jockey Club; Or, A Sketch of the Manners of the Age: By the Author of the Former Jockey Club* (London, n.p., n.d.; repr. New York: Greenleaf, Fellows, and Wayland, 1794).

PIOZZI, HESTER LYNCH, *Anecdotes of the Late Samuel Johnson, LL D During the Last Twenty Years of his Life* (London: Printed for T. Cadell, 1786).

—— *Autobiography, Letters and Literary Remains of Mrs. Piozzi (Thrale)*, ed. A[braham] Hayward, 2 vols. (London: Longman, Green, Longman, and Roberts, 1861).

PIOZZI, HESTER LYNCH, *British Synonymy; or, An Attempt at Regulating the Choice of Words in Familiar Conversation* . . . 2 vols. (London: Printed for G. G. and J. Robinson, 1794).

—— *Letters to and from the Late Samuel Johnson, LL D, to which are Added Some Poems Never Before Printed* . . . 2 vols. (London: Printed for A. Strahan, 1788).

—— *Observations and Reflections Made in the Course of a Journey Through France, Italy, and Germany*, 2 vols. (London: Printed for A. Strahan, and T. Cadell, 1789).

—— *Retrospection; or, A Review of the Most Striking and Important Events, Characters, Situations, and their Consequences, which the Last Eighteen Hundred Years have Presented to the View of Mankind* . . . (London: Printed for J. Stockdale, 1801).

—— *Thraliana: The Diary of Mrs. Hester Lynch Thrale (Later Mrs Piozzi) 1776-1809*, ed. Katharine C. Balderston, 2nd edn., 2 vols. (Oxford: Clarendon Press, 1951).

[POLWHELE, RICHARD], *The Unsex'd Females: A Poem, Addressed to the Author of* The Pursuits of Literature (London: Printed for Cadell and Davies, 1798).

POPE, ALEXANDER, *Correspondence*, ed. George Sherburn, 5 vols. (Oxford: Clarendon Press, 1956).

—— *Imitations of Horace*, ed. John Butt (London: Methuen, 1939).

—— *Poems of Alexander Pope*, vi, *Minor Poems*, ed. Norman Ault and John Butt (London: Methuen; New Haven, Conn.: Yale UP, 1954).

PORTER, KATHERINE H., 'Margaret, Duchess of Portland', thesis (Cornell Univ., 1930).

[PORTEUS, BEILBY], 'A Review of the Life and Character of Archbishop Secker', Thomas Secker, *Sermons on Several Subjects*, ed. Beilby Porteus and George Stinton, i (London: Printed for J. and F. Rivington, 1770), pp. i–xcvii.

POWYS, PHILIP LYBBE, Mrs., *Passages from the Diaries of Mrs. Philip Lybbe Powys of Hardwick House, Oxon., A.D. 1756 to 1808*, ed. Emily J. Climenson (London: Longmans, Green, 1899).

PRESSLY, WILLIAM L., *The Life and Art of James Barry*, Paul Mellon Centre for Studies in British Art (New Haven, Conn.: Yale UP, 1981).

—— *James Barry: The Artist as Hero* (London: The Tate Gallery, 1983).

PYM, BARBARA, *Some Tame Gazelle* (London, 1950. Harper & Row, Perennial Library, 1984).

RAO, ANANDA U., *A Minor Augustan, Being the Life and Works of George, Lord Lyttelton, 1709-1773* (Calcutta: The Book Co., 1934).

RAYMOND, JANICE G., *A Passion for Friends: Toward a Philosophy of Female Affection* (Boston, Mass.: Beacon Press, 1986).

REDFORD, BRUCE, *The Converse of the Pen: Acts of Intimacy in the Eighteenth-Century Familiar Letter* (Chicago, Ill.: Univ. of Chicago Press, 1986).

REYNOLDS, MYRA, *The Learned Lady in England, 1650–1760* (Boston, Mass.: Houghton Mifflin Co., 1920; repr. Gloucester, Mass.: Peter Smith, 1964).

RICH, ADRIENNE, 'Compulsory Heterosexuality and Lesbian Existence', *Signs*, 5 (1980), 631–60.

RICHARDSON, SAMUEL, *The Correspondence of Samuel Richardson, Author of Pamela, Clarissa, and Sir Charles Grandison: Selected from the Original Manuscripts, bequeathed by him to his Family, to which are Prefixed, a Biographical Account of that Author, and Observations on his Writings*, ed. Anna Laetitia Barbauld, 6 vols. (London: Printed for Richard Phillips, 1804).

—— *The History of Sir Charles Grandison*, ed. Jocelyn Harris, 3 vols. (London: OUP, 1972).

—— *Selected Letters*, ed. John Carroll (Oxford: Clarendon Press, 1964).

ROBBIE, MARY L., 'Discovering the Bluestockings: A Neglected Constellation of Clever Women', thesis (Univ. of Edinburgh, 1947).

ROTHSCHILD LIBRARY, *A Catalogue of the Collection of Eighteenth-Century Printed Books and Manuscripts formed by Lord Rothschild*, 2 vols. (Cambridge: Privately printed at the University Press, 1954).

ROWE, ELIZABETH SINGER, *The Miscellaneous Work in Prose and Verse: The Greater Part now First Published, by her Order, from her Original Manuscripts, by Mr. Theophilus Rowe, to which are Added, Poems on Several Occasions, by Mr. Thomas Rowe. and to the Whole is Prefix'd, an Account of the Lives and Writings of the Authors*, 2 vols. (London: Printed for R. Hett and R. Dodsley, 1739).

Royal Society of Arts, *Premiums by the Society, Established at London, for the Encouragement of Arts, Manufactures, and Commerce*, 7 vols. (London: Printed by Order of the Society, 1758; 1759; 1760; 1761; 1764; 1765; 1775).

RUHE, EDWARD, 'Birch, Johnson, and Elizabeth Carter: An Episode of 1738–39', *PMLA* 73 (1958), 491–500.

[SCARGILL, WILLIAM PITT], *Blue-stocking Hall*, 3 vols. (London: Henry Colburn, 1827).

SCHLESINGER, ARTHUR, jun., 'Profiles: Marietta Tree', *Architectural Digest* (Mar. 1984), 131–9.

SCHNORRENBERG, BARBARA BRANDON (Catherine [Sawbridge]

Macaulay), *A Dictionary of British and American Women Writers, 1660–1800*, ed. Janet Todd (Totawa, NJ: Rowman & Allanheld, 1985).

SCOTT, MARY, *The Female Advocate: A Poem, Occasioned by Reading Mr. Duncombe's Feminead* (London: Printed for Joseph Johnson, 1774).

SCOTT, SARAH, *A Description of Millenium Hall . . . by 'A Gentleman on his Travels'*, Introd. Jane Spencer (London: Virago, 1986; first pub. in Great Britain by J. Newbery, 1762).

SCOTT, WALTER, SIR, *Journal (1825–1826)*, ed. J. G. Tait, i (Edinburgh: Oliver & Boyd, 1939).

—— *Journal (1829–1832)*, ed. J. G. Tait, iii (Edinburgh: Oliver & Boyd, 1946).

SEDGWICK, ROMNEY, *The House of Commons, 1715–1754*, 2 vols. (London: HMSO, 1970).

SEIDEL, MICHAEL A., 'Poulain de la Barre's *The Woman as Good as the Man*', *Journal of the History of Ideas*, 35 (1974), 499–508.

SEWARD, THOMAS, 'The Female Right to Literature, in a Letter to a Young Lady, from Florence', *A Collection of Poems in Several Hands*, ii (London: Printed for R. Dodsley, 1748), 295–302.

SHAKESPEARE, WILLIAM, *Shakespeare's Sonnets*, ed. with analytic commentary by Stephen Booth (New Haven, Conn.: Yale UP, 1977, 1978).

[SHARPE, MISS], *Sketch of the Character of Mrs. Elizabeth Carter, who Died in London, on February the 19th, 1806, in the Eighty-Ninth Year of her Age* (Kelso: Printed by A. Ballantyne, 1806).

SHERIDAN, FRANCES. *Memoirs of Miss Sidney Bidulph, Extracted from her Own Journal, and Now First Published*, 3 vols. (London: R. and J. Dodsley, 1761).

SHEVELOW, KATHRYN (Charlotte Lennox), *A Dictionary of British and American Women Writers, 1660–1800*, ed. Janet Todd (Totawa, NJ: Rowan & Allanheld, 1985).

SHOWALTER, ELAINE, *A Literature of their Own: British Women Novelists from Brontë to Lessing* (Princeton, NJ: Princeton UP, 1977).

*Six Odes, Presented to that Justly-Celebrated Historian, Mrs. Catharine Macaulay, on her Birthday, and Publicly Read to a Polite and Brilliant Audience, Assembled April the Second, at Alfred-House, Bath, to Congratulate that Lady on the Happy Occasion* (Bath: Printed and sold by R. Cruttwell, 1777).

SMITH, CHARLOTTE TURNER, *Emmeline, the Orphan of the Castle*, 4 vols. (London: Printed for T. Cadell, 1788).

SMITH, ELIZABETH, *Fragments in Prose and Verse: With Some Account of her Life and Character*, ed. H[enrietta] M[aria] Bowdler (Boston, Mass.: Munroe & Francis, and Samuel H. Parker, 1810).

SMOLLETT, TOBIAS, *The Adventures of Roderick Random*, ed. Paul-Gabriel Bouce (Oxford: OUP, 1979).

SOLIS, ANTONIO, DE, *The History of the Conquest of Mexico by the Spaniards*, tr. Thomas Townsend (London, 1724).

[SOPHIA], *Woman not Inferior to Man; or, A Short and Modest Vindication of the Natural Right of the Fair-Sex to a Perfect Equality of Power, Dignity, and Esteem, with the Men* (London: Printed for John Hawkins, 1739).

SOPHOCLES, *The Tragedies of Sophocles, from the Greek*, tr. Thomas Francklin, 2 vols. (London, 1758–9).

*The Spectator*, ed. Donald F. Bond, 5 vols. (Oxford: Clarendon Press, 1965).

SPENCER, JANE, *The Rise of the Woman Novelist: From Aphra Behn to Jane Austen* (Oxford: Blackwell, 1986).

SPENDER, DALE, *Women of Ideas and What Men Have Done to Them: From Aphra Behn to Adrienne Rich* (London: Routledge & Kegan Paul, 1982).

SPENDER, LYNNE, *Intruders on the Rights of Men: Women's Unpublished Heritage* (London: Pandora Press, 1983).

'Steele's "Ladies" Library', *Bookworm*, 2 (1889), 62–3.

STECHER, HENRY F., *Elizabeth Singer Rowe, the Poetess of Frome: A Study in Eighteenth-Century English Pietism, European University Papers*, 14 (Berne: Herbert Lang; Frankfurt-on-Main: Peter Lang, 1973).

STENTON, DORIS MARY, *The English Woman in History* (London: George Allen and Unwin, 1957; repr. New York: Schocken Books, 1977).

STIMPSON, CATHARINE R., 'Zero Degree Deviancy: The Lesbian Novel in English', *Critical Inquiry*, 8 (1981), 363–79.

STOCK, R. D., *Samuel Johnson and Neoclassical Drama Theory* (Lincoln, Nebr.: Univ. of Nebraska Press, 1973).

STONE, LAWRENCE, *The Family, Sex and Marriage in England, 1500–1800* (London: Weidenfeld & Nicolson, 1977).

SWIFT, JONATHAN, *The Correspondence of Jonathan Swift*, ed. Harold Williams, 5 vols. (Oxford: Clarendon Press, 1963).

TALBOT, CATHERINE, *The Works of the Late Mrs. Catharine Talbot*, new edn. (London: Printed by John Rivington, jun., for John, Francis, and Charles Rivington, 1780).

—— *The Works of the Late Miss Catharine Talbot . . . With Some Few Additional Papers . . . and Some Account of her Life . . .* 7th edn., ed. Montagu Pennington (London: Printed for F. C. and J. Rivington, 1809).

TASSONI, ALESSANDRO, *De pensieri diversi* (Venice: Per il Barezzi, 1646).

TAYLOR, GORDON RATTRAY, *The Angel Makers: A Study in the Psych logical Origins of Historical Change, 1750–1850* (London: Heinemann, 1958).

[TAYLOR, JEREMY], *A Discourse of the Nature, Offices and Measures of Friendship, with Rules of Conducting it, Written in Answer to a Letter from the Most Ingenious and Vertuous M.K.P.* (London: Printed for R. Royston, 1657).

TINKER, CHANCEY BREWSTER, *The Salon and English Letters: Chapters on the Interrelations of Literature and Society in the Age of Johnson* (New York: Macmillan, 1915).

TODD, JANET, *Women's Friendship in Literature* (New York: Columbia UP, 1980).

TOMPKINS, J. M. S., *The Polite Marriage* (Cambridge: CUP, 1938).

TRUMBACH, RANDOLPH, *The Rise of the Egalitarian Family: Aristocratic Kinship and Domestic Relations in Eighteenth-Century England* (New York: Academic Press, 1978).

TURBERVILLE, A. S., *A History of Welbeck Abbey and its Owners*, 2 vols. (London: Faber & Faber, 1939).

VICKERS, BRIAN (ed.), *Shakespeare: The Critical Heritage, 1765–1774*, 5 vols. (London: Routledge & Kegan Paul, 1979), vol. 5.

*Victoria History of the Counties of England: Buckinghamshire*, ed. William Page, 3 vols. (London: St Catherine Press, 1925), vol. 3.

WALLAS, ADA, *Before the Bluestockings* (New York: Macmillan, 1930).

WALLER, EDMUND, *Works in Verse and Prose: Published by Mr. Fenton* (London: Printed for J. Tonson, 1729).

WALPOLE, HORACE, *Correspondence*, ed. W. S. Lewis, *et al.*, 48 vols. (New Haven, Conn.: Yale UP, 1937–1983).

—— *The Duchess of Portland's Museum*, Introd. W. S. Lewis (New York: Grolier Club, 1936).

WARTON, JOSEPH, *An Essay on the Genius and Writings of Pope*, 2 vols., 4th corr. edn. (London: Printed for J. Dodsley, 1782).

WATSON, JAMES D., *The Double Helix: A Personal Account of the Structure of DNA* (New York: Atheneum, 1968; repr. 1980).

WEST, GILBERT, *Observations on the History and Evidences of the Resurrection of Jesus Christ*, 3rd edn., rev. and corr. by the author (London: Printed for R. Dodsley, 1747).

WHEELER, ETHEL ROLT, *Famous Blue-Stockings* (London: Methuen, 1910).

WILBUR, RICHARD (tr.), Jean Baptiste de Molière, *The Learned Ladies* (New York: Harcourt, 1977).

illiam H. Robinson Ltd., *The Library of Mrs. Elizabeth Vesey (1715–791), Catalogue 14*, Introd. Ross Balfour (Newcastle upon Tyne, 6).

MSON, MARILYN L., 'Who's Afraid of Mrs. Barbauld? The

Blue Stockings and Feminism', *International Journal of Women's Studies*, 3 (Jan./Feb. 1980), 89–102.

[WOLCOT, JOHN], *The Works of Peter Pindar, Esq. with a Copious Index: to which is Prefixed Some Account of his Life*, 4 vols. (London: Printed for Walker and Edwards, *et al.*, 1816).

YEARSLEY, ANN, *Poems, on Several Occasions, by Ann Yearsley, a Milk-woman of Bristol* (London: Printed for T. Cadell, 1785).

—— *Poems, on Several Occasions, by Ann Yearsley, a Milkwoman of Bristol*, 4th edn. (London: Printed for G. G. I. and J. Robinson, 1786).

—— *Poems, on Various Subjects, by Ann Yearsley, a Milkwoman of Clifton, near Bristol; Being her Second Work* (London: Printed for the Author, 1787).

YORK, LYLE, 'When Bluestockings Met Blue Collars', Review of the film, 'The Women of Summer', *San Francisco Chronicle Datebook* (1 June 1986), 37.

[YORKE, PHILIP, 2nd Earl Hardwicke, *et al.*], *Athenian Letters; or, The Epistolary Correspondence of an Agent of the King of Persia, Residing at Athens During the Peloponnesian War*, new edn., 2 vols. (London: Printed for T. Cadell, jun., and W. Davies, 1798).

YORKE, PHILIP C., *The Life and Correspondence of Philip Yorke, Earl of Hardwicke, Lord High Chancellor of Great Britain*, 3 vols. (Cambridge: CUP, 1913), i.

ZIMMERMAN, BONNIE, 'What Has Never Been: An Overview of Lesbian Feminist Literary Criticism', *The New Feminist Criticism: Essays on Women, Literature, and Theory*, ed. Elaine Showalter (New York: Pantheon, 1985).

# INDEX

Savage, Richard 58
Scargill, William Pitt 294-6
Schlesinger, Arthur, jun. 301
Scott, George Lewis 103, 136, 138
Scott, Mary 274
Scott, Sarah, *see* Robinson, Sarah
Scott, Sir Walter 290-1
Secker, Catherine, *see* Benson, Catherine
Secker, Revd Thomas, *later* Archbishop
     5, 62-6, 69, 72-4, 108-9, 113-14,
     116, 120, 133, 159, 161-3, 165-6,
     168-9, 215, 228
Seidel, Michael A. 126
self awareness 15, 17, 56, 81, 85, 119,
     123, 140, 149, 234
Sévigné, Marquise de 70, 154, 187, 298
Seward, Anna 127
Seward, Thomas 126-8, 235, 275
sexuality 4, 256-7, 270, 287
     equality 2, 125-6, 142, 146
     lesbianism 18-19, 75
Seymour, Frances Thynne, Countess of
     Hertford *later* Duchess of Somerset
     49, 215, 225
Shakespeare, William 180-1, 185, 194,
     250
     *Essay on the Writings and Genius of
     Shakespear* (Montagu) 11, 155, 186,
     196-206, 233, 252, 256
Sheridan, Elizabeth Linley 276-9
Sheridan, Frances 195
Shevelow, Kathryn 244
Showalter, Elaine 243
sisterhood 121
Smith, Charlotte Turner 149
Smith, Elizabeth 293
Smollett, Tobias G. 4, 42
Solis, Antonio de 191
Sophocles 184-5, 199
Soulie, Frédéric 297
spas 6, 19, 250-1
*Spectator* 123-4, 235
Spencer, Jane 10, 128
Spender, Dale 122
Spender, Lynne 122
spinsterhood 1, 93, 95, 119-20, 230, 234
status 1, 16, 85-6, 134, 163, 259
Steele, Richard 123-4
Sterne, Laurence 265
Stillingfleet, Benjamin 6-7, 179
Stimpson, Catharine R. 18-19
Stock, R. D. 202
stoicism 159, 165-7, 236

Stone, Lawrence 86, 91
study 1, 7, 58, 187, 194, 263, 303
subscription, publication by 129, 133,
     164-5, 168-9, 243, 260-1
Swan, Dr J. 53
Swift, Jonathan 22, 38, 88

Talbot, Catherine 11, 187, 216, 232, 294
     and Ballard, George 133, 144
     and bishops 159-60
     and Carter, Elizabeth 60, 68-78, 116,
          122, 134-5, 173, 175, 192, 213-15,
          217, 220, 222, 227-8, 232
     and Campbell, Jemima 5, 61-8
     and Epictetus 161-4
     and marriage 86-7, 112-17
     in painting 276
     posthumous fame 223-8
     and Robinson, Elizabeth 149, 222
     role models 125, 153-4, 262
     writings 107, 157-8, 207-15
Talbot, Revd Edward 61-2
Talbot, Mary 61-3, 69, 74, 113-14,
     116, 159, 163, 210, 215, 222
Tassoni, Alessandro 4, 140
*Tatler* 123
Taylor, Gordon R. 232
Taylor, Jeremy 61, 85, 120
Thomas, Bishop John 77, 229, 238
Thomas, M. Carey 300
Thornhill, James 22
Thrale, Henry 254-5, 271
Thrale, Hester, *see* Salusbury, Hester
     Lynch
Tinker, Chauncey B. 287
Todd, Janet 17
Torriano, Samuel 6, 179
Tree, Marietta 301
Trilling, Diana 301
Trumbach, Randolph 85, 89, 91
Tunbridge Wells, Kent 19, 30, 102, 177,
     179-80, 189, 251
Turberville, A. S. 89
Twywell, Northamptonshire 76-7

Vernier, Jules 297
Vernon, Anne 25
Vesey, Agmondesham 251-2, 265-7
Vesey, Elizabeth 7-9, 11, 44, 174, 177,
     199, 250-3, 259, 265-6, 283
Vickers, Brian 198-9, 202-3
virtue 17, 127-8, 132, 140, 173, 232,
     245-6, 259, 271, 288, 293